Free Video  Free Video

Essential Test Tips Video from Trivium Test Prep

Dear Customer,

Thank you for purchasing from Trivium Test Prep! We're honored to help you prepare for your GED exam.

To show our appreciation, we're offering a **FREE *GED Essential Test Tips* Video by Trivium Test Prep**.* Our video includes 35 test preparation strategies that will make you successful on the GED. All we ask is that you email us your feedback and describe your experience with our product. Amazing, awful, or just so-so: we want to hear what you have to say!

To receive your **FREE *GED Essential Test Tips* Video**, please email us at 5star@ triviumtestprep.com. Include "Free 5 Star" in the subject line and the following information in your email:

1. The title of the product you purchased.
2. Your rating from 1 – 5 (with 5 being the best).
3. Your feedback about the product, including how our materials helped you meet your goals and ways in which we can improve our products.
4. Your full name and shipping address so we can send your **FREE *GED Essential Test Tips* Video**.

If you have any questions or concerns please feel free to contact us directly at 5star@ triviumtestprep.com.

Thank you!

- Trivium Test Prep Team

*To get access to the free video please email us at 5star@triviumtestprep.com, and please follow the instructions above.

GED Preparation 2019 – 2020 All Subjects Study Guide

GED Test Prep Book and Practice Questions for the GED Exam

TABLE OF CONTENTS

ONLINE RESOURCES

To help you fully prepare for your GED, Accepted, Inc. includes online resources with the purchase of this study guide.

Practice Tests

In addition to the example questions and "Test Your Knowledge" sections included in this book, we also offer two online exam. Since many exams today are computer based, getting to practice your test-taking skills on the computer is a great way to prepare.

Flash Cards

A convenient supplement to this study guide, Accepted Inc.'s flash cards enable you to review important terms easily on your computer or smartphone.

From Stress to Success

Watch "From Stress to Success," a brief but insightful YouTube video that offers the tips, tricks, and secrets experts use to score higher on the exam.

Reviews

Leave a review, send us helpful feedback, or sign up for Accepted, Inc. promotions—including free books!

Access these materials at:

www.acceptedinc.com/ged-2018-online-resources

INTRODUCTION

Congratulations on choosing to take the GED exam! By purchasing this book, you've taken an important step on your path to earning your high school-equivalency credential.

This guide will provide you with a detailed overview of the GED exam so that you know exactly what to expect on test day. We'll take you through all the concepts covered on the exam and give you the opportunity to test your knowledge with practice questions. Even if it's been a while since you last took a major test, don't worry; we'll make sure you're more than ready!

What is the GED?

The General Educational Development, or GED, test is a high school-equivalency test—composed of four subtests—that certifies that the test-taker has high school-level academic skills. Forty states currently offer the GED test. The four subtests can be taken together or separately, but you must pass all four subtests in order to pass the test overall. Once a test-taker in one of those states passes the exam, then that person becomes eligible to receive a high school-equivalency diploma, which can be used in job applications or in applying to colleges or universities. The test is specifically designed for individuals who did not complete a high school diploma, no matter the reason.

What's on the GED?

The GED test gauges high school-level content knowledge and skills in four areas: Reasoning through Language Arts (RLA), Mathematical Reasoning, Science, and Social Studies. Candidates are expected to be able to read closely, write clearly, edit and understand standard written English as it is used in context, and solve quantitative and algebraic problems. You also must show strong content knowledge in life science, physical science, and Earth and space science as well as civics and government, United States history, geography and the world, and economics.

The test includes a variety of question types, including multiple-choice, drag-and-drop, hot spot, and fill-in-the-blank. The multiple-choice questions are a standard style in which the test-taker selects the best answer among a series of choices. In drag-and-drop questions, the test-taker must select the best answer, click on it, and drag it to the appropriate location. This usually involves sorting items into categories or making associations between different concepts. Hot spot questions require the test-taker to click on a specific area of an image. For fill-in-the-blank questions, the test-taker must type in the word or phrase missing from the statement or question. The Reasoning through Language Arts section also includes some questions in which the test-taker must select the best grammatical or punctuation change from a drop-down list of options as well as extended response questions that require the test-taker to type the answer.

Each subtest is taken separately. You must complete one subtest before moving on to the next. You will have 115 minutes for the math test, ninety minutes for the science test, seventy minutes for the social studies test, and 150 minutes for the Reasoning through Language Arts test.

What's on the GED Exam?

Skills Assessed	Topics	Percentage of Exam*
Reasoning Through Language Arts		
◆ Read closely	Informational texts	75%
◆ Write clearly		
◆ Edit and understand the use of standard written English in context	Literature texts	25%
Mathematical Reasoning		
◆ Understand key mathematical concepts	Quantitative problem-solving	45%
◆ Demonstrate skill and fluency with key math procedures		
◆ Apply concepts to realistic situations	Algebraic problem-solving	55%
Science		
◆ Use scientific reasoning (textually and quantitatively)	Life science	40%
	Physical science	40%
◆ Apply scientific reasoning to a variety of realistic situations	Earth and space science	20%
Social Studies		
	Civics and government	50%
◆ Textual analysis	United States history	20%
◆ Data representation		
◆ Inference skills	Economics	15%
◆ Problem-solving using social studies content	Geography and the world	15%

Percentages are approximate.

The Reasoning through Language Arts test assesses your ability to understand a range of texts which can be found in both academic and workplace settings. The test includes literary and informational texts as well as important US founding documents. The texts vary in length from 450 to 900 words. You will be asked to identify details and make logical inferences from—as well as valid claims about—the texts. You also will be asked to define key vocabulary and use textual evidence to analyze the texts in your own words in the form of a written response.

The Mathematical Reasoning test assesses mastery of key fundamental math concepts. Rather than focusing on specific content, the test focuses on reasoning skills and modes of thinking that can be used in a variety of mathematical content areas, specifically algebra, data analysis, and number sense. Questions will assess your ability to make sense of complex problems, use logical thinking to find solutions, recognize structure, and look for and express regularity in repeated reasoning. You also will be evaluated on the precision of your mathematics.

The Science test assesses your mastery of scientific content in life science, physical science, and Earth and space science, as well as your ability to apply scientific reasoning. Each question on the test will focus on one science practice and one content topic. Specifically, questions will relate to two primary themes: Human Health and Living Systems—all concepts related to the health and safety of all living things on the planet—and Energy and Related Systems—all concepts related to sources and uses of energy.

The Social Studies test assesses your mastery of both social studies content and skills. Each question addresses one element of social studies practice and one specific content topic. The primary focus of the test is on American civics and government, with the other three content areas as supplements. The questions address two core themes: Development of Modern Liberties and Democracy—which traces the current ideas of democracy from ancient times to present—and Dynamic Responses in Societal Systems, which addresses how society's systems, structures, and policies have developed and responded to each other.

Unique Question Types

While the majority of the GED exam is made up of multiple-choice questions, it also contains several other types of questions that might be unfamiliar to you. Collectively, these are called "technology-enhanced items" because they require you to interact with a computer. There are four types of these questions: drag-and-drop, hot spot, drop-down or cloze, and fill-in-the-blank. Each type of question is structured a little differently and requires different actions from the test-taker. Each type of question also assesses different skills. While they may seem a little intimidating, once you understand what these questions are testing and how to answer them, you will see they are quite manageable.

Drag-and-Drop

A drag-and-drop question has three parts: the question or prompt, drop target, and tiles or "draggers." Each tile contains a small image, word, or numerical expression. You will read the question or prompt, and then click the tile you think has the correct answer, drag it to the target area, and then let it go. In some cases, you may be able to put more than one tile in a single target area, or you may be able to put the same tile in multiple target areas. If this is the case, a note included with the question will tell you that. For example, imagine a question says, *Classify the following fruits by color*. There is a response area for yellow, blue, green, and red, and tiles that say *apple, strawberry, blueberry, banana,* and *pear*. You would drag both the apple and strawberry tiles to the red target area. You would also put the apple tile in the green area.

Drag-and-drop questions will differ both in structure and in skills assessed, depending on the subtest. On the Mathematics subtest, drag-and-drop questions are primarily used for constructing expressions, equations, and inequalities. For example, the prompt will include a scenario and an incomplete equation. The tiles will contain various numerical and/or alphabetical variables and operators that could complete the equation. You must then drag the appropriate mathematical element to its spot in the equation. You also could be asked to order the steps in a mathematical process or solution or match items from two different sets.

On the Reasoning Through Language Arts (RLA) subtest, drag-and-drop questions will typically focus on sequencing and classifying to assess comprehension and analysis of a reading passage. Some questions may ask you to order events in a passage based on chronology or to illustrate cause and effect. Or you might be asked to classify evidence based on how it relates to the argument of a passage. Drag-and-drop questions on this subtest will usually incorporate graphic organizers, such as Venn diagrams, timelines, or charts.

On the Social Studies subtest, drag-and-drop questions are primarily used for mapping, classifying, and sequencing. For example, you might be asked to put the steps in a political process in the correct order, or you may be asked to sort actions based on the related constitutional freedom. Alternatively, you could be asked to place correct labels on the continents or use information from a brief text to place data points on a graph or chart.

On the Science subtest, drop-and-drag questions are used primarily for sequencing questions: placing the steps of a biological or chemical process in the correct order. These questions can also be used for classification, like sorting animals into mammals and non-mammals. Like on the RLA subtest, science drag-and-drop questions often utilize graphic organizers, like Venn diagrams.

EXAMPLE

The owner of a taco truck decides to use data to determine how many tacos he can make during a two-hour lunch rush. He has determined that the average time it takes to make five tacos is eight minutes.

Complete the equation to show how the taco truck owner determined that he can make seventy-five tacos in two hours.

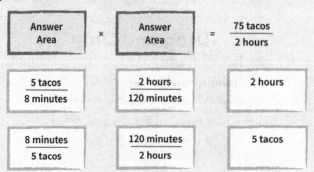

Hot Spot

In a hot spot question, you will be presented with a graphic image. The image is embedded with virtual "sensors" placed at various points. The question will ask you to identify something specific within the image or to select an answer from several listed within the image. You will indicate your selection by clicking on a virtual sensor. For example, the image could be a diagram of the human body. If the question asks where the lungs are located, you would click the chest, activating the sensor there. While hot spot questions are different from a traditional multiple-choice question, they might be easier for you to do. Clicking on part of an image—rather than selecting a choice from A to D—might feel similar to how you express knowledge in the real world.

Hot spot questions appear on every subtest except RLA. On the Mathematics subtest, hot spots are most often used to assess your ability to plot points on coordinate grids, number lines, or scatter plots. For example, the graphic image could be a coordinate grid, and the question would ask you to plot a specific point, like (5, –2). You would then click the spot on the graph associated with (5, –2). Other math questions include identifying specific parts of a scale model, selecting numerical or algebraic expressions that identify parallel equations, or identifying different representations of the same numeric value.

On the Science subtest, hot spot questions may use a graphic image or a block of text. In addition to allowing you to identify information on a model or diagram, they assess your understanding of the relationship between data points or your ability to use data points to support or refute a particular conclusion.

On the Social Studies subtest, hot spots questions often ask you to indicate evidence that supports a particular statement or idea. Like on the Science subtest, you might be asked to demonstrate the relationship between different data points from a short block of text or an image. They are also often used with mapping.

EXAMPLE

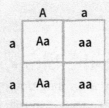

The square above is based on the eye color of two parents: one with brown eyes and one with green. According to this square, this couple's biological children have a 50 percent chance of having green eyes. Click the sections of the square that support this conclusion.

Drop-Down (Cloze)

A drop-down question is an open-stem question, or incomplete statement. This type of question occurs in multiple-choice questions as well. However, in a drop-down question, rather than selecting an answer from the A – D options that appear after the statement, a drop-down box with multiple response options is embedded in the statement. You will select the appropriate word or phrase, which will fill in the blank. You can then read the complete statement to check the accuracy of your response. For example, a question might read, *Bananas are*, followed by a drop-down box with several colors listed—blue, red, yellow, green. You would click yellow, and the statement would then read, *Bananas are yellow.*

On the Mathematics subtest, drop-down questions are most often used to assess math vocabulary or to compare two quantities, in which case the drop-down box will contain less than, greater than, and equal signs. For other drop-down questions, you will be asked to select the correct number to complete a statement.

On the RLA subtest, drop-down questions are used to assess mastery of language skills, such as American English conventions, standard usage, and punctuation. Drop-down questions on this subtest mimic the editing process. So multiple variations of the same phrase will appear in the drop-down box within the text, and you will select the one that is grammatically correct. It is important to read the complete sentence after your selection to ensure your choice makes sense.

On the Science and Social Studies subtests, these questions are also most often used with text. You may be asked to draw a logical conclusion from provided text-based evidence or to make a generalization based on an author's argument.

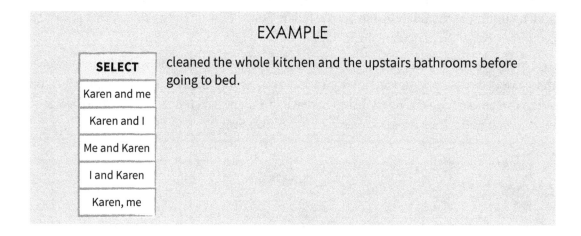

EXAMPLE

SELECT
Karen and me
Karen and I
Me and Karen
I and Karen
Karen, me

cleaned the whole kitchen and the upstairs bathrooms before going to bed.

Fill-in-the-blank (FIB)

A fill-in-the-blank (FIB) question is a combination of a standard item and a constructed response. It is similar to a drop-down question in that it contains an incomplete statement. However, rather than selecting an answer from several options, you type in the answer. Unlike a constructed response, the answer you type will be only one to two words long. Using the example in the drop-down section, if the statement read, *Bananas are*, rather than selecting from several colors, you would simply type *yellow*. FIB can only be used for questions in which the answers have very little variability (so this particular example would not actually appear on the test). Sometimes a question may have more than one blank, requiring you to type two separate responses. FIB questions assess your knowledge without the distraction of incorrect choices.

FIB questions are included in all subtests except the RLA subtest. On the Mathematics subtest, FIB questions may ask you to type a numerical answer to a math problem or to write an equation using the numbers and characters on the keyboard. On the Science subtest, an FIB question may ask you to fill in the specific quantity of something from a graphic representation of data or for a response to a specific calculation.

On the Social Studies subtest, FIB questions are used to assess your understanding of a concept or key vocabulary. Often there will be brief text from which you will have to infer the concept or vocabulary. Other questions will ask you to identify specific information—from a chart, graph, or map—that supports or demonstrates a concept, idea, or trend.

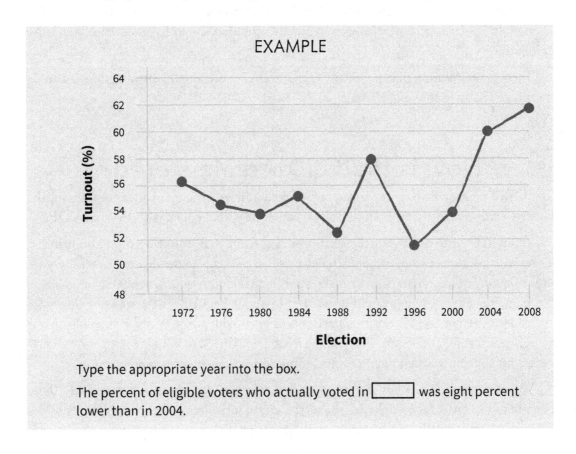

EXAMPLE

Type the appropriate year into the box.

The percent of eligible voters who actually voted in ⬚ was eight percent lower than in 2004.

How is the GED Scored?

You will receive your scores on your GED tests within twenty-four hours of completing the exam.

The number of raw points each question is worth depends on the number of required answers for that question. For example, a question that requires the test-taker to select two items from a drop-down menu would be worth two raw points.

The two science constructed-response questions are scored on a three-point scale. Scores are based on scientific reasoning, the application of relevant scientific skills, and the quality of the evidence or support provided.

The written component of the Reasoning through Language Arts subtest is scored on three traits: analysis of arguments and use of evidence, development of ideas and structure, and clarity and command of standard English. Each trait can earn a raw score of up to two points.

The number of questions can vary between versions of the exam but the number of raw points remains constant. There are sixty-five raw score points on the Reasoning through

Language Arts exam, forty-nine on the Mathematical Reasoning exam, forty on the Science exam, and thirty on the Social Studies exam. The total number of raw points earned is then scaled to a score between 100 and 200. You must earn at least 145 scaled score points in order to qualify for your high school equivalency credential. A score of at least 165 qualifies you as College Ready, and a score of 175 or higher qualifies you as College Ready + Credit, meaning you could qualify to receive college credit.

Each test is scored independently, and points from one test cannot affect the point value of another. You must pass each subtest in order to qualify for your high school-equivalency credential.

There is no guessing penalty on the GED exam, so you should always guess if you do not know the answer to a question.

How is the GED Administered?

The GED exam is a computer-based test offered at a wide range of sites throughout the United States and the world. To find a test center near you, check with Pearson VUE.

You will need to print your registration ticket from your online account and bring it, along with your identification, to the testing site on test day. Some test centers will require other forms or documentation, so make sure to check with your test center in advance. No pens, pencils, erasers, printed or written materials, electronic devices or calculators are allowed. An online scientific calculator will be provided to you at the time of the test as well as a formula reference sheet for the math test. Check in advance with your testing center for specific testing guidelines, including restrictions on dress and accessories.

You may take the subtests all on the same day or individually on separate days. There is no required order for completing the test. Certain jurisdictions may apply limits to the amount of time available for completing all four tests.

There are three versions of each test, so if you want to retake the test, you can do so right away up to two times. You will receive a different version of the test each time. If you still need to retake the test after the third time, you must wait sixty days. Ultimately, you may take each test up to eight times a year. If you do not pass one subtest, you are not required to retake all of the tests—only the one you failed.

About This Guide

This guide will help you to master the most important test topics and also develop critical test-taking skills. We have built features into our books to prepare you for your tests and increase your score. Along with a detailed summary of the test's format, content, and scoring, we offer an in-depth overview of the content knowledge required to pass the test. In the review you'll find sidebars that provide interesting information, highlight key concepts, and review content so that you can solidify your understanding of the exam's concepts. You can also test your knowledge with sample questions throughout the text and practice questions that reflect the content and format of the GED. We're pleased you've chosen Accepted, Inc. to be a part of your journey!

PART I: REASONING THROUGH LANGUAGE ARTS

one

READING

To do well on reading comprehension questions on the GED, you should be able to identify explicit details in a text, draw inferences about the text, grasp the author's intent, and understand the main idea of a text. Just like the rest of the Reasoning Through Language Arts section, about 75 percent of the texts are from informational sources and 25 percent are literary.

The Main Idea

The main idea of a text describes the author's main topic and general concept; it also generalizes the author's point of view about a subject. It is contained within and throughout the text. The reader can find the main idea by considering how the main topic is addressed throughout a passage. On reading questions, you are expected not only to identify the main idea but also to be able to differentiate it from a text's theme and to summarize the main idea clearly and concisely. For instance, you might be asked to pick an answer choice that best summarizes the main idea of a passage.

The author's perspective on the subject of the text and how he or she has framed the argument or story hints at the main idea. For example, if the author framed the story with a description, image, or short anecdote, he or she is hinting at a particular idea or point of view.

The main idea is closely connected to topic sentences and how they are supported in a text. Questions may deal with finding topic sentences, summarizing a text's ideas, or locating supporting details. The sections and practice examples that follow detail the distinctions between these aspects of text.

Identifying the Main Idea

To identify the main idea, first identify the topic. The difference between these two things is simple: the **TOPIC** is the overall subject matter of a passage; the **MAIN IDEA** is what the author wants to say about that topic. The main idea covers the author's direct perspective about a topic, as distinct from the **THEME**, which is a generally true idea that the reader might derive from a text. Most of the time, fiction has a theme, whereas nonfiction has a main idea. This is the case because in a nonfiction text, the author speaks more directly to the audience about a topic—his or her perspective is more visible. For example, the following passage conveys the topic as well as what the author wants to communicate about that topic.

> The "shark mania" of recent years can be largely pinned on the sensationalistic media surrounding the animals: from the release of *Jaws* in 1975 to the week of ultra-hyped shark feeding frenzies and "worst shark attacks" countdowns known as *Shark Week*, popular culture both demonizes and fetishizes sharks until the public cannot get enough. Swimmers and beachgoers may look nervously for the telltale fin skimming the surface, but the reality is that shark bites are extremely rare and they are almost never unprovoked. Sharks attack people at very predictable times and for very predictable reasons. Rough surf, poor visibility, or a swimmer sending visual and physical signals that mimic a shark's normal prey are just a few examples.
>
> Of course, some places are just more dangerous to swim. Shark attack "hot spots," such as the coasts of Florida, South Africa, and New Zealand try a variety of solutions to protect tourists and surfers. Some beaches employ "shark nets," meant to keep sharks away from the beach, though these are controversial because they frequently trap other forms of marine life as well. Other beaches use spotters in helicopters and boats to alert beach officials when there are sharks in the area. In addition, there is an array of products that claim to offer personal protection from sharks, ranging from wetsuits in different colors to devices that broadcast electrical signals in an attempt to confuse the sharks' sensory organs. At the end of the day, though, beaches like these remain dangerous, and swimmers must assume the risk every time they paddle out from shore.

The author of this passage has a clear topic: sharks and their relationship with humans. In order to identify the main idea of the passage, the reader must ask, What does the author want to say about this topic? What is the reader meant to think or understand?

Readers should identify the topic of a text and pay attention to how the details about it relate to one another. A passage may discuss, for example, topic similarities, characteristics, causes, and/ or effects.

The author makes sure to provide information about several different aspects of the relationship between sharks and humans, and points out that humans must respect sharks as dangerous marine animals, without sensationalizing the risk of attack. The reader can figure this out by looking at the various pieces of information the author includes as well as the similarities between them. The passage describes sensationalistic media, then talks about how officials and governments try to protect beaches, and ends with the observation that people must take personal responsibility. These details clarify what the author's main idea is: thanks to safety precautions and their natural behavior, sharks are not as dangerous as they are portrayed to be. Summarizing that main idea by focusing on the connection between the different details helps the reader draw a conclusion.

EXAMPLES

The art of the twentieth and twenty-first centuries demonstrates several aspects of modern social advancement. A primary example is the advent of technology: new technologies have developed new avenues for art making, and the globalization brought about by the internet has both diversified the art world and brought it together simultaneously. Even as artists are able to engage in a global conversation about the categories and characteristics of art, creating a more uniform understanding, they can now express themselves in a diversity of ways for a diversity of audiences. The result has been a rapid change in how art is made and consumed.

1. This passage is primarily concerned with

   A) the importance of art in the twenty-first century.

   B) the use of art to communicate overarching ideals to diverse communities.

   C) the importance of technology to art criticism.

   D) the change in understanding and creation of art in the modern period.

   Answer:

   D) is correct. The art of the modern period reflects the new technologies and globalization possible through the internet.

2. Which of the following best describes the main idea of the passage?

   A) Modern advances in technology have diversified art making and connected artists to distant places and ideas.

   B) Diversity in modern art is making it harder for art viewers to understand and talk about that art.

   C) The use of technology to discuss art allows us to create standards for what art should be.

   D) Art-making before the invention of technology such as the internet was disorganized and poorly understood.

   Answer:

   A) is correct. According to the text, technology and the internet have "diversified the art world and brought it together simultaneously."

Topic and Summary Sentences

Identifying the main idea requires understanding the structure of a piece of writing. In a short passage of one or two paragraphs, the topic and summary sentences quickly relate what the paragraphs are about and what conclusions the author wants the reader to draw. These sentences function as bookends to a paragraph or passage, telling readers what to think and keeping the passage tied tightly together.

Generally, the TOPIC SENTENCE is the first, or very near the first, sentence in a paragraph. It is a general statement that introduces the topic, clearly and specifically directing the reader to access any previous experience with that topic.

A summary is a very brief restatement of the most important parts of an argument or text. Building a summary begins with the most important idea in a text. A longer summary also includes supporting details. The text of a summary should be much shorter than the original.

The SUMMARY SENTENCE, on the other hand, frequently—but not always!—comes at the end of a paragraph or passage, because it wraps up all the ideas presented. This sentence provides an understanding of what the author wants to say about the topic and what conclusions to draw about it. While a topic sentence acts as an introduction to a topic, allowing the reader to activate his or her own ideas and experiences, the summary statement asks the reader to accept the author's ideas about that topic. Because of this, a summary sentence helps the reader quickly identify a piece's main idea.

EXAMPLES

There is nowhere more beautiful and interesting than California. With glimmering azure seas, fertile green plains, endless deserts, and majestic mountains, California offers every landscape. Hikers can explore the wilderness in Yosemite National Park, where a variety of plants and animals make their home. Farmers grow almonds, apricots, cotton, tomatoes, and more in the Central Valley that winds through the middle of the state. Skiers enjoy the slopes and backcountry of the Sierra Nevada and Lake Tahoe area. In the desert of Death Valley, temperatures rise well over one hundred degrees Fahrenheit. And of course, California's famous beaches stretch from the Mexican border to Oregon. Furthermore, California features some of America's most important cities. In the south, Los Angeles is home to the movie industry and Hollywood. Farther north, the San Francisco Bay Area includes Silicon Valley, where the US tech industry is based. Both places are centers of commercial activity. In fact, California is the most populous state in the country. There is no shortage of things to do or sights to see!

1. Which of the following best explains the general idea and focus indicated by the topic sentence?

   A) The diversity of California's landscape allows agriculture to flourish, and the most important crops will be detailed.

   B) California is beautiful and diverse; the reader will read on to find out what makes it so interesting.

   C) California is a peaceful place; its people live with a sense of predictability and the state is prosperous.

   D) The incredible geography of California is the reason it is a rural state, and the reader can expect a discussion of the countryside.

   Answer:

   B) is correct. This option indicates both the main idea and what the reader will focus on while reading.

2. Which of the following best states what the author wants the reader to understand after reading the summary sentence?

   A) Tourists should see everything in California when they visit.

   B) The cities of California are interesting, but the rural parts are better.

   C) The resources of California are nearly exhausted.

   D) California is an inspiring and exciting place.

   Answer:

   D) is correct. The phrase "no shortage of things to do or sights to see" suggests the writer is enthusiastic about the many interesting activities possible in

Supporting Details

Between a topic sentence and a summary sentence, the rest of a paragraph is built with SUPPORTING DETAILS. Supporting details come in many forms; the purpose of the passage dictates the type of details that will support the main idea. A persuasive passage may use facts and data or detail specific reasons for the author's opinion. An informative passage will primarily use facts about the topic to support the main idea. Even a narrative passage will have supporting details—specific things the author says to develop the story and characters.

The most important aspect of supporting details is exactly what it sounds like: they support the main idea. Examining the various supporting details and how they work with one another will reveal how the author views a topic and what the main idea of the passage is. Supporting details are key to understanding a passage.

Supporting details can often be found in texts by looking for SIGNAL WORDS—transitions that explain to the reader how one sentence or idea is connected to another. Signal words can add information, provide counterarguments, create organization in a passage, or draw conclusions. Some common signal words and phrases include *in particular*, *in addition*, *besides*, *contrastingly*, *therefore*, and *because*.

EXAMPLE

Increasingly, companies are turning to subcontracting services rather than hiring full-time employees. This provides companies with advantages like greater flexibility, reduced legal responsibility to employees, and lower possibility of unionization within the company. However, this has led to increasing confusion and uncertainty over the legal definition of employment. Courts have grappled with questions about the hiring company's responsibility in maintaining fair labor practices. Companies argue that they delegate that authority to subcontractors, while unions and other worker advocate groups argue that companies still have a legal obligation to the workers who contribute to their business.

According to the passage, why do companies use subcontractors?

Hiring subcontractors

A) costs less money than hiring full-time employees.

B) increases the need for unionization of employees.

C) reduces the company's legal responsibilities.

D) gives the company greater control over worker's hours.

Answer:

C) is correct. The passage states that hiring subcontractors provides the advantage of "reduced legal responsibility to employees."

The Author's Purpose

The author of a passage sets out with a specific goal in mind: to communicate a particular idea to an audience. The **AUTHOR'S PURPOSE** is determined by asking why the author wants the reader to understand the passage's main idea. There are four basic purposes to which an author can write: narrative, expository, technical, and persuasive. Within each of these general purposes, the author may direct the audience to take a clear action or respond in a certain way.

The purpose for which an author writes a passage is also connected to the structure of that text. In a **NARRATIVE**, the author seeks to tell a story, often to illustrate a theme or idea the reader needs to consider. In a narrative, the author uses characteristics of storytelling, such as chronological order, characters, and a defined setting, and these characteristics communicate the author's theme or main idea.

In an **EXPOSITORY** passage, on the other hand, the author simply seeks to explain an idea or topic to the reader. The main idea will probably be a factual statement or a direct assertion of a broadly held opinion. Expository writing can come in many forms, but one essential feature is a fair and balanced representation of a topic. The author may explore one detailed aspect or a broad range of characteristics, but he or she mainly seeks to prompt a decision from the reader.

Similarly, in **TECHNICAL** writing, the author's purpose is to explain specific processes, techniques, or equipment in order for the reader to use that process or equipment to obtain a desired result. Writing like this employs chronological or spatial structures, specialized vocabulary, and imperative or directive language.

Reading persuasive text requires an awareness of what the author believes about the topic.

In **PERSUASIVE** writing, the author actively seeks to convince the reader to accept an opinion or belief. Much like expository writing, persuasive writing is presented in many organizational forms.

EXAMPLE

University of California, Berkeley, researchers decided to tackle an age-old problem: why shoelaces come untied. They recorded the shoelaces of a volunteer walking on a treadmill by attaching devices to record the acceleration, or g-force, experienced by the knot. The results were surprising. A shoelace knot experiences more g-force from a person walking than any rollercoaster can generate. However, if the person simply stomped or swung their feet—the two movements that make up a walker's stride—the g-force was not enough to undo the knots.

What is the purpose of this passage?

A) to confirm if shoelaces always come undone

B) to compare the force of treadmills and rollercoasters

C) to persuade readers to tie their shoes tighter

D) to describe the results of an experiment on shoelaces

Organization and Text Structures

It's important to analyze the organization and structure of informational texts, as these details can provide valuable insight into the author's purpose and the overall meaning of a text. Several common structures are used in informative texts, and understanding these structures will help readers quickly make sense of new texts. Texts may be organized in one of the following ways:

- **CHRONOLOGICAL** texts describe events in the order they occurred.
- **PROBLEM-SOLUTION** texts begin by describing a problem and then offer a possible solution to the issue.
- **CAUSE-EFFECT** is a text structure that shows a causal chain of events or ideas.
- **GENERAL-TO-SPECIFIC** is a text structure that describes a general topic then provides details about a specific aspect of that topic.
- **COMPARE-CONTRAST** texts give the similarities and differences between two things.

Authors choose the organizational structure of their text according to their purpose. For example, an author who hopes to convince people to begin recycling might begin by talking about the problems that are caused by excessive waste and end by offering recycling as a reasonable solution. On the other hand, the author might choose to use a chronological structure for an article whose purpose is to give an impartial history of recycling.

EXAMPLE

For thirteen years, a spacecraft called *Cassini* was on an exploratory mission to Saturn. The spacecraft was designed not to return but to end its journey by diving into Saturn's atmosphere. This dramatic ending provided scientists with unprecedented information about Saturn's atmosphere and its magnetic and gravitational fields. First, however, *Cassini* passed Saturn's largest moon, Titan, where it recorded data on Titan's curious methane lakes, gathering information about potential seasons on the planet-sized moon. Then it passed through the unexplored region between Saturn itself and its famous rings. Scientists hope to learn how old the rings are and to directly examine the particles that make them up. *Cassini*'s mission ended in 2017, but researchers have new questions for future exploration.

Which of the following best describes the organization of this passage?

A) general-to-specific

B) compare-contrast

C) chronological

D) problem-solution

> **Answer:**
>
> **C) is correct.** The passage describes the journey of *Cassini* in chronological order: it passed by Titan, went through the region between Saturn and its rings, and ended its mission in 2017.

The Audience

The structure, purpose, main idea, and language of a text all converge on one target: the intended AUDIENCE. An author makes decisions about every aspect of a piece of writing based on that audience, and readers can evaluate the writing by considering who the author is writing for. By considering the probable reactions of an intended audience, readers can determine many things:

- whether they are part of that intended audience
- the author's purpose for using specific techniques or devices
- the biases of the author and how they appear in the writing
- how the author uses rhetorical strategies.

When reading a persuasive text, students should maintain awareness of what the author believes about the topic.

The audience for a text can be identified by careful analysis of the text. First, the reader considers who most likely cares about the topic and main idea of the text: who would want or need to know about this topic? The audience may be SPECIFIC (e.g., biologists who study sharks) or more GENERAL (e.g., people with an interest in marine life).

Next, consider the language of the text. The author tailors language to appeal to the intended audience, so the reader can determine from the language who the author is speaking to. A FORMAL style is used in business and academic settings and can make the author seem more credible. Characteristics of a formal style include:

- third person perspective (i.e., no use of *I* or *you*)
- no use of slang or clichés
- follows a clear structure (e.g., an introduction, a body, and a conclusion)
- technically correct grammar and sentence structure
- objective language

An INFORMAL style is used to appeal to readers in a more casual setting, such as a magazine or blog. Using an informal style may make the author seem less credible, but it can help create an emotional connection with the audience. Characteristics of informal writing include:

- use of first or second person (e.g., *I* or *you*)
- use of slang or casual language
- follows an unusual or flexible structure
- bends the rules of grammar
- appeals to audience's emotions

Evaluating Arguments

An author selects details to help support the main idea. The reader must then evaluate these details for relevance and consistency. Though the author generally includes details that support the text's main idea, it's up to the reader to decide whether those details are convincing.

Readers should be able to differentiate between facts and opinions in order to more effectively analyze supporting details. FACTS are based in truth and can usually be proven. They are pieces of information that have been confirmed or validated. An opinion is a judgment, belief, or viewpoint that is not based on evidence. OPINIONS are often stated in descriptive, subjective language that is difficult to define or prove. While opinions can be included in informative texts, they are often of little impact unless they are supported by some kind of evidence.

Sometimes, the author's BIAS—an inclination towards a particular belief—causes the author to leave out details that do not directly support the main idea or that support an opposite idea. The reader has to be able to notice not only what the author says but also what the author leaves out. Discovering the author's bias and how the supporting details reveal that bias is also key to understanding a text.

> Which of the following phrases would be associated with opinions?
> for example, studies have shown, I believe, in fact, it's possible that

Writers will often use specific techniques, or RHETORICAL STRATEGIES, to build an argument. Readers can identify these strategies in order to clearly understand what an author wants them to believe, how the author's perspective and purpose may lead to bias, and whether the passage includes any logical fallacies.

Common rhetorical strategies include the appeals to ethos, logos, and pathos. An author uses these to build trust with the reader, explain the logical points of his or her argument, and convince the reader that his or her opinion is the best option.

An **ETHOS (ETHICAL) APPEAL** uses balanced, fair language and seeks to build a trusting relationship between the author and the reader. An author might explain her or his credentials, include the reader in an argument, or offer concessions to an opposing argument.

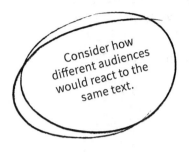

Consider how different audiences would react to the same text.

A **LOGOS (LOGICAL) APPEAL** builds on that trust by providing facts and support for the author's opinion, explaining the argument with clear connections and reasoning. At this point, the reader should beware of logical fallacies that connect unconnected ideas and build arguments on incorrect premises. With a logical appeal, an author strives to convince the reader to accept an opinion or belief by demonstrating that not only is it the most logical option but that it also satisfies her or his emotional reaction to a topic.

A **PATHOS (EMOTIONAL) APPEAL** does not depend on reasonable connections between ideas; rather, it seeks to remind the reader, through imagery, strong language, and personal connections, that the author's argument aligns with her or his best interests.

EXAMPLE

Exercise is critical for healthy development in children. Today in the United States, there is an epidemic of poor childhood health; many of these children will face further illnesses in adulthood that are due to poor diet and lack of exercise now. This is a problem for all Americans, especially with the rising cost of health care.

It is vital that school systems and parents encourage children to engage in a minimum of thirty minutes of cardiovascular exercise each day, mildly increasing their heart rate for a sustained period. This is proven to decrease the likelihood of developmental diabetes, obesity, and a multitude of other health problems. Also, children need a proper diet, rich in fruits and vegetables, so they can develop physically and learn healthy eating habits early on.

Which of the following statements from the passage is a fact, not an opinion?

A) Fruits and vegetables are the best way to help children be healthy.

B) Children today are lazier than they were in previous generations.

C) The risk of diabetes in children is reduced by physical activity.

D) Children should engage in thirty minutes of exercise a day.

Answer:

C) is correct. Choice C is a simple fact stated by the author. It is introduced by the word *proven* to indicate that it is supported by evidence.

Drawing Conclusions

Reading text begins with making sense of the explicit meanings of information or a narrative. Understanding occurs as the reader draws conclusions and makes logical inferences. First, the reader considers the details or facts. He or she then comes to a **CONCLUSION**—the next logical point in the thought sequence. For example, in a Hemingway story, an old man sits alone in a cafe. A young waiter says that the cafe is closing, but the old man continues to drink. The waiter starts closing up, and the old man signals for a refill. Based on these details, the reader might conclude that the old man has not understood the young waiter's desire for him to leave.

An inference is distinguished from a conclusion drawn. An **INFERENCE** is an assumption the reader makes based on details in the text as well as his or her own knowledge. It is more of an educated guess that extends the literal meaning of a text. Inferences begin with the given details; however, the reader uses the facts to determine additional information. What the reader already knows informs what is being suggested by the details of decisions or situations in the text. Returning to the example of the Hemingway story, the reader might *infer* that the old man is lonely, enjoys being in the cafe, and therefore is reluctant to leave.

When reading fictional text, inferring character motivations is essential. The actions of the characters move the plot forward; a series of events is understood by making sense of why the characters did what they did. Hemingway includes contrasting details as the young waiter and an older waiter discuss the old man. The older waiter sympathizes with the old man; both men have no one at home and experience a sense of emptiness in life, which motivates them to seek the cafe.

Another aspect of understanding text is connecting it to other texts. Readers may connect the Hemingway story about the old man in the cafe to other Hemingway stories about individuals struggling to deal with loss and loneliness in a dignified way. They can extend their initial connections to people they know or their personal experiences. When readers read a persuasive text, they often connect the arguments made to counterarguments and opposing evidence of which they are aware. They use these connections to infer meaning.

When considering a character's motivations, the reader should ask what the character wants to achieve, what the character will get by accomplishing this, and what the character seems to value the most.

Conclusions are drawn by thinking about how the author wants the reader to feel. A group of carefully selected facts can cause the reader to feel a certain way.

EXAMPLE

After World War I, political and social forces pushed for a return to normalcy in the United States. The result was disengagement from the larger world and increased focus on American economic growth and personal enjoyment. Caught in the middle were American writers, raised on the values of the prewar world and frustrated with what they viewed as the superficiality and materialism of postwar American culture. Many of them fled to Paris, where they became known as the "lost generation," creating a trove of literary works criticizing their home culture and delving into their own feelings of alienation.

Which conclusion about the effects of war is most likely true, according to the passage?

A) War served as an inspiration for literary works.

B) It was difficult to stabilize countries after war occurred.

C) Writers were torn between supporting war and their own ideals.

D) Individual responsibility and global awareness declined after the war.

Tone and Mood

The TONE of a passage describes the author's attitude toward the topic. In general, the author's tone can be described as positive, negative, or neutral. The MOOD is the pervasive feeling or atmosphere in a passage that provokes specific emotions in the reader. Put simply, tone is how the author feels about the topic. Mood is how the reader feels about the text.

Table 1.1 Words That Describe Tone

POSITIVE	NEUTRAL	NEGATIVE
admiring		angry
approving		annoyed
celebratory		belligerent
earnest		bitter
encouraging		condescending
excited		confused
funny	casual	cynical
hopeful	detached	depressed
humorous	formal	disrespectful
nostalgic	impartial	embarrassed
optimistic	informal	fearful
playful	objective	gloomy
poignant	questioning	melancholy
proud	unconcerned	mournful
relaxed		pessimistic
respectful		skeptical
sentimental		solemn
silly		suspicious
sympathetic		unsympathetic

DICTION, or word choice, helps determine mood and tone in a passage. Many readers make the mistake using the author's ideas alone to determine tone; a much better practice is to look at specific words and try to identify a pattern in the emotion they evoke. Does the writer choose positive words like *ambitious* and *confident*? Or does he describe those concepts with negative words like *greedy* and *overbearing*? The first writer's tone might be described as admiring, while the more negative tone would be disapproving.

When looking at tone, it's important to examine not just the literal definition of words. Every word has not only a literal meaning but also a CONNOTATIVE MEANING, which relies on

To decide the connotation of a word, the reader examines whether the word conveys a positive or negative association in the mind. Adjectives are often used to influence the feelings of the reader, such as in the phrase *an ambitious attempt to achieve.*

the common emotions and experiences an audience might associate with that word. The following words are all synonyms: *dog, puppy, cur, mutt, canine, pet.* Two of these words—*dog* and *canine*—are neutral words, without strong associations or emotions. Two others—*pet* and *puppy*—have positive associations. The last two—*cur* and *mutt*—have negative associations. A passage that uses one pair of these words versus another pair activates the positive or negative reactions of the audience.

EXAMPLES

Day had broken cold and grey, exceedingly cold and grey, when the man turned aside from the main Yukon trail and climbed the high earth-bank, where a dim and little-travelled trail led eastward through the fat spruce timberland. It was a steep bank, and he paused for breath at the top, excusing the act to himself by looking at his watch. It was nine o'clock. There was no sun nor hint of sun, though there was not a cloud in the sky. It was a clear day, and yet there seemed an intangible pall over the face of things, a subtle gloom that made the day dark, and that was due to the absence of sun. This fact did not worry the man. He was used to the lack of sun. It had been days since he had seen the sun, and he knew that a few more days must pass before that cheerful orb, due south, would just peep above the sky-line and dip immediately from view.

—from "To Build a Fire" by Jack London

1. Which of the following best describes the mood of the passage?

    A) exciting and adventurous

    B) unhappy and anxious

    C) bleak but accepting

    D) grim yet hopeful

    Answer:

    C) is correct. The day is described as "cold and grey" with an "intangible pall," which creates a bleak mood. However, the man himself "did not worry" and knew that only "a few more days must pass" before he would see the sun again, suggesting he has accepted his circumstances.

2. The connotation of the words *intangible pall* is

    A) a death-like covering.

    B) a sense of familiarity.

    C) a feeling of communal strength.

    D) an understanding of the struggle ahead.

    Answer:

    A) is correct. Within the context of the sentence "It was a clear day, and yet there seemed an intangible pall over the face of things, a subtle gloom that made the day dark," the words *gloom* and *dark* are suggestive of death; the phrase *over the face* suggests a covering.

Meaning of Words and Phrases

The GED does not specifically ask you to define words, but it is good to know strategies to determine the meaning of unfamiliar words you may encounter when analyzing reading passages and improving paragraphs.

When confronted with unfamiliar words, the passage itself can help clarify their meaning. Often, identifying the tone or main idea of the passage can help eliminate answer choices. For example, if the tone of the passage is generally positive, try eliminating the answer choices with a negative connotation. Or, if the passage is about a particular occupation, rule out words unrelated to that topic.

Passages may also provide specific context clues that can help determine the meaning of a word. One type of context clue is a **DEFINITION**, or **DESCRIPTION**, **CLUE**. Sometimes, authors use a difficult word, then include *that is* or *which is* to signal that they are providing a definition. An author also may provide a synonym or restate the idea in more familiar words:

> Teachers often prefer teaching students with intrinsic motivation; these students have an internal desire to learn.

The meaning of *intrinsic* is restated as *an internal desire*.

Similarly, authors may include an **EXAMPLE CLUE**, providing an example phrase that clarifies the meaning of the word:

> Teachers may view extrinsic rewards as efficacious; however, an individual student may not be interested in what the teacher offers. For example, a student who does not like sweets may not feel any incentive to work when offered a sugary reward.

Efficacious is explained with an example that demonstrates how an extrinsic reward may not be effective.

Another commonly used context clue is the **CONTRAST**, or **ANTONYM**, **CLUE**. In this case, authors indicate that the unfamiliar word is the opposite of a familiar word:

> In contrast to intrinsic motivation, extrinsic motivation is contingent on teachers offering rewards that are appealing.

The phrase *in contrast* tells the reader that extrinsic is the opposite of intrinsic.

EXAMPLES

1. Which of the following is the meaning of *incentivize* as used in the sentence?

   One challenge of teaching is finding ways to incentivize, or to motivate, learning.

   A) encourage
   B) determine
   C) challenge
   D) improve

2. Which of the following is the meaning of *apprehensive* as used in the sentence?

   If an extrinsic reward is extremely desirable, a student may become so apprehensive he or she cannot focus. The student may experience such intense pressure to perform that the reward undermines its intent.

   A) uncertain

   B) distracted

   C) anxious

   D) forgetful

Answer:

C) is correct. The reader can infer that the *pressure to perform* is making the student anxious.

Figurative Language

Figures of speech are expressions that are understood to have a nonliteral meaning. Rather than stating their ideas directly, authors use FIGURATIVE LANGUAGE to suggest meaning by speaking of a subject as if it were something else. For example, when Shakespeare says, "All the world's a stage,/ And all men and women merely players," he is speaking of the world as if it is a stage. Since the world is not literally a stage, the reader has to ask how the two are similar and what Shakespeare might be implying about the world through this comparison. Figures of speech extend the meaning of words by engaging the reader's imagination and adding emphasis to different aspects of their subject.

A METAPHOR is a type of figurative language that describes something that may be unfamiliar to the reader (the topic) by referring to it as though it were something else that is more familiar to the reader (the vehicle). A metaphor stands in as a synonym, interchangeable with its corresponding topic. As the reader reflects on the similarities between the topic and the vehicle, he or she forms a clearer understanding of the topic. For example, in Shakespeare's *Romeo and Juliet*, Romeo says that "Juliet is the sun." By making this comparison, Romeo is comparing Juliet's energy to the brightness of the sun, which is familiar to readers.

A SIMILE is a type of figurative language that directly points to similarities between two things. As with a metaphor, the author uses a familiar vehicle to express an idea about a less familiar topic. Unlike a metaphor, however, a simile does not replace the object with a figurative description; it compares the vehicle and topic using "like," "as," or similar words. For example, in his poem "The Rime of the Ancient Mariner," Coleridge describes his ship as "idle as a painted ship/ Upon a painted ocean." He speaks about the boat as if it were painted (unlike Romeo above, who says explicitly that Juliet is the sun itself). The reader understands that paintings do not move, so Coleridge uses this comparison to show the reader that the ship in the poem is completely motionless.

IMAGERY is vivid description that appeals to the reader's sense of sight, sound, smell, taste, or touch. This type of figurative language allows readers to experience through their senses what is being described; as readers use their imaginations to visualize or recall sensory experience, they are drawn into the scene of the story or poem.

HYPERBOLE is an overstatement, an exaggeration intended to achieve a particular effect. Hyperbole can create humor or add emphasis to a text by drawing the reader's attention to a particular idea. For example, a character might say he or she is "so hungry, [he or she] could eat a horse." Though the character probably cannot literally eat a horse, the reader understands that he or she is extremely hungry.

PERSONIFICATION is a type of figurative language in which human characteristics are attributed to objects, abstract ideas, natural forces, or animals. For example, if a writer refers to "murmuring pine trees," he or she is attributing to the pine trees the human ability of murmuring. The writer is using the familiar vehicle of the sound of murmuring to help the reader understand the sound pine trees make in the wind.

SYMBOLISM is a literary device in which the author uses a concrete object, action, or character to represent an abstract idea. The significance of the symbol reaches beyond the object's ordinary meaning. Familiar symbols are roses representing beauty, light representing truth, and darkness representing evil. As readers notice an author's use of symbolism, they begin to make connections and to formulate ideas about what the author is suggesting.

An **ALLUSION**, not to be confused with illusion, is a reference to a historical person or event, a fictional character or event, a mythological or religious character or event, or an artist or artistic work. When a reader recognizes an allusion, he or she may make associations that contribute to his or her understanding of the text. For example, if a character is described as having a "Mona Lisa smile," an instant image will arise in the minds of most readers. Because allusions can be difficult to recognize, especially for young readers whose experiences are limited, teachers must provide instruction in how to recognize, research, and interpret unfamiliar references.

CLICHÉS are common sayings that lack originality but are familiar and relatable to an audience. Though clichés are not necessarily beneficial to the author who is trying to write a wholly original work, they can be helpful for a writer who is attempting to show that he or she can relate to the audience.

DIALECT and **SLANG** are linguistic qualities that an author might incorporate into his or her writing in order to develop characters or setting. A character's dialect may reveal where he or she is from, while the slang he or she uses may be an indication of social, economic, and educational status.

IRONY comes in different forms. **VERBAL IRONY** is used when a character or narrator says something that is the opposite of what he or she means. **SITUATIONAL IRONY** occurs when something happens that contradicts what the audience expected to happen. **DRAMATIC IRONY** occurs when the audience knows about something of which a character or characters are not aware.

Graphic Sources of Information

Informational texts on the GED may be accompanied by graphic sources of information, including graphs, diagrams, or photographs. There's no simple set of rules for handling these questions, but many of the same strategies that are used for other figures and for text passages are applicable.

Always start with the TITLE of a figure—it will provide information that is likely crucial to understanding the figure. An anatomical diagram might have a title such as *Lobes of the Brain* that tells the viewer that the diagram will likely show the names and locations of the brain's lobes. Similarly, a graph may have a title like *Number of Customers per Month*, which describes the information in the graph.

Also make sure to examine any LABELS, legends, or scales provided with the figure. Graphs, for example, should always include labels on the axes that describe what's shown on each axis, and a flowchart will have arrows indicating an ordered sequence.

Many of the strategies needed to interpret traditional reading passages can also be used for graphic representations of information, particularly those that may be text heavy. When looking at a photograph or advertisement, it will help to identify:

- the purpose of the author
- the intended audience
- rhetorical strategies designed to influence the viewer
- the main idea of the image

A flyer for a local bake sale, for example, may be designed to appeal to the viewer's emotions by including pictures of local schoolchildren. Similarly, a computer advertisement meant to appeal to corporate buyers would probably use more formal language than one aimed at teenagers.

EXAMPLE

As you can see from the graph, my babysitting business has been really successful. The year started with a busy couple of months—several snows combined with a large number of requests for Valentine's Day services boosted our sales quite a bit. The spring months have admittedly been a bit slow, but we're hoping for a big summer once school gets out. Several clients have already put in requests for our services!

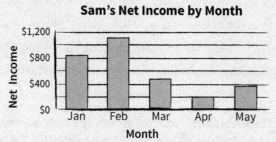

Sam's Net Income by Month

Based on the information in the graph, how much more did Sam's Babysitting Service bring in during February than during April?

A) $200

B) $900

C) $1100

D) $1300

Answer:

B) is correct. In February the service earned $1100, and in April it earned $200. The difference between the two months is $900.

Elements of Fiction

FICTION is a prose genre, made up of narratives whose details are not based in truth but are instead the creation of the author. Just as artists have the tools of color and shape to communicate ideas, so have writers their literary tools. These tools include point of view, plot, setting, character, tone, and figurative language. Each of these elements contributes to the overall idea that is developed in the text and, as such, can provide valuable insight into the theme of the work.

POINT OF VIEW is the perspective from which the action in a story is told. By carefully selecting a particular point of view, writers are able to control what their readers know. Most literature is written in either first person or third person point of view. With the FIRST PERSON POINT OF VIEW, the action is narrated by a character within the story, which can make it feel more believable and authentic to the reader. However, as a result of the first person point of view, the reader's knowledge and understanding are constrained by what the narrator notices and influenced by what the narrator thinks and values.

An author may, on the other hand, choose to tell the story from the THIRD PERSON POINT OF VIEW. A third person narrator is a voice outside the action of the story, an observer who shares what he or she knows, sees, or hears with the reader. A third person narrator might be FULLY OMNISCIENT (able to see into the minds of the characters and share what they are thinking and feeling), PARTIALLY OMNISCIENT (able to see into the minds of just one or a few characters), or LIMITED (unable to see into the minds of any of the characters and only able to share what can be seen and heard).

PLOT STRUCTURE is the way the author arranges the events of a narrative. In a conventional plot line, the story is structured around a central conflict, a struggle between two opposing forces. Conflicts in literature can be categorized in general terms as either internal or external, though most stories have a combination of both. Internal conflicts take place inside the main character's mind; he or she might be making a difficult decision, struggling with change, or sorting out priorities. External conflicts, on the other hand, occur when a character is in conflict with something or someone in the external world—the elements of nature, another character, supernatural forces, destiny, or society.

In a traditional plot structure, the author begins with EXPOSITION: important background information about the setting, the characters, and the current state of the world. Following the exposition, an INCITING INCIDENT introduces the antagonist and establishes the conflict. As the story progresses, the conflict becomes more complicated and tension increases, moving the story toward a CLIMAX or turning point, in which the conflict reaches a crisis point. Finally, there is a RESOLUTION to the conflict, followed by falling actions, events that move the characters away from the conflict and into a new life.

SETTING is the geographical and chronological location of events in a story. When considering setting, readers should examine how characters interact with their surroundings, how they are influenced by the societal expectations of that time and place, and how the location and time period impact the development of the story. Often, setting can seem inseparable from plot; therefore, a helpful question for beginning the discussion of setting is, How would this story change if it were set in a different time or place?

CHARACTER DEVELOPMENT is the process an author uses to create characters that are complex and, to some degree, believable. One way authors develop their characters is directly: they tell the reader explicitly what the character is like by describing traits and assigning values. Sometimes, authors might include the thoughts and feelings of the characters themselves, offering readers even more insight. Authors can also develop their characters indirectly by revealing their actions and interactions with others, sometimes including what one character says or thinks about another and allowing the reader to draw his or her own conclusions. Most authors use a combination of direct and indirect characterization; this ensures that readers know what they need to know while also providing opportunities for reflection and interpretation.

EXAMPLE

Which passage below from *A Mystery of Heroism* by Stephen Crane best demonstrates the third person omniscient point of view?

A) In the midst of it all Smith and Ferguson, two privates of A Company, were engaged in a heated discussion, which involved the greatest questions of the national existence.

B) An officer screamed out an order so violently that his voice broke and ended the sentence in a falsetto shriek.

C) The officer's face was grimy and perspiring, and his uniform was tousled as if he had been in direct grapple with an enemy. He smiled grimly when the men stared at him.

D) No, it could not be true. He was not a hero. Heroes had no shames in their lives, and, as for him, he remembered borrowing fifteen dollars from a friend and promising to pay it back the next day, and then avoiding that friend for ten months.

Answer:

D) is correct. The narrator is reporting the thoughts of the character, as the character's memory about not acting heroic in the past is revealed. The other choices only include descriptions of the characters words or actions.

Test Your Knowledge

Read each passage, and then choose the most correct answer.

The cisco, a foot-long freshwater fish native to the Great Lakes, once thrived throughout the basin but had virtually disappeared by the 1950s. However, today fishermen are pulling them up by the net-load in Lake Michigan and Lake Ontario. It is highly unusual for a native species to revive, and the reason for the cisco's reemergence is even more unlikely. The cisco have an invasive species, quagga mussels, to thank for their return. Quagga mussels depleted nutrients in the lakes, harming other species highly dependent on these nutrients. Cisco, however, thrive in low-nutrient environments. As other species—many invasive—diminished, cisco flourished in their place.

1. It can be inferred from the passage that most invasive species
   A) support the growth of native species.
   B) do not impact the development of native species.
   C) struggle to survive in their new environments.
   D) cause the decline of native species.

When a fire destroyed San Francisco's American Indian Center in October of 1969, American Indian groups set their sights on the recently closed island prison of Alcatraz as a site of a new Indian cultural center and school. Ignored by the government, an activist group known as Indians of All Tribes sailed to Alcatraz in the early morning hours with eighty-nine men, women, and children. They landed on Alcatraz, claiming it for all the tribes of North America. Their demands were ignored, and so the group continued to occupy the island for the next nineteen months, its numbers swelling up to 600 as others joined. By January of 1970, many of the original protestors had left, and on June 11, 1971, federal marshals forcibly removed the last residents.

2. The main idea of this passage is that
   A) the government refused to listen to the demands of American Indians.
   B) American Indians occupied Alcatraz in protest of government policy.
   C) few people joined the occupation of Alcatraz, weakening its effectiveness.
   D) the government took violent action against protestors at Alcatraz.

Archaeologists have discovered the oldest known specimens of bedbugs in a cave in Oregon where humans once lived. The three different species date back to between 5,000 and 11,000 years ago. The finding gives scientists a clue as to how bedbugs became human parasites. These bedbugs, like those that plague humans today, originated as bat parasites. Scientists hypothesize that it was the co-habitation of humans and bats in the caves that encouraged the bugs to begin feeding on the humans. The three species found in the Oregon caves are actually still around today, although they continue to prefer bats. Humans only lived seasonally in the Oregon cave system, however, which might explain why these insects did not fully transfer to human hosts like bedbugs elsewhere did.

3. With which of the following claims about bedbugs would the author most likely agree?

   A) Modern bedbugs that prefer humans thrive better in areas with extensive light.

   B) Bedbugs are a relatively fragile species that has struggled to survive over time.

   C) The transition to humans significantly accelerated the growth of bedbug populations.

   D) Bedbugs that prefer humans originated in caves that humans occupied year-round.

In a remote nature preserve in northeastern Siberia, scientists are attempting to recreate the subarctic steppe grassland ecosystem that flourished there during the last Ice Age. The area today is dominated by forests, but the lead scientists of the project believe the forested terrain was neither a natural development nor environmentally advantageous. They believe that if they can restore the grassland, they will be able to slow climate change by slowing the thawing of the permafrost which lies beneath the tundra. Key to this undertaking is restoring the wildlife to the region, including wild horses, musk oxen, bison, and yak. Most ambitiously, the scientists hope to revive the wooly mammoth species which was key in trampling the ground and knocking down the trees, helping to keep the land free for grasses to grow.

4. In the second sentence, the word *advantageous* most nearly means

   A) beneficial

   B) damaging

   C) useful

   D) appropriate

The heart works by shifting between two states: systole and diastole. In systole, the cardiac muscles are contracting and moving blood from any given chamber. During diastole, the muscles are relaxing and the chamber is expanding to fill with blood. The systole and diastole are responsible blood pressure—the pressure in the major arteries. This is the blood pressure that is measured in a regular exam. The two values are systolic and diastolic pressures, respectively. Because it is measured when blood is being pumped into the arteries, systolic blood pressure is always the higher number.

Systolic blood pressure is correlated with negative health outcomes such as stroke and heart failure. For this reason, doctor's categorize patients based on their systolic blood pressure. These categories are given below.

Categories	Systolic Range
Normal	< 120
Prehypertension	120 – 139
Hypertension Stage 1	140 – 159
Hypertension Stage 2	160 – 179
Hypertensive Crisis	> 180

5. If a person has a blood pressure of 151/95, which category would their doctor place them in?

   A) normal

   B) prehypertension

   C) hypertension stage 1

   D) hypertension stage 2

The odds of success for any new restaurant are slim. Competition in the city is fierce, and the low margin of return means that aspiring restaurateurs must be exact and ruthless with their budget and pricing. The fact that The City Café has lasted as long as it has is a testament to its owners' skills.

6. Which of the following conclusions is well supported by the passage?

   A) The City Café offers the best casual dining in town.

   B) The City Café has a well-managed budget and prices items on its menu appropriately.

   C) The popularity of The City Café will likely fall as new restaurants open in the city.

   D) The City Café has a larger margin of return than other restaurants in the city.

The social and political discourse of America continues to be permeated with idealism. An idealistic viewpoint asserts that the ideals of freedom, equality, justice, and human dignity are the truths that Americans must continue to aspire to. Idealists argue that truth is what should be, not necessarily what is. In general, they work to improve things and to make them as close to ideal as possible.

7. The purpose of the passage is to

   A) advocate for freedom, equality, justice, and human rights

   B) explain what an idealist believes in

   C) explain what's wrong with social and political discourse in America

   D) persuade readers to believe in certain truths

Alexander Hamilton and James Madison called for the Constitutional Convention to write a constitution as the foundation of a stronger federal government. Madison and other Federalists like John Adams believed in separation of powers, republicanism, and a strong federal government. Despite the separation of powers that would be provided for in the US Constitution, anti-Federalists like Thomas Jefferson called for even more limitations on the power of the federal government.

8. In the context of the passage above, which of the following would most likely NOT support a strong federal government?

   A) Alexander Hamilton

   B) James Madison

   C) John Adams

   D) Thomas Jefferson

It's that time again—the annual Friendswood Village Summer Fair is here! Last year we had a record number of visitors, and we're expecting an even bigger turnout this year. The fair will be bringing back all our traditional food and games, including the famous raffle. This year, we'll have a carousel, petting zoo, and climbing wall (for teenagers and adults only, please). We're also excited to welcome Petey's BBQ and Happy Tummy's Frozen Treats, who are both new to the fair this year. Tickets are available online and at local retailers.

9. Which of the following will NOT be a new presence at the Fair this year?
    A) the raffle
    B) the petting zoo
    C) the carousel
    D) the climbing wall

After looking at five houses, Robert and I have decided to buy the one on Forest Road. The first two homes we visited didn't have the space we need—the first had only one bathroom, and the second did not have a guest bedroom. The third house, on Pine Street, had enough space inside but didn't have a big enough yard for our three dogs. The fourth house we looked at, on Rice Avenue, was stunning but well above our price range. The last home, on Forest Road, wasn't in the neighborhood we wanted to live in. However, it had the right amount of space for the right price.

10. What is the author's conclusion about the house on Pine Street?
    A) The house did not have enough bedrooms.
    B) The house did not have a big enough yard.
    C) The house was not in the right neighborhood.
    D) The house was too expensive.

The study showed that private tutoring is providing a significant advantage to those students who are able to afford it. Researchers looked at the grades of students who had received free tutoring through the school versus those whose parents had paid for private tutors. The study included 2500 students in three high schools across four grade levels. The study found that private tutoring corresponded with a rise in grade point average (GPA) of 0.5 compared to students who used the school's free tutor service and 0.7 compared to students who used no tutoring. After reviewing the study, the board is recommending that the school restructure its free tutor service to provide a more equitable education for all students.

11. Which of the following would weaken the author's argument?
    A) the fact that the cited study was funded by a company that provides discounted tutoring through schools
    B) a study showing differences in standardized test scores between students at schools in different neighborhoods
    C) a statement signed by local teachers stating that they do not provide preferential treatment in the classroom or when grading
    D) a study showing that GPA does not strongly correlate with success in college

It could be said that the great battle between the North and South we call the Civil War was a battle for individual identity. The states of the South had their own culture, one based on farming, independence, and the rights of both man and state to determine their own paths. Similarly, the North had forged its own identity as a center of centralized commerce and manufacturing. This clash of lifestyles was bound to create tension, and this tension was bound to lead to war. But people who try to sell you this narrative are wrong. The Civil War was not a battle of cultural identities—it was a battle about slavery. All other explanations for the war are either a direct consequence of the South's desire for wealth at the expense of her fellow man or a fanciful invention to cover up this sad portion of our nation's history. And it cannot be denied that this time in our past was very sad indeed.

12. The purpose of the passage is to

   A) convince readers that slavery was the main cause of the Civil War

   B) illustrate the cultural differences between the North and the South before the Civil War

   C) persuade readers that the North deserved to win the Civil War

   D) demonstrate that the history of the Civil War is too complicated to be understood clearly

East River High School has released its graduation summary for the class of 2016. Out of a total of 558 senior students, 525 (94 percent) successfully completed their degree program and graduated. Of these, 402 (representing 72 percent of the total class) went on to attend to a two- or four-year college or university. The distribution of students among the four main types of colleges and universities—small or large private and small or large public—is shown in the figure below. As the data shows, the majority of East River High School's college-attending graduates chose a large, public institution.

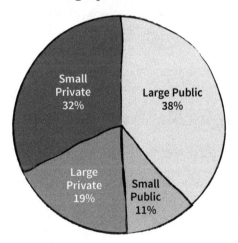

13. According to the figure, how many students from East River High School will attend a small, public college or university?

   A) 4

   B) 44

   C) 440

   D) 4400

The Gatling gun, a forerunner of the modern machine gun, was an early rapid-fire spring loaded, hand-cranked weapon. In 1861, Dr. Richard J. Gatling designed the gun to allow one person to fire many shots quickly. His goal was to reduce the death toll of war by decreasing the number of soldiers needed to fight. The gun consisted of a central shaft surrounded by six rotating barrels. A soldier turned a crank which rotated the shaft. As each barrel reached a particular point in the cycle, it fired, ejected its spent cartridge and loaded another. During this process, it cooled down, preparing it to fire again. The Gatling gun was first used in combat by the Union Army during the Civil War. However, each gun was purchased directly by individual commanders. The US Army did not purchase a Gatling gun until 1866.

14. The purpose of the passage is to
    A)   explain why the Gatling gun was harmful to troops.
    B)   critique the US Army's use of the Gatling gun.
    C)   describe the design and early history of the Gatling gun.
    D)   analyze the success of Dr. Gatling in achieving his goals.

Alan —

I just wanted to drop you a quick note to let you know I'll be out of the office for the next two weeks. Elizabeth and I are finally taking that trip to France we've been talking about for years. It's a bit of a last-minute decision, but since we had the vacation time available, we figured it was now or never.

Anyway, my team's been briefed on the upcoming meeting, so they should be able to handle the presentation without any hiccups. If you have any questions or concerns, you can direct them to Joanie, who'll be handling my responsibilities while I'm out.

Let me know if you want any special treats. I don't know if you can take chocolate and cheese on the plane, but I'm going to try!

Best regards,

Michael

15. Which of the following best describes the writer's tone?
    A)   competitive
    B)   formal
    C)   friendly
    D)   caring

The bacteria, fungi, insects, plants, and animals that live together in a habitat have evolved to share a pool of limited resources. They've competed for water, minerals, nutrients, sunlight, and space—sometimes for thousands or even millions of years. As these communities have evolved, the species in them have developed complex, long-term interspecies interactions known as symbiotic relationships.

Ecologists characterize these interactions based on whether each party benefits. In mutualism, both individuals benefit, while in synnecrosis, both organisms are harmed. A relationship where one individual benefits and the other is harmed is known as parasitism. Examples of these relationships can easily be seen in any ecosystem. Pollination, for example, is mutualistic—pollinators get nutrients from the flower, and the plant is able to reproduce—while tapeworms, which steal nutrients from their host, are parasitic.

There's yet another class of symbiosis that is <u>controversial</u> among scientists. As it's long been defined, commensalism is a relationship where one species benefits and the other is unaffected. But is it possible for two species to interact and for one to remain completely unaffected? Often, relationships described as commensal include one species that feeds on another species' leftovers; remoras, for instance, will attach themselves to sharks and eat the food particles they leave behind. It might seem like the shark gets nothing from the relationship, but a closer look will show that sharks in fact benefit from remoras, which clean the sharks' skin and remove parasites. In fact, many scientists claim that relationships currently described as commensal are just mutualistic or parasitic in ways that haven't been discovered yet.

16. What is the meaning of the word *controversial* in the last paragraph?
    A) debatable
    B) disbelieved
    C) confusing
    D) upsetting

17. The purpose of the passage is to
    A) argue that commensalism isn't actually found in nature
    B) describe the many types of symbiotic relationships
    C) explain how competition for resources results in long-term interspecies relationships
    D) provide examples of the many different ways individual organisms interact

18. Which of the following is NOT a fact stated in the passage?
    A) Mutualism is an interspecies relationship where both species benefit.
    B) Synnecrosis is an interspecies relationship where both species are harmed.
    C) The relationship between plants and pollinators is mutualistic.
    D) The relationship between remoras and sharks is parasitic.

19. Epiphytes are plants that attach themselves to trees and derive nutrients from the air and surrounding debris. Sometimes, the weight of epiphytes can damage the trees on which they're growing. The relationship between epiphytes and their hosts would be described as _____.
    A) mutualism
    B) commensalism
    C) parasitism
    D) synnecrosis

20. What can the reader conclude from this passage about symbiotic relationships?

A) Scientists cannot decide how to classify symbiotic relationships among species.

B) The majority of interspecies interactions are parasitic because most species do not get along.

C) If two species are involved in a parasitic relationship, one of the species will eventually become extinct.

D) Symbiotic relationships evolve as the species that live in a community adapt to their environments and each other.

Answer Key

1. **D) is correct.**

   The author writes that "the reason for the cisco's reemergence is even more unlikely. The cisco have an invasive species, quagga mussels, to thank for their return."

2. **B) is correct.**

   The author states, "Ignored by the government, an activist group known as Indians of All Tribes sailed to Alcatraz in the early morning hours with eighty-nine men, women, and children." The author goes on to describe the nineteen-month occupation of the island.

3. **D) is correct.**

   The author writes, "Humans only lived seasonally in the Oregon cave system, however, which might explain why these insects did not fully transfer to human hosts like bedbugs elsewhere did."

4. **A) is correct.**

   The author goes on to explain that the development of forests was not good for the environment: scientists believe grasslands would slow climate change.

5. **C) is correct.**

   A systolic blood pressure reading of 151 (the higher number) places the patient in the hypertension stage 1 category.

6. **B) is correct.**

   The passage states that restaurateurs must be "exact and ruthless with their budget and pricing." The success of The City

Café implies that its owners have done that.

7. **B) is correct.**

   The purpose of the passage is to explain what an idealist believes in. The author does not offer any opinions or try to persuade readers about the importance of certain values.

8. **D) is correct.**

   In the passage, Thomas Jefferson is defined as an anti-Federalist, in contrast with Federalists who believed in a strong federal government.

9. **A) is correct.**

   The raffle is the only feature described as an event the organizers will be "bringing back[.]"

10. **B) is correct.**

    The author says that the house on Pine Street "had enough space inside but didn't have a big enough yard for [their] three dogs."

11. **A) is correct.**

    A company that profits from private tutoring might introduce bias into a study on the effects of private tutoring in schools.

12. **A) is correct.**

    The author writes, "But people who try to sell you this narrative are wrong. The Civil War was not a battle of cultural identities—it was a battle about slavery."

13. **B) is correct.**

The passage states that 402 students went on to attend college or university, and 11 percent of 402 is approximately 44 students.

14. **C) is correct.**

The author explains why the gun was created, how it functions, and how it was initially used.

15. **C) is correct.**

The author and Alan have a friendly relationship, as evidenced by the author's informal tone and his offer to bring Alan a gift from his vacation.

16. **A) is correct.**

The author writes that "[t]here's yet another class of symbiosis that is controversial among scientists" and goes on to say that "many scientists claim that relationships currently described as commensal are just mutualistic or parasitic in ways that haven't been discovered yet." This implies that scientists debate about the topic of commensalism.

17. **B) is correct.**

The author writes that "[a]s these communities have evolved, the species in them have developed complex, long-term interspecies interactions known as symbiotic relationships." She then goes on to describe the different types of symbiotic relationships that exist.

18. **D) is correct.**

The author writes, "Often, relationships described as commensal include one species that feeds on another species' leftovers; remoras, for instance, will attach themselves to sharks and eat the food particles they leave behind. It might seem like the shark gets nothing from the relationship, but a closer look will show that sharks in fact benefit from remoras, which clean the sharks' skin and remove parasites."

19. **C) is correct.**

The author writes, "A relationship where one individual benefits and the other is harmed is known as parasitism."

20. **D) is correct.**

The author writes, "The bacteria, fungi, insects, plants, and animals that live together in a habitat have evolved to share a pool of limited resources...As these communities have evolved, the species in them have developed complex, long-term interspecies interactions known as symbiotic relationships."

two

GRAMMAR AND SENTENCE STRUCTURE

The Reasoning Through Language Arts test of the GED will test your understanding of the basic rules of grammar. You will be asked to improve paragraphs by choosing the best way to complete sentences. To do so correctly, you must know the basic rules of grammar, mechanics, and sentence structure.

Parts of Speech

The **PARTS OF SPEECH** are the building blocks of sentences, paragraphs, and entire texts. Grammarians have typically defined eight parts of speech—nouns, pronouns, verbs, adverbs, adjectives, conjunctions, prepositions, and interjections—all of which play unique roles in the context of a sentence. Thus, a fundamental understanding of the parts of speech is necessary for comprehending basic sentence construction.

Though some words fall easily into one category or another, many words can function as different parts of speech based on their usage within a sentence.

Nouns and Pronouns

NOUNS are the words that describe people, places, things, and ideas. Most often, nouns fill the position of subject or object within a sentence. Nouns have several subcategories: common nouns (*chair, car, house*), proper nouns (*Julie, David*), noncountable nouns (*money, water*), and countable nouns (*dollars, cubes*), among others. There is much crossover among these subcategories (for example, *chair* is common and countable), and other subcategories do exist.

PRONOUNS replace nouns in a sentence or paragraph, allowing a writer to achieve a smooth flow throughout a text by avoiding unnecessary repetition. While there are countless nouns in the English language, there are only a few types of pronouns. The ones important for the GED follow:

PERSONAL PRONOUNS act as subjects or objects in a sentence.

She received a letter; I gave the letter to her.

POSSESSIVE PRONOUNS indicate possession.

The apartment is hers, but the furniture is mine.

REFLEXIVE or **INTENSIVE PRONOUNS** intensify a noun or reflect back on a noun.

I made the dessert myself.

INDEFINITE PRONOUNS simply replace nouns to avoid unnecessary repetition.

Several came to the party to see both.

Table 2.1. Personal, Possessive, and Reflexive Pronouns

CASE	FIRST PERSON		SECOND PERSON		THIRD PERSON	
	Singular	Plural	Singular	Plural	Singular	Plural
Subject	I	we	you	you (all)	he, she, it	they
Object	me	us	you	you (all)	him, her, it	them
Possessive	mine	ours	yours	yours	his, hers, its	theirs
Reflexive/ intensive	myself	ourselves	yourself	yourselves	himself, herself, itself	themselves

EXAMPLES

1. What purpose do nouns usually serve in a sentence?

    A) They indicate possession.

    B) They act as subject or object.

    C) They intensify other nouns.

    D) They clarify when an action occurs.

    Answer:

    B) is correct. Nouns are people, places, things, or ideas; they usually act as the subject or object in a sentence.

2. Which pronoun best completes the sentence?

    _____ baked the cookies ourselves and ate most of them.

    A) She

    B) Her

    C) I

    D) We

    Answer:

    D) is correct. The reflexive pronoun *ourselves* refers back to the subject of the sentence. Because it is in the first person plural, the subject should also be in the first person plural (*we*).

Verbs

VERBS express action (*run, jump, play*) or state of being (*is, seems*). Verbs that describe action are **ACTION VERBS**, and those that describe being are **LINKING VERBS**.

ACTION: My brother <u>plays</u> tennis.

LINKING: He <u>is</u> the best player on the team.

Verbs are conjugated to indicate PERSON, which refers to the point of view of the sentence. First person is the speaker (*I, we*); second person is the person being addressed (*you*); and third person is outside the conversation (*they, them*). Verbs are also conjugated to match the NUMBER (singular or plural) of their subject. HELPING VERBS (*to be, to have, to do*) are used to conjugate verbs. An unconjugated verb is called an INFINITIVE and includes the word *to* in front (*to be, to break*).

PARTICIPLES are verb forms lacking number and person. The PAST PARTICIPLE is usually formed by adding the suffix *–ed* to the verb stem (*type* becomes *typed; drop* becomes *dropped*). The PRESENT PARTICIPLE is always formed by adding the suffix *–ing* to the verb stem (*typing, dropping*). Participles are used in verb conjugation to indicate the state of an action (*she is going; we had waited*).

Participles also act in *participial phrases* that act as descriptors in sentences:

<u>Seated</u> politely, Ron listened to his friend's boring story.

Maya petted the <u>sleeping</u> cat.

When a present participle acts as a noun, it is called a GERUND. In the following sentence, *running* is a noun and serving as the subject of the sentence:

<u>Running</u> is my favorite form of exercise.

A common error in sentence structure is the *dangling participle*: when a participial phrase is disconnected from the word or phrase it modifies.

INCORRECT: <u>Discussing the state of the nation,</u> I listened to the president's speech.

Here, the president, not the narrator, is discussing the state of the nation; the narrator is simply *listening*. However, the participial phrase "Discussing the state of the nation" is disconnected from the word it modifies, *president*. Thus it is *dangling* in the sentence—a dangling participle.

To fix a dangling particle, rearrange the sentence so that the modifying phrase is next to the word it modifies.

CORRECT: I listened to the president's speech <u>discussing the state of the nation</u>.

Table 2.2. Verb Conjugation (Present Tense)

PERSON	SINGULAR	PLURAL
First person	I give	we give
Second person	you give	you (all) give
Third person	he/she/it/ gives	they give

Verbs are also conjugated to indicate TENSE, or when the action has happened. Actions can happen in the past, present, or future. Tense also describes over how long a period the action took place:

- ◆ SIMPLE verbs describe something that happened once or general truths.
- ◆ CONTINUOUS verbs describe an ongoing action.

- ◆ **PERFECT** verbs describe repeated actions or actions that started in the past and have been completed.
- ◆ **PERFECT CONTINUOUS** verbs describe actions that started in the past and are continuing.

Table 2.3. Verb Tenses

TENSE	PAST	PRESENT	FUTURE
Simple	I <u>gave</u> her a gift yesterday.	I <u>give</u> her a gift every day.	I <u>will give</u> her a gift on her birthday.
Continuous	I <u>was giving</u> her a gift when you got here.	I <u>am giving</u> her a gift; come in!	I <u>will be giving</u> her a gift at dinner.
Perfect	I <u>had given</u> her a gift before you got there.	I <u>have given</u> her a gift already.	I <u>will have given</u> her a gift by midnight.
Perfect continuous	Her friends <u>had been giving</u> her gifts all night when I arrived.	I <u>have been giving</u> her gifts every year for nine years.	I <u>will have been giving</u> her gifts on holidays for ten years next year.

Verbs that follow the standard rules of conjugation are called **REGULAR** verbs. **IRREGULAR** verbs do not follow these rules, and their conjugations must be memorized. Some examples of irregular verbs are given in Table 2.4.

Table 2.4. Irregular Verbs

PRESENT	PAST	HAS/HAVE/HAD
am	was	been
do	did	done
see	saw	seen
write	wrote	written
break	broke	broken
grow	grew	grown
speak	spoke	spoken
begin	began	begun
run	ran	run
buy	bought	bought

TRANSITIVE VERBS take a **DIRECT OBJECT**, which receives the action of the verb. Intransitive verbs have no object. The person or thing that receives the direct object is the **INDIRECT OBJECT**.

Transitive: Alex <u>gave</u> the ball to his brother. (The *ball* is the direct object; *his* brother is the indirect object.)

Intransitive: She <u>jumped</u> over the fence.

Identify the type of nouns, pronouns, and verbs used in the following sentence: Marcus and Paula offered to pick up the cake—they are driving that way anyway—but I told them I would do it myself.

EXAMPLES

1. Which verb phrase best completes the sentence?

   By this time tomorrow, we _____ in New York.

   A) will have arrived

   B) have arrived

   C) arrive

   D) was arriving

   Answer:

   A) is correct. The phrase *by this time tomorrow* describes as action that will take place and be completed in the future, so the future perfect tense (*will have arrived*) should be used.

2. Identify the direct object in the following sentence:

   My friends brought me a package of souvenirs from their trip to Spain.

   A) friends

   B) me

   C) package

   D) trip

   Answers:

   C) is correct. *Package* is the direct object of the verb *brought*.

Adjectives and Adverbs

ADJECTIVES modify or describe nouns and pronouns. In English, adjectives are usually placed before the word being modified, although they can also appear after a linking verb such as *is* or *smells*.

> The beautiful blue jade necklace will go perfectly with my dress.

> I think that lasagna smells delicious.

When multiple adjectives are used, they should be listed in the following order:

1. Determiners: articles (*a*, *an*, and *the*), possessive adjectives (e.g., *my*, *her)*, and descriptors of quantity (e.g., *three*, *several*)

2. Opinions: modifiers that imply a value (e.g., *beautiful*, *perfect*, *ugly*)

3. Size: descriptions of size (e.g., *small*, *massive)*

4. Age: descriptions of age (e.g., *young, five-year-old*)

5. Shape: descriptions of appearance or character (e.g., *smooth*, *loud)*

6. Color: descriptions of color (e.g., *blue*, *dark)*

7. Origin: modifiers that describe where something came from (e.g., *American*, *homemade)*

8. Material: modifiers that describe what something is made from (e.g., *cotton*, *metallic)*

9. Purpose: adjectives that function as part of the noun to describe its purpose (e.g., sewing *machine*, rocking *chair)*

ADVERBS, which are often formed by adding the suffix –*ly*, modify any word or set of words that is not a noun or pronoun. They can modify verbs, adjectives, other adverbs, phrases, or clauses.

He <u>quickly</u> ran to the house next door. (*Quickly* modifies the verb *ran*.)

Her <u>very</u> effective speech earned her a promotion. (*Very* modifies the adjective *effective*.)

<u>Finally</u>, the table was set and dinner was ready. (*Finally* modifies the clause *the table was set and dinner was ready*.)

> Adjectives answer the questions what kind, how many, or which one? Adverbs answer the questions how, when, where, why, or to what extent?

COMPARATIVE adjectives and adverbs compare two items. For most one- or two-syllable words, the suffix –*er* is added to make it comparative; the word may be followed by *than*.

SUPERLATIVE adjectives and adverbs compare three or more items. Most one- or two-syllable words are made superlative by adding a suffix, –*est*.

Comparative: My brother is <u>taller</u> than my sister.

Superlative: My brother is the <u>tallest</u> of my five siblings.

Longer adjectives and adverbs must be preceded by *more* to form the comparative and *most* to form the superlative.

Comparative: My bed at home is <u>more comfortable</u> than the one at the hotel.

Superlative: The bed in your guestroom is the <u>most comfortable</u> bed I've ever slept in!

Some adjectives and adverbs form irregular comparatives and superlatives (see Table 2.5.).

Comparative: The weather is bad today, but it was <u>worse</u> yesterday.

Superlative: The <u>worst</u> day this week was Monday, when it rained.

Table 2.5. Irregular Comparative and Superlative Adjectives and Adverbs

ADJECTIVE/ADVERB	COMPARATIVE	SUPERLATIVE
much	more	most
bad	worse	worst
good	better	best
little	less	least
far	further/farther	furthest/farthest

EXAMPLES

1. Which of the following sentences is CORRECTLY constructed?
   A) Between my mom and dad, my father is the oldest.
   B) I ran less than usual today.
   C) Henry's cat is more fatter than mine.
   D) After taking medicine, she felt worser.

   Answer:

   B) is correct. The speaker is comparing today's run to the norm, not to any additional instances, so the comparative is acceptable here. Furthermore, the word *than* appears, a clue that the comparative is appropriate. *Less* is the irregular comparative form of *little*.

2. Read the following sentence:

    He carelessly sped around the flashing yellow light.

    Which is the adverb in this sentence?

    A) flashing

    B) yellow

    C) around

    D) carelessly

    Answer:

    D) is correct. *Carelessly* is an adverb modifying *sped* and explaining *how* the driving occurred. The subject was not mindful as he drove; he raced through a yellow light when he should have exercised caution.

Conjunctions

CONJUNCTIONS join words into phrases, clauses, and sentences. The *coordinating conjunctions* (FANBOYS) join two independent clauses: **F**or, **A**nd, **N**or, **B**ut, **O**r, **Y**et, **S**o.

Marta went to the pool, <u>and</u> Alex decided to go shopping.

Aisha didn't want to eat tacos for dinner, <u>so</u> she picked up a pizza on her way home.

Subordinating conjunctions join dependent clauses to the independent clauses to which they are related.

We chose that restaurant <u>because</u> Juan loves pizza.

Table 2.6. Subordinating Conjunctions

Time	after, as, as long as, as soon as, before, since, until, when, whenever, while
Manner	as, as if, as though
Cause	because
Condition	although, as long as, even if, even though, if, provided that, though, unless, while
Purpose	in order that, so that, that
Comparison	as, than

EXAMPLES

1. The following sentence contains an error. How should it be rewritten?

    He liked to cook and baking was his specialty.

    A) He liked to cook, and baking was his specialty.

    B) He liked to cook so baking was his specialty.

    C) He liked to cook; and baking was his specialty.

    D) He liked to cook, baking was his specialty.

Answer:

A) is correct. This sentence includes two independent clauses: "He liked to cook" and "baking was his specialty." They can be connected with a comma and coordinating conjunction (the conjunction *and* is appropriate here). The sentence could also be written with a semicolon and no conjunction.

2. Identify the underlined part of speech in the following sentence:

    Anne and Peter drank their coffee languidly <u>while</u> they read the paper.

    A) subordinating conjunction

    B) coordinating conjunction

    C) irregular verb

    D) adverb

Answer:

A) is correct. "While they read the paper" is a dependent clause; the subordinating conjunction *while* connects it to the independent clause "Anne and Peter drank their coffee languidly."

Prepositions

PREPOSITIONS set up relationships in time (*after the party*) or space (*under the cushions*) within a sentence. A preposition will always function as part of a prepositional phrase—the preposition along with the object of the preposition.

Table 2.7. Common Prepositions

PREPOSITIONS

about	by	off	toward
among	despite	on	under
around	down	onto	underneath
at	during	out	until
before	except	outside	up
behind	for	over	upon
below	from	past	with
beneath	in	since	within
beside	into	through	
between	near	till	
beyond	of	to	

COMPOUND PREPOSITIONS

according to	because of	in place of	on account of
as of	by means of	in respect to	out of
as well as	in addition to	in spite of	prior to
aside from	in front of	instead of	with regard to

Interjections

INTERJECTIONS have no grammatical attachment to the sentence itself other than to add expressions of emotion. These parts of speech may be punctuated with commas or exclamation points and may fall anywhere within the sentence.

<u>Ouch!</u> He stepped on my toe.

Constructing Sentences

Phrases

A PHRASE is a group of words that communicates a partial idea and lacks either a subject or a predicate. Several phrases may be strung together, one after another, to add detail and interest to a sentence.

Phrases are categorized based on the main word in the phrase. A PREPOSITIONAL PHRASE begins with a preposition and ends with an object of the preposition; a VERB PHRASE is composed of the main verb along with its helping verbs; and a NOUN PHRASE consists of a noun and its modifiers.

PREPOSITIONAL PHRASE: The dog is hiding <u>under the porch</u>.

VERB PHRASE: The chef <u>wanted to cook</u> a different dish.

NOUN PHRASE: <u>The big, red barn</u> rests beside <u>the vacant chicken house</u>.

An **APPOSITIVE PHRASE** is a particular type of noun phrase that renames the word or group of words that precedes it. Appositive phrases usually follow the noun they describe and are set apart by commas.

Appositive phrase: My dad, <u>a clock maker</u>, loved antiques.

VERBAL PHRASES begin with a word that would normally act as a verb but is instead filling another role within the sentence. These phrases can act as nouns, adjectives, or adverbs.

NOUN: <u>To become a doctor</u> had always been her goal.

ADJECTIVE: <u>Enjoying the stars that filled the sky</u>, Ben lingered outside for quite a while.

EXAMPLE

Identify the type of phrase underlined in the following sentence:

<u>Dodging traffic</u>, Rachel drove to work on back roads.

A) prepositional phrase

B) noun phrase

C) verb phrase

D) verbal phrase

Answer:

D) is correct. The phrase is a verbal phrase modifying the noun *Rachel*. It begins with the word *dodging*, derived from the verb to *dodge*.

Clauses and Types of Sentences

CLAUSES contain both a subject and a predicate. They can be either independent or dependent. An **INDEPENDENT** (or main) **CLAUSE** can stand alone as its own sentence:

The dog ate her homework.

Dependent (or subordinate) clauses cannot stand alone as their own sentences. They start with a subordinating conjunction, relative pronoun, or relative adjective, which will make them sound incomplete:

<u>Because</u> the dog ate her homework

Table 2.8. Words That Begin Dependent Clauses

SUBORDINATING CONJUNCTIONS	RELATIVE PRONOUNS AND ADJECTIVES
after, before, once, since, until, when, whenever, while, as, because, in order that, so, so that, that, if, even if, provided that, unless, although, even though, though, whereas, where, wherever, than, whether	who, whoever, whom, whomever, whose, which, that, when, where, why, how

Sentences can be classified based on the number and type of clauses they contain. A **SIMPLE SENTENCE** will have only one independent clause and no dependent clauses. The sentence may contain phrases, complements, and modifiers, but it will comprise only one independent clause, one complete idea.

The cat ran under the porch.

A **COMPOUND SENTENCE** has two or more independent clauses and no dependent clauses.

The cat ran under the porch, and the dog ran after him.

A **COMPLEX SENTENCE** has only one independent clause and one or more dependent clauses.

The cat, who is scared of the dog, ran under the porch.

A **COMPOUND-COMPLEX SENTENCE** has two or more independent clauses and one or more dependent clauses.

The cat, who is scared of the dog, ran under the porch, and the dog ran after him.

Table 2.9. Sentence Structure and Clauses

SENTENCE STRUCTURE	INDEPENDENT CLAUSES	DEPENDENT CLAUSES
Simple	1	0
Compound	2 +	0
Complex	1	1 +
Compound-complex	2 +	1 +

EXAMPLE

Which of the following is a compound sentence?
- **A)** The turtle swam slowly around the pond.
- **B)** Alligators generally lie still, but they can move with lightning speed.
- **C)** Mice are most likely to come out at night after other animals have gone to sleep.
- **D)** Squirrels, to prepare for winter, gather and hide seeds and nuts underground.

Answer:

B) is correct. "Alligators...still" and "they...speed" are two independent clauses connected by a comma and the coordinating conjunction *but*.

Punctuation

Terminal punctuation marks are used to end sentences. The **PERIOD** (.) ends declarative (statement) and imperative (command) sentences. The **QUESTION MARK** (?) terminates interrogative sentences (questions). Lastly, **EXCLAMATION POINTS** end exclamatory sentences, in which the writer or speaker is exhibiting intense emotion or energy.

Sarah and I are attending a concert.

How many people are attending the concert?

What a great show that was!

The colon and the semicolon, though often confused, each have a unique set of rules for their use. While both punctuation marks are used to join clauses, the construction of the clauses and the relationship between them is different. The SEMICOLON (;) is used to join two independent clauses (IC; IC) that are closely related.

I need to buy a new car soon; my old car broke down last month.

The COLON (:) is used to introduce a list, definition, or clarification. The clause preceding the colon has to be independent, but what follows the colon can be an independent clause, a dependent clause, or a phrase.

The buffet offers three choices: ham, turkey, or roast beef.

He decided to drive instead of taking the train: he didn't think the train would arrive in time.

COMMAS show pauses in the text or set information apart from the main text. There are lots of rules for comma usage, so only the most common are summarized below.

1. Commas separate two independent clauses along with a coordinating conjunction.
   George ordered the steak, <u>but</u> Bruce preferred the ham.

2. Commas separate coordinate adjectives.
   She made herself a big bowl of <u>cold, delicious</u> ice cream.

3. Commas separate items in a series.
   The list of groceries included <u>cream, coffee, donuts, and tea</u>.

4. Commas separate introductory words and phrases from the rest of the sentence.
   <u>For example</u>, we have thirty students who demand a change.

5. Commas set off non-essential information and appositives.
   Estelle, <u>our newly elected chairperson</u>, will be in attendance.

6. Commas set off the day and month of a date within a text.
   I was born on February <u>16, 1988</u>.

7. Commas set up numbers in a text of more than four digits.
   We expect <u>25,000</u> visitors to the new museum.

8. Commas set off the names of cities from their states, territories, or provinces.
   She lives in <u>Houston, Texas</u>.

QUOTATION MARKS have a number of different purposes. They enclose titles of short, or relatively short, literary works such as short stories, chapters, and poems. (The titles of longer works, like novels and anthologies, are italicized.) Additionally, quotation marks are used to enclose direct quotations within the text of a document where the quotation is integrated into the text. Writers also use quotation marks to set off dialogue.

We will be reading the poem "Bright Star" in class today.

The poem opens with the line "Bright star, would I were steadfast as thou art."

APOSTROPHES, sometimes referred to as single quotation marks, have several different purposes.

1. They show possession.

   boy's watch, Ronald and Maria's house

2. They replace missing letters, numerals, and signs.

   do not = don't, 1989 = '89

3. They form plurals of letters, numerals, and signs.

   A's, 10's

Less commonly used punctuation marks include:

◆ EN DASH (–): indicates a range

◆ EM DASH (—): shows an abrupt break in a sentence and emphasizes the words within the em dashes

◆ PARENTHESES ( ): enclose nonessential information

◆ BRACKETS [ ]: enclose added words to a quotation and add insignificant information within parentheses

◆ SLASH (/): separates lines of poetry within a text or indicates interchangeable terminology

◆ ELLIPSES (…): indicates that information has been removed from a quotation or creates a reflective pause

EXAMPLES

1. Which sentence includes an improperly placed comma?

   A) Ella, Cassie, and Cameron drove to South Carolina together.

   B) Trying to impress his friends, Carl ended up totaling his car.

   C) Ice cream is my favorite food, it is so cold and creamy.

   D) Mowing the lawn, Navid discovered a family of baby rabbits.

   Answer:

   C) is correct. "Ice cream...food" and "it...creamy" are two independent clauses. The writer should include a coordinating conjunction like *for* or separate the clauses with a semicolon.

2. The following sentence contains an error. How should it be rewritten?

   Oak trees—with proper care—can grow taller than thirty feet; providing shade for people, shelter for animals, and perches for birds.

   A) replace the em dashes with commas

   B) remove the comma after *people*

   C) insert an apostrophe at the end of *animals*

   D) replace the semicolon with a comma

   Answer:

   D) is correct. "Providing shade..." is not an independent clause; therefore it cannot be preceded by a semicolon.

Capitalization

CAPITALIZATION is writing the first letter of a word in uppercase and the remaining letters in lowercase. Capitalization is used in three main contexts. The first, and most common, is in the first word after a period or the first word of a text. For example, the first word in each sentence of this paragraph is capitalized.

The second most common usage of capitalization is for proper nouns or adjectives derived from proper nouns. For instance, *France*—as the name of a country—is capitalized. Similarly, *French*, the adjective derived from the proper noun *France*, is also capitalized. There is an exception to this rule: when the adjective has taken on a meaning independent of the original proper noun. For example, the term *french fries* is not capitalized.

The third usage of capitalization is in a title or honorific that appears before a name: "**P**resident George Washington never lived in the capital." If, however, that same title is used *instead of* the name, or if the name and title are separated by a comma, it remains lowercase. For example, "The first **p**resident, George Washington, never lived in the capital" or "The **p**resident did not originally live in the capital."

EXAMPLE

Which sentence CORRECTLY uses capitalization?

A) Robert and Kelly raced across the River in their small boats.

B) ducks flying in a V-formation cross the Midwest in the fall.

C) The Chairwoman of the board, Keisha Johnson, will lead today's meeting.

D) The Senators from Virginia and Louisiana strongly favor the bill.

Answer:

C) is correct. *Keisha Johnson*, as a proper noun, should be capitalized, but "chairwoman of the board" should not be because it is separated from the name by a comma.

Common Language Errors

Subject-Verb Agreement

Verbs must agree in number with their subjects. Common rules for subject/verb agreement are given below.

1. Single subjects agree with single verbs; plural subjects agree with plural verbs.

   The <u>girl walks</u> her dog.

   The <u>girls walk</u> their dogs.

2. Ignore words between the subject and the verb: agreement must exist between the subject and verb.

   The new <u>library</u> ~~with its many books and rooms~~ <u>fills</u> a long-felt need.

3. Compound subjects joined by *and* typically take a plural verb unless considered one item.

   <u>Correctness and precision are required</u> for all good writing.

   <u>Macaroni and cheese makes</u> a great snack for children.

4. The linking verbs agree with the subject and not the subject complement (predicate nominative).

   My <u>favorite</u> is strawberries and apples.

   My <u>favorites are</u> strawberries and apples.

5. When a relative pronoun (*who, whom, which, that*) is used as the subject of the clause, the verb will agree with the antecedent of the relative pronoun.

   This is the <u>student who is receiving</u> an award.

   These are the <u>students who are receiving</u> awards.

6. All single, indefinite pronouns agree with single verbs.

   <u>Neither</u> of the students <u>is</u> happy about the play.

   <u>Each</u> of the many cars <u>is</u> on the grass.

   Every <u>one</u> of the administrators <u>speaks</u> highly of Trevor.

EXAMPLE

Which sentence in the following list is CORRECT in its subject and verb agreement?

A) My sister and my best friend lives in Chicago.

B) My parents or my brother is going to pick me up from the airport.

C) Neither of the students refuse to take the exam.

D) The team were playing a great game until the rain started.

Answer:

B) is correct. The verb agrees with the closest subject—in this case, the singular *brother*.

Pronoun-Antecedent Agreement

Similarly, pronouns must agree with their antecedents (the words they replaced) in number; however, some pronouns also require gender agreement (*him, her*). **PRONOUN/ANTECEDENT AGREEMENT** rules can be found below:

1. Antecedents joined by *and* typically require a plural pronoun.

   The <u>children and their dogs</u> enjoyed <u>their</u> day at the beach.

   If the two nouns refer to the same person, a singular pronoun is preferable.

   My <u>best friend and confidant</u> still lives in <u>her</u> log cabin.

2. For compound antecedents joined by *or*, the pronoun agrees with the nearer or nearest antecedent.

   Either the resident mice <u>or the manager's cat</u> gets <u>itself</u> a meal of good leftovers.

3. When indefinite pronouns function in a sentence, the pronoun must agree with the number of the indefinite pronoun.

Neither student finished his or her assignment.

Both students finished their assignments.

4. When collective nouns function as antecedents, the pronoun choice will be singular or plural depending on the function of the collective.

The audience was cheering as it rose to its feet in unison.

Our family are spending their vacations in Maine, Hawaii, and Rome.

5. When *each* and *every* precede the antecedent, the pronoun agreement will be singular.

Each and every man, woman, and child brings unique qualities to his or her family.

Every creative writer, technical writer, and research writer is attending his or her assigned lecture.

How would you complete the following sentence? "Every boy and girl should check _____ homework before turning it in." Many people would use the pronoun *their*. But since the antecedent is "every boy and girl," technically, the correct answer would be *his or her*. Using *they* or *their* in similar situations is increasingly accepted in formal speech, however. It is unlikely that you will see questions like this appear on the GED, but if you do, it is safest to use the technically correct response.

EXAMPLE

1. Which sentence in the following list is CORRECT in its pronoun and antecedent agreement?

   A) The grandchildren and their cousins enjoyed their day at the park.

   B) Most of the grass has lost their deep color.

   C) The jury was relieved as their commitment came to a close.

   D) Every boy and girl must learn to behave themselves in school.

   Answer:

   A) is correct. The plural antecedents *grandchildren* and *cousins* match the plural possessive pronoun *their*.

2. Which sentence in the following list is CORRECT in its pronoun and antecedent agreement?

   A) Either my brother or my dad will bring their van to pick us up.

   B) The university is having their tenth fundraiser tonight.

   C) Alyssa and Jacqueline bought herself a big lunch today.

   D) Each dog, cat, and rabbit has its own bowl and blanket.

   Answer:

   D) is correct. When *each* precedes the antecedent, the pronoun agreement is singular. The pronoun *its* therefore agrees with the antecedents *Each dog, cat, and rabbit*.

Verb Tense Agreement

In any passage, verb tense should be consistent and make sense in context of other verbs, adverbs, and general meaning. Verb tense questions appear frequently on the GED, so pay attention to the context of the entire passage.

> INCORRECT: Deborah <u>was speaking</u> with her colleague when her boss <u>will appear</u>, demanding a meeting.

In this sentence, the subject, *Deborah*, is acting in an ongoing event in the past, so the verb describing this action, *speaking*, is conjugated in the continuous past tense. In the context of the sentence, the appearance of her boss is a completed event that happens during the conversation. The verb describing the boss' appearance should be conjugated in the simple past tense. The corrected sentence reads as follows:

> CORRECT: Deborah <u>was speaking</u> with her colleague when her boss <u>appeared</u>, demanding a meeting.

One clue to the correct conjugation of the verb *appeared* is the adverb *when*, which implies that a completed event occurred to interrupt the ongoing event (in this case, Deborah's talk with her colleague).

Pay attention to how verbs are conjugated in the beginning of a sentence or passage, and look for clues to spot any errors in verb tense agreement.

EXAMPLE

The following sentence contains an error. How should it be rewritten?
Veronica attended cooking classes, and she goes to yoga classes too.

A) Veronica attends cooking classes, and she went to yoga classes too.

B) Veronica attended cooking classes, and she went to yoga classes too.

C) Veronica attended cooking classes; she goes to yoga classes too.

D) Veronica attended cooking classes. She goes to yoga classes too.

Answer:

B) is correct. In this sentence, the verbs *attended* and *went* are both correctly conjugated in the simple past tense.

Parallelism

Errors in PARALLELISM prevent a writer from creating a smooth flow, or coherence, from word to word and sentence to sentence. Writers should create parallel structure in words, phrases, and clauses wherever two or more similar and equally important ideas exist next to each other in a sentence. Errors in parallel structure frequently appear in sentences with verb phrases, prepositional phrases, and correlative conjunctions like *either...or, neither... nor,* and *not only...but also.*

> INCORRECT: Adia could <u>program</u> computers, <u>repair</u> cars, and <u>knew how to make</u> croissants.

> CORRECT: Adia could <u>program</u> computers, <u>repair</u> cars, and <u>bake</u> croissants.

In the corrected sentence, the verbs are aligned in parallel structure. Furthermore, the first sentence contains a verb error. By omitting "program computers, repair cars," the sentence reads "Adia could…knew how to make croissants" Rewriting the sentence in parallel structure corrects the verb error.

In sentences with multiple prepositional phrases in a parallel series, the preposition must be repeated unless the same preposition begins each phrase.

INCORRECT: You can park your car <u>in</u> the garage, the carport, or <u>on</u> the street.

CORRECT: You can park your car <u>in</u> the garage, <u>in</u> the carport, or <u>on</u> the street.

EXAMPLE

The following sentence contains an error. How should it be rewritten?
Shelly achieved more at nursing school because she was going to bed earlier, eating healthy food, and she started to stay home and study more.

A) Shelly achieved more at nursing school. She was going to bed earlier, eating healthy food, and she started to stay home and study more.

B) Shelly achieved more at nursing school because she was going to bed earlier, eating healthy food, and studying more.

C) Shelly achieved more at nursing school; she was going to bed earlier, eating healthy food, and she started to stay home and study more.

D) Shelly achieved more at nursing school; she was going to bed earlier, and she started to eat healthy food and studying more.

Answer:

B) is correct. In this sentence, three related clauses are written in parallel structure using the participles *going, eating,* and *studying*.

Sentence Construction Errors

SENTENCE ERRORS fall into three categories: fragments, comma splices (comma fault), and fused sentences (run-on). A FRAGMENT occurs when a group of words is not a complete sentence but is punctuated like one. The fragment might be a phrase or a dependent clause. To fix a fragment, an independent clause needs to be created.

FRAGMENT (PHRASE): The girl in my class who asks a lot of questions.

CORRECT: The girl in my class who asks a lot of questions sits in the back row.

FRAGMENT (DEPENDENT CLAUSE): Because of the big storm we had last weekend.

CORRECT: Because of the big storm we had last weekend, the park will be closed.

A COMMA SPLICE (comma fault) occurs when two independent clauses are joined together in a paragraph with only a comma to "splice" them together. FUSED (run-on) sentences occur when two independent clauses are joined with no punctuation whatsoever. To fix a comma splice or fused sentence, add the correct punctuation and/or conjunction.

COMMA SPLICE: My family eats turkey at <u>Thanksgiving, we</u> eat ham at Christmas.

CORRECT: My family eats turkey at <u>Thanksgiving, and we</u> eat ham at Christmas.

CORRECT: My family eats turkey at <u>Thanksgiving. We</u> eat ham at Christmas.

CORRECT: My family eats turkey at <u>Thanksgiving; we</u> eat ham at Christmas.

FUSED SENTENCE: I bought a chocolate pie from the <u>bakery it</u> was delicious.

CORRECT: I bought a chocolate pie from the <u>bakery. It</u> was delicious.

CORRECT: I bought a chocolate pie from the <u>bakery, and it</u> was delicious.

CORRECT: I bought a chocolate pie from the <u>bakery; it</u> was delicious.

EXAMPLE

Which of the following is CORRECTLY punctuated?

A) Since she went to the store.

B) The football game ended in a tie, the underdog caught up in the fourth quarter.

C) The mall is closing early today so we'll have to go shopping tomorrow.

D) When the players dropped their gloves, a fight broke out on the ice hockey rink floor.

Answer:

D) is correct. This is a complete sentence that is punctuated properly with a comma between the dependent and independent clauses.

Easily Confused Words

A, AN: *a* precedes words beginning with consonants or consonant sounds; *an* precedes words beginning with vowels or vowel sounds.

AFFECT, EFFECT: *affect* is most often a verb; *effect* is usually a noun. (*The experience affected me significantly* OR *The experience had a significant effect on me.*)

AMONG, AMONGST, BETWEEN: *among* is used for a group of more than two people or items; *amongst* is an uncommon, archaic term; *between* distinguishes two people or items.

AMOUNT, NUMBER: *amount* is used for noncountable sums; *number* is used with countable nouns.

CITE, SITE: the verb *cite* credits an author of a quotation, paraphrase, or summary; the noun *site* is a location.

EVERY DAY, EVERYDAY: *every day* is an indefinite adjective modifying a noun; *everyday* is a one-word adjective implying frequent occurrence. (*Our visit to the Minnesota State Fair is an everyday activity during August.*)

FEWER, LESS: *fewer* is used with a countable noun; *less* is used with a noncountable noun. (*Fewer parents are experiencing stress since the new teacher was hired; parents are experiencing less stress since the new teacher was hired*).

GOOD, WELL: good is always the adjective; *well* is always the adverb except in cases of health. (*He writes well. She felt well after the surgery.*)

IMPLIED, INFERRED: *implied* is something a speaker does; *inferred* is something the listener does after assessing the speaker's message. (*The speaker implied something mysterious, but I inferred the wrong thing.*)

IRREGARDLESS, REGARDLESS: *irregardless* is nonstandard usage and should be avoided; *regardless* is the proper usage of the transitional statement.

ITS, IT'S: *its* is a possessive pronoun; *it's* is a contraction for *it is*.

PRINCIPAL, PRINCIPLE: as a noun, *principal* is an authority figure, often the head of a school; as an adjective, *principal* means *main*; the noun *principle* means idea or belief. (*The principal of the school spoke on the principal meaning of the main principles of the school.*)

QUOTE, QUOTATION: *quote* is a verb; *quotation* is a noun.

SHOULD OF, SHOULD HAVE: *should of* is improper usage—*of* is not a helping verb and therefore cannot complete the verb phrase; *should have* is the proper usage. (*He should have driven.*)

THAN, THEN: *than* sets up a comparison; *then* indicates a reference to a point in time. (*When I said that I liked the hat better than the gloves, my sister laughed; then she bought both for me.*)

THEIR, THERE, THEY'RE: *their* is the possessive case of the pronoun *they*. *There* is the demonstrative pronoun indicating location or place. *They're* is a contraction of the words *they are*.

TO LIE (TO RECLINE), TO LAY (TO PLACE): *to lie* is the intransitive verb meaning *to recline*; *to lay* is the transitive verb meaning *to place something*. (*I lie out in the sun; I lay my towel on the beach.*)

WHO, WHOM: *who* is the subject relative pronoun. (*My son, who is a good student, studies hard.*) Here, the son is carrying out the action of studying, so the pronoun is a subject pronoun (*who*). *Whom* is the object relative pronoun. (*My son, whom the other students admire, studies hard.*) Here, *son* is the object of the other students' admiration, so the pronoun standing in for him, *whom*, is an object pronoun.

YOUR, YOU'RE: *your* is the possessive case of the pronoun *you*. *You're* is a contraction of the words *you are*.

EXAMPLE

Which of the following sentences contains an error?

A)   I invited fewer people to my birthday party this year.

B)   The students asked the principle to postpone the meeting.

C)   My sister baked cookies then asked me to help clean the kitchen.

D)   She paints well even though she has no formal training.

Answer:

B) is correct. A principle is a belief; a principal is the head of a school.

Test Your Knowledge

Select the underlined portion of the sentence that contains a grammatical error. If the sentence is correct, choose (D) No error.

1. Ukrainians **(A)**celebrate a holiday called Malanka during which men **(B)** dress in costumes and **(C)**plays tricks on their neighbors. **(D)**No error

2. Because of **(A)**its distance from the sun, the planet Neptune **(B)**has seasons that last the **(C)**equivalent of forty-one Earth years. **(D)**No error

3. In addition to the disastrous effects an active volcano can have on **(A)**it's immediate surroundings, an eruption can also pose a threat to passing aircraft and **(B)**can temporarily change the temperature of **(C)**Earth's atmosphere. **(D)**No error

4. The employer **(A)**decided that, **(B)** due to the high cost of health care, he could not afford to offer **(C)**no other benefits to his employees. **(D)**No error

5. Though Puerto Rico is known popularly for **(A)**its beaches, its landscape also **(B)**includes mountains, which are home to many of the **(C)**island's rural villages. **(D)**No error

6. The photographer **(A)**, specializes in shooting portraits and taking still lifes, but she also **(B)**likes to accept more challenging assignments, such as **(C)**photographing wildlife. **(D)**No error

7. In the fight **(A)**against obesity, **(B)** countries' around the world are imposing taxes on sodas and other sugary drinks **(C)**in hopes of curbing unhealthy habits. **(D)**No error

8. The **(A)**Black Death, often thought of as a concern of times past, **(B)** continued to spread among rodent populations even today, occasionally making **(C)**its way into a human host. **(D)**No error

9. The storm chasers, who **(A)**stressed and emphasized the importance of caution in their work, **(B)**decided not to go out when the sheets of rain made visibility **(C)**too low. **(D)**No error

10. James **(A)**having already been awake for nineteen hours, after a **(B)**twelve-hour work day, when he **(C)**received the news. **(D)**No error

Select the answer choice that best completes the sentence.

11. The famously high death toll at the end of the Civil War was not due only to battle losses; _____ large numbers of soldiers and civilians fell ill and died as a result of living conditions during the war.

   A)   in addition,

   B)   therefore,

   C)   however,

   D)   on the other hand,

12. The public defense attorney was able to maintain her optimism despite _____.

    A) her dearth of courtroom wins, lack of free time she had, and growing list of clients she was helping.

    B) her dearth of courtroom wins, lack of free time, and growing list of clients.

    C) her dearth of courtroom wins, the free time she lacked, and the list of clients she was growing.

    D) the losses she had experienced, the free time she lacked, and her growing client list.

13. _____ the stethoscope underwent a number of reiterations before the modern form of the instrument was introduced in the 1850s.

    A) Being invented in France in the early nineteenth century,

    B) It was invented in France in the early nineteenth century,

    C) Though it was invented in France in the nineteenth century,

    D) Invented in France in the early nineteenth century,

14. In 1983, almost twenty years after his death, T. S. Eliot won two Tony Awards for his contributions to the well-loved musical *Cats*, _____

    A) it was based on a book of his poetry.

    B) which was based on a book of his poetry.

    C) being based on a book of his poetry.

    D) having been based on a book of his poetry.

15. Parrots, among the most intelligent birds in the world, have been prized pets for many _____

    A) centuries, in fact, the first recorded instance of parrot training was written in the thirteenth century.

    B) centuries, but the first recorded instance of parrot training was written in the thirteenth century.

    C) centuries, writing the first recorded instance of parrot training in the thirteenth century.

    D) centuries; in fact, the first recorded instance of parrot training was written in the thirteenth century.

16. Typically, water _____ before falling to Earth again as precipitation.

    A) remain in the sky in cloud form for fewer than ten days

    B) remain in the sky in cloud form for fewer then ten days

    C) remains in the sky in cloud form for fewer than ten days

    D) will remain in the sky in cloud form for fewer then ten days

17. _____ research into automating vehicle processes began as early as the 1920s.

    A) Before self-driving vehicles are just now being introduced on the automotive market,

    B) Though self-driving vehicles are just now being introduced on the automotive market,

    C) Because self-driving vehicles are just now being introduced on the automotive market,

    D) Self-driving vehicles are just now being introduced on the automotive market,

18. The exotic pet _____ is a significant concern for environmentalists and animal rights advocates around the world.

  A) trade, which involves both the capturing of wild animals and the captive breeding of wild species,

  B) trade, which involves both the capturing of wild animals and they breed wild species in captivity,

  C) trade involves both the capturing of wild animals and the captive breeding of wild species, it

  D) trade, it involves both the capturing of wild animals and the captive breeding of wild species,

19. Hurricanes, _____ have been the cause of almost two million deaths in the last two hundred years.

  A) which costs the United States roughly $5 billion per year in damages,

  B) having cost the United States roughly $5 billion per year in damages,

  C) which cost the United States roughly $5 billion per year in damages,

  D) have cost the United States roughly $5 billion per year in damages,

20. In 1903, Pennsylvania _____ in response, however, artists like Walt McDougall began depicting politicians in an even less flattering light—as inanimate objects such as trees and mugs.

  A) depicting politicians as animals, passed a law prohibiting cartoonists in order to curb criticism by the press;

  B) prohibiting cartoonists from depicting politicians as animals, passed a law in order to curb criticism by the press;

  C) passed a law prohibiting cartoonists from depicting politicians in order to curb criticism as animals by the press;

  D) passed a law prohibiting cartoonists from depicting politicians as animals in order to curb criticism by the press;

Select the answer choice that best completes the sentence in the passage.

Anyone who has been given a nickname knows that these informal labels can sometimes be difficult to shake. In the 1980s, one group of young actors earned a group nickname—the Brat Pack—that would follow them for decades. While some members of the Brat Pack still went on to have successful **(21)**_____ struggled to make their own names stand out against the backdrop of the group.

The members of the Brat Pack earned their fame by appearing together in a series of films made for teen and young adult audiences. **(22)**_____ one of these movies was made in the early 1980s, the Brat Pack label did not appear until 1985, when *New York Magazine* writer David Blum wrote an article about his experience socializing with some of the group members. The article **(23)**_____ these young actors as immature, unprofessional, and spoiled, and though Blum's experience with them was limited to one night with just three individuals, his label quickly caught on and tarnished the reputations of many of the other young actors who worked alongside the three. Many of these individuals struggled professionally as a result of the negative label, and most of them denied being a part of any such group.

Today, despite the initial repercussions of the unfortunate nickname, the Brat Pack label is still in use, largely because of the **(24)**_____ relevance and significance of the Brat Pack films. Most of these films are coming-of-age stories, in which one or more of the characters gains experience or learns an important lesson about adult life. For example, in the most famous of these films, *The Breakfast Club*, the five main characters, **(25)**_____ are all from different social circles at one high school, learn to look past labels and appearances and find that they have more in common than they ever imagined.

Because of the talent and the relatability of the Brat Pack members, these characters and their stories continue to appeal to young people and influence popular culture in the new millennium. Thus, the Brat Pack nickname has been freed of its negative connotations by the actors who once despised and wore the label.

21.
- **A)** careers; others
- **B)** careers, others
- **C)** careers, but others
- **D)** careers. Others

22.
- **A)** Though the first
- **B)** The first
- **C)** Because the first
- **D)** Consequently, the first

23.
- **A)** is portraying
- **B)** would portray
- **C)** was portraying
- **D)** portrayed

24.
- **A)** ongoing and perpetual
- **B)** perpetually ongoing
- **C)** never-ending, perpetual
- **D)** ongoing

25.
- **A)** whom
- **B)** who
- **C)** which
- **D)** and

Answer Key

1. **C) is correct.**

   Plays is a singular verb and does not correctly pair with the plural subject *men*; *men dress* and *play*.

2. **D) is correct.**

   No errors are present in this sentence.

3. **A) is correct.**

   It's is a contraction of the phrase *it is*; this context requires the possessive form (*its surroundings*).

4. **C) is correct.**

   Because it is a negative, *no other* inaccurately discounts the first negative (*not*) and creates a double negative (*could not afford no other*); it should be changed to *any other*.

5. **D) is correct.**

   No error exists in this sentence.

6. **A) is correct.**

   A comma should not be included in this location, as it separates the subject (*photographer*) and the verb (*specializes*).

7. **B) is correct.**

   Countries' is a plural possessive but should be acting as a plural subject; the correct format of the word is *countries* (*around the world*).

8. **B) is correct.**

   Continued is a past-tense verb; however, it should be present tense (*continues*) in order to align with the time mentioned later in the sentence (*even today*).

9. **A) is correct.**

   Stressed and emphasized have similar definitions in this context; only one word needs to be used.

10. **A) is correct.**

    Having, a participle, turns this sentence into a fragment by removing the verb; to improve the sentence, *having* should be replaced with *had*.

11. **A) is correct.**

    In addition is the appropriate introductory phrase to signify the additive relationship between the two clauses.

12. **B) is correct.**

    In this iteration, all items in the list are nouns (*dearth*, *lack*, and *list*), followed by prepositions (*of*) and objects of the prepositions (*wins*, *time*, and *clients*).

13. **D) is correct.**

    Invented, the past participle of *invent*, appropriately introduces this participial phrase that provides more information about the subject of the sentence (*stethoscope*).

14. **B) is correct.**

    Which is used correctly here to introduce an additional, nonrestrictive clause about an element of the sentence (*the musical*).

15. **D) is correct.**

    The semicolon is used appropriately here to join two independent, related clauses; *in fact* signifies an interesting detail to follow.

16. **C) is correct.**

Remains is a singular, present-tense verb that agrees with its subject *water*, which is noncountable and therefore singular; *than* is a conjunction used correctly here to express inequality between two things (amount of time the water is in the sky and ten days).

17. **B) is correct.**

Though is used correctly in this sentence to show a slight contradiction between the assumption (that self-driving cars are new) and the truth (that vehicle automation has been a topic of study for many decades).

18. **A) is correct.**

The appositive phrase is correctly enclosed with commas; the items inside the commas are parallel (*the capturing of wild animals and the captive breeding of wild species*).

19. **C) is correct.**

Which cost is a clear, concise way to set off the nonrestrictive appositive phrase.

20. **D) is correct.**

Modifying relationships are clear: *Pennsylvania* is followed by its verb *passed* and the description of the

law (*prohibiting cartoonists from…*) immediately follows the word *law*; the reason for the law (*in order to…*) comes after the description of the law.

21. **B) is correct.**

The comma following *careers* correctly separates the independent clause from the following dependent clause.

22. **A) is correct.**

The subordinating conjunction *though* correctly begins the sentence; it creates a relationship that makes good sense between the opening subordinate clause and the independent clause that follows.

23. **D) is correct.**

The past-tense verb *portrayed* agrees with the past-tense verbs *was* and *caught* that appear later in the sentence.

24. **D) is correct.**

Since the two adjectives are synonyms, using just one of them is sufficient. Using both would be redundant.

25. **B) is correct.**

The subject form of the relative pronoun *who* correctly appears here. The word functions as a subject, not an object.

three

THE ESSAY

The GED requires an essay in the Reasoning Through Language Arts section. You will be provided with a prompt and asked to take a position on it. To do well on the essay, take a clear side on the issue put forth in the prompt. Support your perspective with strong arguments and specific examples. An effective essay is clearly organized and structured, displays strong vocabulary, and features complex sentences.

There are two common types of essays:

◆ an expository essay explains an issue without taking sides or promoting a perspective

◆ a persuasive essay argues in favor of or against an issue or perspective

For the GED, you'll be writing a persuasive essay.

Writing a Thesis Statement

A THESIS STATEMENT articulates the main argument of the essay. No essay is complete without it: the structure and organization of the essay revolves around the thesis statement. The thesis statement is simply the writer's main idea or argument. It usually appears at the end of the introduction.

In a good thesis statement, the author states his or her idea or argument and why it is correct or true.

EXAMPLE

Take a position on the following topic in your essay. You can choose to write about either of the two viewpoints discussed in the prompt, or you may argue for a third point of view.

Many scientists argue that recent unusual weather patterns, such as powerful hurricanes and droughts, are due to climate change triggered by human activity. They argue that automobiles, oil and gas production, and manufacturing generate carbon emissions that artificially heat the atmosphere, resulting in extreme weather patterns. Others disagree. Some researchers and media pundits argue that climate change is natural, and that extreme weather has always been a feature of Earth's atmosphere.

Possible thesis statements:

Around the world more people than ever before are driving cars, and industrial production is at an all-time high: it is obvious that human activity is affecting the atmosphere and causing extreme weather events.

I believe that temperatures and storms are more extreme than ever because of the environmental impact of human activity; not only do scientists have overwhelming evidence that climate change is unnatural, but I can also personally remember when there were fewer storms and variations in temperature.

Society needs cars and manufacturing, but governments should restrict harmful emissions released into the atmosphere so we can slow down climate change and save lives.

Structuring the Essay

On the GED, a strong essay will have an introduction, a body, and a conclusion. While there are many ways to organize an essay, on this exam it is most important that the essay is clearly structured. There is no need to get too complicated: this simple structure will do.

Introductions

Some writers struggle with the introduction, but it is actually an opportunity to present your idea or argument. On the GED, the introduction can be one paragraph that ends with the thesis statement. In the rest of the paragraph, the writer provides some context for his or her argument. This context might include counterarguments, a preview of specific examples to be discussed later on, acknowledgement of the complexities of the issue, or even a reference to personal experience. The writer can reexamine some of these issues in the conclusion.

If you're not sure what to include in your introduction, start your essay with just the thesis statement. You can go back and complete the introduction once the rest of the essay is finished.

EXAMPLE

In the example below, the writer has written an introduction that includes context for her argument: background information, a counterargument, and personal experience. As a result, the reader has a better idea of how complex the issue is and why the writer feels the way she does. The thesis statement appears at the end of the paragraph; as a result of the introduction as a whole, the thesis statement has more impact.

A century ago, there were barely any cars on the road. Oil had just been discovered in a few parts of the world. Industrial production existed but had not yet exploded with the introduction of the assembly line. Refineries and factories were not yet churning out the chemical emissions they are today. Certainly, hurricanes and droughts occurred, but the populations and infrastructure affected were far smaller. Now, scientists have evidence that human activity—like pollution from industry and cars—is affecting the atmosphere and making weather more extreme. In 2017, millions of people were affected by hurricanes and wildfires. It is true that some researchers disagree that human activity has caused these and other extreme weather events. But why take the risk? If we can limit destruction now and in the future, we should. Extreme weather events are a danger to people all around the world. Society needs cars and manufacturing, but governments should restrict harmful emissions released into the atmosphere so we can slow down climate change and save lives.

The Body Paragraphs

Most writers find the body of the essay the easiest part to write. The body of the essay is simply several paragraphs, each beginning with a topic sentence. Each paragraph usually addresses an example that supports the argument made in the thesis statement or, in the case of an expository essay, explains the writer's reasoning. On the GED, you may use specific examples or personal anecdotes, present problems and solutions, or compare and contrast ideas. You do not need to refer to any outside literature or documentation.

To strengthen the body of the essay, writers will maintain consistency in paragraphs, always beginning with a topic sentence, which introduces the main idea of each paragraph. Each paragraph deals with its own main topic, but writers should use transition words and phrases to link paragraphs with each other. A good essay maintains readability and flow.

EXAMPLE

This example body paragraph is related to the introduction provided above. It provides reasoning and historical evidence for the author's argument that human activity is impacting the earth and causing climate change.

Human industrial activity has been growing exponentially, putting more pollution into the atmosphere than ever. Over the past forty years, large countries like China and India have become industrialized and manufacture many of the world's products. As their populations become more prosperous, demand for automobiles also rises, putting more cars on the road—and exhaust in the air. While industrial development has benefited Asia and other areas, carbon emissions that cause climate change have multiplied. Meanwhile, previously industrialized countries in Europe and North America continue to produce carbon emissions. In the nineteenth century, only a few countries had industrial sectors; today, global industry strains the environment like never before. The past 150 years have seen unprecedented industrial growth. Even if the climate changes naturally over time, it cannot be denied that recent human activity has suddenly generated enormous amounts of carbon emissions that have impacted the atmosphere. Scientists say that the earth is warming as a result.

Conclusions

The conclusion does not need to be long. Its purpose is to wrap up the essay, reminding the reader why the topic and the writer's argument is important. It is an opportunity for the writer to reexamine the thesis statement and ideas in the introduction. It is a time to reinforce the argument, not just to repeat the introduction.

EXAMPLE

This example is taken from the same essay as the introduction and body paragraph above. It reinforces the writer's argument without simply repeating what she said in the introduction. The writer does address the topics she spoke about in the introduction (climate change and protecting people from extreme weather) but she does not simply rewrite the thesis: she calls for action.

No doubt, scientists, pundits, and politicians will continue to argue over the reasons for extreme weather. Meanwhile, Mother Nature will continue to wreak havoc on vulnerable areas regardless of what we think. Because we have proof that climate change is related to extreme weather and we know that extreme weather threatens people's lives, the time to act is now. We can take steps to mitigate pollution without lowering quality of life. Doing anything else is irresponsible—and for some, deadly.

Providing Supporting Evidence

As discussed above, a good essay should have specific evidence or examples that support the thesis statement. On the GED, a specific example should be something related to the idea of the paragraph and the essay, not a new idea. A specific example can be from your general knowledge; you do not need to know about specific academic issues to do well on the essay. Remember, you are being tested on your reasoning and argumentative skills.

The following are some examples of general statements and specific statements that provide more detailed support:

GENERAL: Human industrial activity has been growing exponentially, putting more pollution into the atmosphere than ever.

SPECIFIC: Over the past forty years, large countries like China and India have become industrialized and manufacture many of the world's products. As their populations become more prosperous, demand for automobiles also rises, putting more cars on the road—and exhaust in the air.

SPECIFIC: Meanwhile, previously industrialized countries in Europe and North America continue to produce carbon emissions. In the nineteenth century, only a few countries had industrial sectors; today, global industry strains the environment like never before.

GENERAL: More people than ever are affected by extreme weather.

SPECIFIC: In 2017, several hurricanes affected the United States and the Caribbean. In Texas, Hurricane Harvey led to historic flooding in Houston and the Texas Coast. Millions of people were affected; thousands lost their homes, jobs, and livelihoods.

SPECIFIC: Hurricane Irma damaged the US Virgin Islands and neighboring Caribbean nations. Soon after, Hurricane Maria catastrophically devastated Puerto Rico. Months later, Puerto Ricans were still without power and basic necessities. It is still not clear how many have died due to the storm and related damage.

EXAMPLE

In the example below, the paragraph is structured with a topic sentence and specific supporting ideas. This paragraph supports the introduction in the example above.

More people than ever are affected by extreme weather. In 2017, several hurricanes affected the United States and the Caribbean. In Texas, Hurricane Harvey led to historic flooding in Houston and the Texas Coast. Millions of people were affected; thousands lost their homes, jobs, and livelihoods. Hurricane Irma damaged Florida, the US Virgin Islands, and neighboring Caribbean nations. Soon after, Hurricane Maria catastrophically devastated Puerto Rico. Months later, Puerto Ricans were still without power and basic necessities. It is still not clear how many have died due to the storm and related damage. In California, severe droughts led to exceptionally large wildfires that threatened Los Angeles and destroyed neighboring communities. Meanwhile, those same areas—Southern California, the Texas Coast, and Florida—continue to grow, putting more people at risk when the next hurricane or fire strikes.

Writing Well

Using transitions, complex sentences, and certain words can turn a good essay into a great one. Transitions, syntax, word choice, and tone all help clarify and amplify a writer's argument or point and improve the flow of an essay.

Transitions

An essay consists of several paragraphs. TRANSITIONS are words and phrases that help connect the paragraphs and ideas of the text. Most commonly, transitions would appear at the beginning of a paragraph, but writers should also use them throughout a text to connect ideas. Common transitions are words like *also, next, still, although, in addition to,* and *in other words.* A transition shows a relationship between ideas, so writers should pay close attention to the transition words and phrases they choose. Transitions may show connections or contrasts between words and ideas.

Table 3.1. Common Transitions

TRANSITION TYPE	EXAMPLES
addition	additionally, also, as well, further, furthermore, in addition, moreover
cause and effect	as a result, because, consequently, due to, if/then, so, therefore, thus
concluding	briefly, finally, in conclusion, in summary, thus, to conclude

Table 3.1. Common Transitions (continued)

Transition Type	Examples
contrast	but, however, in contrast, on the other hand, nevertheless, on the contrary, yet
examples	in other words, for example, for instance
similarity	also, likewise, similarly
time	after, before, currently, later, recently, subsequently, since, then, while

Syntax

SYNTAX refers to how words and phrases are arranged in writing or speech. Writing varied sentences is essential to capturing and keeping a reader's interest. A good essay features different types of sentences: simple, complex, compound, and compound-complex. Sentences need not always begin with the subject; they might start with a transition word or phrase, for instance. Variety is key.

Still, writers should keep in mind that the point of an essay is to get an idea across to the reader, so it is most important that writing be clear. They should not sacrifice clarity for the sake of flowery, overly wordy language or confusing syntax.

Word Choice and Tone

Like syntax, word choice makes an impression on readers. The GED does not test on specific vocabulary or require writers to use specific words on the essay. However, the essay is a good opportunity to use strong vocabulary pertaining to the prompt or issue under discussion. Writers should be careful, though, that they understand the words they are using. Writers should also avoid vague, imprecise, or generalizing language like *good, bad, a lot, a little, very, normal,* and so on.

Editing, Revising, and Proofreading

On the GED, the writer has a limited amount of time to complete the essay. If there is time for editing or proofreading, writers should hunt for grammar, spelling, or punctuation mistakes that could change the meaning of the text or make it difficult to understand. These include sentence fragments, run-on sentences, subject-verb disagreement, and pronoun-antecedent disagreement.

Test Your Knowledge

Topic: Driving Age — Is Sixteen Too Young?

PASSAGE 1: THE CASE FOR TEEN DRIVERS BY RIYA SIDANA

A recent spate of articles appearing in major publications are raising the question of whether states should change the driving age for teens, raising it by one or even two years. The proposals cite statistics about the risks of impulsive, distractible, inexperienced drivers on the road harming themselves and others. Unfortunately, these proposals fail to account for the hardships the change might impose on parents and teens in some families. For instance, some teens provide income by working a part-time job that they might need a car for. Furthermore, the proposals completely overlook other, potentially more useful solutions to the issue.

Teens are indeed inexperienced and impulsive decision makers, and car accidents are the number one cause of death for teens, but raising the driving age will not automatically instill more experience and stronger decision-making. Solutions such as graduated licensing and improved driver's education courses have reduced teen fatalities and road accidents in states that have implemented them, such as New Jersey and Connecticut. These states employ changing requirements for teen drivers that are stricter and harsher for younger drivers and more relaxed as drivers grow more competent. In addition to greater penalties, increasing the amount of supervised driving time and limiting the number of passengers a teen can carry help to gradually improve that teen's skills on the road.

Before eliminating a beloved rite of passage for American teens, inconveniencing families, and demonstrating to teens that that they cannot be trusted, states should seek to address dangers and problems with solutions that have been proven to work.

PASSAGE 2: RAISING THE DRIVING AGE BY THOMAS MADDOW

In 2010, 33 percent of deaths of teens aged sixteen to nineteen were caused by motor vehicle crashes.

Talking on a phone can double the likelihood of an accident, and more than 56 percent of teens admit to using a cell phone while driving.

Of all these groups, sixteen-year-olds have higher crash rates than any other age.

These are just a few of the statistics that demonstrate the need for serious consideration of the age at which we allow our teens to drive. The driving age should be legally raised to seventeen or even eighteen, giving teens time to develop a stronger ability to make responsible choices on the road, avoid the pressures of showing off dangerously for friends, and gain a greater understanding of the responsibilities of a driver. While teens understandably long for the freedom of the road and feel that another year of waiting may be impossible to bear, many other industrialized nations impose an older driving age, and it is the responsibility of adults and lawmakers to do what is best for teens—despite their protests.

The author of passage 1 argues that rather than changing the driving age, states should add limitations and rules for younger drivers. The writer of passage 2 suggests that the correct course is to raise the driving age.

In your response, analyze both texts. Write a persuasive essay explaining which side is more convincing, using examples from each text to support your argument.

Sample Essay

The argument over whether or not to raise the driving age is not simple, with arguments and statistics supporting both sides. The two passages given both offer compelling reasons why their argument is more correct; however, passage 1 by Riya Sidana offers a more complete argument that addresses a broad audience and includes clear evidence and explanation.

Thomas Maddow's article begins with clear statistics that support his argument, stating them directly and starkly; however, the statistics are missing any context that can help the reader understand how they fit into a larger picture. Sidana, on the other hand, fleshes out her argument that there are better ways to address the issues Maddow lists. She says that "solutions such as graduated licensing and improved driver's education courses have reduced teen fatalities," giving clear examples of how the issues can be addressed without raising the driver's age. By addressing the issues themselves, she makes her argument more complex and complete.

Additionally, Sidana mentions New Jersey and Connecticut to provide specific examples of states that have already done what she suggests. She says these states "employ changing requirements" and that "increasing the amount of supervised driving time and limiting the number of passengers" also helps improve teens' driving skills. In contrast, Maddow calls for action from like-minded adults, citing their responsibilities, but not explaining how the changes will help. Sidana's explanations are more persuasive because they provide more detail.

Finally, Sidana's argument seems to be addressed to a broader audience, both teens who believe they should have the freedom to drive and parents or lawmakers charged with making the changes suggested. Sidana acknowledges the problem rather than dismissing it, but also acknowledges the difficulties that might be faced by families and teens, mentioning that a teen "may provide income." Her language paints teens as potentially responsible, helpful members of the family, but does not deny that they are "inexperienced and impulsive decision makers." By describing both sides impartially, Sidana widens her audience and allows both sides to agree to a compromise.

Because she addresses both sides fairly, makes a more complex argument, and supports it with evidence, Sidana's argument is simply more effective than Maddow's, despite his clear, straightforward statistics. Passage 1 does a better job of persuading its audience.

Follow the link below for your second Reasoning Through Language Arts GED practice test:
www.acceptedinc.com/ged-2018-online-resources

PART II: MATHEMATICAL REASONING

four

NUMBERS AND OPERATIONS

This chapter provides a review of the basic yet critical components of mathematics such as manipulating fractions, comparing numbers, and using units. These concepts will provide the foundation for more complex mathematical operations in later chapters.

Types of Numbers

Numbers are placed in categories based on their properties.

- A **NATURAL NUMBER** is greater than 0 and has no decimal or fraction attached. These are also sometimes called counting numbers $\{1, 2, 3, 4, ...\}$.

- **WHOLE NUMBERS** are natural numbers and the number 0 $\{0, 1, 2, 3, 4, ...\}$.

- **INTEGERS** include positive and negative natural numbers and 0 $\{..., -4, -3, -2, -1, 0, 1, 2, 3, 4, ...\}$.

- A **RATIONAL NUMBER** can be represented as a fraction. Any decimal part must terminate or resolve into a repeating pattern. Examples include -12, $-\frac{4}{5}$, 0.36, $7.\overline{7}$, $26\frac{1}{2}$, etc.

- An **IRRATIONAL NUMBER** cannot be represented as a fraction. An irrational decimal number never ends and never resolves into a repeating pattern. Examples include $-\sqrt{7}$, π, and $0.34567989135...$

- A **REAL NUMBER** is a number that can be represented by a point on a number line. Real numbers include all the rational and irrational numbers.

- An **IMAGINARY NUMBER** includes the imaginary unit i, where $i = \sqrt{-1}$ Because $i^2 = -1$, imaginary numbers produce a negative value when squared. Examples of imaginary numbers include $-4i$, $0.75i$, $i\sqrt{2}$ and $\frac{8}{3}i$.

- A **COMPLEX NUMBER** is in the form $a + bi$, where a and b are real numbers. Examples of complex numbers include $3 + 2i$, $-4 + i$, $\sqrt{3} - i\sqrt[3]{5}$ and $\frac{5}{8} - \frac{7i}{8}$. All imaginary numbers are also complex.

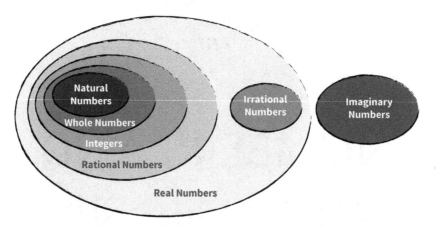

Figure 4.1. Types of Numbers

The **FACTORS** of a natural number are all the numbers that can multiply together to make the number. For example, the factors of 24 are 1, 2, 3, 4, 6, 8, 12, and 24. Every natural number is either prime or composite. A **PRIME NUMBER** is a number that is only divisible by itself and 1. (The number 1 is not considered prime.) Examples of prime numbers are 2, 3, 7, and 29. The number 2 is the only even prime number. A **COMPOSITE NUMBER** has more than two factors. For example, 6 is composite because its factors are 1, 6, 2, and 3. Every composite number can be written as a unique product of prime numbers, called the **PRIME FACTORIZATION** of the number. For example, the prime factorization of 90 is $90 = 2 \times 3^2 \times 5$. All integers are either even or odd. An even number is divisible by 2; an odd number is not.

If a real number is a natural number (e.g., 50), then it is also a whole number, an integer, and a rational number.

Properties of Number Systems

A system is **CLOSED** under an operation if performing that operation on two elements of the system results in another element of that system. For example, the integers are closed under the operations of addition, subtraction, and multiplication but not division. Adding, subtracting, or multiplying two integers results in another integer. However, dividing two integers could result in a rational number that is not an integer $\left(-2 \div 3 = \frac{-2}{3}\right)$.

- The rational numbers are closed under all four operations (except for division by 0).
- The real numbers are closed under all four operations.
- The complex numbers are closed under all four operations.
- The irrational numbers are NOT closed under ANY of the four operations.

The **COMMUTATIVE PROPERTY** holds for an operation if order does not matter when performing the operation. For example, multiplication is commutative for integers: (–2)(3)= (3)(–2).

The **ASSOCIATIVE PROPERTY** holds for an operation if elements can be regrouped without changing the result. For example, addition is associative for real numbers: –3 + (–5 + 4) = (–3 + –5) + 4.

The **DISTRIBUTIVE PROPERTY** of multiplication over addition allows a product of sums to be written as a sum of products: $a(b + c) = ab + ac$. The value a is distributed over the sum $(b + c)$. The acronym FOIL (First, Outer, Inner, Last) is a useful way to remember the distributive property.

When an operation is performed with an **IDENTITY ELEMENT** and another element a, the result is a. The identity element for multiplication on real numbers is $a \times 1 = a$), and for addition is 0 $(a + 0 = a)$.

An operation of a system has an **INVERSE ELEMENT** if applying that operation with the inverse element results in the identity element. For example, the inverse element of a for addition is $-a$ because $a + (-a) = 0$. The inverse element of a for multiplication is $\frac{1}{a}$ because $a \times \frac{1}{a} = 1$.

EXAMPLES

1. Classify the following numbers as natural, whole, integer, rational, or irrational. (The numbers may have more than one classification.)

   A) 72

   B) $-\frac{2}{3}$

   C) $\sqrt{5}$

   Answers:

   A) The number is **natural**, **whole**, an **integer**, and **rational**.

   B) The fraction is **rational**.

   C) The number is **irrational**. (It cannot be written as a fraction, and written as a decimal is approximately 2.2360679...)

2. Determine the real and imaginary parts of the following complex numbers.

   A) 20

   B) $10 - i$

   C) $15i$

   Answers:

   A complex number is in the form of $a + bi$, where a is the real part and bi is the imaginary part.

   A) $20 = 20 + 0i$
   The real part is 20, and there is no imaginary part.

   B) $10 - i = 10 - 1i$
   The real part is 10, and $-1i$ is the imaginary part.

   C) $15i = 0 + 15i$
   The real part is 0, and the imaginary part is $15i$.

3. Answer True or False for each statement:

   A) The natural numbers are closed under subtraction.

   B) The sum of two irrational numbers is irrational.

   C) The sum of a rational number and an irrational number is irrational.

Answers:

A) **False.** Subtracting the natural number 7 from 2 results in
2 − 7 = −5, which is an integer, but not a natural number.

B) **False.** For example, $(5 - 2\sqrt{3}) + (2 + 2\sqrt{3}) = 7$. The sum of two irrational numbers in this example is a whole number, which is not irrational. The sum of a rational number and an irrational number is sometimes rational and sometimes irrational.

C) **True.** Because irrational numbers have decimal parts that are unending and with no pattern, adding a repeating or terminating decimal will still result in an unending decimal without a pattern.

4. Answer true or false for each statement:

   A) The associative property applies for multiplication in the real numbers.

   B) The commutative property applies to all real numbers and all operations.

Answers:

A) **True.** For all real numbers, $a \times (b \times c) = (a \times b) \times c$. Order of multiplication does not change the result.

B) **False.** The commutative property does not work for subtraction or division on real numbers. For example, 12 − 5 = 7, but 5 − 12 = −7, and 10 ÷ 2 = 5, but $2 \div 10 = \frac{1}{5}$.

Operations with Complex Numbers

Operations with complex numbers are similar to operations with real numbers in that complex numbers can be added, subtracted, multiplied, and divided. When adding or subtracting, the imaginary parts and real parts are combined separately. When multiplying, the distributive property (FOIL) can be applied. Note that multiplying complex numbers often creates the value i^2 which can be simplified to −1.

To divide complex numbers, multiply both the top and bottom of the fraction by the COMPLEX CONJUGATE of the divisor (bottom number). The complex conjugate is the complex number with the sign of the imaginary part changed. For example, the complex conjugate of $3 + 4i$ would be $3 - 4i$. Since both the top and the bottom of the fraction are multiplied by the same number, the fraction is really just being multiplied by 1. When simplified, the denominator of the fraction will now be a real number.

EXAMPLES

1. Simplify: $(3 - 2i) - (-2 + 8i)$

   Answer:

$(3 - 2i) - (-2 + 8i)$	
$= (3 - 2i) - 1(-2 + 8i)$	Distribute the −1.
$= 3 - 2i + 2 - 8i$	
$= \mathbf{5 - 10}\boldsymbol{i}$	Combine like terms.

2. Simplify: $\dfrac{4i}{(5-2i)}$

Answer:

$\dfrac{4i}{(5-2i)}$	
$= \dfrac{4i}{5-2i}\left(\dfrac{5+2i}{5+2i}\right)$ $= \dfrac{20i+8i^2}{25+10i-10i-4i^2}$	Multiply the top and bottom of the fraction by the complex conjugate of $5 + 2i$.
$= \dfrac{20i+8(-1)}{25+10i-10i-4(-1)}$ $= \dfrac{20i-8}{25+10i-10i+4}$	Simplify the result using the identity $i^2 = -1$.
$= \dfrac{20i-8}{29}$	Combine like terms.
$= \dfrac{-8}{29} + \dfrac{20}{29}i$	Write the answer in the form $a + bi$.

Scientific Notation

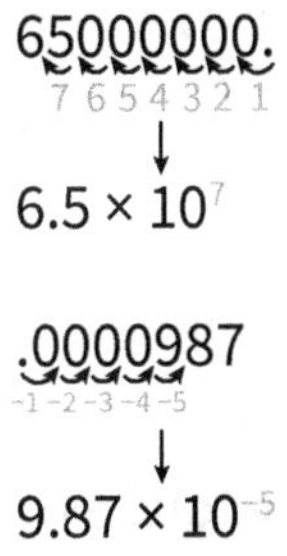

$$65\underset{7\;6\;5\;4\;3\;2\;1}{000000.}$$
$$\downarrow$$
$$6.5 \times 10^{7}$$

$$.\underset{-1\;-2\;-3\;-4\;-5}{0000987}$$
$$\downarrow$$
$$9.87 \times 10^{-5}$$

**Figure 4.2.
Scientific Notation**

SCIENTIFIC NOTATION is a method of representing very large and small numbers in the form $a \times 10^n$, where a is a value between 1 and 10, and n is a nonzero integer. For example, the number 927,000,000 is written in scientific notation as 9.27×10^8. Multiplying 9.27 by 10 eight times gives 927,000,000. When performing operations with scientific notation, the final answer should be in the form $a \times 10^n$.

When adding and subtracting numbers in scientific notation, the power of 10 must be the same for all numbers. This results in like terms in which the a terms are added or subtracted and the 10^n remains unchanged. When multiplying numbers in scientific notation, multiply the a factors, and then multiply that answer by 10 to the sum of the exponents. For division, divide the a factors and subtract the exponents.

When multiplying numbers in scientific notation, add the exponents. When dividing, subtract the exponents.

EXAMPLES

1. Simplify: $(3.8 \times 10^3) + (4.7 \times 10^2)$

Answer:

$(3.8 \times 10^3) + (4.7 \times 10^2)$	
$3.8 \times 10^3 = 3.8 \times 10 \times 10^2 = 38 \times 10^2$	To add, the exponents of 10 must be the same.
$38 \times 10^2 + 4.7 \times 10^2 = 42.7 \times 10^2$	Add the a terms together.

= 4.27 × 10³	Write the number in proper scientific notation.

2. Simplify: $(8.1 \times 10^{-5})(1.4 \times 10^7)$

   Answer:

$(8.1 \times 10^{-5})(1.4 \times 10^7)$	
$8.1 \times 1.4 = 11.34$ $-5 + 7 = 2$ $= 11.34 \times 10^2$	Multiply the *a* factors and add the exponents on the base of 10.
= 1.134 × 10³	Write the number in proper scientific notation.

Positive and Negative Numbers

POSITIVE NUMBERS are greater than 0, and **NEGATIVE NUMBERS** are less than 0. Both positive and negative numbers can be shown on a **NUMBER LINE**.

Figure 4.3. Number Line

The **ABSOLUTE VALUE** of a number is the distance the number is from 0. Since distance is always positive, the absolute value of a number is always positive. The absolute value of *a* is denoted $|a|$. For example, $|-2| = 2$ since –2 is two units away from 0.

Positive and negative numbers can be added, subtracted, multiplied, and divided. The sign of the resulting number is governed by a specific set of rules shown in the table below.

Table 4.1. Operations with Positive and Negative Numbers

ADDING REAL NUMBERS		SUBTRACTING REAL NUMBERS	
Positive + Positive = Positive	$7 + 8 = 15$	Negative – Positive = Negative	$-7 - 8 =$ $-7 + (-8) = -15$
Negative + Negative = Negative	$-7 + (-8) = -15$	Positive – Negative = Positive	$7 - (-8) =$ $7 + 8 = 15$
Negative + Positive OR Positive + Negative = Keep the sign of the number with larger absolute value	$-7 + 8 = 1$ $7 + -8 = -1$	Negative – Negative = Change the subtraction to addition and change the sign of the second number; then use addition rules.	$-7 - (-8) =$ $-7 + 8 = 1$ $-8 - (-7) = -8 +$ $7 = -1$

MULTIPLYING REAL NUMBERS		DIVIDING REAL NUMBERS	
Positive × Positive = Positive	$8 \times 4 = 32$	Positive ÷ Positive = Positive	$8 \div 4 = 2$
Negative × Negative = Positive	$-8 \times (-4) = 32$	Negative ÷ Negative = Positive	$-8 \div (-4) = 2$

Multiplying Real Numbers		Dividing Real Numbers	
Positive × Negative OR Negative × Positive = Negative	$8 \times (-4) = -32$ $-8 \times 4 = -32$	Positive ÷ Negative OR Negative ÷ Positive = Negative	$8 \div (-4) = -2$ $-8 \div 4 = -2$

EXAMPLES

1. Add or subtract the following real numbers:

   A) $-18 + 12$

   B) $-3.64 + (-2.18)$

   C) $9.37 - 4.25$

   D) $86 - (-20)$

   Answers:

   A) Since $|-18| > |12|$, the answer is negative: $|-18| - |12| = 6$. So the answer is **−6**.

   B) Adding two negative numbers results in a negative number. Add the values: **−5.82**.

   C) The first number is larger than the second, so the final answer is positive: **5.12**.

   D) Change the subtraction to addition, change the sign of the second number, and then add: $86 - (-20) = 86 + (+20) = $ **106**.

2. Multiply or divide the following real numbers:

   A) $\left(\frac{10}{3}\right)\left(-\frac{9}{5}\right)$

   B) $\frac{-64}{-10}$

   C) $(2.2)(3.3)$

   D) $-52 \div 13$

   Answers:

   A) Multiply the numerators, multiply the denominators, and simplify: $\frac{-90}{15} = $ **−6**.

   B) A negative divided by a negative is a positive number: **6.4**.

   C) Multiplying positive numbers gives a positive answer: **7.26**.

   D) Dividing a negative by a positive number gives a negative answer: **−4**.

Order of Operations

The **ORDER OF OPERATIONS** is simply the order in which operations are performed. **PEMDAS** is a common way to remember the order of operations:

1.	Parentheses	4.	Division
2.	Exponents	5.	Addition
3.	Multiplication	6.	Subtraction

Multiplication and division, and addition and subtraction, are performed together from left to right. So, performing multiple operations on a set of numbers is a four-step process:

1. **P:** Calculate expressions inside parentheses, brackets, braces, etc.
2. **E:** Calculate exponents and square roots.
3. **MD:** Calculate any remaining multiplication and division in order from left to right.
4. **AS:** Calculate any remaining addition and subtraction in order from left to right.

Always work from left to right within each step when simplifying expressions.

EXAMPLES

1. Simplify: $2(21 - 14) + 6 \div (-2) \times 3 - 10$

   Answer:

$2(21 - 14) + 6 \div (-2) \times 3 - 10$	
$= 2(7) + 6 \div (-2) \times 3 - 10$	Calculate expressions inside parentheses.
$= 14 + 6 \div (-2) \times 3 - 10$ $= 14 + (-3) \times 3 - 10$ $= 14 + (-9) - 10$	There are no exponents or radicals, so perform multiplication and division from left to right.
$= 5 - 10$ $= -5$	Perform addition and subtraction from left to right.

2. Simplify: $-(3)^2 + 4(5) + (5 - 6)^2 - 8$

   Answer:

$-(3)^2 + 4(5) + (5 - 6)^2 - 8$	
$= -(3)^2 + 4(5) + (-1)^2 - 8$	Calculate expressions inside parentheses.
$= -9 + 4(5) + 1 - 8$	Simplify exponents and radicals.
$= -9 + 20 + 1 - 8$	Perform multiplication and division from left to right.
$= 11 + 1 - 8$ $= 12 - 8$ $= 4$	Perform addition and subtraction from left to right.

3. Simplify: $\dfrac{(7 - 9)^3 + 8(10 - 12)}{4^2 - 5^2}$

   Answer:

$\dfrac{(7 - 9)^3 + 8(10 - 12)}{4^2 - 5^2}$	
$= \dfrac{(-2)^3 + 8(-2)}{4^2 - 5^2}$	Calculate expressions inside parentheses.
$= \dfrac{-8 + (-16)}{16 - 25}$	Simplify exponents and radicals.

$= \frac{-24}{-9}$	Perform addition and subtraction from left to right.
$= \frac{8}{3}$	Simplify.

Units of Measurement

The standard units for the metric and American systems are shown below, along with the prefixes used to express metric units.

Table 4.2. Units and Conversion Factors

DIMENSION	AMERICAN	SI
length	inch/foot/yard/mile	meter
mass	ounce/pound/ton	gram
volume	cup/pint/quart/gallon	liter
force	pound-force	newton
pressure	pound-force per square inch	pascal
work and energy	cal/British thermal unit	joule
temperature	Fahrenheit	kelvin
charge	faraday	coulomb

Table 4.3. Metric Prefixes

PREFIX	SYMBOL	MULTIPLICATION FACTOR
tera	T	1,000,000,000,000
giga	G	1,000,000,000
mega	M	1,000,000
kilo	k	1,000
hecto	h	100
deca	da	10
base unit	--	--
deci	d	0.1
centi	c	0.01
milli	m	0.001
micro	μ	0.000001
nano	n	0.000000001
pico	p	0.000000000001

Units can be converted within a single system or between systems. When converting from one unit to another unit, a conversion factor (a numeric multiplier used to convert a value with a unit to another unit) is used. The process of converting between units using a conversion factor is sometimes known as dimensional analysis.

Table 4.4. Conversion Factors

1 in. = 2.54 cm	1 lb. = 0.454 kg
1 yd. = 0.914 m	1 cal = 4.19 J
1 mi. = 1.61 km	$1°F = \frac{9}{5}°C + 32°C$
1 gal. = 3.785 L	$1 cm^3 = 1 mL$
1 oz. = 28.35 g	1 hr = 3600 s

EXAMPLES

1. Convert the following measurements in the metric system.

    A)   4.25 kilometers to meters

    B) $8 m^2$ to mm^2

    Answers:

    A) $4.25 \text{ km} \left(\frac{1000 \text{ m}}{1 \text{ km}}\right) = \textbf{4250 m}$

    B) $\frac{8 m^2}{1} \times \frac{1000 \text{ mm}}{1 \text{ m}} \times \frac{1000 \text{ mm}}{1 \text{ m}} = \textbf{8,000,000 mm}^2$

    Since the units are square units (m^2), multiply by the conversion factor twice, so that both meters cancel.

2. Convert the following measurements in the American system.

    A)   12 feet to inches

    B) $7 yd^2$ to ft^2

    Answers:

    A) $12 \text{ ft}\left(\frac{12 \text{ in}}{1 \text{ ft}}\right) = \textbf{144 in}$

    B) $7 \text{ yd}^2\left(\frac{3 ft^2}{1 yd^2}\right)\left(\frac{3 ft^2}{1 yd^2}\right) = \textbf{63 ft}^2$

    Since the units are square units (ft^2), multiply by the conversion factor twice.

3. Convert the following measurements in the metric system to the American system.

    A)   23 meters to feet

    B) $10 m^2$ to yd^2

    Answers:

    A) $23 \text{ m} \left(\frac{3.28 \text{ ft}}{1 \text{ m}}\right) = \textbf{75.44 ft}$

    B) $\frac{10 \text{ } m^2}{1} \times \frac{1.094 \text{ yd}}{1 \text{ m}} \times \frac{1.094 \text{ yd}}{1 \text{ m}} = \textbf{11.97 yd}^2$

4. Convert the following measurements in the American system to the metric system.

    A) $8 in^3$ to milliliters

    B)   16 kilograms to pounds

Decimals and Fractions

Decimals

A DECIMAL is a number that contains a decimal point. A decimal number is an alternative way of writing a fraction. The place value for a decimal includes TENTHS (one place after the decimal), HUNDREDTHS (two places after the decimal), THOUSANDTHS (three places after the decimal), etc.

Table 4.5. Place Values

1,000,000	10^6	millions
100,000	10^5	hundred thousands
10,000	10^4	ten thousands
1,000	10^3	thousands
100	10^2	hundreds
10	10^1	tens
1	10^0	ones
.		decimal
$\frac{1}{10}$	10^{-1}	tenths
$\frac{1}{100}$	10^{-2}	hundredths
$\frac{1}{1000}$	10^{-3}	thousandths

Decimals can be added, subtracted, multiplied, and divided:

- To add or subtract decimals, line up the decimal point and perform the operation, keeping the decimal point in the same place in the answer.
- To multiply decimals, first multiply the numbers without the decimal points. Then, sum the number of decimal places to the right of the decimal point in the original numbers and place the decimal point in the answer so that there are that many places to the right of the decimal.

> To determine which way to move the decimal after multiplying, remember that changing the decimal should always make the final answer smaller.

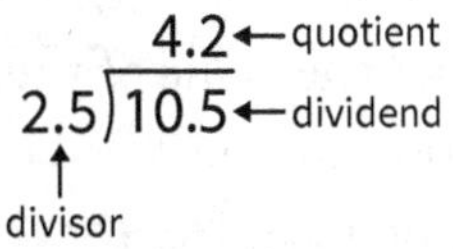

- When dividing decimals move the decimal point to the right in order to make the divisor a whole number and move the decimal the same number of places in the dividend. Divide the numbers without regard to the decimal. Then, place the decimal point of the quotient directly above the decimal point of the dividend.

$$4.2 \leftarrow \text{quotient}$$
$$2.5 \overline{)10.5} \leftarrow \text{dividend}$$
$$\uparrow$$
$$\text{divisor}$$

Figure 4.4. Division Terms

EXAMPLES

1. Simplify: 24.38 + 16.51 − 29.87

   Answer:

24.38 + 16.51 − 29.87	
24.38 + 16.51 = 40.89	Align the decimals and apply the order of operations left to right.
40.89 − 29.87 = **11.02**	

2. Simplify: (10.4)(18.2)

   Answer:

(10.4)(18.2)	
104 × 182 = 18,928	Multiply the numbers ignoring the decimals.
18,928 → 189.28	The original problem includes two decimal places (one in each number), so move the decimal point in the answer so that there are two places after the decimal point.

Estimating is a good way to check the answer: 10.4 ≈ 10, 18.2 ≈ 18, and 10 × 18 = 180.

3. Simplify: 80 ÷ 2.5

   Answer:

80 ÷ 2.5	
80 → 800 2.5 → 25	Move both decimals one place to the right (multiply by 10) so that the divisor is a whole number.
800 ÷ 25 = 32	Divide normally.

Fractions

A **FRACTION** is a number that can be written in the form $\frac{a}{b}$, where b is not equal to 0. The a part of the fraction is the **NUMERATOR** (top number) and the b part of the fraction is the **DENOMINATOR** (bottom number).

If the denominator of a fraction is greater than the numerator, the value of the fraction is less than 1 and it is called a **PROPER FRACTION** (for example, $\frac{3}{5}$ is a proper fraction). In an **IMPROPER FRACTION**, the denominator is less than the numerator and the value of the fraction is greater than 1 ($\frac{8}{3}$ is an improper fraction). An improper fraction can be written as a **MIXED NUMBER**, which has a whole number part and a proper fraction part. Improper fractions can be converted to mixed numbers by dividing the numerator by the denominator, which gives the whole number part, and the remainder becomes the numerator of the proper fraction part. (For example, the improper fraction $\frac{25}{9}$ is equal to mixed number $2\frac{7}{9}$ because 9 divides into 25 two times, with a remainder of 7.)

Conversely, mixed numbers can be converted to improper fractions. To do so, determine the numerator of the improper fraction by multiplying the denominator by the whole number, and then adding the numerator. The final number is written as the (now larger) numerator over the original denominator.

To convert mixed numbers to improper fractions:
$$a\frac{m}{n} = \frac{n \times a + m}{n}$$

Fractions with the same denominator can be added or subtracted by simply adding or subtracting the numerators; the denominator will remain unchanged. To add or subtract fractions with different denominators, find the **LEAST COMMON DENOMINATOR** (**LCD**) of all the fractions. The LCD is the smallest number exactly divisible by each denominator. (For example, the least common denominator of the numbers 2, 3, and 8 is 24.) Once the LCD has been found, each fraction should be written in an equivalent form with the LCD as the denominator.

To multiply fractions, the numerators are multiplied together and denominators are multiplied together. If there are any mixed numbers, they should first be changed to improper fractions. Then, the numerators are multiplied together and the denominators are multiplied together. The fraction can then be reduced if necessary. To divide fractions, multiply the first fraction by the reciprocal of the second.

Any common denominator can be used to add or subtract fractions. The quickest way to find a common denominator of a set of values is simply to multiply all the values together. The result might not be the least common denominator, but it will allow the problem to be worked.

$$\frac{a}{b} \pm \frac{c}{b} = \frac{a \pm c}{b}$$
$$\frac{a}{b} \times \frac{c}{d} = \frac{ac}{bd}$$
$$\frac{a}{b} \div \frac{c}{d} = \left(\frac{a}{b}\right)\left(\frac{d}{c}\right) = \frac{ad}{bc}$$

EXAMPLES

1. Simplify: $2\frac{3}{5} + 3\frac{1}{4} - 1\frac{1}{2}$

Answer:

$2\frac{3}{5} + 3\frac{1}{4} - 1\frac{1}{2}$	
$= 2\frac{12}{20} + 3\frac{5}{20} - 1\frac{10}{20}$	Change each fraction so it has a denominator of 20, which is the LCD of 5, 4, and 2.
$2 + 3 - 1 = 4$ $\frac{12}{20} + \frac{5}{20} - \frac{10}{20} = \frac{7}{20}$	Add and subtract the whole numbers together and the fractions together.
$4\frac{7}{20}$	Combine to get the final answer (a mixed number).

2. Simplify: $\frac{7}{8} \times 3\frac{1}{3}$

Answer:

$$\frac{7}{8} \times 3\frac{1}{3}$$

$3\frac{1}{3} = \frac{10}{3}$	Change the mixed number to an improper fraction.
$\frac{7}{8}\left(\frac{10}{3}\right) = \frac{7 \times 10}{8 \times 3}$ $= \frac{70}{24}$	Multiply the numerators together and the denominators together.
$= \frac{35}{12}$ $= 2\frac{11}{12}$	Reduce the fraction.

3. Simplify: $4\frac{1}{2} \div \frac{2}{3}$

    Answer:

    $4\frac{1}{2} \div \frac{2}{3}$

$4\frac{1}{2} = \frac{9}{2}$	Change the mixed number to an improper fraction.
$\frac{9}{2} \div \frac{2}{3}$ $= \frac{9}{2} \times \frac{3}{2}$ $= \frac{27}{4}$	Multiply the first fraction by the reciprocal of the second fraction.
$= 6\frac{3}{4}$	Simplify.

Converting Between Fractions and Decimals

A fraction is converted to a decimal by using long division until there is no remainder and no pattern of repeating numbers occurs.

A decimal is converted to a fraction using the following steps:

- ◆ Place the decimal value as the numerator in a fraction with a denominator of 1.
- ◆ Multiply the fraction by $\frac{10}{10}$ for every digit in the decimal value, so that there is no longer a decimal in the numerator.
- ◆ Reduce the fraction.

EXAMPLES

1. Write the fraction $\frac{7}{8}$ as a decimal.

    Answer:

$\begin{array}{r} 0.875 \\ 8\overline{)7000} \\ -64\downarrow \\ \hline 60 \\ -56\downarrow \\ \hline 40 \end{array}$	Divide the denominator into the numerator using long division.

2. Write the fraction $\frac{5}{11}$ as a decimal.

Answer:

$$
\begin{array}{r}
0.\overline{4545} \\
11)\overline{50000} \\
-44 \\
\hline
60 \\
-55 \\
\hline
50 \\
-44 \\
\hline
60
\end{array}
$$

Dividing using long division yields a repeating decimal.

3. Write the decimal 0.125 as a fraction.

Answer:

0.125	
$= \frac{0.125}{1}$	Create a fraction with 0.125 as the numerator and 1 as the denominator.
$\frac{0.125}{1} \times \frac{10}{10} \times \frac{10}{10} \times \frac{10}{10} = \frac{125}{1000}$	Multiple by $\frac{10}{10}$ three times (one for each numeral after the decimal).
$= \frac{1}{8}$	Simplify.

Alternatively, recognize that 0.125 is read "one hundred twenty-five thousandths" and can therefore be written in fraction form as $\frac{125}{1000}$.

Rounding and Estimation

ROUNDING is a way of simplifying a complicated number. The result of rounding will be a less precise value with which it is easier to write or perform operations. Rounding is performed to a specific place value, for example the thousands or tenths place.

The rules for rounding are as follows:
1. Underline the place value being rounded to.
2. Locate the digit one place value to the right of the underlined value. If this value is less than 5, then keep the underlined value and replace all digits to the right of the underlined value with 0. If the value to the right of the underlined digit is greater than or equal to 5, then increase the underlined digit by one and replace all digits to the right of it with 0.

ESTIMATION is when numbers are rounded and then an operation is performed. This process can be used when working with large numbers to find a close, but not exact, answer.

Estimation can often be used to eliminate answer choices on multiple-choice tests without having to work the problem to completion.

EXAMPLES

1. Round the number 138,472 to the nearest thousands.

Answer:

138,472 ≈ **138,000**	The 8 is in the thousands place, and the number to its right is 4. Because 4 is less than 5, the 8 remains and all numbers to the right become 0.

2. The populations of five local towns are 12,341, 8975, 9431, 10,521, and 11,427. Estimate the total population to the nearest 1000 people.

Answer:

12,341 ≈ 12,000 8975 ≈ 9000 9431 ≈ 9000 10,521 ≈ 11,000 11,427 ≈ 11,000	Round each value to the thousands place.
12,000 + 9000 + 9000 + 11,000 + 11,000 = **52,000**	Add.

Ratios

A **RATIO** is a comparison of two numbers and can be represented as $\frac{a}{b}$, $a:b$, or a to b. The two numbers represent a constant relationship, not a specific value: for every a number of items in the first group, there will be b number of items in the second. For example, if the ratio of blue to red candies in a bag is 3:5, the bag will contain 3 blue candies for every 5 red candies. So, the bag might contain 3 blue candies and 5 red candies, or it might contain 30 blue candies and 50 red candies, or 36 blue candies and 60 red candies. All of these values are representative of the ratio 3:5 (which is the ratio in its lowest, or simplest, terms).

To find the "whole" when working with ratios, simply add the values in the ratio. For example, if the ratio of boys to girls in a class is 2:3, the "whole" is five: 2 out of every 5 students are boys, and 3 out of every 5 students are girls.

EXAMPLES

1. There are 10 boys and 12 girls in a first-grade class. What is the ratio of boys to the total number of students? What is the ratio of girls to boys?

Answer:

number of boys: 10 number of girls: 12 number of students: 22	Identify the variables.
number of boys : number of students = 10 : 22 = $\frac{10}{22}$ = $\frac{5}{11}$	Write out and simplify the ratio of boys to total students.

number of girls : number of boys $= 12 : 10$ $= \frac{12}{10}$ $= \frac{6}{5}$	Write out and simplify the ratio of girls to boys.

2. A family spends \$600 a month on rent, \$400 on utilities, \$750 on groceries, and \$550 on miscellaneous expenses. What is the ratio of the family's rent to their total expenses?

Answer:

rent = 600 utilities = 400 groceries = 750 miscellaneous = 550 total expenses = 600 + 400 + 750 + 550 = 2300	Identify the variables.
rent : total expenses $= 600 : 2300$ $= \frac{600}{2300}$ $= \frac{6}{23}$	Write out and simplify the ratio of rent to total expenses.

Proportions

A **PROPORTION** is an equation which states that two ratios are equal. A proportion is given in the form $\frac{a}{b} = \frac{c}{d}$, where the a and d terms are the extremes and the b and c terms are the means. A proportion is solved using cross-multiplication ($ad = bc$) to create an equation with no fractional components. A proportion must have the same units in both numerators and both denominators.

EXAMPLES

1. Solve the proportion for x: $\frac{3x-5}{2} = \frac{x-8}{3}$.

Answer:

$\frac{(3x-5)}{2} = \frac{(x-8)}{3}$	
$3(3x-5) = 2(x-8)$	Cross-multiply.
$9x - 15 = 2x - 16$ $7x - 15 = -16$ $7x = -1$ $x = -\frac{1}{7}$	Solve the equation for x.

2. A map is drawn such that 2.5 inches on the map equates to an actual distance of 40 miles. If the distance measured on the map between two cities is 17.25 inches, what is the actual distance between them in miles?

Answer:

$\frac{2.5}{40} = \frac{17.25}{x}$	Write a proportion where x equals the actual distance and each ratio is written as inches : miles.
$2.5x = 690$ $x = 276$ The two cities are **276 miles apart**.	Cross-multiply and divide to solve for x.

3. A factory knows that 4 out of 1000 parts made will be defective. If in a month there are 125,000 parts made, how many of these parts will be defective?

Answer:

$\frac{4}{1000} = \frac{x}{125,000}$	Write a proportion where x is the number of defective parts made and both ratios are written as defective : total.
$1000x = 500,000$ $x = 500$ There are **500 defective parts** for the month.	Cross-multiply and divide to solve for x.

Percentages

A **PERCENT** (or percentage) means per hundred and is expressed with a percent symbol (%). For example, 54% means 54 out of every 100. A percent can be converted to a decimal by removing the % symbol and moving the decimal point two places to the left, while a decimal can be converted to a percent by moving the decimal point two places to the right and attaching the % sign. A percent can be converted to a fraction by writing the percent as a fraction with 100 as the denominator and reducing. A fraction can be converted to a percent by performing the indicated division, multiplying the result by 100, and attaching the % sign.

The equation for finding percentages has three variables: the part, the whole, and the percent (which is expressed in the equation as a decimal). The equation, as shown below, can be rearranged to solve for any of these variables.

- part = whole × percent
- percent = $\frac{\text{part}}{\text{whole}}$
- whole = $\frac{\text{part}}{\text{percent}}$

This set of equations can be used to solve percent word problems. All that's needed is to identify the part, whole, and/or percent, and then to plug those values into the appropriate equation and solve.

EXAMPLES

1. Change the following values to the indicated form:

   A) 18% to a fraction

   B) $\frac{3}{5}$ to a percent

   C) 1.125 to a percent

   D) 84% to a decimal

   Answers:

   A) The percent is written as a fraction over 100 and reduced:
   $\frac{18}{100} = \frac{9}{50}$.

   B) Dividing 5 by 3 gives the value 0.6, which is then multiplied by 100: **60%**.

   C) The decimal point is moved two places to the right:
   $1.125 \times 100 = \textbf{112.5\%}$.

   D) The decimal point is moved two places to the left:
   $84 \div 100 = \textbf{0.84}$.

2. In a school of 650 students, 54% of the students are boys. How many students are girls?

   Answer:

Percent of students who are girls = 100% − 54% = 46%	
percent = 46% = 0.46	Identify the variables.
whole = 650 students	
part = ?	
part = whole × percent = 0.46 × 650 = 299 **There are 299 girls.**	Plug the variables into the appropriate equation.

Percent Change

Percent change problems involve a change from an original amount. Often percent change problems appear as word problems that include discounts, growth, or markups. In order to solve percent change problems, it's necessary to identify the percent change (as a decimal), the amount of change, and the original amount. (Keep in mind that one of these will be the value being solved for.) These values can then be plugged into the equations below:

Key terms associated with percent change problems include discount, sales tax, and markup.

- ◆ amount of change = original amount × percent change

- ◆ percent change = $\dfrac{\text{amount of change}}{\text{original amount}}$

- ◆ original amount = $\dfrac{\text{amount of change}}{\text{percent change}}$

EXAMPLES

1. An HDTV that originally cost $1,500 is on sale for 45% off. What is the sale price for the item?

   Answer:

original amount =$1,500 percent change = 45% = 0.45 amount of change = ?	Identify the variables.
amount of change = original amount × percent change = 1500 × 0.45 = 675	Plug the variables into the appropriate equation.
1500 − 675 = 825 **The final price is $825.**	To find the new price, subtract the amount of change from the original price.

2. A house was bought in 2000 for $100,000 and sold in 2015 for $120,000. What was the percent growth in the value of the house from 2000 to 2015?

   Answer:

original amount = $100,000 amount of change = 120,000 − 100,000 = 20,000 percent change = ?	Identify the variables.
percent change = $\frac{\text{amount of change}}{\text{original amount}}$ = $\frac{20,000}{100,000}$ = 0.20	Plug the variables into the appropriate equation.
0.20 × 100 = **20%**	To find the percent growth, multiply by 100.

Comparison of Rational Numbers

Rational numbers can be ordered from least to greatest (or greatest to least) by placing them in the order in which they fall on a number line. When comparing a set of fractions, it's often easiest to convert each value to a common denominator. Then, it's only necessary to compare the numerators of each fraction.

Drawing a number line can help when comparing numbers: the final list should go in order from left to right (least to greatest) or right to left (greatest to least) on the line.

When working with numbers in multiple forms (for example, a group of fractions and decimals), convert the values so that the set contains only fractions or only decimals. When ordering negative numbers, remember that the negative numbers with the largest absolute values are farthest from 0 and are therefore the smallest numbers. (For example, −75 is smaller than −25.)

EXAMPLES

1. Order the following numbers from greatest to least: $-\frac{2}{3}$, 1.2, 0, -2.1, $\frac{5}{4}$, -1, $\frac{1}{8}$.

Answer:

$-\frac{2}{3} = -0.\overline{66}$ $\frac{5}{4} = 1.25$ $\frac{1}{8} = 0.125$	Change each fraction to a decimal.
1.25, 1.2, 0.125, 0, $-0.\overline{66}$, -1, -2.1	Place the decimals in order from greatest to least.
$\frac{5}{4}$, **1.2**, $\frac{1}{8}$, **0,** $-\frac{2}{3}$, **-1, -2.1**	Convert back to fractions if the problem requires it.

2. Order the following numbers from least to greatest: $\frac{1}{3}$, $-\frac{5}{6}$, $1\frac{1}{8}$, $\frac{7}{12}$, $-\frac{3}{4}$, $-\frac{3}{2}$.

Answer:

$\frac{1}{3} = \frac{8}{24}$ $-\frac{5}{6} = -\frac{20}{24}$ $1\frac{1}{8} = \frac{9}{8} = \frac{27}{24}$ $\frac{7}{12} = \frac{14}{24}$ $-\frac{3}{4} = -\frac{18}{24}$ $-\frac{3}{2} = -\frac{36}{24}$	Convert each value using the least common denominator of 24.
$-\frac{36}{24}, -\frac{20}{24}, -\frac{18}{24}, \frac{8}{24}, \frac{14}{24}, \frac{27}{24}$	Arrange the fractions in order from least to greatest by comparing the numerators.
$-\frac{3}{2}, -\frac{5}{6}, -\frac{3}{4}, \frac{1}{3}, \frac{7}{12}, 1\frac{1}{8}$	Put the fractions back in their original form if the problem requires it.

Exponents and Radicals

Exponents

An expression in the form b^n is in an exponential notation where b is the BASE and n is an EXPONENT. To perform the operation, multiply the base by itself the number of times indicated by the exponent. For example, 2^3 is equal to $2 \times 2 \times 2$ or 8.

GO ON

Table 4.6. Operations with Exponents

RULE	EXAMPLE	EXPLANATION
$a^0 = 1$	$5^0 = 1$	Any base (except 0) to the 0 power is 1.
$a^{-n} = \frac{1}{a^n}$	$5^{-3} = \frac{1}{5^3}$	A negative exponent becomes positive when moved from numerator to denominator (or vice versa).
$a^m a^n = a^{m+n}$	$5^3 5^4 = 5^{3+4} = 5^7$	Add the exponents to multiply two powers with the same base.
$(a^m)^n = a^{m \times n}$	$(5^3)^4 = 5^{3(4)} = 5^{12}$	Multiply the exponents to raise a power to a power.
$\frac{a^m}{a^n} = a^{m-n}$	$\frac{5^4}{5^3} = 5^{4-3} = 5^1$	Subtract the exponents to divide two powers with the same base.
$(ab)^n = a^n b^n$	$(5 \times 6)^3 = 5^3 6^3$	Apply the exponent to each base to raise a product to a power.
$\left(\frac{a}{b}\right)^n = \frac{a^n}{b^n}$	$\left(\frac{5}{6}\right)^3 = \frac{5^3}{6^3}$	Apply the exponent to each base to raise a quotient to a power.
$\left(\frac{a}{b}\right)^{-n} = \left(\frac{b}{a}\right)^n$	$\left(\frac{5}{6}\right)^{-3} = \left(\frac{6}{5}\right)^3$	Invert the fraction and change the sign of the exponent to raise a fraction to a negative power.
$\frac{a^m}{b^n} = \frac{b^{-n}}{a^{-m}}$	$\frac{5^3}{6^4} = \frac{6^{-4}}{5^{-3}}$	Change the sign of the exponent when moving a number from the numerator to denominator (or vice versa).

EXAMPLES

1. Simplify: $\frac{(10^2)^3}{(10^2)^2}$

    Answer:

$\frac{(10^2)^3}{(10^2)^2}$	
$= \frac{10^6}{10^{-4}}$	Multiply the exponents raised to a power.
$= 10^{6-(-4)}$	Subtract the exponent in the denominator from the one in the numerator.
$= 10^{10}$ $= \mathbf{10{,}000{,}000{,}000}$	Simplify.

2. Simplify: $\frac{(x^{-2}y^2)^2}{x^3 y}$

    Answer:

$\frac{(x^{-2}y^2)^2}{x^3 y}$	
$= \frac{x^{-4}y^4}{x^3 y}$	Multiply the exponents raised to a power.
$= x^{-4-3}y^{4-1}$ $= x^{-7}y^3$	Subtract the exponent in the denominator from the one in the numerator.
$= \frac{y^3}{x^7}$	Move negative exponents to the denominator.

Radicals

RADICALS are expressed as $\sqrt[b]{a}$, where b is called the INDEX and a is the RADICAND. A radical is used to indicate the inverse operation of an exponent: finding the base which can be raised to b to yield a. For example, $\sqrt[3]{125}$ is equal to 5 because 5 × 5 × 5 equals 125. The same operation can be expressed using a fraction exponent, so $\sqrt[b]{a} = a^{\frac{1}{b}}$. Note that when no value is indicated for b, it is assumed to be 2 (square root).

When b is even and a is positive, $\sqrt[b]{a}$ is defined to be the positive real value n such that $n^b = a$ (example: $\sqrt{16} = 4$ only, and not –4, even though $(-4)(-4) = 16$). If b is even and a is negative, $\sqrt[b]{a}$ will be a complex number (example: $\sqrt{-9} = 3i$). Finally if b is odd, $\sqrt[b]{a}$ will always be a real number regardless of the sign of a. If a is negative, $\sqrt[b]{a}$ will be negative since a number to an odd power is negative (example: $\sqrt[5]{-32} = -2$ since $(-2)^5 = -32$).

$\sqrt[n]{x}$ is referred to as the nth root of x.

- ◆ $n = 2$ is the square root
- ◆ $n = 3$ is the cube root
- ◆ $n = 4$ is the fourth root
- ◆ $n = 5$ is the fifth root

The following table of operations with radicals holds for all cases EXCEPT the case where b is even and a is negative (the complex case).

Table 4.7. Operations with Radicals

RULE	EXAMPLE	EXPLANATION
$\sqrt[b]{ac} = \sqrt[b]{a}\,\sqrt[b]{c}$	$\sqrt[3]{81} = \sqrt[3]{27}\,\sqrt[3]{3} = 3\sqrt[3]{3}$	The values under the radical sign can be separated into values that multiply to the original value.
$\sqrt[b]{\frac{a}{c}} = \frac{\sqrt[b]{a}}{\sqrt[b]{c}}$	$\sqrt{\frac{4}{81}} = \frac{\sqrt{4}}{\sqrt{81}} = \frac{2}{9}$	The b-root of the numerator and denominator can be calculated when there is a fraction under a radical sign.
$\sqrt[b]{a^c} = (\sqrt[b]{a})^c = a^{\frac{c}{b}}$	$\sqrt[3]{6^2} = (\sqrt[3]{6})^2 = 6^{\frac{2}{3}}$	The b-root can be written as a fractional exponent. If there is a power under the radical sign, it will be the numerator of the fraction.
$\frac{c}{\sqrt[b]{a}} \times \frac{\sqrt[b]{a}}{\sqrt[b]{a}} = \frac{c\sqrt[b]{a}}{a}$	$\frac{5}{\sqrt{2}}\,\frac{\sqrt{2}}{\sqrt{2}} = \frac{5\sqrt{2}}{2}$	To rationalize the denominator, multiply the numerator and denominator by the radical in the denominator until the radical has been canceled out.
$\frac{c}{b - \sqrt{a}} \times \frac{b + \sqrt{a}}{b + \sqrt{a}}$ $= \frac{c(b + \sqrt{a})}{b^2 - a}$	$\frac{4}{3 - \sqrt{2}}\,\frac{3 + \sqrt{2}}{3 + \sqrt{2}}$ $= \frac{4(3 + \sqrt{2})}{9 - 2} = \frac{12 + 4\sqrt{2}}{7}$	To rationalize the denominator, the numerator and denominator are multiplied by the conjugate of the denominator.

EXAMPLES

1. Simplify: $\sqrt{48}$

    Answer:

    $\sqrt{48}$

$= \sqrt{16 \times 3}$	Determine the largest square number that is a factor of the radicand (48) and write the radicand as a product using that square number as a factor.
$= \sqrt{16}\sqrt{3}$ $= 4\sqrt{3}$	Apply the rules of radicals to simplify.

2. Simplify: $\frac{6}{\sqrt{8}}$

Answer:

$\frac{6}{\sqrt{8}}$	
$= \frac{6}{\sqrt{4}\sqrt{2}}$ $= \frac{6}{2\sqrt{2}}$	Apply the rules of radicals to simplify.
$= \frac{6}{2\sqrt{2}}\left(\frac{\sqrt{2}}{\sqrt{2}}\right)$ $= \frac{3\sqrt{2}}{2}$	Multiply by $\frac{\sqrt{2}}{\sqrt{2}}$ to rationalize the denominator.

Factorials

A **FACTORIAL** of a number n is denoted by $n!$ and is equal to $1 \times 2 \times 3 \times 4 \times \ldots \times n$. Both $0!$ and $1!$ are equal to 1 by definition. Fractions containing factorials can often be simplified by crossing out the portions of the factorials that occur in both the numerator and denominator.

EXAMPLES

1. Simplify: $8!$

    Answer:

$8!$ $= 8 \times 7 \times 6 \times 5 \times 4 \times 3 \times 2 \times 1$ $= 40{,}320$	Expand the factorial and multiply.

2. Simplify: $\frac{10!}{7!3!}$

    Answer:

$\frac{10!}{7!3!}$	
$= \frac{10 \times 9 \times 8 \times 7!}{7! \times 3 \times 2 \times 1}$	Expand the factorial.
$= \frac{10 \times 9 \times 8}{3 \times 2 \times 1}$	Cross out values that occur in both the numerator and denominator.

$= \dfrac{720}{6}$	Multiply and simplify.
$= \mathbf{120}$	

Sequences and Series

Sequences can be thought of as a set of numbers (called TERMS) with a rule that explains the particular pattern between the terms. The terms of a sequence are separated by commas. There are two types of sequences that will be examined, arithmetic and geometric. The sum of an arithmetic sequence is known as an ARITHMETIC SERIES; similarly the sum of a geometric sequence is known as a GEOMETRIC SERIES.

Arithmetic Sequences

ARITHMETIC GROWTH is constant growth, meaning that the difference between any one term in the series and the next consecutive term will be the same constant. This constant is called the COMMON DIFFERENCE. Thus, to list the terms in the sequence, one can just add (or subtract) the same number repeatedly. For example, the series {20, 30, 40, 50} is arithmetic since 10 is added each time to get from one term to the next. One way to represent this sequence is using a RECURSIVE definition, which basically says: *next term = current term + common difference*. For this example, the recursive definition would be $a_{n+1} = a_n + 10$ because the *next* term a_{n+1} in the sequence is the current term a_n plus 10. In general, the recursive definition of a series is:

$$a_{n+1} = a_n + d, \text{ where } d \text{ is the common difference.}$$

Often, the objective of arithmetic sequence questions is to find a specific term in the sequence or the sum of a certain series of terms. The formulas to use are:

Table 4.8. Formulas for Arithmetic Sequences and Series

FINDING THE *N*TH TERM . . .

$a_n = a_1 + d(n-1)$ $a_n = a_m + d(n-m)$	d = the common difference of the sequence a_n = the nth term in the sequence n = the number of the term a_m = the mth term in the sequence m = the number of the term a_1 = the first term in the sequence

FINDING THE PARTIAL SUM . . .

$S_n = \dfrac{n(a_1 + a_n)}{2}$	S_n = sum of the terms through the nth term a_n = the nth term in the sequence n = the number of the term a_1 = the first term in the sequence

EXAMPLES

1. Find the ninth term of the sequence: −57, −40, −23, −6 …

   Answer:

$a_1 = -57$ $d = -57 - (-40) = 17$ $n = 9$	Identify the variables given.
$a_9 = -57 + 17(9 - 1)$	Plug these values into the formula for the specific term of an arithmetic sequence.
$a_9 = -57 + 17(8)$ $a_9 = -57 + 136$ $\boldsymbol{a_9 = 79}$	Solve for a_9.

2. If the 23rd term in an arithmetic sequence is 820, and the 5th term is 200, find the common difference between each term.

   Answer:

$a_5 = 200$ $a_{23} = 820$ $n = 23$ $m = 5$ $d = ?$	Idenfity the variables given.
$a_n = a_m + d(n - m)$ $820 = 200 + d(23 - 5)$ $620 = d(18)$ $\boldsymbol{d = 34.\overline{44}}$	Plug these values into the equation for using one term to find another in an arithmetic sequence.

3. Evaluate $\sum_{n=14}^{45} 2n + 10$.

   Answer:

$a_1 = 2(1) + 10 = 12$ $n = 45$ $a_n = 2(45) + 10 = 100$ $S_n = \dfrac{n(a_1 + a_n)}{2}$ $= \dfrac{45(12 + 100)}{2}$ $= 2520$	Find the partial sum of the first 45 terms.

$a_1 = 2(1) + 10 = 12$ $n = 13$ $a_n = 2(13) + 10 = 36$ $S_n = \dfrac{n(a_1 + a_n)}{2}$ $= \dfrac{13(12 + 36)}{2}$ $= 312$	Find the partial sum of the first 13 terms.
$S_{45} - S_{13} = 2520 - 312$ $= \mathbf{2208}$	The sum of the terms between 14 and 45 will be the difference between S_{45} and S_{13}.

Geometric Sequences

While an arithmetic sequence has an additive pattern, a GEOMETRIC SEQUENCE has a multiplicative pattern. This means that to get from any one term in the sequence to the next term in the sequence, the term is multiplied by a fixed number (called the COMMON RATIO). The following sequence is a geometric sequence: {8, 4, 2, 1, .5, .25, .125}. In this case, the multiplier (or common ratio) is $\frac{1}{2}$. The multiplier can be any real number other than 0 or 1. To find the common ratio, simply choose any term in the sequence and divide it by the previous term (this is the ratio of two consecutive terms—thus the name common *ratio*). In the above example, the ratio between the second and third terms is $\frac{2}{4} = \frac{1}{2}$.

Geometric sequences require their own formulas to find the next term and a sum of a specific series.

Table 4.9. Geometric Sequences: Formulas

FINDING THE *N*TH TERM . . .

$a_n = a_1 \times r^{n-1}$ $a_n = a_m \times r^{n-m}$	r = the common ratio of the sequence a_n = the nth term in the sequence n = the number of the term a_m = the mth term in the sequence m = the number of the term a_1 = the first term in the sequence

FINDING THE PARTIAL SUM . . .

$S_n = \dfrac{a_1(1 - r^n)}{1 - r}$	S_n = sum of the terms through the nth term r = the common ratio of the sequence a_n = the nth term in the sequence n = the number of the term a_1 = the first term in the sequence

FINDING THE SUM OF AN INFINITE SERIES . . .

$S_\infty = \dfrac{a}{1 - r}$ $(|r| < 1)$	S_∞ = sum of all terms r = the common ratio of the sequence a = the fifth term in the sequence

The finite sum formula works similarly to the arithmetic sequence sum. However, sometimes the INFINITE SUM of the sequence must be found. The sum of an infinite number of terms of a sequence is called a SERIES. If the infinite terms of the sequence add up to a finite number, the series is said to CONVERGE to that number. If the sum of the terms is infinite, then the series DIVERGES. Another way to say this is to ask: is there a limit to the finite sum S_n as n goes to infinity? For geometric series in the form $\sum_{n=1}^{\infty} a \times r^n$, the series converges only when $|r| < 1$ (or $-1 < r < 1$). If r is greater than 1, the sum will approach infinity, so the series diverges.

Compared to arithmetic growth, geometric growth is much faster. As seen in the formulas used to find a geometric term, geometric growth is exponential, whereas arithmetic growth is linear.

EXAMPLES

1. Find the 8th term in the sequence: {13, 39, 117, 351 . . .}

   Answer:

$a_1 = 13$ $n = 8$ $r = \frac{39}{13} = 3$	Identify the variables given.
$a_8 = 13 \times 3^{8-1}$ $a_8 = 13 \times 2187 = 28{,}431$	Plug these values into the equation to find a specific term in a geometric sequence.

   The eighth term of the given sequence is **28,431**.

2.) Find the sum of the first 10 terms of this sequence: {−4, 16, −64, 256 . . .}

   Answer:

$a_1 = -4$ $n = 10$ $r = \frac{16}{-4} = -4$	Identify the variables given.
$S_{10} = \frac{-4(1 - (-4)^{10})}{1 - (-4)}$ $= \frac{-4(1 - 1{,}048{,}576)}{5}$ $= \frac{4{,}194{,}300}{5}$ $= \mathbf{838{,}860}$	Plug these values into the equation for the partial sum of a geometric sequence.

Test Your Knowledge

Work the problem, and then choose the most correct answer.

1. Simplify: $\frac{7.2 \times 10^6}{1.6 \times 10^{-3}}$

   A) 4.5×10^{-9}

   B) 4.5×10^{-3}

   C) 4.5×10^3

   D) 4.5×10^9

2. Simplify: $(3^2 \div 1^3) - (4 - 8^2) + 2^4$

   A) -35

   B) -4

   C) 28

   D) 85

3. In a theater, there are 4,500 lower-level seats and 2,000 upper-level seats. What is the ratio of lower-level seats to total seats?

   A) $\frac{4}{9}$

   B) $\frac{4}{13}$

   C) $\frac{9}{13}$

   D) $\frac{9}{4}$

4. If a student answers 42 out of 48 questions correctly on a quiz, what percentage of questions did she answer correctly?

   A) 82.5%

   B) 85%

   C) 87.5%

   D) 90%

5. A worker was paid $15,036 for 7 months of work. If he received the same amount each month, how much was he paid for the first 2 months?

   A) $2,148

   B) $4,296

   C) $6,444

   D) $8,592

6. Simplify: $\frac{(3x^2y^2)^2}{3^3x^{-2}y^3}$

   A) $3x^6y$

   B) $\frac{x^6y}{3}$

   C) $\frac{x^4}{3y}$

   D) $\frac{3x^4}{y}$

7. Simplify: $\frac{5^2(3) + 3(-2)^2}{4 + 3^2 - 2(5 - 8)}$

   Write in the answer: _____

8. Convert 55 meters to feet (round to the nearest tenth of a foot).

   Write in the answer: _____

GO ON

Answer Key

1. **D) is correct.**

Divide the digits and subtract the exponents.

$$\frac{7.2 \times 10^6}{1.6 \times 10^{-3}}$$

$$7.2 \div 1.6 = 4.5$$

$$6 - (-3) = 9$$

$$\mathbf{4.5 \times 10^9}$$

2. **D) is correct.**

Simplify using PEMDAS.

$$(3^2 \div 1^3) - (4 - 8^2) + 2^4$$

$$= (9 \div 1) - (4 - 64) + 16$$

$$= 9 - (-60) + 16 = \mathbf{85}$$

3. **C) is correct.**

$$\text{total seats} = 4,500 + 2,000$$

$$\frac{\text{lower seats}}{\text{all seats}} = \frac{4,500}{6,500} = \frac{\mathbf{9}}{\mathbf{13}}$$

4. **C) is correct.**

Use the formula for percentages.

$$\text{percent} = \frac{\text{part}}{\text{whole}}$$

$$= \frac{42}{48}$$

$$= 0.875 = \mathbf{87.5\%}$$

5. **B) is correct.**

Write a proportion and then solve for x.

$$\frac{15,036}{7} = \frac{x}{2}$$

$$7x = 30,072$$

$$x = \mathbf{4,296}$$

6. **B) is correct.**

Use the rules of exponents to simplify the expression.

$$\frac{(3x^2y^2)^2}{3^3x^{-2}y^3} = \frac{3^2x^4y^4}{3^3x^{-2}y^3} = \frac{x^6y}{3}$$

7. $\frac{87}{19}$ **is correct.**

Simplify using PEMDAS.

$$\frac{5^2(3) + 3(-2)^2}{4 + 3^2 - 2(5 - 8)}$$

$$= \frac{5^2(3) + 3(-2)^2}{4 + 3^2 - 2(-3)}$$

$$= \frac{25(3) + 3(4)}{4 + 9 - 2(-3)}$$

$$= \frac{75 + 12}{13 + 6} = \frac{87}{19}$$

8. **180.4 feet is correct.**

Multiply by the converstion factor to get from meters to feet.

$$55 \text{ m} \left(\frac{3.28 \text{ ft.}}{1 \text{ m}}\right) = \mathbf{180.4 \text{ feet}}$$

five

ALGEBRA

lgebra, meaning "restoration" in Arabic, is the mathematical method of finding the unknown. The first algebraic book in Egypt was used to figure out complex inheritances that were to be split among many individuals. Today, algebra is just as necessary when dealing with unknown amounts.

Algebraic Expressions

The foundation of algebra is the **VARIABLE**, an unknown number represented by a symbol (usually a letter such as x or a). Variables can be preceded by a **COEFFICIENT**, which is a constant (i.e., a real number) in front of the variable, such as $4x$ or $-2a$. An **ALGEBRAIC EXPRESSION** is any sum, difference, product, or quotient of variables and numbers (for example $3x^2$, $2x + 7y - 1$, and $\frac{5}{x}$ are algebraic expressions). **TERMS** are any quantities that are added or subtracted (for example, the terms of the expression $x^2 - 3x + 5$ are x^2, $3x$, and 5). A **POLYNOMIAL EXPRESSION** is an algebraic expression where all the exponents on the variables are whole numbers. A polynomial with only two terms is known as a **BINOMIAL**, and one with three terms is a **TRINOMIAL**. A **MONOMIAL** has only one term.

Simplified expressions are ordered by variable terms alphabetically with highest exponent first then down to constants.

    EVALUATING EXPRESSIONS is another way of saying "find the numeric value of an expression if the variable is equal to a certain number." To evaluate the expression, simply plug the given value(s) for the variable(s) into the equation and simplify. Remember to use the order of operations when simplifying:

1. Parentheses
2. Exponents
3. Multiplication
4. Division
5. Addition
6. Subtraction

If $m = 4$, find the value of the following expression: $5(m - 2)^3 + 3m^2 - \frac{m}{4} - 1$

Answer:

$5(m - 2)^3 + 3m^2 - \frac{m}{4} - 1$	
$= 5(4 - 2)^3 + 3(4)^2 - \frac{4}{4} - 1$	Plug the value 4 in for m in the expression.
$= 5(2)^3 + 3(4)^2 - \frac{4}{4} - 1$	Calculate all the expressions inside the parentheses.
$= 5(8) + 3(16) - \frac{4}{4} - 1$	Simplify all exponents.
$= 40 + 48 - 1 - 1$	Perform multiplication and division from left to right.
$= \mathbf{86}$	Perform addition and subtraction from left to right.

Operations with Expressions

Adding and Subtracting

Expressions can be added or subtracted by simply adding and subtracting LIKE TERMS, which are terms with the same variable part (the variables must be the same, with the same exponents on each variable). For example, in the expressions $2x + 3xy - 2z$ and $6y + 2xy$, the like terms are $3xy$ and $2xy$. Adding the two expressions yields the new expression $2x + 6xy - 2z + 6y$. Note that the other terms did not change; they cannot be combined because they have different variables.

EXAMPLE

If $a = 12x + 7xy - 9y$ and $b = 8x - 9xz + 7z$, what is $a + b$?

Answer:

$a + b =$	The only like terms in both expressions are $12x$
$(12x + 8x) + 7xy - 9y - 9xz + 7z =$	and $8x$, so these two terms will be added, and all
$\mathbf{20x + 7xy - 9y - 9xz + 7z}$	other terms will remain the same.

Distributing and Factoring

Distributing and factoring can be seen as two sides of the same coin. DISTRIBUTION multiplies each term in the first factor by each term in the second factor to get rid of parentheses. FACTORING reverses this process, taking a polynomial in standard form and writing it as a product of two or more factors.

Operations with polynomials can always be checked by evaluating equivalent expressions for the same value.

When distributing a monomial through a polynomial, the expression outside the parentheses is multiplied by each term inside the parentheses. Using the rules of exponents, coefficients are multiplied and exponents are added.

When simplifying two polynomials, each term in the first polynomial must multiply each term in the second polynomial.

A binomial (two terms) multiplied by a binomial, will require 2 × 2 or 4 multiplications. For the binomial × binomial case, this process is sometimes called **FOIL**, which stands for first, outside, inside, and last. These terms refer to the placement of each term of the expression: multiply the first term in each expression, then the outside terms, then the inside terms, and finally the last terms. A binomial (two terms) multiplied by a trinomial (three terms), will require 2 × 3 or 6 products to simplify. The first term in the first polynomial multiplies each of the three terms in the second polynomial, then the second term in the first polynomial multiplies each of the three terms in the second polynomial. A trinomial (three terms) by a trinomial will require 3 × 3 or 9 products, and so on.

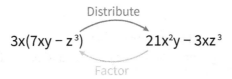

Distribute

$$3x(7xy - z^3) \qquad 21x^2y - 3xz^3$$

Factor

Figure 5.1. Distribution and Factoring

Factoring is the reverse of distributing: the first step is always to remove ("undistribute") the GCF of all the terms, if there is a GCF (besides 1). The GCF is the product of any constants and/or variables that <u>every</u> term shares. (For example, the GCF of $12x^3$, $15x^2$ and $6xy^2$ is $3x$ because $3x$ evenly divides all three terms.) This shared factor can be taken out of each term and moved to the outside of the parentheses, leaving behind a polynomial where each term is the original term divided by the GCF. (The remaining terms for the terms in the example would be $4x^2$, $5x$, and $2xy$.) It may be possible to factor the polynomial in the parentheses further, depending on the problem.

EXAMPLES

1. Expand the following expression: $5x(x^2 - 2c + 10)$

   Answer:

$5x(x^2 - 2c + 10)$	
$(5x)(x^2) = 5x^3$	Distribute and multiply the term outside the parentheses to all three terms inside the parentheses.
$(5x)(-2c) = -10xc$	
$(5x)(10) = 50x$	
$= 5x^3 - 10xc + 50x$	

2. Expand the following expression: $(x^2 - 5)(2x - x^3)$

   Answer:

$(x^2 - 5)(2x - x^3)$	
$(x^2)(2x) = 2x^3$	
$(x^2)(-x^3) = -x^5$	Apply FOIL: first, outside, inside, and last.
$(-5)(2x) = -10x$	
$(-5)(-x^3) = 5x^3$	
$= 2x^3 - x^5 - 10x + 5x^3$	Combine like terms and put them in order.

$$= -x^5 + 7x^3 - 10x$$

3. Factor the expression $16z^2 + 48z$

    Answer:

$16z^2 + 48z$ $= 16z(z + 3)$	Both terms have a z, and 16 is a common factor of both 16 and 48. So the greatest common factor is $16z$. Factor out the GCF.

4. Factor the expression $6m^3 + 12m^3n - 9m^2$

    Answer:

$6m^3 + 12m^3n - 9m^2$ $= 3m^2(2m + 4mn - 3)$	All the terms share the factor m^2, and 3 is the greatest common factor of 6, 12, and 9. So, the GCF is $3m^2$.

Factoring Trinomials

If the leading coefficient is $a = 1$, the trinomial is in the form $x^2 + bx + c$ and can often be rewritten in the factored form, as a product of two binomials: $(x + m)(x + n)$. Recall that the product of two binomials can be written in expanded form $x^2 + mx + nx + mn$. Equating this expression with $x^2 + bx + c$, the constant term c would have to equal the product mn. Thus, to work backward from the trinomial to the factored form, consider all the numbers m and n that multiply to make c. For example, to factor $x^2 + 8x + 12$, consider all the pairs that multiply to be 12 ($12 = 1 \times 12$ or 2×6 or 3×4). Choose the pair that will make the coefficient of the middle term (8) when added. In this example 2 and 6 add to 8, so making $m = 2$ and $n = 6$ in the expanded form gives:

$x^2 + 8x + 12 = x^2 + 2x + 6x + 12$	
$= (x^2 + 2x) + (6x + 12)$	Group the first two terms and the last two terms.
$= x(x + 6) + 2(x + 6)$	Factor the GCF out of each set of parentheses.
$= (x + 6)(x + 2)$	The two terms now have the common factor $(x + 6)$, which can be removed, leaving $(x + 2)$ and the original polynomial is factored.

In general:

$x^2 + bx + c = x^2 + mx + nx + mn$, where $c = mn$ and $b = m + n$	
$= (x^2 + mx) + (nx + mn)$	Group.
$= x(x + m) + n(x + m)$	Factor each group.
$= (x + m)(x + n)$	Factor out the common binomial.

Note that if none of the factors of c add to the value b, then the trinomial cannot be factored, and is called PRIME.

If the leading coefficient is not 1 ($a \neq 1$), first make sure that any common factors among the three terms are factored out. If the a-value is negative, factor out –1 first as well. If the *a*-value of the new polynomial in the parentheses is still not 1, follow this rule: Identify two values *r* and *s* that multiply to be *ac* and add to be *b*. Then write the polynomial in this form: $ax^2 + bx + c = ax^2 + rx + sx + c$, and proceed by grouping, factoring, and removing the common binomial as above.

There are a few special factoring cases worth memorizing: difference of squares, binomial squared, and the sum and difference of cubes.

- ◆ **DIFFERENCE OF SQUARES** (each term is a square and they are subtracted):
  - ❖ $a^2 - b^2 = (a + b)(a - b)$
  - ❖ Note that a SUM of squares is never factorable.
- ◆ **BINOMIAL SQUARED:**
  - ❖ $a^2 + 2ab + b^2 = (a + b)(a + b) = (a + b)^2$
- ◆ **SUM AND DIFFERENCE OF CUBES:**
  - ❖ $a^3 + b^3 = (a + b)(a^2 - ab + b^2)$
  - ❖ $a^3 - b^3 = (a - b)(a^2 + ab + b^2)$
  - ❖ Note that the second factor in these factorizations will never be able to be factored further.

EXAMPLES

1. Factor: $16x^2 + 52x + 30$

   Answer:

$16x^2 + 52x + 30$	
$= 2(8x^2 + 26x + 15)$	Remove the GCF of 2.
$= 2(8x^2 + 6x + 20x + 15)$	To factor the polynomial in the parentheses, calculate $ac = (8)(15) = 120$, and consider all the pairs of numbers that multiply to be 120: 1×120, 2×60, 3×40, 4×30, 5×24, 6×20, 8×15, and 10×12. Of these pairs, choose the pair that adds to be the *b*-value 26 (6 and 20).
$= 2[(8x^2 + 6x) + (20x + 15)]$	Group.
$= 2[(2x(4x + 3) + 5(4x + 3)]$	Factor out the GCF of each group.
$= 2[(4x + 3)(2x + 5)]$	Factor out the common binomial.
$\mathbf{2(4x + 3)(2x + 5)}$	

   If there are no values *r* and *s* that multiply to be *ac* and add to be *b*, then the polynomial is prime and cannot be factored.

2. Factor: $-21x2 - x + 10$

   Answer:

$-21x^2 - x + 10$	
$= -(21x^2 + x - 10)$	Factor out the negative.

	Factor the polynomial in the parentheses.
$= -(21x^2 - 14x + 15x - 10)$	$ac = 210$ and $b = 1$ The numbers 15 and −14 can be multiplied to get 210 and subtracted to get 1.
$= -[(21x2 - 14x) + (15x - 10)]$	Group.
$= -[7x(3x - 2) + 5(3x - 2)]$	Factor out the GCF of each group.
$= -(3x - 2)(7x + 5)$	Factor out the common binomial.

Linear Equations

An EQUATION states that two expressions are equal to each other. Polynomial equations are categorized by the highest power of the variables they contain: the highest power of any exponent of a linear equation is 1, a quadratic equation has a variable raised to the second power, a cubic equation has a variable raised to the third power, and so on.

Solving Linear Equations

Solving an equation means finding the value or values of the variable that make the equation true. To solve a linear equation, it is necessary to manipulate the terms so that the variable being solved for appears alone on one side of the equal sign while everything else in the equation is on the other side.

The way to solve linear equations is to "undo" all the operations that connect numbers to the variable of interest. Follow these steps:

On multiple choice tests, it is often easier to plug the possible values into the equation and determine which solution makes the equation true than to solve the equation.

1. Eliminate fractions by multiplying each side by the least common multiple of any denominators.

2. Distribute to eliminate parentheses, braces, and brackets.

3. Combine like terms.

4. Use addition or subtraction to collect all terms containing the variable of interest to one side, and all terms not containing the variable to the other side.

5. Use multiplication or division to remove coefficients from the variable of interest.

Sometimes there are no numeric values in the equation or there are a mix of numerous variables and constants. The goal is to solve the equation for one of the variables in terms of the other variables. In this case, the answer will be an expression involving numbers and letters instead of a numeric value.

EXAMPLES

1. Solve for x: $\frac{100(x + 5)}{20} = 1$

Answer:

$\dfrac{100(x+5)}{20} = 1$	
$(20)\left(\dfrac{100(x+5)}{20}\right) = (1)(20)$ $100(x+5) = 20$	Multiply both sides by 20 to cancel out the denominator.
$100x + 500 = 20$	Distribute 100 through the parentheses.
$100x = -480$	"Undo" the +500 by subtracting 500 on both sides of the equation to isolate the variable term.
$x = \dfrac{-480}{100}$	"Undo" the multiplication by 100 by dividing by 100 on both sides to solve for x.
$x = -4.8$	

2. Solve for x: $2(x+2)^2 - 2x^2 + 10 = 42$

   Answer:

$2(x+2)^2 - 2x^2 + 10 = 42$	
$2(x+2)(x+2) - 2x^2 + 10 = 42$	Eliminate the exponents on the left side.
$2(x^2 + 4x + 4) - 2x^2 + 10 = 42$	Apply FOIL.
$2x^2 + 8x + 8 - 2x^2 + 10 = 42$	Distribute the 2.
$8x + 18 = 42$	Combine like terms on the left-hand side.
$8x = 24$	Isolate the variable. "Undo" +18 by subtracting 18 on both sides.
$x = 3$	"Undo" multiplication by 8 by dividing both sides by 8.

3. Solve the equation for D: $\dfrac{A(3B+2D)}{2N} = 5M - 6$

   Answer:

$\dfrac{A(3B+2D)}{2N} = 5M - 6$	
$3AB + 2AD = 10MN - 12N$	Multiply both sides by 2N to clear the fraction, and distribute the A through the parentheses.
$2AD = 10MN - 12N - 3AB$	Isolate the term with the D in it by moving 3AB to the other side of the equation.
$D = \dfrac{(10MN - 12N - 3AB)}{2A}$	Divide both sides by 2A to get D alone on the right-hand side.

Graphs of Linear Equations

The most common way to write a linear equation is SLOPE-INTERCEPT FORM, $y = mx + b$. In this equation, m is the slope, which describes how steep the line is, and b is the y-intercept. Slope is often described as "rise over run" because it is calculated as the difference in y-values (rise) over the difference in x-values (run). The slope of the line is also the rate of change of the dependent variable y with respect to the independent variable x. The y-intercept is the point where the line crosses the y-axis, or where x equals zero.

Use the phrase "Begin, Move" to remember that b is the y-intercept (where to begin) and m is the slope (how the line moves).

To graph a linear equation, identify the y-intercept and place that point on the y-axis. If the slope is not written as a fraction, make it a fraction by writing it over 1 $\left(\frac{m}{1}\right)$. Then use the slope to count up (or down, if negative) the "rise" part of the slope and over the "run" part of the slope to find a second point. These points can then be connected to draw the line.

To find the equation of a line, identify the y-intercept, if possible, on the graph and use two easily identifiable points to find the slope. If the y-intercept is not easily identified, identify the slope by choosing easily identifiable points; then choose one point on the graph, plug the point and the slope values into the equation, and solve for the missing value b.

- standard form: $Ax + By = C$
- $m = -\dfrac{A}{B}$
- x-intercept $= \dfrac{C}{A}$
- y-intercept $= \dfrac{C}{B}$

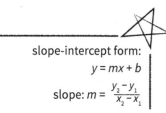

slope-intercept form:
$$y = mx + b$$
slope: $m = \dfrac{y_2 - y_1}{x_2 - x_1}$

Another way to express a linear equation is standard form: $Ax + By = C$. In order to graph equations in this form, it is often easiest to convert them to point-slope form. Alternately, it is easy to find the x- or y-intercept from this form, and once these two points are known, a line can be drawn through them. To find the x-intercept, simply make $y = 0$ and solve for x. Similarly, to find the y-intercept, make $x = 0$ and solve for y.

EXAMPLES

1. What is the equation of the following line?

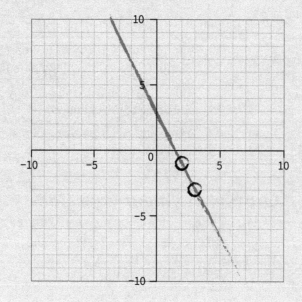

Answer:

$b = 3$	The y-intercept can be identified on the graph as $(0, 3)$.
$m = \frac{(-3) - (-1)}{3 - 2} = \frac{-2}{1} = -2$	To find the slope, choose any two points and plug the values into the slope equation. The two points chosen here are $(2, -1)$ and $(3, -3)$.
$y = -2x + 3$	Replace m with -2 and b with 3 in $y = mx + b$.

2. What is the slope of the line whose equation is $6x - 2y - 8 = 0$?

   Answer:

$6x - 2y - 8 = 0$	
$-2y = -6x + 8$ $y = \frac{-6x + 8}{-2}$ $y = 3x - 4$	Rearrange the equation into slope-intercept form by solving the equation for y.
$m = 3$	The slope is 3, the value attached to x.

3. Write the equation of the line which passes through the points $(-2, 5)$ and $(-5, 3)$.

   Answer:

$(-2, 5)$ and $(-5, 3)$	
$m = \frac{3 - 5}{(-5) - (-2)}$ $= \frac{-2}{-3}$ $= \frac{2}{3}$	Calculate the slope.
$5 = \frac{2}{3}(-2) + b$ $5 = \frac{-4}{3} + b$ $b = \frac{19}{3}$	To find b, plug into the equation $y = mx + b$ the slope for m and a set of points for x and y.
$y = \frac{2}{3}x + \frac{19}{3}$	Replace m and b to find the equation of the line.

4. What is the equation of the following graph?

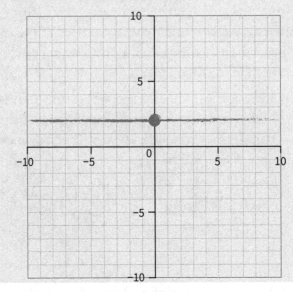

Answer:	
$y = 0x + 2$, or $y = 2$	The line has a rise of 0 and a run of 1, so the slope is $\frac{0}{1}$ = 0. There is no x-intercept. The y-intercept is $(0, 2)$, meaning that the b-value in the slope-intercept form is 2.

Systems of Linear Equations

Systems of equations are sets of equations that include two or more variables. These systems can only be solved when there are at least as many equations as there are variables. Systems involve working with more than one equation to solve for more than one variable. For a system of linear equations, the solution to the system is the set of values for the variables that satisfies every equation in the system. Graphically, this will be the point where every line meets. If the lines are parallel (and hence do not intersect), the system will have no solution. If the lines are multiples of each other, meaning they share all coordinates, then the system has infinitely many solutions (because every point on the line is a solution).

Plug answers back into both equations to ensure the system has been solved properly.

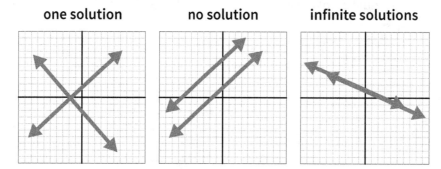

| one solution | no solution | infinite solutions |

Figure 5.2. Systems of Equations

There are three common methods for solving systems of equations. To perform SUBSTITUTION, solve one equation for one variable, and then plug in the resulting expression for that variable in the second equation. This process works best for systems of two equations with two variables where the coefficient of one or more of the variables is 1.

To solve using ELIMINATION, add or subtract two equations so that one or more variables are eliminated. It's often necessary to multiply one or both of the equations by a scalar (constant) in order to make the variables cancel. Equations can be added or subtracted as many times as necessary to find each variable.

Yet another way to solve a system of linear equations is to use a MATRIX EQUATION. In the matrix equation $AX = B$, A contains the system's coefficients, X contains the variables, and B contains the constants (as shown below). The matrix equation can then be solved by multiplying B by the inverse of A: $X = A^{-1}B$

$$\begin{matrix} ax + by = e \\ cx + dy = f \end{matrix} \rightarrow A = \begin{bmatrix} a & b \\ c & d \end{bmatrix} \quad X = \begin{bmatrix} x \\ y \end{bmatrix} \quad B = \begin{bmatrix} e \\ f \end{bmatrix} \rightarrow AX = B$$

This method can be extended to equations with three or more variables. Technology (such as a graphing calculator) is often employed when solving using this method if more than two variables are involved.

EXAMPLES

1. Solve for x and y:

$2x - 4y = 28$

$4x - 12y = 36$

Answer:

$2x - 4y = 28$ $x = 2y + 14$	Solve the system with substitution. Solve one equation for one variable.
$4x - 12y = 36$ $4(2y + 14) - 12y = 36$ $8y + 56 - 12y = 36$ $-4y = -20$ $y = 5$	Plug in the resulting expression for x in the second equation and simplify.
$2x - 4y = 28$ $2x - 4(5) = 28$ $2x - 20 = 28$ $2x = 48$ $x = 24$ The answer is $y = 5$ and $x = 24$ or **(24, 5)**.	Plug the solved variable into either equation to find the second variable.

2. Solve for the system for x and y:

$3 = -4x + y$

$16x = 4y + 2$

Answer:

$3 = -4x + y$ $y = 4x + 3$	Isolate the variable in one equation.
$16x = 4y + 2$ $16x = 4(4x + 3) + 2$ $16x = 16x + 12 + 2$ $0 = 14$ **No solution exists.**	Plug the expression into the second equation. Both equations have slope 4. This means the graphs of the equations are parallel lines, so no intersection (solution) exists.

3. Solve the system of equations:

$6x + 10y = 18$

$4x + 15y = 37$

Answer:

Because solving for x or y in either equation will result in messy fractions, this problem is best solved using elimination. The goal is to eliminate one of the variables by making the coefficients in front of one set of variables the same, but with different signs, and then adding both equations.

$6x + 10y = 18 \xrightarrow{(-2)} {}^{-12}x {}^{-20}y = {}^{-36}$ $4x + 15y = 37 \xrightarrow{(3)} {}^{12}x {}^{+45}y = {}^{1}\underline{11}$	To eliminate the x's in this problem, find the least common multiple of coefficients 6 and 4. The smallest number that both 6 and 4 divide into evenly is 12. Multiply the top equation by −2, and the bottom equation by 3.
$25y = 75$	Add the two equations to eliminate the x's.
$y = 3$	Solve for y.
$6x + 10(3) = 18$ $6x + 30 = 18$ $x = -2$	Replace y with 3 in either of the original equations.
The solution is **(−2, 3)**.	

4. Solve the following systems of equations using matrix arithmetic:

$2x - 3y = -5$

$3x - 4y = -8$

Answer:

$\begin{bmatrix} 2 & -3 \\ 3 & -4 \end{bmatrix} \begin{bmatrix} x \\ y \end{bmatrix} = \begin{bmatrix} -5 \\ -8 \end{bmatrix}$	Write the system in matrix form, $AX = B$.
$\begin{bmatrix} 2 & -3 \\ 3 & -4 \end{bmatrix}^{-1}$ $= \dfrac{1}{(2)(-4) - (-3)(3)} \begin{bmatrix} -4 & 3 \\ -3 & 2 \end{bmatrix} = \begin{bmatrix} -4 & 3 \\ -3 & 2 \end{bmatrix}$	Calculate the inverse of Matrix A.
$\begin{bmatrix} x \\ y \end{bmatrix} = \begin{bmatrix} -4 & 3 \\ -3 & 2 \end{bmatrix} \begin{bmatrix} -5 \\ -8 \end{bmatrix} = \begin{bmatrix} -4 \\ -1 \end{bmatrix}$	Multiply B by the inverse of A.
$x = -4$ $y = -1$	Match up the 2 × 1 matrices to identify x and y.

Building Equations

In word problems, it is often necessary to translate a verbal description of a relationship into a mathematical equation. No matter the problem, this process can be done using the same steps:

1. Read the problem carefully and identify what value needs to be solved for.

2. Identify the known and unknown quantities in the problem, and assign the unknown quantities a variable.

3. Create equations using the variables and known quantities.

4. Solve the equations.

5. Check the solution: Does it answer the question asked in the problem? Does it make sense?

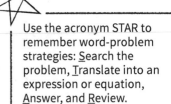

Use the acronym STAR to remember word-problem strategies: Search the problem, Translate into an expression or equation, Answer, and Review.

EXAMPLES

1. A school is holding a raffle to raise money. There is a $3 entry fee, and each ticket costs $5. If a student paid $28, how many tickets did he buy?

Answer:

Number of tickets = x Cost per ticket = 5 Cost for x tickets = $5x$ Total cost = 28 Entry fee = 3	Identify the quantities.
$5x + 3 = 28$	Set up equations. The total cost for x tickets will be equal to the cost for x tickets plus the $3 flat fee.
$5x + 3 = 28$ $5x = 25$ $x = 5$	Solve the equation for x.
The student bought **5 tickets**.	

2. Kelly is selling shirts for her school swim team. There are two prices: a student price and a nonstudent price. During the first week of the sale, Kelly raised $84 by selling 10 shirts to students and 4 shirts to nonstudents. She earned $185 in the second week by selling 20 shirts to students and 10 shirts to nonstudents. What is the student price for a shirt?

Answer:

Student price = s Nonstudent price = n $10s + 4n = 84$ $20s + 10n = 185$	Assign variables. Create two equations using the number of shirts Kelly sold and the money she earned.
$10s + 4n = 84$ $10n = -20s + 185$ $n = -2s + 18.5$ $10s + 4(-2s + 18.5) = 84$	Solve the system of equations using substitution.

$10s - 8s + 74 = 84$ $2s + 74 = 84$ $2s = 10$ $s = 5$	Solve the system of equations using substitution (continued).
The student cost for shirts is **$5**.	

Linear Inequalities

Solving Linear Inequalities

An inequality shows the relationship between two expressions, much like an equation. However, the equal sign is replaced with an inequality symbol that expresses the following relationships:

- < less than
- > greater than

- ≤ less than or equal to
- ≥ greater than or equal to

Inequalities are read from left to right. For example, the inequality $x \le 8$ would be read as "x is less than or equal to 8," meaning x has a value smaller than or equal to 8. The set of solutions of an inequality can be expressed using a number line. The shaded region on the number line represents the set of all the numbers that make an inequality true. One major difference between equations and inequalities is that equations generally have a finite number of solutions, while inequalities generally have infinitely many solutions (an entire interval on the number line containing infinitely many values).

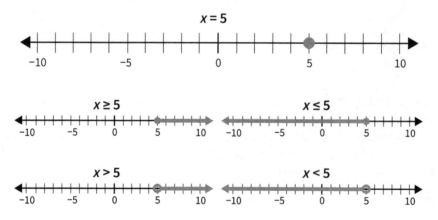

Figure 5.3. Inequalities on a Number Line

Linear inequalities can be solved in the same way as linear equations, with one exception. When multiplying or dividing both sides of an inequality by a negative number, the direction of the inequality sign must reverse—"greater than" becomes "less than" and "less than" becomes "greater than."

1. Solve for z: $3z + 10 < -z$

Answer:

$3z + 10 < -z$	
$3z < -z - 10$	Collect nonvariable terms to one side.
$4z < -10$	Collect variable terms to the other side.
$z < -2.5$	Isolate the variable.

-2.5

2. Solve for x: $2x - 3 > 5(x - 4) - (x - 4)$

Answer:

$2x - 3 > 5(x - 4) - (x - 4)$	
$2x - 3 > 5x - 20 - x + 4$	Distribute 5 through the parentheses and −1 through the parentheses.
$2x - 3 > 4x - 16$	Combine like terms.
$-2x > -13$	Collect x-terms to one side, and constant terms to the other side.
$x < 6.5$	Divide both sides by −2; since dividing by a negative, reverse the direction of the inequality.

6.5

Compound Inequalities

Compound inequalities have more than one inequality expression. Solutions of compound inequalities are the sets of all numbers that make *all* the inequalities true. Some compound inequalities may not have any solutions, some will have solutions that contain some part of the number line, and some will have solutions that include the entire number line.

Table 5.1. Unions and Intersections

INEQUALITY	MEANING IN WORDS	NUMBER LINE
$a < x < b$	All values x that are greater than a and less than b	
$a \leq x \leq b$	All values x that are greater than or equal to a and less than or equal to b	
$x < a$ or $x > b$	All values of x that are less than a or greater than b	
$x \leq a$ or $x \geq b$	All values of x that are less than or equal to a or greater than or equal to b	

Compound inequalities can be written, solved, and graphed as two separate inequalities. For compound inequalities in which the word *and* is used, the solution to the compound inequality will be the set of numbers on the number line where both inequalities have solutions (where both are shaded). For compound inequalities where *or* is used, the solution to the compound inequality will be *all* the shaded regions for *either* inequality.

EXAMPLES

1. Solve the compound inequalities: $2x + 4 < -18$ *or* $4(x + 2) > 18$

   Answer:

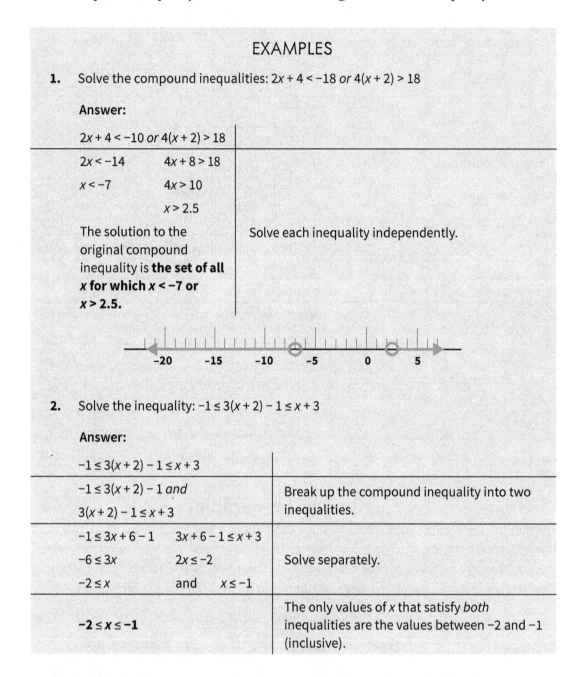

$2x + 4 < -10$ *or* $4(x + 2) > 18$	
$2x < -14$ $4x + 8 > 18$ $x < -7$ $4x > 10$ $x > 2.5$	Solve each inequality independently.
The solution to the original compound inequality is **the set of all x for which $x < -7$ or $x > 2.5$.**	

2. Solve the inequality: $-1 \leq 3(x + 2) - 1 \leq x + 3$

   Answer:

$-1 \leq 3(x + 2) - 1 \leq x + 3$	
$-1 \leq 3(x + 2) - 1$ *and* $3(x + 2) - 1 \leq x + 3$	Break up the compound inequality into two inequalities.
$-1 \leq 3x + 6 - 1$ $3x + 6 - 1 \leq x + 3$ $-6 \leq 3x$ $2x \leq -2$ $-2 \leq x$ and $x \leq -1$	Solve separately.
$-2 \leq x \leq -1$	The only values of x that satisfy *both* inequalities are the values between -2 and -1 (inclusive).

Graphing Linear Inequalities in Two Variables

Linear inequalities in two variables can be graphed in much the same way as linear equations. Start by graphing the corresponding equation of a line (temporarily replace the inequality with an equal sign, and then graph). This line creates a boundary line of two half-planes. If the inequality is a "greater/less than," the boundary should not be included and a dotted line is used. A solid line is used to indicate that the boundary should be included in the solution when the inequality is "greater/less than or equal to."

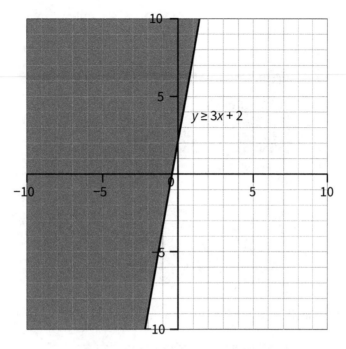

Figure 5.4. Graphing Inequalities

One side of the boundary is the set of all points (x, y) that make the inequality true. This side is shaded to indicate that all these values are solutions. If y is greater than the expression containing x, shade above the line; if it is less than, shade below. A point can also be used to check which side of the line to shade.

A set of two or more linear inequalities is a **SYSTEM OF INEQUALITIES**. Solutions to the system are all the values of the variables that make every inequality in the system true. Systems of inequalities are solved graphically by graphing all the inequalities in the same plane. The region where all the shaded solutions overlap is the solution to the system.

 A dotted line is used for "greater/less than" because the solution may approach that line, but the coordinates on the line can never be a solution.

EXAMPLES

1. Graph the following inequality: $3x + 6y \leq 12$.

    Answer:

$3x + 6y \leq 12$	
$3(0) + 6y = 12$	
$y = 2$	
y-intercept: $(0, 2)$	Find the x- and y-intercepts.
$3x + 6(0) \leq 12$	
$x = 4$	
x-intercept: $(4, 0)$	

    Graph the line using the intercepts, and shade below the line.

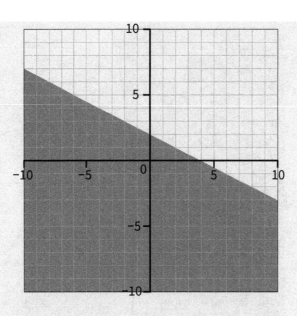

2. What is the inequality represented on the graph below?

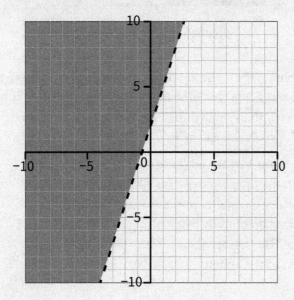

Answer:

y-intercept: $(0, 2)$ slope: 3 $y = 3x + 2$	Determine the equation of the boundary line.
$y > 3x + 2$	Replace the equal sign with the appropriate inequality: the line is dotted and the shading is above the line, indicating that the symbol should be "greater than." Check a point: for example $(1, 5)$ is a solution since $5 > 3(-1) + 2$.

3. Graph the system of inequalities: $-x + y \leq 1, x \geq -1, y > 2x - 4$

Answer:

To solve the system, graph all three inequalities in the same plane; then identify the area where the three solutions overlap. All points (x, y) in this area will be solutions to the system since they satisfy all three inequalities.

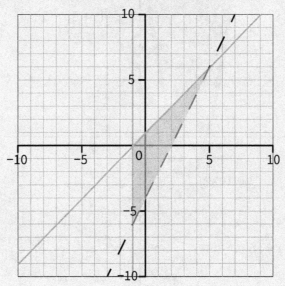

Quadratic Equations

Quadratic equations are degree 2 polynomials; the highest power on the dependent variable is two. While linear functions are represented graphically as lines, the graph of a quadratic function is a **PARABOLA**. The graph of a parabola has three important components. The **VERTEX** is where the graph changes direction. In the parent graph $y = x^2$, the origin $(0, 0)$ is the vertex. The **AXIS OF SYMMETRY** is the vertical line that cuts the graph into two equal halves. The line of symmetry always passes through the vertex. On the parent graph, the y-axis is the axis of symmetry. The **ZEROS** or **ROOTS** of the quadratic are the x-intercepts of the graph.

Forms of Quadratic Equations

Quadratic equations can be expressed in two forms:

- **STANDARD FORM:** $y = ax^2 + bx + c$

  Axis of symmetry: $x = -\frac{b}{2a}$ 　　　Vertex: $(-\frac{b}{2a}, f(-\frac{b}{2a}))$

- **VERTEX FORM:** $y\ a(x - h)^2 + k$

  Vertex: (h, k) 　　　　　　Axis of symmetry: $x = h$

In both equations, the sign of a determines which direction the parabola opens: if a is positive, then it opens upward; if a is negative, then it opens downward. The wideness or narrowness is also determined by a. If the absolute value of a is less than one (a proper fraction), then the parabola will get wider the closer $|a|$ is to zero. If the absolute value of a is greater than one, then the larger $|a|$ becomes, the narrower the parabola will be.

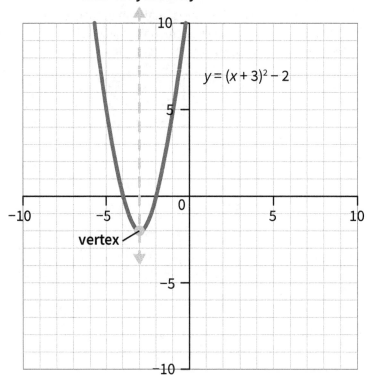

axis of symmetry

$y = (x + 3)^2 - 2$

vertex

Figure 5.5. Parabola

Equations in vertex form can be converted to standard form by squaring out the $(x - h)^2$ part (using FOIL), distributing the a, adding k, and simplifying the result.

Equations can be converted from standard form to vertex form by **COMPLETING THE SQUARE**. Take an equation in standard form, $y = ax^2 + bc + c$.

1. Move c to the left side of the equation.
2. Divide the entire equation through by a (to make the coefficient of x^2 be 1).
3. Take half of the coefficient of x, square that number, and then add the result to both sides of the equation.
4. Convert the right side of the equation to a perfect binomial squared, $(x + m)^2$.
5. Isolate y to put the equation in proper vertex form.

EXAMPLES

1. What is the line of symmetry for $y = -2(x + 3)^2 + 2$?

   Answer:
   This quadratic is given in vertex form, with $h = -3$ and $k = 2$. The vertex of this equation is $(-3, 2)$. The line of symmetry is the vertical line that passes through this point. Since the x-value of the point is -3, the line of symmetry is $\boldsymbol{x = -3}$.

2. What is the vertex of the parabola $y = -3x^2 + 24x - 27$?

Answer:

$y = -3x^2 + 24x - 27$	
$x = -\dfrac{b}{2a}$ where $a = -3$, $b = 24$ $x = -\dfrac{24}{2(-3)} = 4$	This quadratic equation is in standard form. Use the formula for finding the x-value of the vertex.
$y = -3(4)^2 + 24(4) - 27 = 21$ The vertex is at **(4, 21)**.	Plug $x = 4$ into the original equation to find the corresponding y-value.

3. Write $y = -3x^2 + 24x - 27$ in vertex form by completing the square.

Answer:

$y = -3x^2 + 24x - 27$	
$y + 27 = -3x^2 + 24x$	Move c to the other side of the equation.
$\dfrac{y}{-3} - 9 = x^2 - 8x$	Divide through by a (–3 in this example).
$\dfrac{y}{-3} - 9 + 16 = x^2 - 8x + 16$	Take half of the new b, square it, and add that quantity to both sides: $\frac{1}{2}(-8) = -4$. Squaring it gives $(-4)^2 = 16$.
$\dfrac{y}{-3} + 7 = (x - 4)^2$	Simplify the left side, and write the right side as a binomial squared.
$y = -3(x - 4)^2 + 21$	Subtract 7, and then multiply through by –3 to isolate y.

Solving Quadratic Equations

Solving the quadratic equation $ax^2 + bx + c = 0$ finds x-intercepts of the parabola (by making $y = 0$). These are also called the **ROOTS** or **ZEROS** of the quadratic function. A quadratic equation may have zero, one, or two real solutions. There are several ways of finding the zeros. One way is to factor the quadratic into a product of two binomials, and then use the zero product property. (If $m \times n = 0$, then either $m = 0$ or $n = 0$.) Another way is to complete the square and square root both sides. One way that works every time is to memorize and use the **QUADRATIC FORMULA**:

$$x = \frac{-b \pm \sqrt{b^2 - 4ac}}{2a}$$

The a, b, and c come from the standard form of quadratic equations above. (Note that to use the quadratic equation, the right-hand side of the equation must be equal to zero.)

The part of the formula under the square root radical ($b^2 - 4ac$) is known as the **DISCRIMINANT**. The discriminant tells how many and what type of roots will result without actually calculating the roots.

With all graphing problems, putting the function into the $y =$ window of a graphing calculator will aid the process of elimination when graphs are examined and compared to answer choices with a focus on properties like axis of symmetry, vertices, and roots of formulas.

Table 5.2. Discriminants

If $B^2 - 4AC$ is	There will be	And the parabola
zero	only 1 real root	has its vertex on the x-axis
positive	2 real roots	has **two** x-intercepts
negative	0 real roots 2 complex roots	has **no** x-intercepts

EXAMPLES

1. Find the zeros of the quadratic equation: $y = -(x + 3)^2 + 1$.

   Answer:

   Method 1: Make $y = 0$; isolate x by square rooting both sides:

$0 = -(x + 3)^2 + 1$	Make $y = 0$.
$-1 = -(x + 3)^2$	Subtract 1 from both sides.
$1 = (x + 3)^2$	Divide by -1 on both sides.
$(x + 3) = \pm 1$	Square root both sides. Don't forget to write plus OR minus 1.
$(x + 3) = 1$ or $(x + 3) = -1$	Write two equations using $+1$ and -1.
$x = -2$ or $x = -4$	Solve both equations. These are the zeros.

   Method 2: Convert vertex form to standard form, and then use the quadratic formula.

$y = -(x + 3)^2 + 1$ $y = -(x^2 + 6x + 9) + 1$ $y = -x^2 - 6x - 8$	Put the equation in standard form by distributing and combining like terms.
$x = \dfrac{-b \pm \sqrt{(b^2 - 4ac)}}{2a}$ $x = \dfrac{-(-6) \pm \sqrt{(-6)^2 - 4(-1)(-8)}}{2(-1)}$ $x = \dfrac{6 \pm \sqrt{36 - 32}}{-2}$ $x = \dfrac{6 \pm \sqrt{4}}{-2}$ $x = -4, -2$	Find the zeros using the quadratic formula.

2. Find the root(s) for: $z^2 - 4z + 4 = 0$

   Answer:

   This polynomial can be factored in the form $(z - 2)(z - 2) = 0$, so the only root is $z = 2$. There is only one x-intercept, and the vertex of the graph is *on* the x-axis.

3. Write a quadratic function that has zeros at $x = -3$ and $x = 2$ that passes through the point $(-2, 8)$.

Answer:

If the quadratic has zeros at $x = -3$ and $x = 2$, then it has factors of $(x + 3)$ and $(x - 2)$. The quadratic function can be written in the factored form $y = a(x + 3)(x - 2)$. To find the a-value, plug in the point $(-2, 8)$ for x and y:

$8 = a(-2 + 3)(-2 - 2)$

$8 = a(-4)$

$a = -2$

The quadratic function is $y = -2(x + 3)(x - 2)$.

Graphing Quadratic Equations

The final expected quadratic skills are graphing a quadratic function given its equation and determining the equation of a quadratic function from its graph. The equation's form determines which quantities are easiest to obtain:

Table 5.3 Obtaining Quantities from Quadratic Functions

NAME OF FORM	EQUATION OF QUADRATIC	EASIEST QUANTITY TO FIND	HOW TO FIND OTHER QUANTITIES
vertex form	$y = a(x - h)^2 + k$	vertex at (h, k) and axis of symmetry $x = h$	Find zeros by making $y = 0$ and solving for x.
factored form	$y = a(x - m)(x - n)$	x – intercepts at $x = m$ and $x = n$	Find axis of symmetry by averaging m and n: $x = \frac{m + n}{2}$. This is also the x-value of the vertex.
standard form	$y = ax^2 + bx + c$	y – intercept at $(0, c)$	Find axis of symmetry and x-value of the vertex using $x = \frac{-b}{2a}$. Find zeros using quadratic formula.

To graph a quadratic function, first determine if the graph opens up or down by examining the a-value. Then determine the quantity that is easiest to find based on the form given, and find the vertex. Then other values can be found, if necessary, by choosing x-values and finding the corresponding y-values. Using symmetry instantly doubles the number of points that are known.

Given the graph of a parabola, the easiest way to write a quadratic equation is to identify the vertex and insert the h- and k-values into the vertex form of the equation. The a-value can be determined by finding another point the graph goes through, plugging these values in for x and y, and solving for a.

EXAMPLES

1. Graph the quadratic $y = 2(x - 3)^2 + 4$.

Answer:

Start by marking the vertex at (3, 4) and recognizing this parabola opens upward. The line of symmetry is $x = 3$. Now, plug in an easy value for x to get one point on the curve; then use symmetry to find another point. In this case, choose $x = 2$ (one unit to the left of the line of symmetry) and solve for y:

$y = 2(2 - 3)^2 + 4$

$y = 2(1) + 4$

$y = 6$

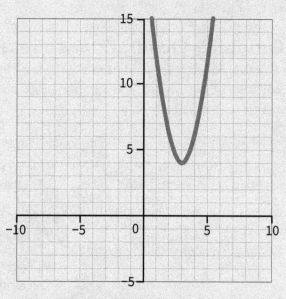

Thus the point (2, 6) is on the curve. Then use symmetry to find the corresponding point one unit to the right of the line of symmetry, which must also have a y value of 6. This point is (4, 6). Draw a parabola through the points.

2. What is the vertex form of the equation shown on the following graph?

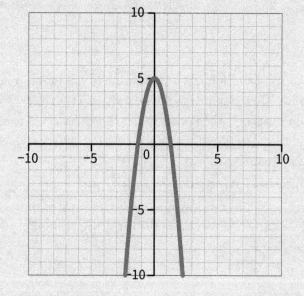

Answer:

$(h, k) = (0, 5)$ $y = a(x - h)^2 + k$ $y = a(x - 0)^2 + 5$ $y = ax^2 + 5$	Locate the vertex and plug values for h and k into the vertex form of the quadratic equation.
$(x, y) = (1, 2)$ $y = ax^2 + 5$ $2 = a(1)^2 + 5$ $a = -3$	Choose another point on the graph to plug into this equation to solve for a.
$y = -3x^2 + 5$	Plug a into the vertex form of the equation.

Functions

Working with Functions

Functions can be thought of as a process: when something is put in, an action (or operation) is performed, and something different comes out. A FUNCTION is a relationship between two quantities (for example x and y) in which, for every value of the independent variable (usually x), there is exactly one value of the dependent variable (usually y). Briefly, each input has *exactly one* output. Graphically this means the graph passes the VERTICAL LINE TEST: anywhere a vertical line is drawn on the graph, the line hits the curve at exactly one point.

The notation $f(x)$ or $g(t)$, etc., is often used when a function is being considered. This is FUNCTION NOTATION. The input value is x and the output value y is written as $y = f(x)$. Thus, $f(2)$ represents the output value (or y value) when $x = 2$, and $f(2) = 5$ means that when $x = 2$ is plugged into the $f(x)$ function, the output (y value) is 5. In other words, $f(2) = 5$ represents the point $(2, 5)$ on the graph of $f(x)$.

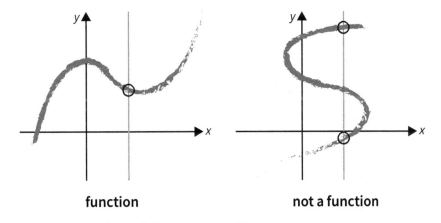

function   not a function

Figure 5.6. Vertical Line Test

Every function has an INPUT DOMAIN and OUTPUT RANGE. The domain is the set of all the possible x values that can be used as input values (these are found along the horizontal axis on the graph), and the range includes all the y values or output values that result from applying $f(x)$ (these are found along the vertical axis on the graph). Domain and range are usually intervals of numbers and are often expressed as inequalities, such as $x < 2$ (the domain is all values less than 2) or $3 < x < 15$ (all values between 3 and 15).

A function $f(x)$ is EVEN if $f(-x) = f(x)$. Even functions have symmetry across the y-axis. An example of an even function is the parent quadratic $y = x^2$, because any value of x (for example, 3) and its opposite $-x$ (for example, –3) have the same y value (for example, $3^2 = 9$ and $(-3)^2 = 9$). A function is ODD if $f(-x) = -f(x)$. Odd functions have symmetry about the origin. For example, $f(x) = x^3$ is an odd function because $f(3) = 27$, and $f(-3) = -27$. A function may be even, odd, or neither.

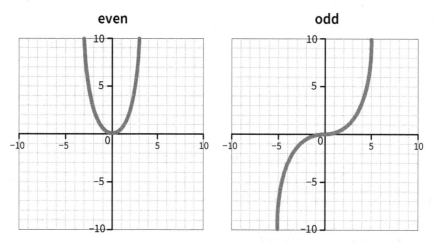

Figure 5.7. Even and Odd Functions

EXAMPLES

1. What are the domain and range of the following function?

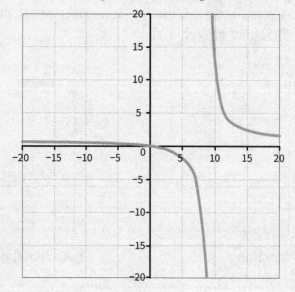

Answer:

This function has an asymptote at $x = 9$, so is not defined there. Otherwise, the function is defined for all other values of x.

D: $-\infty < x < 9$ or $9 < x < \infty$

Interval notation can also be used to show domain and range. Round brackets indicate that an end value is not included, and square brackets show that it is. The symbol ∪ means *or*, and the symbol ∩ means *and*. For example, the statement (−infinity, 4) ∪ (4, infinity) describes the set of all real numbers except 4.

Since the function has a horizontal asymptote at $y = 1$ that it never crosses, the function never takes the value 1, so the range is all real numbers except 1: **R**: $-\infty < y < 1$ *or* $1 < y < \infty$.

2. What is the domain and the range of the following graph?

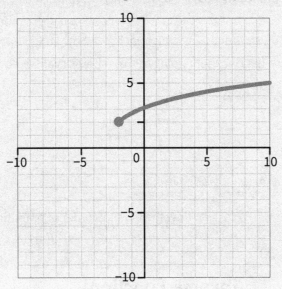

Answer:

For the domain, this graph goes on to the right to positive infinity. Its leftmost point, however, is $x = -2$. Therefore, its domain is all real numbers equal to or greater than −2,

D: $-2 \le x < \infty$, or [−2, ∞).

The lowest range value is $y = 2$. Although it has a decreasing slope, this function continues to rise. Therefore, the domain is all real numbers greater than 2, **R: $2 \le y < \infty$ or [2, ∞).**

3. Which of the following represents a function?

A.

X	G(X)
0	0
1	1
2	2
1	3

B.

X	F(X)
0	1
0	2
0	3
0	4

C.

T	F(T)
1	1
2	2
3	3
4	4

D.

X	F(X)
0	0
5	1
0	2
5	3

Answer:

For a set of numbers to represent a function, every input must generate a unique output. Therefore, if the same input (*x*) appears more than once in the table, determine if that input has two different outputs. If so, then the table does not represent a function.

A.   This table is not a function because input value 1 has two different outputs (1 and 3).

B.   Table B is not function because 0 is the only input and results in four different values.

C.   This table shows a function because each input has one output.

D.   This table also has one input going to two different values, so it is not a function.

4.   Evaluate: $f(4)$ if $f(x) = x^3 - 2x + \sqrt{x}$

Answer:

$f(x) = x^3 - 2x + \sqrt{x}$	
$f(4) = (4)^3 - 2(4) + \sqrt{(4)}$	Plug in 4.
$= 64 - 8 + 2$	Follow the PEMDAS order of operations.
$= 58$	

Inverse Functions

INVERSE FUNCTIONS switch the inputs and the outputs of a function. If $f(x) = k$ then the inverse of that function would read $f^{-1}(k) = x$. The domain of $f^{-1}(x)$ is the range of $f(x)$, and

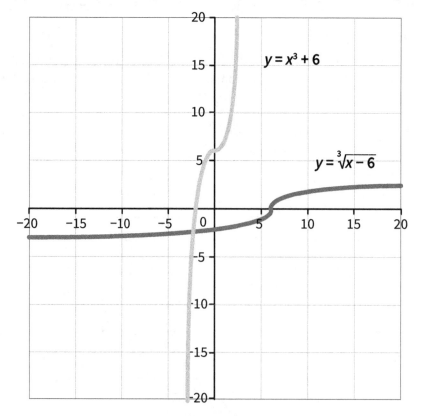

$y = x^3 + 6$

$y = \sqrt[3]{x - 6}$

Figure 5.8. Inverse Functions

the range of $f^{-1}(x)$ is the domain of $f(x)$. If point (a, b) is on the graph of $f(x)$, then point (b, a) will be on the graph of $f^{-1}(x)$. Because of this fact, the graph of $f^{-1}(x)$ is a reflection of the graph of $f(x)$ across the line $y = x$. Inverse functions "undo" all the operations of the original function.

The steps for finding an inverse function are:

1. Replace $f(x)$ with y to make it easier manipulate the equation.

2. Switch the x and y.

3. Solve for y.

4. Label the inverse function as $f^{-1}(x) =$.

Inverse graphs can be tested by taking any point on one graph and flipping coordinates to see if that new point is on the other curve. For example, the coordinate point $(5, -2)$ is on the function and $(-2, 5)$ is a point on its inverse.

EXAMPLES

1. What is the inverse of function of $f(x) = 5x + 5$?

Answer:

$y = 5x + 5$	Replace $f(x)$ with y
$x = 5y + 5$	Switch the places of y and x.
$x = 5y + 5$ $x - 5 = 5y$ $y = \frac{x}{5} - 1$	Solve for y.
$f^{-1}(x) = \frac{x}{5} - 1$	

2. Find the inverse of the graph of $f(x) = -1 - \frac{1}{5}x$

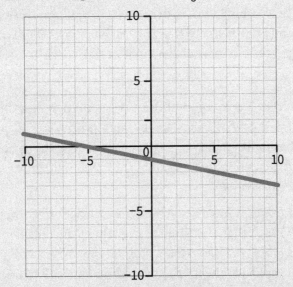

Answer:

This is a linear graph with some clear coordinates: $(-5, 0)$, $(0, -1)$, $(5, -2)$, and $(10, -3)$. This means the inverse function will have coordinate $(0, -5)$, $(-1, 0)$, $(-2, 5)$, and $(-3, 10)$. The inverse function is reflected over the line $y = x$ and is the line $f^{-1}(x) = -5(x + 1)$ below.

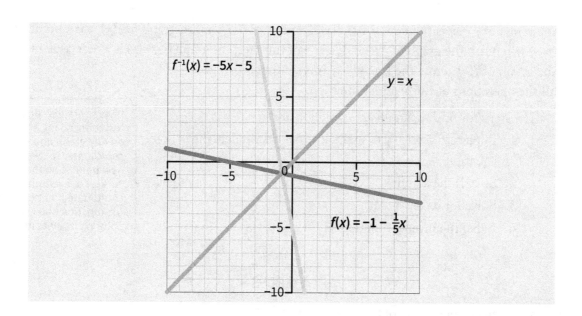

Compound Functions

COMPOUND FUNCTIONS take two or more functions and combine them using operations or composition. Functions can be combined using addition, subtraction, multiplication, or division:

$$\text{addition: } (f + g)(x) = f(x) + g(x)$$

$$\text{subtraction: } (f - g)(x) = f(x) - g(x)$$

$$\text{multiplication: } (fg)(x) = f(x)g(x)$$

$$\text{division: } \left(\frac{f}{g}\right)(x) = \frac{f(x)}{g(x)} \text{ (note that } g(x) \neq 0)$$

Functions can also be combined using COMPOSITION. Composition of functions is indicated by the notation $(f \circ g)(x)$. Note that the $\circ$ symbol does NOT mean multiply. It means take the output of $g(x)$ and make it the input of $f(x)$:

$$(f \circ g)(x) = f(g(x))$$

This equation is read f of g of x, and will be a new function of x. Note that order is important. In general, $f(g(x)) \neq g(f(x))$. They *will* be equal when $f(x)$ and $g(x)$ are inverses of each other, however, as both will simplify to the original input x. This is because performing a function on a value and then using that output as the input to the inverse function should bring you back to the original value.

The domain of a composition function is the set of x values that are in the domain of the "inside" function $g(x)$ such that $g(x)$ is in the domain of the outside function $f(x)$. For example, if $f(x) = \frac{1}{x}$ and $g(x) = \sqrt{x}$, $f(g(x))$ has a domain of $x > 0$ because $g(x)$ has a domain of $x \geq 0$. But when $f(x)$ is applied to the $\sqrt{x}$ function, the composition function becomes $\frac{1}{\sqrt{x}}$ and the value $x = 0$ is no longer allowed because it would result in 0 in the denominator, so the domain must be further restricted.

1. If $z(x) = 3x - 3$ and $y(x) = 2x - 1$, find $(y \circ z)(-4)$.

Answer:

$(y \circ z)(-4) = y(z(-4))$	
$z(-4)$ $= 3(-4) - 3$ $= -12 - 3$ $= -15$	Starting on the inside, evaluate z.
$y(z(-4))$ $= y(-15)$ $= 2(-15) - 1$ $= -30 - 1$ $\mathbf{= -31}$	Replace $z(-4)$ with -15, and simplify.

2. Find $(k \circ t)(x)$ if $k(x) = \frac{1}{2}x - 3$ and $t(x) = \frac{1}{2}x - 2$.

Answer:

$(k \circ t)(x) = k(t(x))$ $= k\left(\frac{1}{2}x - 2\right)$ $= \frac{1}{2}\left(\frac{1}{2}x - 2\right) - 3$	Replace x in the $k(x)$ function with $\left(\frac{1}{2}x - 2\right)$
$= \frac{1}{4}x - 1 - 3$ $= \frac{1}{4}x - 4$	Simplify.
$\mathbf{(k \circ t)(x) = \frac{1}{4}x - 4}$	

3. The wait (W) (in minutes) to get on a ride at an amusement park depends on the number of people (N) in the park. The number of people in the park depends on the number of hours, t, that the park has been open. Suppose $N(t) = 400t$ and $W(N) = 5(1.2)^{\frac{N}{100}}$. What is the value and the meaning in context of $N(4)$ and $W(N(4))$?

Answer:

$N(4) = 400(4) = 1600$ and means that 4 hours after the park opens there are 1600 people in the park. $W(N(4)) = W(1600) = 96$ and means that 4 hours after the park opens the wait time is about **96 minutes** for the ride.

Transforming Functions

Many functions can be graphed using simple transformation of parent functions. Transformations include reflections across axes, vertical and horizontal translations (or shifts), and vertical or horizontal stretches or compressions. The table gives the effect of each transformation to the graph of any function $y = f(x)$.

Table 5.4. Effects of Transformations

EQUATION	EFFECT ON GRAPH
$y = -f(x)$	reflection across the x-axis (vertical reflection)
$y = f(x) + k$	vertical shift up k units ($k > 0$) or down k units ($k < 0$)
$y = kf(x)$	vertical stretch (if $k > 1$) or compression (if $k < 1$)
$y = f(-x)$	reflection across the y-axis (horizontal reflection)
$y = f(x + k)$	horizontal shift right k units ($k < 0$) or left k units ($k > 0$)
$y = f(kx)$	horizontal stretch ($k < 1$) or compression ($k > 1$)

Note that the first three equations have an operation applied to the *outside* of the function $f(x)$ and these all cause *vertical changes* to the graph of the function that are *intuitive* (for example, adding a value moves it up). The last three equations have an operation applied to the *inside* of the function $f(x)$ and these all cause *horizontal changes* to the graph of the function that are *counterintuitive* (for example, multiplying the x's by a fraction results in stretch, not compression, which would seem more intuitive). It is helpful to group these patterns together to remember how each transformation affects the graph.

EXAMPLES

1. Graph: $y = |x + 1| + 4$

    Answer:

    This function is the absolute value function with a vertical shift up of 4 units (since the 4 is outside the absolute value bars), and a horizontal shift left of 1 unit (since it is inside the bars). The vertex of the graph is at $(-1, 4)$ and the line $x = -1$ is an axis of symmetry.

    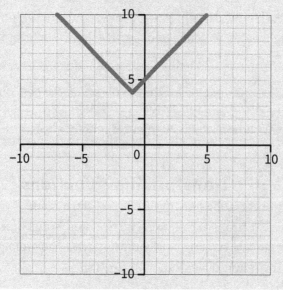

2. Graph: $y = -3|x - 2| + 2$

Answer:

The negative sign in front of the absolute value means the graph will be reflected across the x-axis, so it will open down. The 3 causes a vertical stretch of the function, which results in a narrower graph. The basic curve is shifted 2 units right (since the −2 is an inside change) and 2 units up (since the +2 is an outside change), so the vertex is at (2, 2).

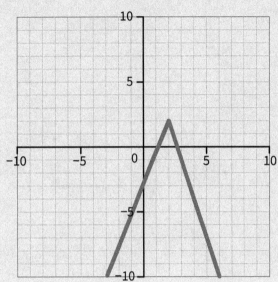

GO ON

Test Your Knowledge

Work the problem, and then choose the most correct answer.

1. Which of the following is equivalent to $z^3(z+2)^2 - 4z^3 + 2$?

    A) 2

    B) $z^5 + 4z^4 + 4z^3 + 2$

    C) $z^6 + 4z^3 + 2$

    D) $z^5 + 4z^4 + 2$

2. Which of the following represents a linear equation?

    A) $\sqrt[3]{y} = x$

    B) $\sqrt[3]{x} = y$

    C) $\sqrt[3]{y} = x^2$

    D) $y = \sqrt[3]{x^3}$

3. Which of the following is the y-intercept of the given equation?

    $7y - 42x + 7 = 0$

    A) $(0, \frac{1}{6})$

    B) $(6, 0)$

    C) $(0, -1)$

    D) $(-1, 0)$

4. What is the slope of the graph below?

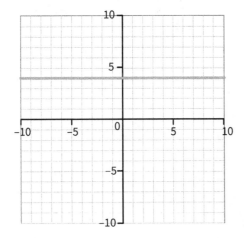

5. 50 shares of a financial stock and 10 shares of an auto stock are valued at $1,300. If 10 shares of the financial stock and 10 shares of the auto stock are valued at $500, what is the value of 50 shares of the auto stock?

    Write in the answer: _____

6. What are the real zero(s) of the following polynomial?

    $2n^2 + 2n - 12 = 0$

    A) {2}

    B) {-3, 2}

    C) {2, 4}

    D) There are no real zeros of n.

7. What is the solution set for the inequality $2x^2 - 4x - 6 < 0$?

    A) $(-1, 3)$

    B) $(-\infty, \infty)$

    C) $\varnothing$

    D) $(-\infty, -1) \cup (3, \infty)$

8. Which expression is equivalent to $5^2 \times (-5)^{-2} - (2+3)^{-1}$?

    A) 0

    B) 1

    C) $\frac{5}{4}$

    D) $\frac{4}{5}$

Answer Key

1. **D) is correct.**

Simplify using PEMDAS.

$z^3(z + 2)^2 - 4z^3 + 2$

$z^3(z^2 + 4z + 4) - 4z^3 + 2$

$z^5 + 4z^4 + 4z^3 - 4z^3 + 2$

$\mathbf{z^5 + 4z^4 + 2}$

2. **D) is correct.**

Solve each equation for y and find the equation with a power of 1.

$\sqrt[3]{y} = x \rightarrow y = x^3$

$\sqrt[3]{x} = y \rightarrow y = \sqrt[3]{x}$

$\sqrt[3]{y} = x^2 \rightarrow y = x^6$

$y = \sqrt[3]{x^3} \rightarrow \mathbf{y = x}$

3. **C) is correct.**

Plug 0 in for x and solve for y.

$7y - 42x + 7 = 0$

$7y - 42(0) + 7 = 0$

$y = -1$

The y-intercept is at $\mathbf{(0, -1)}$.

4. **C) is correct.**

The slope of a horizontal line is always 0.

5. **D) is correct.**

Set up a system of equations and solve using elimination.

f = the cost of a financial stock

a = the cost of an auto stock

$50f + 10a = 1300$

$10f + 10a = 500$

$\begin{aligned} 50f + 10a &= 1300 \\ + -50f - 50a &= -2500 \\ \hline -40a &= -1,200 \\ a &= 30 \end{aligned}$

$50(30) = \mathbf{1,500}$

6. **B) is correct.**

Factor the trinomial and set each factor equal to 0.

$2n^2 + 2n - 12 = 0$

$2(n^2 + n - 6) = 0$

$2(n + 3)(n - 2) = 0$

$\mathbf{n = -3}$ and $\mathbf{n = 2}$

7. **A) is correct.**

Use the zeros of the function to find the intervals where it is less than 0.

$2x^2 - 4x - 6 = 0$

$(2x - 6)(x + 1) = 0$

$x = 3$ and $x = -1$

$(-\infty, -1) \rightarrow 2x^2 - 4x - 6 > 0$

$(-1, 3) \rightarrow 2x^2 - 4x - 6 < 0$

$(3, \infty) \rightarrow 2x^2 - 4x - 6 > 0$

The function is less than 0 on the interval $\mathbf{(-1, 3)}$.

8. **D) is correct.**

Simplify using PEMDAS.

$5^2 \times (-5)^{-2} - 5^{-1}$

$= 25 \times \frac{1}{25} - \frac{1}{5}$

$= 1 - \frac{1}{5}$

$= \mathbf{\frac{4}{5}}$

six

GEOMETRY

Properties of Shapes

Basic Definitions

The basic figures from which many other geometric shapes are built are points, lines, and planes. A **POINT** is a location in a plane. It has no size or shape, but is represented by a dot. It is labeled using a capital letter.

A **LINE** is a one-dimensional collection of points that extends infinitely in both directions. At least two points are needed to define a line, and any points that lie on the same line are **COLINEAR**. Lines are represented by two points, such as *A* and *B*, and the line symbol: ($\overleftrightarrow{AB}$). Two lines on the same plane will intersect unless they are **PARALLEL**, meaning they have the same slope. Lines that intersect at a 90 degree angle are **PERPENDICULAR**.

A **LINE SEGMENT** has two endpoints and a finite length. The length of a segment, called the measure of the segment, is the distance from *A* to *B*. A line segment is a subset of a line, and is also denoted with two points, but with a segment symbol: ($\overline{AB}$). The **MIDPOINT** of a line segment is the point at which the segment is divided into two equal parts. A line, segment, or plane that passes through the midpoint of a segment is called a **BISECTOR** of the segment, since it cuts the segment into two equal segments.

A **RAY** has one endpoint and extends indefinitely in one direction. It is defined by its endpoint, followed by any other point on the ray: $\overrightarrow{AB}$. It is important that the first letter represents the endpoint. A ray is sometimes called a half line.

Table 6.1. Basic Geometric Figures

TERM	DIMENSIONS	GRAPHIC	SYMBOL
point	zero	●	$\cdot A$
line segment	one	*A* —— *B*	$\overline{AB}$
ray	one	*A* —— *B* →	$\overrightarrow{AB}$

Table 6.1. Basic Geometric Figures (continued)

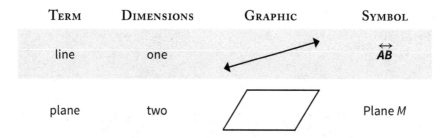

TERM	DIMENSIONS	GRAPHIC	SYMBOL
line	one		$\overleftrightarrow{AB}$
plane	two		Plane M

A **PLANE** is a flat sheet that extends indefinitely in two directions (like an infinite sheet of paper). A plane is a two-dimensional (2D) figure. A plane can always be defined through any three noncollinear points in three-dimensional (3D) space. A plane is named using any three points that are in the plane (for example, plane **ABC**). Any points lying in the same plane are said to be **COPLANAR**. When two planes intersect, the intersection is a line.

EXAMPLE

Which points and lines are not contained in plane M in the diagram below?

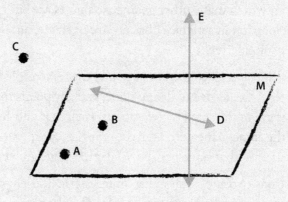

Answer:

Points A and B and line D are all on plane M. Point C is above the plane, and line E cuts through the plane and thus does not lie on plane M. The point at which line E intersects plane M is on plane M but the line as a whole is not.

Angles

ANGLES are formed when two rays share a common endpoint. They are named using three letters, with the vertex point in the middle (for example $\angle ABC$, where B is the vertex). They can also be labeled with a number or named by their vertex alone (if it is clear to do so). Angles are also classified based on their angle measure. A **RIGHT ANGLE** has a measure of exactly 90°. **ACUTE ANGLES** have measures that are less than 90°, and **OBTUSE ANGLES** have measures that are greater than 90°.

Angles can be measured in degrees or radian. Use the conversion factor 1 rad = 57.3 degrees to convert between them.

Any two angles that add to make 90° are called **COMPLE-MENTARY ANGLES**. A 30° angle would be complementary to a

60° angle. **SUPPLEMENTARY ANGLES** add up to 180°. A supplementary angle to a 60° angle would be a 120° angle; likewise, 60° is the **SUPPLEMENT** of 120°. The complement and supplement of any angle must always be positive. For example, a 140 degree has no complement. Angles that are next to each other and share a common ray are called **ADJACENT ANGLES**. Angles that are adjacent and supplementary are called a **LINEAR PAIR** of angles. Their nonshared rays form a line (thus the *linear* pair). Note that angles that are supplementary do not need to be adjacent; their measures simply need to add to 180°.

VERTICAL ANGLES are formed when two lines intersect. Four angles will be formed; the vertex of each angle is at the intersection point of the lines. The vertical angles across from each other will be equal in measure. The angles adjacent to each other will be linear pairs and therefore supplementary.

A ray, line, or segment that divides an angle into two equal angles is called an **ANGLE BISECTOR**.

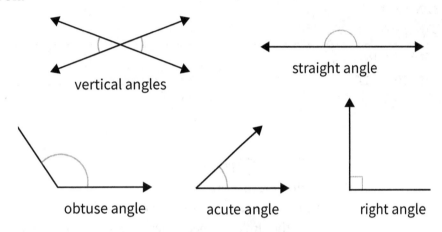

Figure 6.1. Types of Angles

EXAMPLES

1. How many linear pairs of angles are there in the following figure?

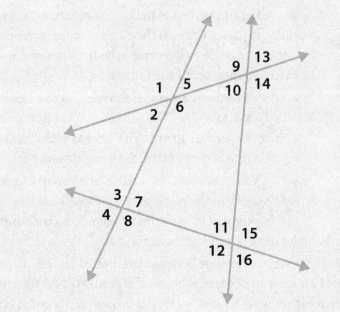

2. If angles *M* and *N* are supplementary and ∠*M* is 30° less than twice ∠*N*, what is the degree measurement of each angle?

Answer:

$\angle M + \angle N = 180°$ $\angle M = 2\angle N - 30°$	Set up a system of equations.
$\angle M + \angle N = 180°$ $(2\angle N - 30°) + \angle N = 180°$ $3\angle N - 30° = 180°$ $3\angle N = 210°$ $\angle N = 70°$	Use substitution to solve for ∠*N*.
$\angle M + \angle N = 180°$ $\angle M + 70° = 180°$ $\boldsymbol{\angle M = 110°}$	Solve for ∠*M* using the original equation.

Circles

A **CIRCLE** is the set of all the points in a plane that are the same distance from a fixed point called the **CENTER**. The distance from the center to any point on the circle is the **RADIUS** of the circle. The distance around the circle (the perimeter) is called the **CIRCUMFERENCE**.

The ratio of a circle's circumference to its diameter is a constant value called pi (π), an irrational number which is commonly rounded to 3.14. The formula to find a circle's circumference is $C = 2\pi r$. The formula to find the enclosed area of a circle is $A = \pi r^2$.

Circles have a number of unique parts and properties:

Trying to square a circle means attempting to create a square that has the same area as a circle. Because the area of a circle depends on π, which is an irrational number, this task is impossible. The phrase is often used to describe trying to do something that can't be done.

♦ The **DIAMETER** is the largest measurement across a circle. It passes through the circle's center, extending from one side of the circle to the other. The measure of the diameter is twice the measure of the radius.

♦ A line that cuts across a circle and touches it twice is called a **SECANT** line. The part of a secant line that lies within a circle is called a **CHORD**. Two chords within a circle are of equal length if they are the same distance from the center.

♦ A line that touches a circle or any curve at one point is **TANGENT** to the circle or the curve. These lines are always exterior to the circle. A line tangent to a circle and a radius drawn to the point of tangency meet at a right angle (90°).

♦ An **ARC** is any portion of a circle between two points on the circle. The **MEASURE** of an arc is in degrees, whereas the **LENGTH OF THE ARC** will be in linear measurement (such as centimeters or inches). A **MINOR ARC** is the small arc between the two points (it measures less than 180°), whereas a MAJOR ARC is the large arc between the two points (it measures greater than 180°).

◆ An angle with its vertex at the center of a circle is called a CENTRAL ANGLE. For a central angle, the measure of the arc intercepted by the sides of the angle (in degrees) is the same as the measure of the angle.

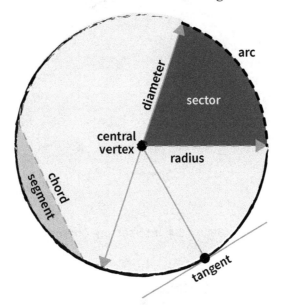

Figure 6.2. Parts of a Circle

◆ A SECTOR is the part of a circle *and* its interior that is inside the rays of a central angle (its shape is like a slice of pie).

	Area of Sector	Length of an Arc
Degrees	$A = \dfrac{\theta}{360°} \times \pi r^2$	$s = \dfrac{\theta}{360°} \times 2\pi r$
Radians	$A = \dfrac{1}{2}\pi^2\theta$	$s = r\theta$

◆ An INSCRIBED ANGLE has a vertex on the circle and is formed by two chords that share that vertex point. The angle measure of an inscribed angle is one-half the angle measure of the central angle with the same endpoints on the circle.

◆ A CIRCUMSCRIBED ANGLE has rays tangent to the circle. The angle lies outside of the circle.

◆ Any angle outside the circle, whether formed by two tangent lines, two secant lines, or a tangent line and a secant line, is equal to half the difference of the intercepted arcs.

◆ Angles are formed within a circle when two chords intersect in the circle. The measure of the smaller angle formed is half the sum of the two smaller arc measures (in degrees). Likewise, the larger angle is half the sum of the two larger arc measures.

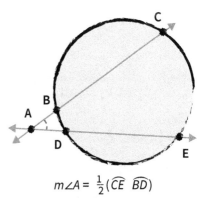

$m\angle A = \frac{1}{2}(\overset{\frown}{CE}\ \overset{\frown}{BD})$

Figure 6.3. Angles Outside a Circle

- If a chord intersects a line tangent to the circle, the angle formed by this intersection measures one half the measurement of the intercepted arc (in degrees).

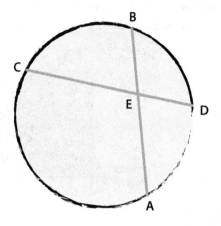

$$m\angle E = \tfrac{1}{2}(\widehat{AC} + \widehat{BD})$$

Figure 6.4. Intersecting Chords

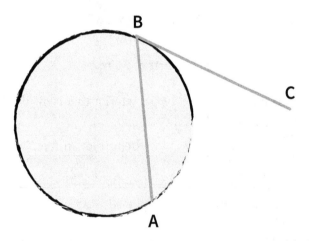

$$m\angle ABC = \tfrac{1}{2} m\widehat{AB}$$

Figure 6.5. Intersecting Chord and Tangent

EXAMPLES

1. Find the area of the sector *NHS* of the circle below with center at *H*:

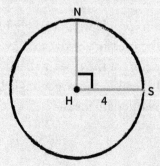

Answer:

$r = 4$	Identify the important parts of the circle.
$\angle NHS = 90°$	
$A = \dfrac{\theta}{360°} \times \pi r^2$	Plug these values into the formula for the area of a sector.
$= \dfrac{90}{360} \times \pi(4)^2$	
$= \dfrac{1}{4} \times 16\pi$	Plug these values into the formula for the area of a sector (continued).
$= \mathbf{4\pi}$	

2. In the circle below with center O, the minor arc ACB measures 5 feet. What is the measurement of $m\angle AOB$?

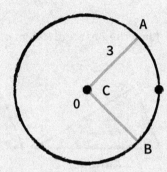

Answer:

$r = 3$	Identify the important parts of the circle.
length of $\overline{ACB} = 5$	
$s = \dfrac{\theta}{360°} \times 2\pi r$	
$5 = \dfrac{\theta}{360°} \times 2\pi(3)$	
$\dfrac{5}{6\pi} = \dfrac{\theta}{360°}$	Plug these values into the formula for the length of an arc and solve for θ.
$\theta = 95.5°$	
$m\angle AOB = \mathbf{95.5°}$	

Triangles

Much of geometry is concerned with triangles as they are commonly used shapes. A good understanding of triangles allows decomposition of other shapes (specifically polygons) into triangles for study.

Triangles have three sides, and the three interior angles always sum to 180°. The formula for the area of a triangle is $A = \dfrac{1}{2}bh$ or one-half the product of the base and height (or altitude) of the triangle.

Some important segments in a triangle include the angle bisector, the altitude, and the median. The **ANGLE BISECTOR** extends from the side opposite an angle to bisect that angle. The **ALTITUDE** is the shortest distance from a vertex of the triangle to the line containing the base side opposite that vertex. It is perpendicular to that line and can occur on the outside of the triangle. The **MEDIAN** extends from an angle to bisect the opposite side.

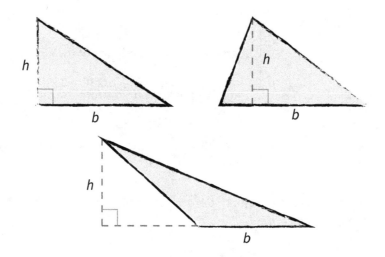

Figure 6.6. Finding the Base and Height of Triangles

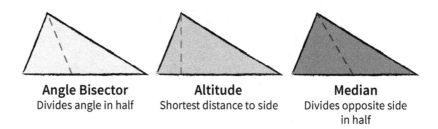

| **Angle Bisector** | **Altitude** | **Median** |
| Divides angle in half | Shortest distance to side | Divides opposite side in half |

Figure 6.7. Important Segments in a Triangle

Triangles have two "centers." The ORTHOCENTER is formed by the intersection of a triangle's three altitudes. The CENTROID is where a triangle's three medians meet.

Triangles can be classified in two ways: by sides and by angles.

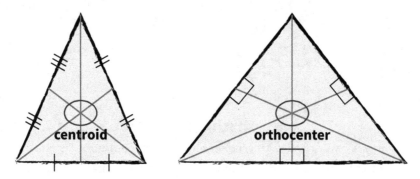

Figure 6.8. Centroid and Orthocenter of a Triangle

A SCALENE TRIANGLE has no equal sides or angles. An ISOSCELES TRIANGLE has two equal sides and two equal angles, often called BASE ANGLES. In an EQUILATERAL TRIANGLE, all three sides are equal as are all three angles. Moreover, because the sum of the angles of a triangle is always 180°, each angle of an equilateral triangle must be 60°.

A RIGHT TRIANGLE has one right angle (90°) and two acute angles. An ACUTE TRIANGLE has three acute angles (all angles are less than 90°). An OBTUSE TRIANGLE has one obtuse angle (more than 90°) and two acute angles.

Triangles Based on Sides

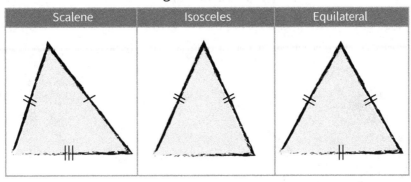

Triangles Based on Angles

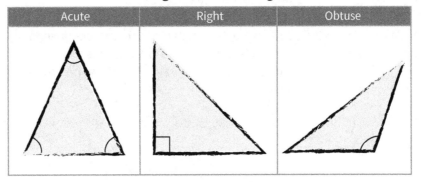

Figure 6.9. Types of Triangles

For any triangle, the side opposite the largest angle will have the longest length, while the side opposite the smallest angle will have the shortest length. The TRIANGLE INEQUALITY THEOREM states that the sum of any two sides of a triangle must be greater than the third side. If this inequality does not hold, then a triangle cannot be formed. A consequence of this theorem is the THIRD-SIDE RULE: if b and c are two sides of a triangle, then the measure of the third side a must be between the sum of the other two sides and the difference of the other two sides: $c - b < a < c + b$.

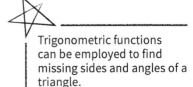

Trigonometric functions can be employed to find missing sides and angles of a triangle.

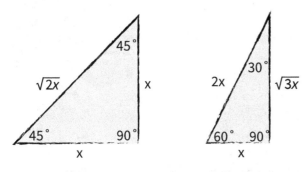

Figure 6.10. Special Right Triangles

Solving for missing angles or sides of a triangle is a common type of triangle problem. Often a right triangle will come up on its own or within another triangle. The relationship among a right triangle's sides is known as the PYTHAGOREAN THEOREM: $a^2 + b^2 = c^2$, where c is the hypotenuse and is across from the 90° angle. Right triangles with angle measurements of 90° – 45° – 45° and 90° – 60° – 30° are known as "special" right triangles and have specific relationships between their sides and angles.

EXAMPLES

1. What are the minimum and maximum values of x to the nearest hundredth?

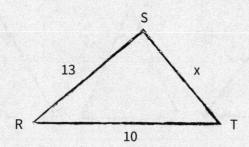

Answers:

The sum of two sides is 23 and their difference is 3. To connect the two other sides and enclose a space, x must be less than the sum and greater than the difference (that is, $3 < x < 23$). Therefore, **x's minimum value to the nearest hundredth is 3.01 and its maximum value is 22.99.**

2. Given the diagram, if $XZ = 100$, $WZ = 80$, and $XU = 70$, then $WY = ?$

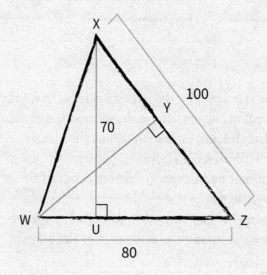

Answer:

$WZ = b_1 = 80$

$XU = h_1 = 70$

$XZ = b_2 = 100$

$WY = h_2 = ?$

$A = \frac{1}{2}bh$

$A_1 = \frac{1}{2}(80)(70) = 2800$

$A_2 = \frac{1}{2}(100)(h_2)$

The given values can be used to write two equation for the area of $\triangle WXZ$ with two sets of bases and heights.

$$2800 = \frac{1}{2}(100)(h_2)$$

$h_2 = 56$

$WY = 56$

Set the two equations equal to each other and solve for WY.

3. Examine and classify each of the following triangles:

1.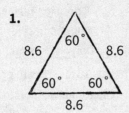

2.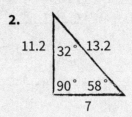

3.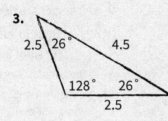

4.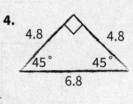

Answers:

Triangle 1 is an equilateral triangle (all 3 sides are equal, and all 3 angles are equal)

Triangle 2 is a scalene, right triangle (all 3 sides are different, and there is a 90° angle)

Triangle 3 is an obtuse, isosceles triangle (there are 2 equal sides and, consequently, 2 equal angles)

Triangle 4 is a right, isosceles triangle (there are 2 equal sides and a 90° angle)

Quadrilaterals

All closed, four-sided shapes are QUADRILATERALS. The sum of all internal angles in a quadrilateral is always 360°. (Think of drawing a diagonal to create two triangles. Since each triangle contains 180°, two triangles, and therefore the quadrilateral, must contain 360°.) The AREA OF ANY QUADRILATERAL is $A = bh$, where b is the base and h is the height (or altitude).

A PARALLELOGRAM is a quadrilateral with two pairs of parallel sides. A rectangle is a parallelogram with two pairs of equal sides and four right angles. A KITE also has two pairs of equal sides, but its equal sides are consecutive. Both a SQUARE and a RHOMBUS have four equal sides. A square has four right angles, while a rhombus has a pair of acute opposite angles and a pair of obtuse opposite angles. A TRAPEZOID has exactly one pair of parallel sides.

All squares are rectangles and all rectangles are parallelograms; however, not all parallelograms are rectangles and not all rectangles are squares.

Table 6.2 Properties of Parallelograms

Term	Shape	Properties
Parallelogram		Opposite sides are parallel. Consecutive angles are supplementary. Opposite angles are equal. Opposite sides are equal. Diagonals bisect each other.
Rectangle		All parallelogram properties hold. Diagonals are congruent *and* bisect each other. All angles are right angles.
Square		All rectangle properties hold. All four sides are equal. Diagonals bisect angles. Diagonals intersect at right angles and bisect each other.
Kite		One pair of opposite angles is equal. Two pairs of consecutive sides are equal. Diagonals meet at right angles.
Rhombus		All four sides are equal. Diagonals bisect angles. Diagonals intersect at right angles and bisect each other.
Trapezoid		One pair of sides is parallel. Bases have different lengths. Isosceles trapezoids have a pair of equal sides (and base angles).

EXAMPLES

1. In parallelogram *ABCD*, the measure of angle m is is $m° = 260°$. What is the measure of $n°$?

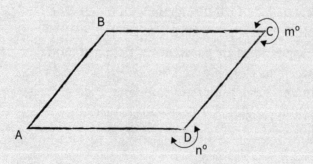

Answers:

$260° + m\angle C = 360°$ $m\angle C = 100°$	Find $\angle C$ using the fact that the sum of $\angle C$ and m is 360°.
$m\angle C + m\angle D = 180°$ $100° + m\angle D = 180°$ $m\angle D = 80°$	Solve for $\angle D$ using the fact that consecutive interior angles in a quadrilateral are supplementary.
$m\angle D + n = 360°$ **$n = 280°$**	Solve for n by subtracting $m\angle D$ from 360°.

2. A rectangular section of a football field has dimensions of x and y and an area of 1000 square feet. Three additional lines drawn vertically divide the section into four smaller rectangular areas as seen in the diagram below. If all the lines shown need to be painted, calculate the total number of linear feet, in terms of x, to be painted.

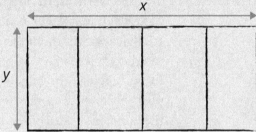

Answer:

$A = 1000 = xy$ $L = 2x + 5y$	Find equations for the area of the field and length of the lines to be painted (L) in terms of x and y.
$y = \frac{1000}{x}$ $L = 2x + 5y$ $L = 2x + 5\left(\frac{1000}{x}\right)$ **$L = 2x + \frac{5000}{x}$**	Substitute to find L in terms of x.

Polygons

Any closed shape made up of three or more line segments is a polygon. In addition to triangles and quadrilaterals, HEXAGONS and OCTAGONS are two common polygons.

The two polygons depicted in Figure 6.11 are REGULAR POLYGONS, meaning that they are equilateral (all sides having equal lengths) and equiangular (all angles having equal measurements). Angles inside a polygon are INTERIOR ANGLES, whereas those formed by one side of the polygon and a line extending outside the polygon are EXTERIOR ANGLES:

The sum of the all the exterior angles of a polygon is always 360°. Dividing 360° by the number of a polygon's sides finds the measure of the polygon's exterior angles.

Breaking an irregular polygon down into triangles and quadrilaterals helps in finding its area.

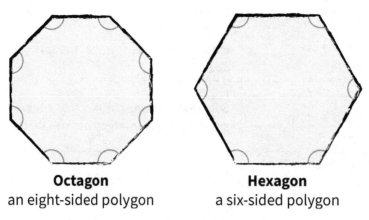

Octagon
an eight-sided polygon

Hexagon
a six-sided polygon

Figure 6.11. Common Polygons

To determine the sum of a polygon's interior angles, choose one vertex and draw diagonals from that vertex to each of the other vertices, decomposing the polygon into multiple triangles. For example, an octagon has six triangles within it, and therefore the sum of the interior angles is 6 × 180° = 1080°. In general, the formula for finding the sum of the angles in a polygon is *sum of angles* = $(n - 2) \times 180°$, where n is the number of sides of the polygon.

To find the measure of a single interior angle in a regular polygon, simply divide the sum of the interior angles by the number of angles (which is the same as the number of sides). So, in the octagon example, each angle is $\frac{1080}{8}$ = 135°.

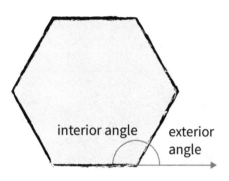

interior angle   exterior angle

Figure 6.12 Interior and Exterior Angles

In general, the formula to find the measure of a regular polygon's interior angles is: *interior angle* = $\frac{(n - 2)}{n} \times 180°$ where n is the number of sides of the polygon.

To find the area of a polygon, it is helpful to know the perimeter of the polygon (p), and the APOTHEM (a). The apothem is the shortest (perpendicular) distance from the polygon's center to one of the sides of the polygon. The formula for the area is: *area* = $\frac{ap}{2}$.

Finally, there is no universal way to find the perimeter of a polygon (when the side length is not given). Often, breaking the polygon down into triangles and adding the base of each triangle all the way around the polygon is the easiest way to calculate the perimeter.

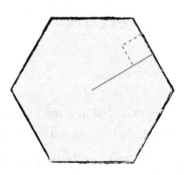

Figure 6.13. Apothem in a Hexagon

EXAMPLES

1. What is the measure of an exterior angle and an interior angle of a regular 400-gon?

    Answer:

    The sum of the exterior angles is 360°. Dividing this sum by 400 gives $\frac{360°}{400}$ = **0.9°**. Since an interior angle is supplementary to an exterior angle, all the interior angles have measure 180 − 0.9 = **179.1°**. Alternately, using the formula for calculating the interior angle gives the same result:

    interior angle = $\frac{400-2}{400}$ × 180° = 179.1°

2. The circle and hexagon below both share center point *T*. The hexagon is entirely inscribed in the circle. The circle's radius is 5. What is the area of the shaded area?

    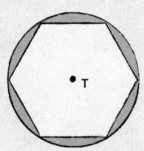

    Answer:

$A_c = \pi r^2$ $= \pi(5)^2$ $= 25\pi$	The area of the shaded region will be the area of the circle minus the area of the hexagon. Use the radius to find the area of the circle.
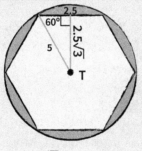 $a = 2.5\sqrt{3}$ $A_H = \frac{ap}{2}$ $= \frac{(2.5\sqrt{3})(30)}{2}$ $= 64.95$	To find the area of the hexagon, draw a right triangle from the vertex, and use special right triangles to find the hexagon's apothem. Then, use the apothem to calculate the area.
$= A_c - A_H$ $= 25\pi - 2.5\sqrt{3}$ $\approx$ **13.59**	Subtract the area of the hexagon from the circle to find the area of the shaded region.

Three-Dimensional Shapes

THREE-DIMENSIONAL SHAPES have depth in addition to width and length. **VOLUME** is expressed as the number of cubic units any solid can hold—that is, what it takes to fill it up. **SURFACE AREA** is the sum of the areas of the two-dimensional figures that are found on its surface. Some three-dimensional shapes also have a unique property called a slant height (ℓ), which is the distance from the base to the apex along a lateral face.

Finding the surface area of a three-dimensional solid can be made easier by using a **NET**. This two-dimensional "flattened" version of a three-dimensional shape shows the component parts that comprise the surface of the solid.

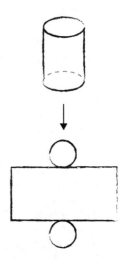

Figure 6.14. Net of a Cylinder

Table 6.3 Three-Dimensional Shapes and Formulas

TERM	SHAPE	FORMULA	
Prism		$V = Bh$ $SA = 2lw + 2wh + 2lh$ $d^2 = a^2 + b^2 + c^2$	B = area of base h = height l = length w = width d = longest diagonal
Cube		$V = s^3$ $SA = 6s^2$	s = cube edge
Sphere		$V = \frac{4}{3}\pi r^3$ $SA = 4\pi r^2$	r = radius
Cylinder		$V = Bh = \pi r^2 h$ $SA = 2\pi r^2 + 2\pi rh$	B = area of base h = height r = radius
Cone		$V = \frac{1}{3}\pi r^2 h$ $SA = \pi r^2 + \pi rl$	r = radius h = height l = slant height
Pyramid		$V = \frac{1}{3}Bh$ $SA = B + \frac{1}{2}(p)l$	B = area of base h = height p = perimeter l = slant height

EXAMPLES

1. A sphere has a radius z. If that radius is increased by t, by how much is the surface area increased? Write the answer in terms of z and t.

   Answer:

$SA_1 = 4\pi z^2$	Write the equation for the area of the original sphere.
$SA_2 = 4\pi(z + t)^2$ $= 4\pi(z^2 + 2zt + t^2)$ $= 4\pi z^2 + 8\pi zt + 4\pi t^2$	Write the equation for the area of the new sphere.
$A_2 - A_1 = 4\pi z^2 + 8\pi zt + 4\pi t^2$ $- 4\pi z^2$ $\mathbf{= 4\pi t^2 + 8\pi zt}$	To find the difference between the two, subtract the original from the increased surface area:

2. A cube with volume 27 cubic meters is inscribed within a sphere such that all of the cube's vertices touch the sphere. What is the length of the sphere's radius?

   Answer:

   Since the cube's volume is 27, each side length is equal to $\sqrt[3]{27} = 3$. The long diagonal distance from one of the cube's vertices to its opposite vertex will provide the sphere's diameter:

   $$d = \sqrt{3^2 + 3^2 + 3^2} = \sqrt{27} = 5.2$$

   Half of this length is the radius, which is **2.6 meters**.

Test Your Knowledge

Work the problem, and then choose the most correct answer.

1. Line *a* and line *b* are perpendicular and intersect at the point (−100, 100). If (−95, 115) is a point on line *b*, which of the following could be a point on line *a*?

A) (104, 168)

B) (−95, 115)

C) (−112, 104)

D) (−112, −104)

2. Which of the angles in the figure below are congruent?

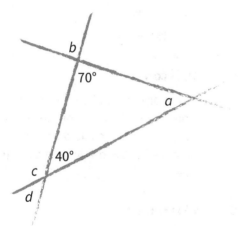

A) *a* and *d*

B) *b* and *d*

C) *a* and *b*

D) *c* and *b*

3. A cube is inscribed in a sphere such that each vertex on the cube touches the sphere. If the volume of the sphere is 972π cm³, what is the approximate volume of the cube in cubic centimeters?

A) 9

B) 10.4

C) 1125

D) 1729

4. If angles *a* and *b* are congruent, what is the measurement of angle *c*?

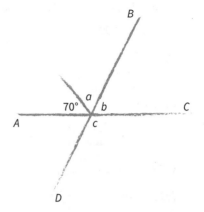

5. In the *xy*-coordinate plane, how many points have a distance of four from the origin?

A) 0

B) 2

C) 4

D) ∞

6. Which of the following sets of shapes are NOT all similar to each other?

A) right triangles

B) spheres

C) 30–60–90 triangles

D) squares

7. Cone *A* is similar to cone *B* with a scale factor of 3:4. If the volume of cone *A* is 54π, what is the volume of cone *B*?

Write in the answer: _____

8. If the surface area of a cylinder with radius of 4 feet is 48π square feet, what is its volume?

Write in the answer: _____

Answer Key

1. **C) is correct.**

Find the slope of line b, take the negative reciprocal to find the slope of a, and test each point.

$(x_1, y_1) = (-100, 100)$

$(x_2, y_2) = (-95, 115)$

$m_b = \frac{115 - 100}{-95 - (-100)} = \frac{15}{5} = 3$

$m_a = -\frac{1}{3}$

$(104, 168): \frac{100 - 168}{-100 - (104)} = \frac{1}{3}$

$(-95, 115): \frac{100 - 115}{-100 - (-95)} = 3$

$(-112, 104): \frac{100 - 104}{-100 - (-112)} = -\frac{1}{3}$

$(-112, -104): \frac{100 - (-104)}{-100 - (-112)} = 17$

2. **C) is correct.**

Find the measure of each angle.

$m\angle a = 180 - (70 + 40) = 70°$

$m\angle b = 70°$

$m\angle c = 180 - 40 = 140°$

$m\angle d = 40°$

$\angle a \cong \angle b$

3. **C) is correct.**

Use the formula for the volume of a sphere to find its radius.

$V = \frac{4}{3}\pi r^3$

$972\pi = \frac{4}{3}\pi r^3$

$r = 9$

Use the super Pythagorean theorem to find the side of the cube.

$d^2 = a^2 + b^2 + c^2$

$18^2 = 3s^2$

$s \approx 10.4$

Use the length of the side to find the volume of the cube.

$V = s^3$

$V \approx (10.4)^3$

$V \approx \mathbf{1{,}125}$

4. **B) is correct.**

Use the two sets of linear angles to find b and then c.

$a = b$

$a + b + 70 = 180$

$2a + 70 = 180$

$a = b = 55°$

$b + c = 180°$

$55 + c = 180$

$c = \mathbf{125°}$

5. **D) is correct.**

There are an infinite number of points with distance four from the origin, all of which lie on a circle centered at the origin with a radius of 4.

6. **A) is correct.**

A) Corresponding angles in right triangles are not necessarily the same, so they do not have to be similar.

B) All spheres are similar.

C) Corresponding angles in 30–60–90 triangles are the same, so all 30–60–90 triangles are similar.

D) Corresponding angles in a square are all the same (90°), so all squares are similar.

7. **$x = 128\pi$ is correct.**

Set up a proportion. Cube the scale factor when calculating volume.

$$\frac{54\pi}{x} = \frac{3^3}{4^3}$$

$x = 128\pi$

8. **32π ft.³ is correct**

Find the height of the cylinder using the equation for surface area.

$SA = 2\pi rh + 2\pi r^2$

$48\pi = 2\pi(4)h + 2\pi(4)^2$

$h = 2$

Find the volume using the volume equation.

$V = \pi r^2 h$

$V = \pi(4)^2(2) = $ **32π ft.³**

seven

STATISTICS AND PROBABILITY

Describing Sets of Data

Measures of Central Tendency

Measures of central tendency help identify the center, or most typical, value within a data set. There are three such central tendencies that describe the "center" of the data in different ways. The MEAN is the arithmetic average and is found by dividing the sum of all measurements by the number of measurements. The mean of a population is written as μ and the mean of a sample is written as $\bar{x}$.

$$\text{population mean} = \mu = \frac{x_1 + x_2 + ...x_N}{N} = \frac{\Sigma x}{N}$$

$$\text{sample mean} = \bar{x} = \frac{x_1 + x_2 + ...x_n}{n} = \frac{\Sigma x}{n}$$

The data points are represented by x's with subscripts; the sum is denoted using the Greek letter sigma (Σ); N is the number of data points in the entire population; and n is the number of data points in a sample set.

The MEDIAN divides the measurements into two equal halves. The median is the measurement right in the middle of an odd set of measurements or the average of the two middle numbers in an even data set. When calculating the median, it is important to order the data values from least to greatest before attempting to locate the middle value. The MODE is simply the measurement that occurs most often. There can be many modes in a data set, or no mode. Since measures of central tendency describe a *center* of the data, all three of these measures will be between the lowest and highest data values (inclusive).

When the same value is added to each term in a set, the mean increases by that value and the standard deviation is unchanged. When each term in a set is multiplied by the same value, both the mean and standard deviation will also be multiplied by that value.

Unusually large or small values, called OUTLIERS, will affect the mean of a sample more than the mode. If there is a high outlier, the mean will be greater than the median; if there is a low outlier, the mean will be lower than the median. When outliers are present, the median is a better measure of the data's center than the mean because the median will be closer to the terms in the data set.

EXAMPLES

1. What is the mean of the following data set? {1000, 0.1, 10, 1}

   Answer:

   Use the equation to find the mean of a sample:

   $\frac{1000 + 0.1 + 10 + 1}{4}$ = **252.78**

2. What is the median of the following data set? {1000, 10, 1, 0.1}

   Answer:

   Since there are an even number of data points in the set, the median will be the mean of the two middle numbers. Order the numbers from least to greatest: 0.1, 1, 10, and 1000. The two middle numbers are 1 and 10, and their mean is:

   $\frac{1 + 10}{2}$ = **5.5**

3. Josey has an average of 81 on four equally weighted tests she has taken in her statistics class. She wants to determine what grade she must receive on her fifth test so that her mean is 83, which will give her a B in the course, but she does not remember her other scores. What grade must she receive on her fifth test?

   Answer:

   Even though Josey does not know her test scores, she knows her average. Therefore it can be assumed that each test score was 81, since four scores of 81 would average to 81. To find the score, x, that she needs use the equation for the mean of a sample:

   $\frac{4(81) + x}{5}$ = 83

   $324 + x = 415$

   $x = $**91**

Measures of Variation

The values in a data set can be very close together (close to the mean), or very spread out. This is called the SPREAD or DISPERSION of the data. There are a few MEASURES OF VARIATION (or MEASURES OF DISPERSION) that quantify the spread within a data set. RANGE is the difference between the largest and smallest data points in a set:

$$R = \text{largest data point} - \text{smallest data point}$$

Notice range depends on only two data points (the two extremes). Sometimes these data points are outliers; regardless, for a large data set, relying on only two data points is not an exact tool.

The understanding of the data set can be improved by calculating QUARTILES. To calculate quartiles, first arrange the data in ascending order and find the set's median (also called quartile 2 or Q2). Then find the median of the lower half of the data, called quartile 1 (Q1), and the median of the upper half of the data, called quartile 3 (Q3). These three points divide the data into four equal groups of data (thus the word *quartile*). Each quartile contains 25% of the data.

INTERQUARTILE RANGE (**IQR**) provides a more reliable range that is not as affected by extremes. IQR is the difference between the third quartile data point and the first quartile data point and gives the spread of the middle 50% of the data:

$$IQR = Q_3 - Q_1$$

The VARIANCE of a data set is simply the square of the standard variation:

$$V = \sigma^2 = \frac{1}{N} \sum_{i=1}^{N} (x_i - \mu)^2$$

Variance measures how narrowly or widely the data points are distributed. A variance of zero means every data point is the same; a large variance means the data is widely spread out.

EXAMPLES

What are the range and interquartile range of the following set? {3, 9, 49, 64, 81, 100, 121, 144, 169}

Answer:

R = largest point – smallest point = 169 – 3 = **166**	Use the equation for range.
3 9 → Q1 = $\frac{49+9}{2}$ = 29 49 64 81 → Q2 100 121 → Q3 = $\frac{121+144}{2}$ = 132.5 144 169	Place the terms in numerical order and identify Q1, Q2, and Q3.
IQR = Q3 – Q1 = 132.5 – 29 = **103.5**	Find the IQR by subtracting Q1 from Q3.

Graphs, Charts, and Tables

Pie Charts

A pie chart simply states the proportion of each category within the whole. To construct a pie chart, the categories of a data set must be determined. The frequency of each category must be found and that frequency converted to a percent of the total. To draw the pie chart, determine the angle of each slice by multiplying the percentage by 360°.

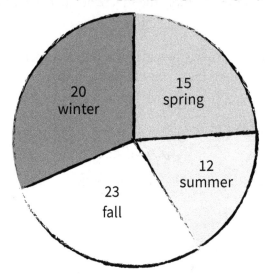

Figure 7.1. Pie Chart

EXAMPLE

A firm is screening applicants for a job by education-level attainment. There are 125 individuals in the pool: 5 have a doctorate, 20 have a master's degree, 40 have a bachelor's degree, 30 have an associate degree, and 30 have a high school degree. Construct a pie chart showing the highest level of education attained by the applicants.

Answer:

Create a frequency table to find the percentages and angle measurement for each category.

Category	Frequency	Percent	Angle Measure
High School	30	24%	86.4
Associate	30	24%	86.4
Bachelor's	40	32%	115.2
Master's	20	16%	57.6
Doctorate	5	4%	14.4

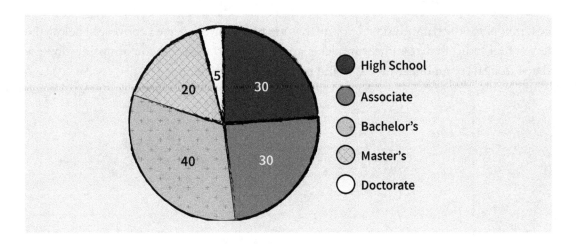

Scatter Plots

A scatter plot is displayed in the first quadrant of the xy-plane where all numbers are positive. Data points are plotted as ordered pairs, with one variable along the horizontal axis and the other along the vertical axis. Scatter plots can show if there is a correlation between two variables. There is a **POSITIVE CORRELATION** (expressed as a positive slope) if increasing one variable appears to result in an increase in the other variable. A **NEGATIVE CORRELATION** (expressed as a negative slope) occurs when an increase in one variable causes a decrease in the other. If the scatter plot shows no discernible pattern, then there is no correlation (a zero, mixed, or indiscernible slope).

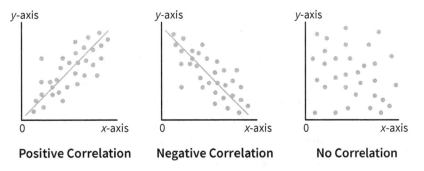

Figure 7.2. Scatter Plots and Correlation

Calculators or other software can be used to find the linear regression equation, which describes the general shape of the data. Graphing this equation produces the regression line, or line of best fit. The equation's **CORRELATION COEFFICIENT** (r) can be used to determine how closely the equation fits the data. The value of r is between –1 and 1. The closer r is to 1 (if the line has a positive slope) or –1 (if the line has a negative slope), the better the regression line fits the data. The closer the r value is to 0, the weaker the correlation between the line and the data. Generally, if the absolute value of the correlation coefficient is 0.8 or higher, then it is considered to be a strong correlation, while an |r| value of less than 0.5 is considered a weak correlation.

To determine which curve is the "best fit" for a set of data, **RESIDUALS** are calculated. The calculator automatically calculates and saves these values to a list called RESID. These values are all the differences between the actual y-value of data points and the y-value calculated by the best-fit line or curve for that x-value. These values can be plotted on an xy-plane to produce a **RESIDUAL PLOT**. The residual plot helps determine if a line is the best model for the data. Residual points that are randomly dispersed above and below the horizontal indicate that a linear model is appropriate, while a *u* shape or upside-down *u* shape indicate a nonlinear model would be more appropriate.

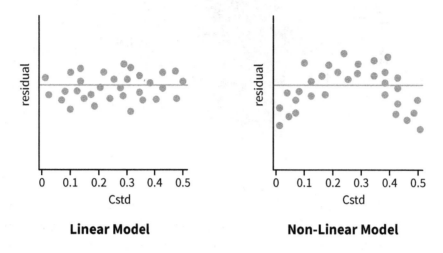

Figure 7.3. Residual Plots

Once a best-fit line is established, it can be used to estimate output values given an input value within the domain of the data. For a short extension outside that domain, reasonable predictions may be possible. However, the further from the domain of the data the line is extended, the greater the reduction in the accuracy of the prediction.

It is important to note here that just because two variables have a strong positive or negative correlation, it cannot necessarily be inferred that those two quantities have a *causal* relationship—that is, that one variable changing *causes* the other quantity to change. There are often other factors that play into their relationship. For example, a positive correlation can be found between the number of ice cream sales and the number of shark attacks at a beach. It would be incorrect to say that selling more ice cream *causes* an increase in shark attacks. It is much more likely that on hot days more ice cream is sold, and many more people are swimming, so one of them is more likely to get attacked by a shark. Confusing correlation and causation is one of the most common statistical errors people make.

A graphing calculator can provide the regression line, *r* value, and residuals list.

EXAMPLE

Based on the scatter plot on the following page, where the *x*-axis represents hours spent studying per week and the *y*-axis represents the average percent grade on exams during the school year, is there a correlation between the amount of studying for a test and test results?

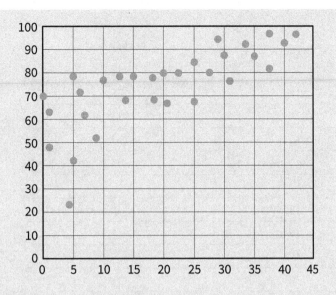

Answer:

There is a somewhat weak positive correlation. As the number of hours spent studying increases, the average percent grade also generally increases.

Line Graphs

Line graphs are used to display a relationship between two variables, such as change over time. Like scatter plots, line graphs exist in quadrant I of the *xy*-plane. Line graphs are constructed by graphing each point and connecting each point to the next consecutive point by a line. To create a line graph, it may be necessary to consolidate data into single bivariate data points. Thus, a line graph is a function, with each *x*-value having exactly one *y*-value, whereas a scatter plot may have multiple *y*-values for one *x*-value.

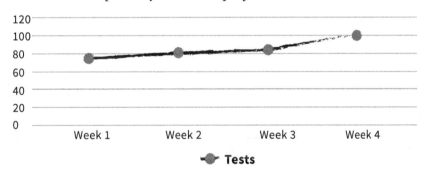

Figure 7.4. Line Graph

EXAMPLE

Create a line graph based on the following survey values, where the first column represents an individual's age and the other represents that individual's reported happiness level on a 20-point scale (0 being the least happy that person has been and 20 being the happiest). Then interpret the resulting graph to determine whether the following statement is true or false: *On average, middle-aged people are less happy than young or older people are.*

AGE	HAPPINESS
12	16
13	15
20	18
15	12
40	5
17	17
18	18
19	15
42	7
70	17
45	10
60	12
63	15
22	14
27	15
33	10
44	8
55	10
80	10
15	13
40	8
17	15
18	17
19	20
22	16
27	15
36	9
33	10
44	6

Answer:

To construct a line graph, the data must be ordered into consolidated categories by averaging the data of people who have the same age so that the data is one-to-one. For example, there are 2 twenty-two-year-olds who are reporting. Their average happiness level is 15. When all the data has been consolidated and ordered from least to greatest, the table and graph below can be presented.

Age	Happiness
12	16
13	15
15	12.5
17	16
18	17.5
19	17.5
20	18
22	15
27	15
33	10
36	10.5
40	6.5
42	7
44	7
45	10
55	10
60	12
63	15
70	17
80	10

Average Happiness Rating Versus Age

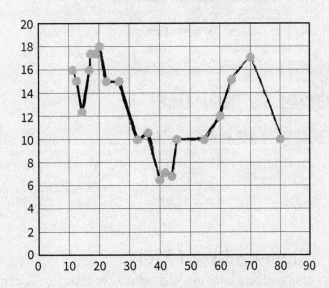

The statement that, on average, middle-aged people are less happy than young or older people appears to be true. According to the graph, people in their thirties, forties, and fifties are less happy than people in their teens, twenties, sixties, and seventies.

Bar Graphs

Bar graphs compare differences between categories or changes over a time. The data is grouped into categories or ranges and represented by rectangles. A bar graph's rectangles can be vertical or horizontal, depending on whether the dependent variable is placed on the *x*- or *y*-axis. Instead of the *xy*-plane, however, one axis is made up of categories (or ranges) instead of a numeric scale. Bar graphs are useful because the differences between categories are easy to see: the height or length of each bar shows the value for each category.

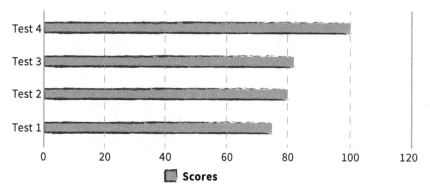

Figure 7.5. Bar Graph

EXAMPLE

A company X had a profit of $10,000 in 2010, $12,000 in 2011, $15,600 in 2012, and $20,280 in 2013. Create a bar graph displaying the profit from each of these four years.

Answer:

Place years on the independent axis, and profit on the dependent axis, and then draw a box showing the profit for each year.

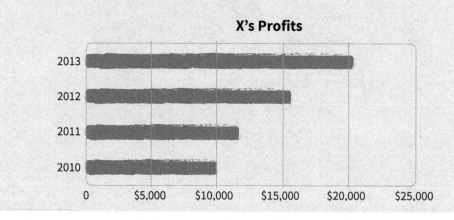

Stem-and-Leaf Plots

Stem-and-leaf plots are ways of organizing large amounts of data by grouping it into classes. All data points are broken into two parts: a stem and a leaf. For instance, the number 512 might be broken into a stem of 5 and a leaf of 12. All data in the 500 range would appear in the same row (this group of data is a class). Usually a simple key is provided to explain how the data is being represented. For instance, 5|12 = 512 would show that the stems are representing hundreds. The advantage of this display is that it shows general density and shape of the data in a compact display, yet all original data points are preserved and available. It is also easy to find medians and quartiles from this display.

STEM	LEAF
0	5
1	6, 7
2	8, 3, 6
3	4, 5, 9, 5, 5, 8, 5
4	7, 7, 7, 8
5	5, 4
6	0

Figure 7.6. Stem and Leaf Plot

EXAMPLE

The table gives the weights of wrestlers (in pounds) for a certain competition. What is the mean, median, and IQR of the data?

2	05, 22, 53, 40
3	07, 22, 29, 45, 89, 96, 98
4	10, 25, 34
6	21

Key: 2|05 = 205 pounds

Answer:

$\mu = \frac{\Sigma x}{N}$ $= \frac{5281}{15}$ **= 353.1 lbs.**	Find the mean using the equation for the population mean.
Q1 = 253 Q2 = 345 Q3 = 410 IQR = 410 − 253 = 157 **The median is 345 lbs.** **The IQR is 157 lbs.**	Find the median and IQR by counting the leaves and identifying Q1, Q2, and Q3.

Frequency Tables and Histograms

The frequency of a particular data point is the number of times that data point occurs. Constructing a frequency table requires that the data or data classes be arranged in ascending order in one column and the frequency in another column.

A histogram is a graphical representation of a frequency table used to compare frequencies. A histogram is constructed in quadrant I of the *xy*-plane, with data in each equal-width class presented as a bar and the height of each bar representing the frequency of that class. Unlike bar graphs, histograms cannot have gaps between bars. A histogram is used to determine the distribution of data among the classes.

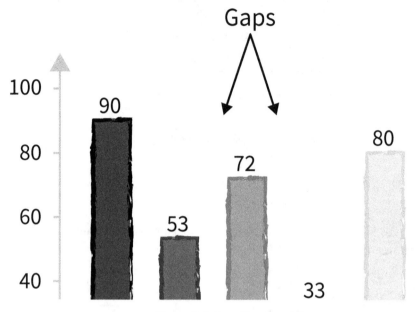

Figure 7.7. Bar Chart vs. Histogram

Histograms can be symmetrical, skewed left or right, or multimodal (data spread around). Note that SKEWED LEFT means the peak of the data is on the *right*, with a tail to the left, while SKEWED RIGHT means the peak is on the *left*, with a tail to the right. This seems counterintuitive to many; the "left" or "right" always refers to the tail of the data. This is because a long tail to the right, for example, means there are high outlier values that are skewing the data to the right.

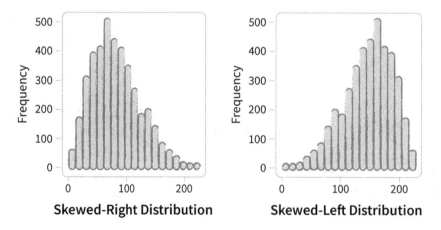

Figure 7.8. Histrograms

A TWO-WAY FREQUENCY TABLE compares CATEGORICAL DATA (data in more than one category) of two related variables (bivariate data). Two-way frequency tables are also called CONTINGENCY TABLES and are often used to analyze survey results. One category is displayed along the top of the table and the other category down along the side. Rows and columns are added and the sums appear at the end of the row or column. The sum of all the row data must equal the sum of all the column data.

From a two-way frequency table, the JOINT RELATIVE FREQUENCY of a particular category can be calculated by taking the number in the row and column of the categories in question and dividing by the total number surveyed. This gives the percent of the total in that particular category. Sometimes the CONDITIONAL RELATIVE FREQUENCY is of interest. In this case, calculate the relative frequency confined to a single row or column.

Students by Grade and Gender

	9TH GRADE	10TH GRADE	11TH GRADE	12TH GRADE	TOTAL
Male	57	63	75	61	256
Female	54	42	71	60	227
Total	111	105	146	121	483

Figure 7.9. Two-Way Frequency Table

EXAMPLES

1. Cineflix movie theater polled its moviegoers on a weeknight to determine their favorite type of movie. The results are in the two-way frequency table below.

MOVIEGOERS	COMEDY	ACTION	HORROR	TOTALS
Male	15	24	21	60
Female	8	18	17	43
Totals	23	42	38	103

Determine whether each of the following statements is true or false.

A) Action films are the most popular type of movie

B) About 1 in 5 moviegoers prefers comedy films

C) Men choose the horror genre more frequently than women do

Answer:

A) **True.** More people (42) chose action movies than comedy (23) or horror (38).

B) **True.** Find the ratio of total number of people who prefer comedy to total number of people. $\frac{23}{103}$ = 0.22; 1 in 5 is 20%, so 22% is about the same.

C) **False.** The percentage of men who choose horror is less than the percentage of women who do.

part = number of men who prefer horror =21

whole = number of men surveyed = 60

percent = $\frac{part}{whole}$

= $\frac{21}{60}$ = 0.35 = 35%

part = number of women who prefer horror =17

whole = number of women surveyed = 43

percent = $\frac{part}{whole}$

= $\frac{17}{43}$ = 0.40 = 40%

2. A café owner tracked the number of customers he had over a twelve-hour period in the following frequency table. Display the data in a histogram and determine what kind of distribution there is in the data.

TIME	NUMBER OF CUSTOMERS
6 a.m. – 8 a.m.	5
8 a.m. – 9 a.m.	6
9 a.m. – 10 a.m.	5
10 a.m. – 12 p.m.	23
12 p.m. – 2 p.m.	24
2 p.m. – 4 p.m.	9
4 p.m. – 6 p.m.	4

Answer:

Since time is the independent variable, it is on the *x*-axis and the number of customers is on the *y*-axis. For the histogram to correctly display data continuously, categories on the *x*-axis must be equal 2-hour segments. The 8 a.m. – 9 a.m. and 9 a.m. – 10 a.m. categories must be combined for a total of 11 customers in that time period. Although not perfectly symmetrical, the amount of customers peaks in the middle and is therefore considered symmetrical.

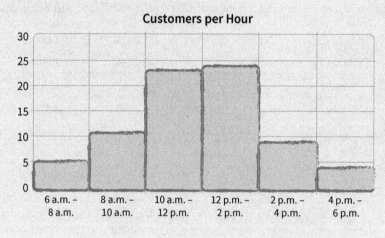

Probability

Probability describes how likely something is to happen. In probability, an **EVENT** is the single result of a trial, and an **OUTCOME** is a possible event that results from a trial. The collection of all possible outcomes for a particular trial is called the **SAMPLE SPACE**. For example, when rolling a die, the sample space is the numbers 1 – 6. Rolling a single number, such as 4, would be a single event.

Counting Principles

Counting principles are methods used to find the number of possible outcomes for a given situation. The **FUNDAMENTAL COUNTING PRINCIPLE** states that, for a series of independent events, the number of outcomes can be found by multiplying the number of possible outcomes for each event. For example, if a die is rolled (6 possible outcomes) and a coin is tossed (2 possible outcomes), there are 6 × 2 = 12 total possible outcomes.

Combinations and permutations describe how many ways a number of objects taken from a group can be arranged. The number of objects in the group is written n, and the number of objects to be arranged is represented by r (or k). In a **COMBINATION**, the order of the selections does not matter because every available slot to be filled is the same. Examples of combinations include:

- picking 3 people from a group of 12 to form a committee (220 possible committees)
- picking 3 pizza toppings from 10 options (120 possible pizzas)

Figure 7.10. Fundamental Counting Principle

In a **PERMUTATION**, the order of the selection matters, meaning each available slot is different. Examples of permutations include:

- handing out gold, silver, and bronze medals in a race with 100 participants (970,200 possible combinations)
- selecting a president, vice-president, secretary, and treasurer from among a committee of 12 people (11,880 possible combinations)

The formulas for the both calculations are similar. The only difference—the $r!$ in the denominator of a combination—accounts for redundant outcomes. Note that both permutations and combinations can be written in several different shortened notations.

$$\text{Permutation: } P(n, r) = {}_nP_r = \frac{n!}{(n - r)!}$$

$$\text{Combination: } C(n, r) = {}_nC_r = \left(\frac{n}{r}\right) = \frac{n!}{(n - r)!r!}$$

EXAMPLES

1. A personal assistant is struggling to pick a shirt, tie, and cufflink set that go together. If his client has 70 shirts, 2 ties, and 5 cufflinks, how many possible combinations does he have to consider?

   Answer:

   Multiply the number of outcomes for each individual event:

   $(70)(2)(5) = $ **700 outfits**

2. If there are 20 applicants for 3 open positions, in how many different ways can a team of 3 be hired?

   Answer:

   The order of the items doesn't matter, so use the formula for combinations:

   $C(n, r) = \frac{n!}{(n - r)!r!}$

   $C(20, 3) = \frac{20!}{(20 - 3)!3!}$

   $= \frac{20!}{(17! \, 3!)}$

   $= \frac{(20)(19)(18)}{3!} = $ **1140 possible teams**

3. Calculate the number of unique permutations that can be made with five of the letters in the word *pickle*.

Answer:

To find the number of unique permutations of 5 letters in pickle, use the permutation formula:

$$P(n, r) = \frac{n!}{(n-r)!}$$

$$P(6, 5) = \frac{6!}{(6-5)!}$$

$$= \frac{720}{1} = \mathbf{720}$$

4. Find the number of permutations that can be made out of all the letters in the word *cheese*.

Answer:

The letter *e* repeats 3 times in the word *cheese*, meaning some permutations of the 6 letters will be indistinguishable from others. The number of permutations must be divided by the number of ways the three *e*'s can be arranged to account for these redundant outcomes:

$$\text{total number of permutations} = \frac{\text{number of ways of arranging 6 letters}}{\text{number of ways of arranging 3 letters}} = \frac{6!}{3!} = 6 \times 5 \times 4 = \mathbf{120}$$

Probability of a Single Event

The probability of a single event occurring is the number of outcomes in which that event occurs (called FAVORABLE EVENTS) divided by the number of items in the sample space (total possible outcomes):

$$P \text{ (an event)} = \frac{\text{number of favorable outcomes}}{\text{total number of possible outcomes}}$$

The probability of any event occurring will always be a fraction or decimal between 0 and 1. It may also be expressed as a percent. An event with 0 probability will never occur and an event with a probability of 1 is certain to occur. The probability of an event not occurring is referred to as that event's COMPLEMENT. The sum of an event's probability and the probability of that event's complement will always be 1.

EXAMPLES

1. What is the probability that an even number results when a six-sided die is rolled? What is the probability the die lands on 5?

Answer:

$$P(\text{rolling even}) = \frac{\text{number of favorable outcomes}}{\text{total number of possible outcomes}} = \frac{3}{6} = \frac{1}{2}$$

$$P(\text{rolling 5}) = \frac{\text{number of favorable outcomes}}{\text{total number of possible outcomes}} = \mathbf{\frac{1}{6}}$$

2. Only 20 tickets were issued in a raffle. If someone were to buy 6 tickets, what is the probability that person would not win the raffle?

Answer:

$$P(\text{not winning}) = \frac{\text{number of favorable outcomes}}{\text{total number of possible outcomes}} = \frac{14}{20} = \frac{7}{10}$$

or

$P(not\ winning) = 1 - P(winning) = 1 - \frac{6}{20} = \frac{14}{20} = \frac{7}{10}$

3. A bag contains 26 tiles representing the 26 letters of the English alphabet. If 3 tiles are drawn from the bag without replacement, what is the probability that all 3 will be consonants?

Answer:

$P = \dfrac{number\ of\ favorable\ outcomes}{total\ number\ of\ possible\ outcomes}$

$= \dfrac{number\ of\ 3\text{-}consonant\ combinations}{number\ of\ 3\text{-}tile\ combinations}$

$= \dfrac{{}_{21}C_3}{{}_{26}C_3}$

$= \dfrac{1330}{2600}$

$= 0.51 = \mathbf{51\%}$

Test Your Knowledge

Use the following graph for questions 1 and 2.

Number of Months with 3 or Fewer Than 3 Inches of Rain

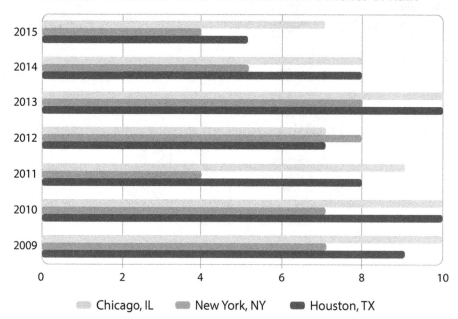

Chicago, IL   New York, NY   Houston, TX

1. New York had the fewest months with less than 3 inches of rain in every year except:

   A) 2012

   B) 2013

   C) 2014

   D) 2015

2. From 2009 to 2015, what is the average number of months that Chicago had 3 or less inches of rain?

   A) 6

   B) 7

   C) 8

   D) 9

3. What is the relationship between the mean and the median in a data set that is skewed right?

   A) The mean is greater than the median.

   B) The mean is less than the median.

   C) The mean and median are equal.

   D) The mean may be greater than, less than, or equal to the median.

4. A bag contains 6 blue, 8 silver, and 4 green marbles. Two marbles are drawn from the bag. What is the probability that the second marble drawn will be green if replacement is not allowed?

   A) $\frac{2}{9}$

   B) $\frac{4}{17}$

   C) $\frac{11}{17}$

   D) $\frac{7}{9}$

5. A pair of 6-sided dice is rolled 10 times. What is the probability that in exactly 3 of those rolls, the sum of the dice will be 5?

A) 0.14%

B) 7.2%

C) 11.1%

D) 60%

6. A restaurant offers burritos on a corn or a flour tortilla, 5 types of meat, 6 types of cheese, and 3 different toppings. When ordering, customers can choose 1 type of tortilla, 1 meat, and 1 cheese. They can then add any of the 3 toppings. How many different burrito combinations are possible?

Write in the answer: _____

7. How many unique ways can the letters in the word *FOGGIER* be arranged?

Write in the answer: _____

8. The mean of 13 numbers is 30. The mean of 8 of these numbers is 42. What is the mean of the other 5 numbers?

Write in the answer: _____

Answer Key

1. **A) is correct.**

   In 2012, New York had more months with less than 3 inches of rain than either Chicago or Houston.

2. **D) is correct.**

   Use the graph to find the number of months Chicago had less than 3 inches of rain year, and then find the average.

   months with < 3 inches rain in Chicago: {7, 8, 10, 7, 9, 10, 10}

   $$\frac{(7 + 8 + 10 + 7 + 9 + 10 + 10)}{7} = 8.7 \approx \mathbf{9}$$

3. **A) is correct.**

   If the data is skewed right, the set includes extremes values that are to the right, or high. The median is unaffected by these high values, but the mean includes these high values and would therefore be greater.

4. **A) is correct.**

   Find the probability that the second marble will be green if the first marble is blue, silver, or green, and then add these probabilities together.

   P(first blue and second green) = P(blue) × P(green|first blue) = $\frac{6}{18} \times \frac{4}{17} = \frac{4}{51}$

   P(first silver and second green) = P(silver) × P(green|first silver) = $\frac{8}{18} \times \frac{4}{17} = \frac{16}{153}$

   P(first green and second green) = P(green) × P(green|first green) = $\frac{4}{18} \times \frac{3}{17} = \frac{2}{51}$

   P(second green) = $\frac{4}{51} + \frac{16}{153} + \frac{2}{51}$
   = $\frac{2}{9}$

5. **B) is correct**

   Use the equation for Bernoulli trials (binomial distribution).

   $P = {}_nC_r(p^r)(q^{n-r})$

   $n = 10$

   $r = 3$

   $p = \frac{4}{36} = \frac{1}{9}$

   $q = \frac{8}{9}$

   $P = {}_{10}C_3\left(\frac{1}{9}\right)^3\left(\frac{8}{9}\right)^7 = 0.072 = \mathbf{7.2\%}$

6. **480 is correct.**

   Use the fundamental counting principle. Each topping has two possible choices (yes or no).

   $2(5)(6)(2)(2)(2) = \mathbf{480}$

7. **2520 is correct.**

   Use the fundamental counting principle to find the number of ways the letters can be arranged. Because the two G's are indistinguishable, divide by the number of ways those 2 letters can be arranged.

   $\frac{7!}{2!} = (7)(6)(5)(4)(3) = \mathbf{2520}$

8. **10.8 is correct.**

   Find the sum of the 13 numbers whose mean is 30.

   $13 \times 30 = 390$

   Find the sum of the 8 numbers whose mean is 42.

   $8 \times 42 = 336$

   Find the sum and mean of the remaining 5 numbers.

   $390 - 336 = 54$

   $\frac{54}{5} = \mathbf{10.8}$

Follow the link below for your second Mathematics GED practice test:
www.acceptedinc.com/ged-2018-online-resources

PART III: SCIENCE

eight

SCIENTIFIC PRACTICES

Scientific Inquiry

Science is defined simply as the study of the natural world. Although there are many disciplines within science, all scientific understanding is reached using a systematic gathering of observations and evidence. The investigations scientists use to gather this information can be descriptive, comparative, or experimental in nature. Once scientists conduct investigations using a range of methods and technology, they can begin to form explanations about natural phenomena. Over time, these explanations are collected in the general body of scientific knowledge and are used to form laws, or generalizations of the natural world, and theories, or explanations of laws.

SCIENTIFIC INQUIRY is defined as the myriad ways in which scientists conduct their studies and form explanations. There is no one set path that all scientists must follow, but the SCIENTIFIC METHOD provides a general framework for conducting scientific inquiry. The scientific method has five steps:

1. FORM A QUESTION.

   OBSERVATIONS about the natural world lead to questions about how or why the observed actions occur. The scientist should also do RESEARCH on current knowledge of the topic in the scientific community. Together, observations and research can be used to create a question to be answered.

2. FORM A HYPOTHESIS.

   A proposed explanation of natural phenomena is also known as a HYPOTHESIS. A hypothesis consists of more than an educated guess; it is a testable proposition that scientists use as the basis for an investigation. If a proposition cannot be tested scientifically, it is not a hypothesis.

3. CONDUCT AN EXPERIMENT.

   The next step is to design and conduct an experiment that tests the hypothesis. A scientific investigation contains an EXPERIMENTAL VARIABLE, which scientists can manipulate during the course of the investigation, and EXPERI-MENTAL CONTROLS, which are variables that are kept constant.

4. **COLLECT AND ANALYZE DATA.**

   Data should be collected during the experiment. This data can then be analyzed to look for statistically valid relationships and patterns.

5. **DRAW A CONCLUSION.**

   Finally, experimental data is used to draw conclusions about the hypothesis. The hypothesis may be proven false, or the data may support the hypothesis.

EXAMPLE

Which of the following best defines a hypothesis?

A) an educated guess

B) a study of the natural world

C) an explanation of natural phenomena

D) a testable proposed scientific explanation

Answer:

D) is correct. A hypothesis must be testable and propose an explanation of observed natural phenomena.

Designing Experiments

Scientists use a rigorous set of rules to design experiments. The protocols of EXPERIMENTAL DESIGN are meant to ensure that scientists are actually testing what they set out to test. A well-designed experiment will measure the impact of a single factor on a system, thus allowing the experimenter to draw conclusions about that factor.

Every experiment includes variables—the factors or treatments that may affect the outcome of the experiment. INDEPENDENT VARIABLES are controlled by the experimenter. They are usually the factors the experimenter has hypothesized will have an effect on the system. Often, a design will include a treatment group and a CONTROL GROUP, which does not receive the treatment. The DEPENDENT VARIABLES are factors that are influenced by the independent variable.

For example, in an experiment investigating which type of fertilizer has the greatest effect on plant growth, the independent variable is the type of fertilizer used. The scientist is controlling, or manipulating, the type of fertilizer. The dependent variable is plant growth because the amount of plant growth depends on the type of fertilizer. The type of plant, the amount of water, and the amount of sunlight the plants receive are controls because those variables of the experiment are kept the same for each plant.

Reproducibility is an essential feature of a scientific finding. Under the same conditions and using the same experimental methods, multiple researchers should be able to produce identical results.

When designing an experiment, scientists must identify possible sources of EXPERIMENTAL ERROR. These can be

CONFOUNDING VARIABLES—factors that act much like the independent variable and thus can make it appear that the independent variable has a greater effect than it actually does. The design may also include unknown variables that are not controlled by the scientists. Finally, scientists must be aware of HUMAN ERROR, particularly in collecting data and making observations, and of possible equipment errors.

EXAMPLE

A chemistry student is conducting an experiment in which she tests the relationship between reactant concentration and heat produced by a reaction. In her experiment, she alters the reactant concentration and measures heat produced. The independent variable in the experiment is the

A) reactant concentration.

B) reaction rate.

C) amount of heat produced by the reaction.

D) product concentration.

Answer:

A) is correct. The independent variable is deliberately changed in the course of the experiment. Here, the student is changing the reactant concentration. The heat produced is the dependent variable.

Facts, Theories, and Laws

Scientific facts, *theories*, and *laws* are terms with specific, distinct definitions. SCIENTIFIC FACTS are objective observations that have been repeatedly confirmed by DATA collected by multiple scientific INVESTIGATIONS. Facts are generally accepted as truth, but they are never considered final proof. Facts are the observations themselves, rather than the explanations for a natural phenomenon.

Explanations of natural phenomena are the realm of hypotheses and theories. Hypotheses, as earlier defined, are proposed testable explanations of natural phenomena. In order to be testable, a hypothesis must contain specific observations researchers could expect to see if the hypothesis were confirmed. Hypotheses that are tested and confirmed time and time again could eventually accumulate enough data to be considered a THEORY. A theory is a well-founded explanation that is supported by large amounts of data and incorporates multiple sources of evidence. Unlike the everyday definition of *theory*, which suggests just an idea, a scientific theory is widely accepted as a valid explanation of phenomena.

Unlike theories, which are *explanations* of phenomena, scientific LAWS are a generalized *description* of natural phenomena based on multiple observations over time. Laws are distinguished from facts by their durability—or ability to stay constant over time—and their predictive nature. If multiple investigations are run under the exact same conditions over and over, the new observations will conform to the scientific law. If results are not as predicted, then the law can be modified and narrowed to incorporate the new information.

EXAMPLE

Why is the germ theory of disease considered to be a theory?

A) There is insufficient evidence to support it.

B) Valid alternative explanations exist.

C) It is strongly supported by existing evidence.

D) It has only limited clinical application.

Answer:

C) is correct. A scientific theory is typically strongly supported by evidence, despite public misunderstanding to the contrary.

Test Your Knowledge

Read the question, and then choose the most correct answer.

1. Which of the following is the first step of the scientific method?

   A) construct a hypothesis

   B) make observations

   C) analyze data

   D) form a question

2. A woman has been suffering from heartburn and thinks that a particular food is causing it. She decides that for each week during a single month, she will not eat a specific food and see if she has heartburn that week. In her experiment, the food she removes from her diet would be which of the following types of variable?

   A) controlled variable

   B) dependent variable

   C) independent variable

   D) experimental variable

3. A scientist discovers a new species of snail that lives in the ocean. He tested the ability of this species to handle heat by measuring its growth rate as he increased the temperature of the water. He also tested two different concentrations of salt to determine which type of marine environment the snail would be best suited for.
   Which of the following is the dependent variable in the experiments described above?

   A) salt concentration

   B) temperature

   C) growth rate

   D) number of snails

4. Which of the following types of variables is changed in a scientific experiment?

   A) controlled variable

   B) measured variable

   C) dependent variable

   D) independent variable

5. A chemist plans to determine the concentration of the acid by performing an acid–base titration reaction. To perform this reaction, he adds a known volume and concentration of strong base to the acid while measuring the pH of the combined acid and base. Once a neutral pH is obtained, the reaction has proceeded to completion and the concentration of the acid may be calculated. In this reaction, what is the dependent variable?

   A) the acid concentration

   B) the volume of base added to reach reaction completion

   C) the concentration of the base

   D) the pH of the reaction mixture

6. Which of the following is an example of human error in an experiment?

   A) an imperfectly calibrated scale

   B) contaminating a sterile sample by breathing on it

   C) a draft in the laboratory slightly changing the temperature of a liquid

   D) failure to account for wind speed when measuring distance traveled

7. A chemist hypothesizes that elevating the temperature of the reaction vessel will increase the mass of product produced during a reaction. He conducts experiments to test this hypothesis and finds that the mass of product remains constant regardless of the temperature of reaction. He later discovers that the balance used to determine the masses of the product samples was calibrated incorrectly. What step should the chemist take next?

A) He should repeat the experiment because his data is flawed.

B) The calibration of the scale identically affected each sample, so he can ignore the error.

C) He should repeat the experiment using a different reaction vessel.

D) He should estimate the true product masses based on the calibration of the balance.

8. Which of the following is a description of a natural phenomenon based on multiple observations?

A) law

B) theory

C) model

D) hypothesis

GO ON

Answer Key

1. **B) is correct.**

Making observations is the first step of the scientific method; observations enable the researcher to form a question and begin the research process.

2. **C) is correct.**

The independent variable is the single variable that is altered during an experiment. The woman is altering her diet to see if her heartburn (the dependent variable) is affected.

3. **C) is correct.**

The growth rate is the variable that is dependent on the changes to water temperature and concentration of salt in the water.

4. **D) is correct.**

The independent variable is changed by the researcher during an experiment; this change may or may not cause a direct change in the dependent variable.

5. **D) is correct.**

The dependent variable is the variable that is directly measured or observed in the course of the experiment. In the case of this reaction, pH is directly measured.

6. **B) is correct.**

Contaminating a sample by breathing on it is an example of human error, or error that occurs when the researcher makes a mistake.

7. **A) is correct.**

The mass data collected cannot be trusted, and the experiments should be repeated and the data collected with a properly calibrated balance.

8. **A) is correct.**

Scientific laws, like Newton's laws of gravity or Mendel's laws of heredity, describe phenomena in the natural world that have repeatedly occurred with no known exceptions.

nine

LIFE SCIENCE

Biological Molecules

Molecules that contain carbon bound to hydrogen are ORGANIC MOLECULES. Large organic molecules that contain many atoms and repeating units are MACROMOLECULES. Many macromolecules are POLYMERS composed of repeating small units called MONOMERS. There are four basic biological macromolecules that are common between all organisms: carbohydrates, lipids, proteins, and nucleic acids.

CARBOHYDRATES, also called sugars, are polymers made of carbon, hydrogen, and oxygen atoms. The monomer for carbohydrates are MONOSACCHARIDES, such as glucose and fructose, that combine to form more complex sugars called POLYSACCHARIDES. Carbohydrates store energy and provide support to cellular structures.

LIPIDS, commonly known as fats, are composed mainly of hydrogen and carbon. They serve a number of functions depending on their particular structure: they make up the membrane of cells and can act as fuel, as steroids, and as hormones. Lipids are hydrophobic, meaning they repel water.

PROTEINS serve an incredibly wide variety of purposes within the body. As enzymes, they play key roles in important processes like DNA replication, cellular division, and cellular metabolism. Structural proteins provide rigidity to cartilage, hair, nails, and the cytoskeletons (the network of molecules that holds the parts of a cell in place). They are also involved in communication between cells and in the transportation of molecules.

An **enzyme** is a protein that accelerates a specific chemical reaction.

Proteins are composed of individual AMINO ACIDS, which are joined together by peptide bonds to form POLYPEPTIDES. There are twenty amino acids, and the order of the amino acids in the polypeptide determines the shape and function of the molecule.

NUCLEIC ACIDS store hereditary information and are composed of monomers called NUCLEOTIDES. Each nucleotide includes a sugar, a phosphate group, and a nitrogenous base.

There are two types of nucleic acids. DEOXYRIBONUCLEIC ACID (DNA) contains the genetic instructions to produce proteins. It is composed of two strings of nucleotides wound into a double helix shape. The "backbone" of the helix is made from the nucleotide's sugar (deoxyribose) and phosphate groups. The "rungs" of the ladder are made from one of four nitrogenous bases: adenine, thymine, cytosine, and guanine. These bases bond together in specific pairs: adenine with thymine and cytosine with guanine.

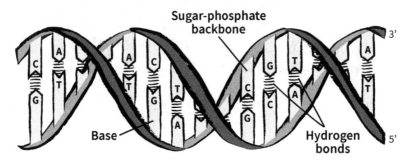

Figure 9.1. The Structure of DNA

RIBONUCLEIC ACID (RNA) transcribes information from DNA and plays several vital roles in the replication of DNA and the manufacturing of proteins. RNA nucleotides contain a sugar (ribose), a phosphate group, and one of four nitrogenous bases: adenine, uracil, cytosine, and guanine. It is usually found as a single-stranded molecule. There are three main differences between DNA and RNA:

1. DNA contains the nucleotide thymine; RNA contains the nucleotide uracil.

2. DNA is double-stranded; RNA is single-stranded.

3. DNA is made from the sugar deoxyribose; RNA is made from the sugar ribose.

EXAMPLES

1. Macromolecules are formed from small subunits called monomers. Which of the following are the monomers that make up a protein?

    A) monosaccharides

    B) nucleotides

    C) amino acids

    D) polypeptides

    Answer:

    C) is correct. Amino acid monomers are the building blocks of proteins.

2. Which of the following is NOT true of RNA?

    A) Hydrogen bonds form between A – T and G – C bases.

    B) A sequence of RNA will not contain T bases but will contain U bases.

    C) RNA is single-stranded.

    D) RNA stores genetic information.

Nucleic Acids

DNA stores information by coding for proteins using blocks of three nucleotides called CODONS. Each codon codes for a specific amino acid; together, all the codons needed to make a specific protein are called a GENE. In addition to codons for specific amino acids, there are also codons that signal "start" and "stop."

The production of a protein starts with TRANSCRIPTION. During transcription, the two sides of the DNA helix unwind and a complementary strand of messenger RNA (mRNA) is manufactured using the DNA as a template.

This mRNA then travels outside the nucleus where it is "read" by a ribosome during TRANSLATION. Each codon on the mRNA is matched to an anti-codon on a strand of tRNA, which carries a specific amino acid. The amino acids bond as they are lined up next to each other, forming a polypeptide.

When it is not being transcribed, DNA is tightly wound around proteins called HISTONES to create NUCLEOSOMES, which are in turn packaged into CHROMATIN. The structure of chromatin allows large amounts of DNA to be stored in a very small space and helps regulate transcription by controlling access to specific sections of DNA. Tightly folding the DNA also helps prevent damage to the genetic code. Chromatin is further bundled into packages of DNA called CHROMOSOMES. During cell division, DNA is replicated to create two identical copies of each chromosome called CHROMATIDS.

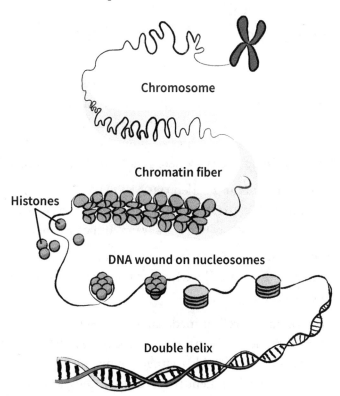

Figure 9.2. DNA, Chromatin, and Chromosomes

Somatic (body) cells are DIPLOID, meaning they carry two copies of each chromosome—one inherited from each parent. Gametes, which are reproductive cells, are HAPLOID and carry only one copy of each chromosome. Human somatic cells have forty-six chromosomes, while human egg and sperm each carry twenty-three chromosomes.

A MUTATION causes a change in the sequence of nucleotides within DNA. For example, the codon GAC codes for the amino acid aspartic acid. However, if the cytosine is swapped for adenine, the codon now reads GAA, which corresponds to the amino acid glutamic acid. Germ-line mutations, or mutations that occur in a cell that will become a gamete, can be passed on to the offspring of an organism. Somatic mutations cannot be passed on to the offspring of an organism.

EXAMPLE

Which of the following processes uses the information stored in RNA to produce a protein?

A) replication

B) translation

C) transcription

D) mutation

Answer:

B) is correct. Translation is the process of matching codons in RNA to the correct anti-codon to manufacture a protein.

Structure and Function of Cells

A CELL is the smallest unit of life that can reproduce on its own. Unicellular organisms, such as amoebae, are made up of only one cell, while multicellular organisms are comprised of many cells. There are two basic types of cells: prokaryotic and eukaryotic. PROKARYOTIC CELLS, which include most bacteria, do not have a nucleus. The DNA in a prokaryotic cell is carried in the CYTOPLASM, which is the fluid that makes up the volume of the cell. EUKARYOTIC CELLS contain a nucleus where genetic material is stored.

Cells contain smaller structures called ORGANELLES that perform specific functions within the cell. These include MITOCHONDRIA, which produce energy; RIBOSOMES, which produce proteins; and VACUOLES, which store water and other molecules.

Plant cells include a number of structures not found in animal cells. These include the CELL WALL, which provides the cell with a hard outer structure, and CHLOROPLASTS, where photosynthesis occurs.

The outer surface of human cells is made up of a PLASMA MEMBRANE, which gives the cell its shape. This membrane is primarily composed of a PHOSPHOLIPID BILAYER, which itself is made up of two layers of lipids that face opposing directions. This functions to separate the inner cellular environment from the extracellular space, the space between cells. Molecules travel through the cell membrane using a number of different methods:

- **DIFFUSION** occurs when molecules pass through the membrane from areas of high to low concentration.
- **FACILITATED DIFFUSION** occurs with the assistance of proteins embedded in the membrane.
- **OSMOSIS** is the movement of water from areas of high to low concentration.
- During **ACTIVE TRANSPORT,** proteins in the membrane use energy (in the form of ATP) to move molecules across the membrane.

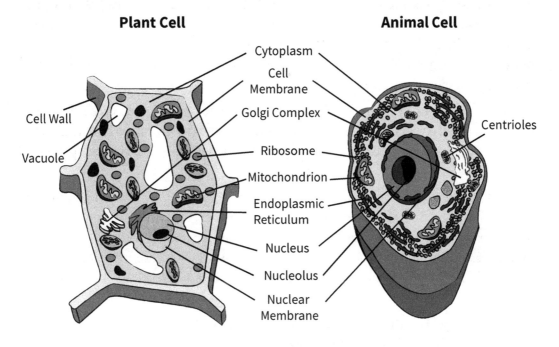

Figure 9.3. Cell Organelles

EXAMPLES

1. Which of the following structures produces proteins and is found in both prokaryotic and eukaryotic cells?

   A) nucleus

   B) chloroplast

   C) ribosome

   D) vacuole

   Answer:

   C) is correct. Ribosomes consist of two subunits built from ribosomal RNA and protein. They are not bound by a membrane.

2. The chromosomes of a eukaryotic organism would be found in the

   A) chloroplast.

   B) nucleus.

   C) mitochondria.

   D) cytoplasm.

Cellular Respiration

Organisms use chains of chemical reactions called BIOCHEMICAL PATHWAYS to acquire, store, and use energy. The molecule most commonly used to store energy is ADENOSINE TRIPHOSPHATE **(ATP)**. When a phosphate group (Pi) is removed from ATP, creating ADENOSINE DIPHOSPHATE **(ADP)**, energy is released. The cell harnesses this energy to perform processes such as transport, growth, and replication.

Cells also transfer energy using the molecules NICOTINAMIDE ADENINE DINUCLEO-TIDE PHOSPHATE **(NADPH)** and NICOTINAMIDE ADENINE DINUCLEOTIDE **(NADH)**. These molecules are generally used to carry energy-rich electrons during the process of creating ATP.

In CELLULAR RESPIRATION, food molecules such as glucose are broken down, and the electrons harvested from these molecules are used to make ATP. The first stage of cellular respiration is an ANAEROBIC (does not require oxygen) process called GLYCOLYSIS. Glycolysis takes place in the cytoplasm of a cell and transforms glucose into two molecules of pyruvate. In the process, two molecules of ATP and two molecules of NADH are produced.

Under anaerobic conditions, pyruvate is reduced to acids and sometimes gases and/or alcohols in a process called FERMENTATION. However, this process is less efficient than aerobic cellular respiration and produces only two ATP.

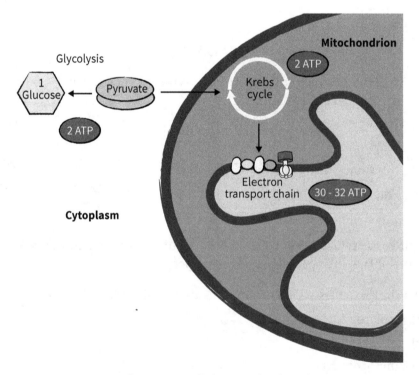

Figure 9.4. Cellular Respiration

Under aerobic conditions, pyruvate enters the second stage of cellular respiration—the KREBS CYCLE. The Krebs cycle takes place in the mitochondria, or tubular organelles, of a eukaryotic cell. Here, pyruvate is oxidized completely to form six molecules of carbon dioxide (CO_2). This set of reactions also produces two more molecules of ATP, ten molecules of NADH, and two molecules of $FADH_2$ (an electron carrier).

The electrons carried by NADH and $FADH_2$ are transferred to the ELECTRON TRANSPORT CHAIN, where they cascade through carrier molecules embedded in the inner mitochondrial membrane. Oxygen is the final electron receptor in the chain; it reacts with these electrons and hydrogen to form water. This sequential movement of electrons drives the formation of a proton (H^+) gradient, which is used by the enzyme ATP synthase to produce ATP. The electron transport chain produces thirty to thirty-two molecules of ATP.

The balanced chemical equation for cellular respiration is:

$$C_6H_{12}O_6 + 6O_2 \rightarrow 6CO_2 + 6H_2O$$

EXAMPLE

Which of the following stages of cellular respiration produces the largest number of ATP molecules?

A) glycolysis

B) fermentation

C) Krebs cycle

D) electron transport chain

Answer:

D) is correct. The electron transport chain produces thirty to thirty-two molecules of ATP made during cellular respiration. The other choices each produce only two molecules of ATP.

Photosynthesis

The sun powers nearly all biological systems on this planet. Plants, along with some bacteria and algae, harness the energy of sunlight and transform it into chemical energy through the process of PHOTOSYNTHESIS.

Inside each chloroplast are stacks of flat, interconnected sacs called THYLAKOIDS. Within the membrane of each thylakoid sac are light-absorbing pigments called CHLOROPHYLL.

In the light-dependent reactions of photosynthesis, light penetrates the chloroplast and strikes the chlorophyll. The energy in the sunlight excites electrons, boosting them to a higher energy level. These excited electrons then cascade through the ELECTRON TRANSPORT CHAIN, creating energy in the form of ATP and NADPH. This reaction also splits water to release O_2.

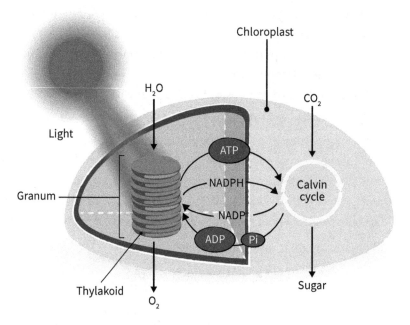

Figure 9.5. Photosynthesis

The ATP and NADPH created by the light-dependent stage of photosynthesis enters the **CALVIN CYCLE**, which uses the energy to produce the carbohydrate glucose ($C_6H_{12}O_6$). The carbon needed for this reaction comes from atmospheric CO_2.

The balanced chemical equation for photosynthesis is:

$$6CO_2 + 6H_2O \rightarrow C_6H_{12}O_6 + 6O_2$$

EXAMPLE

All of the following molecules are used in the Calvin cycle EXCEPT

A) O_2.

B) CO_2.

C) ATP.

D) NADPH.

Answer:

A) is correct. O_2 is released during the light-dependent stage of photosynthesis and is not used during the Calvin cycle. The other choices are all used during the Calvin cycle to produce glucose.

Cell Division

The process of cell growth and reproduction is the **CELL CYCLE**. Eukaryotic cells spend the majority of their lifespan in **INTERPHASE**, during which the cell performs necessary functions and grows. During interphase, the cell also copies its DNA. Then, during **MITOSIS** the two identical sets of DNA are pulled to opposite sides of the cell. The cell then splits during CYTOKINESIS, resulting in two cells that have identical copies of the original cell's DNA.

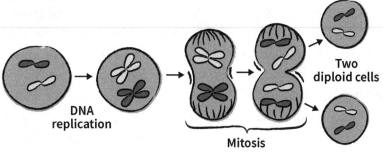

Figure 9.6. Mitosis

MEIOSIS is the process of sexual reproduction, or the formation of gametes (egg and sperm cells). During meiosis, the replicated DNA is separated to form two diploid cells. These cells in turn will separate again, with each cell retaining a single set of chromosomes. The result is four haploid cells.

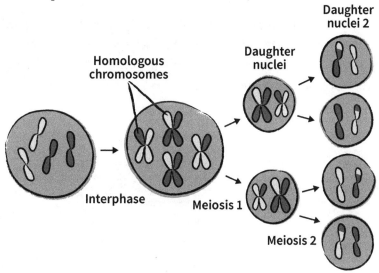

Figure 9.7. Meiosis

EXAMPLE

The result of mitosis and cytokinesis is

A) two haploid cells.

B) four haploid cells.

C) two diploid cells.

D) four diploid cells.

Answer:

C) is correct. The daughter cells produced during mitosis are genetically identical to their diploid (2n) parent.

Genetics

GENETICS is the study of heredity—how characteristics are passed from parents to offspring. These characteristics, or traits, are determined by genes. Each individual has two versions of the same gene, called ALLELES, with one contributed by each parent. An individual is HOMOZYGOUS for a particular gene if both alleles are the same, and HETEROZYGOUS if the two alleles are different.

For a particular gene, the DOMINANT allele will always be expressed, and the RECESSIVE allele will only be expressed if the other allele is also recessive. In other words, a recessive trait is only expressed if the individual is homozygous for that allele.

_____

Alleles are written as a single letter with the dominant allele capitalized (A) and the recessive allele lowercase (a).

The full set of genetic material in an organism is its GENOTYPE. The organism's PHENOTYPE is the set of observable traits in the organism. For example, brown hair is a phenotype. The genotype of this trait is a set of alleles that contain the genetic information for brown hair.

The genotype, and resulting phenotype, of sexually reproducing organisms can be tracked using PUNNETT SQUARES, which show the alleles of the parent generation on each of two axes. The possible genotype of the resulting offspring, called the F1 generation, are then shown in the body of the square.

Parent #1: Rr

	R	r
R	RR	Rr
r	Rr	rr

Parent #2: Rr

Figure 9.8. Punnett Square

In Figure 2.8., two heterozygous parents for trait R are mated, resulting in the following genotypes and phenotypes for the offspring:

- 1 homozygous dominant (dominant phenotype)
- 2 heterozygous (dominant phenotype)
- 1 homozygous recessive (recessive phenotype)

_____

Many of the rules of genetics were discovered by Gregor Mendel, a nineteenth century abbot who used pea plants to show how traits are passed down through generations.

Non-Mendelian inheritance describes patterns that do not follow the ratios described above. These patterns can occur for a number of reasons. Alleles might show INCOMPLETE DOMINANCE, where one allele is not fully expressed over the other, resulting in a third phenotype (for example, a red flower and white flower cross to create a pink flower). Alleles can also be CODOMINANT, meaning both are fully expressed (such as the AB blood type).

The expression of genes can also be regulated by mechanisms other than the dominant/recessive relationship. For example, some genes may inhibit the expression of other genes, a process called EPISTASIS. The environment can also impact gene expression. For example, organisms with the same genotype may grow to different sizes depending on the nutrients available to them.

EXAMPLES

1. Which of the following is NOT a scenario in which the dominant allele will be expressed as a trait?

    A) a recessive allele from the father paired with a recessive allele from the mother

    B) a dominant allele from the father paired with a dominant allele from the mother

    C) a dominant allele from the father paired with a recessive allele from the mother

    D) a recessive allele from the father paired with a dominant allele from the mother

    Answer:

    A) is correct. This genotype is homozygous, and the recessive trait is the only trait that can be expressed.

2. Alleles for brown eyes (B) are dominant over alleles for blue eyes (b). If two parents are both heterozygous for this gene, what is the percent chance that their offspring will have brown eyes?

    A) 25

    B) 50

    C) 75

    D) 100

    Answer:

    C) is correct. The Punnett square shows that there is a 75 percent chance the child will have the dominant B gene, and thus have brown eyes.

	B	b
B	BB	Bb
b	Bb	bb

Evolution

EVOLUTION is the gradual genetic change in species over time. Natural selection alters the variation and frequency of certain alleles and phenotypes within a population. This increased variation and frequency leads to varying reproductive success, in which individuals with certain traits survive over others. Combined, these mechanisms lead to a gradual changes in the genotype of individual populations that, over time, can result in the creation of a new species.

NATURAL SELECTION is a process in which only the members of a population best adapted to their environment tend to survive and reproduce, which ensures that their favorable traits will be passed on to future generations of the species. There are four basic conditions that must be met in order for natural selection to occur:

1. inherited variation
2. overproduction of offspring
3. fitness to environment
4. differential reproduction

Why might a harmful mutation continue to exist in a population?

The offspring with inherited variations best suited for their environment will be more likely to survive than others and are therefore more likely to pass on their successful genes to future populations through reproduction. This is referred to as FITNESS. An organism that is considered biologically "fit" will be more successful passing on its genes through reproduction compared to other members of the population. The frequency of certain alleles in a gene pool will change as a result.

ARTIFICIAL SELECTION occurs in a species when humans get involved in the reproductive process. Over time, humans have intentionally bred organisms with the same desirable traits in a process called selective breeding. This has led to the evolution of many common crops and farm animals that are bred specifically for human consumption, as well as among domesticated animals, such as horses or dogs.

EXAMPLE

Which of the following is NOT an example of natural selection?

A) peahens selecting the most brightly colored peacocks as mates

B) large bears chasing smaller rivals away from food sources

C) sparrows with a certain beak shape reaching plentiful food sources

D) farmers planting seeds only from the most productive corn plants

Answer:

D) is correct. Farmers choosing specific traits in plants is an example of artificial selection.

Ecology

ECOLOGY is the study of organisms' interactions with each other and the environment. Ecologists break down the groups of organisms and abiotic features into hierarchal groups.

Groups of organisms of the same species living in the same geographic area are called POPULATIONS. These organisms will compete with each other for resources and mates and will display characteristic patterns in growth related to their interactions with the environment. For example, many populations exhibit a carrying capacity, which is the highest number of individuals that the resources in a given environment can support. Populations that outgrow their carrying capacity are likely to experience increased death rates until the population reaches a stable level again.

Populations of different species living together in the same geographic region are called COMMUNITIES. Within a community there are many different interactions among individuals of different species. PREDATORS consume PREY for food, and some species are in COMPETITION for the same limited pool of resources. In a SYMBIOTIC relationship, two species have evolved to share a close relationship. Two species may also have a PARASITIC relationship in which one organism benefits to the detriment of the other, such as ticks feeding off a dog. Both species benefit in a MUTUALISTIC relationship, and in a COMMEN-SALISTIC relationship, one species benefits and the other feels the effects.

Within a community, a species exists in a FOOD WEB: every species either consumes or is consumed by another (or others). The lowest trophic level in the web is occupied by PRODUCERS, which include plants and algae that produce energy directly from the sun. The next level are PRIMARY CONSUMERS (herbivores), which consume plant matter. The next trophic level includes SECONDARY CONSUMERS (carnivores), which consume herbivores.

A food web may also contain another level of TERTIARY CONSUMERS (carnivores that consume other carnivores). In a real community, these webs can be extremely complex, with species existing on multiple trophic levels. Communities also include DECOMPOSERS, which are organisms that break down dead matter.

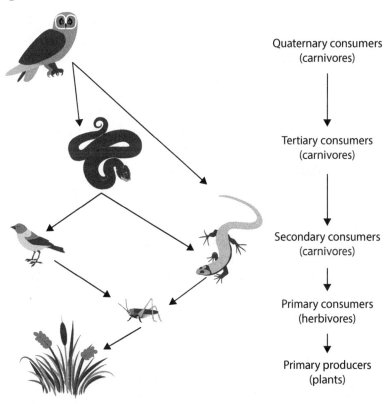

Figure 9.9. Food Web

The collection of biotic (living) and abiotic (nonliving) features in a geographic area is called an ECOSYSTEM. For example, in a forest, the ecosystem consists of all the organisms (animals, plants, fungi, bacteria, etc.), in addition to the soil, groundwater, rocks, and other abiotic features.

BIOMES are collections of plant and animal communities that exist within specific climates. They are similar to ecosystems, but they do not include abiotic components and can exist within and across continents. For example, the Amazon rainforest is a specific ecosystem, while tropical rainforests in general are considered a biome that includes a set of similar communities across the world. Together, all the living and nonliving parts of the earth are known as the BIOSPHERE.

Terrestrial biomes are usually defined by distinctive patterns in temperature and rainfall, and aquatic biomes are defined by the type of water and organisms found there. Examples of biomes include:

- DESERTS: extreme temperatures and very low rainfall with specialized vegetation and small mammals
- TROPICAL RAINFORESTS: hot and wet with an extremely high diversity of species
- TEMPERATE GRASSLANDS: moderate precipitation and distinct seasons with grasses and shrubs dominating
- TEMPERATE FORESTS: moderate precipitation and temperatures with deciduous trees dominating
- TUNDRA: extremely low temperatures and short growing seasons with little or no tree growth
- CORAL REEFS: a marine (saltwater) system with high levels of diversity
- LAKE: an enclosed body of fresh water

If the delicate balance of an ecosystem is disrupted, the system may not function properly. For example, if all the secondary consumers disappear, the population of primary consumers would increase, causing the primary consumers to overeat the producers and eventually starve. KEYSTONE SPECIES are especially important in a particular community, and removing them decreases the overall diversity of the ecosystem.

EXAMPLES

1. Which of the following is an example of an abiotic environmental factor that influences population size?
    A) food availability
    B) rate of precipitation
    C) interspecific competition
    D) competition

    Answer:

    B) is correct. Precipitation is a nonliving (abiotic) factor that influences population size.

2. Which of the following terrestrial biomes is characterized by moderate rainfall and the dominance of deciduous trees?

A) desert

B) tropical rainforest

C) temperate forest

D) tundra

Answer:

C) is correct. Temperate forests have moderate rainfall and are dominated by deciduous trees.

Human Anatomy and Physiology

In a multicellular organism, cells are grouped together into TISSUES, and these tissues are grouped into ORGANS, which perform specific FUNCTIONS. The heart, for example, is the organ that pumps blood throughout the body. Organs are further grouped into ORGAN SYSTEMS, such as the digestive or respiratory systems.

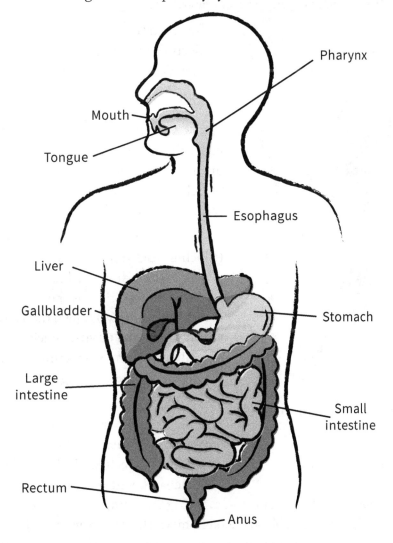

Figure 9.10. Digestive System

ANATOMY is the study of the structure of organisms, and PHYSIOLOGY is the study of how these structures function. Both disciplines study the systems that allow organisms to perform a number of crucial functions, including the exchange of energy, nutrients, and waste products with the environment. This exchange allows organisms to maintain HOMEOSTASIS, or the stabilization of internal conditions.

In science, a **system** is a collection of interconnected parts that make up a complex whole with defined boundaries. Systems may be closed, meaning nothing passes in or out of them, or open, meaning they have inputs and outputs.

The human body has a number of systems that perform vital functions, including the digestive, excretory, respiratory, circulatory, skeletal, muscular, immune, nervous, endocrine, and reproductive systems.

The DIGESTIVE SYSTEM breaks food down into nutrients for use by the body's cells. Food enters through the MOUTH and moves through the ESOPHAGUS to the STOMACH, where it is physically and chemically broken down. The food particles then move into the SMALL INTESTINE, where the majority of nutrients are absorbed. Finally, the remaining particles enter the LARGE INTESTINE, which mostly absorbs water, and waste exits through the RECTUM and ANUS. This system also includes other organs, such as the LIVER, GALLBLADDER, and PANCREAS, that manufacture substances needed for digestion.

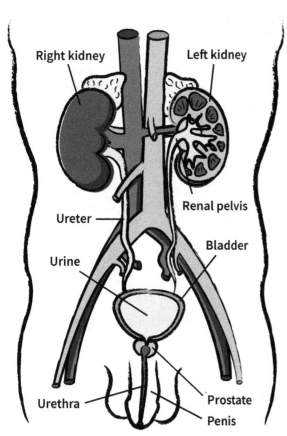

Figure 9.11. Genitourinary System

The GENITOURINARY SYSTEM removes waste products from the body. Its organs include the liver, which breaks down harmful substances, and the KIDNEYS, which filter waste from the bloodstream. The excretory system also includes the BLADDER and URINARY TRACT, which expel the waste filtered by the kidneys; the lungs, which expel the carbon dioxide created by cellular metabolism; and the skin, which secretes salt in the form of perspiration.

The RESPIRATORY SYSTEM takes in oxygen (which is needed for cellular functioning) and expels carbon dioxide. Humans take in air primarily through the nose but also through the mouth. This air travels down the TRACHEA and BRONCHI into the LUNGS, which are composed of millions of small structures called alveoli that allow for the exchange of gases between the blood and the air.

The circulatory system carries oxygen, nutrients, and waste products in the blood to and from all the cells of the body. The HEART is a four-chambered muscle that pumps blood throughout the body. The four chambers are the right atrium, right ventricle, left atrium, and left ventricle. Deoxygenated blood (blood from which all the oxygen has been extracted and used) enters the right atrium and then is sent from the right ventricle through the pulmonary artery to the lungs, where it collects oxygen. The oxygen-rich blood then returns to the left atrium of the heart and is pumped out the left ventricle to the rest of the body.

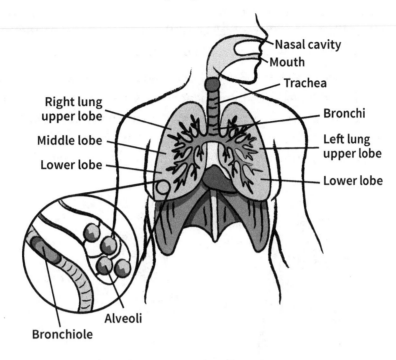

Figure 9.12. Respiratory System

Blood travels through a system of vessels. ARTERIES branch directly off the heart and carry blood away from it. The largest artery is the aorta, which carries blood from the heart

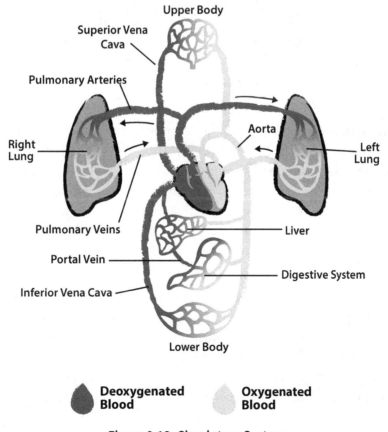

Figure 9.13. Circulatory System

to the rest of the body. **Veins** carry blood back to the heart from other parts of the body. Most veins carry deoxygenated blood, but the pulmonary veins carry oxygenated blood from the lungs back to the heart to then be pumped to the rest of the body. Arteries and veins branch into smaller and smaller vessels until they become **capillaries**, which are the smallest vessels and the site where gas exchange occurs.

The **skeletal system**, which is composed of the body's **bones** and **joints**, provides support for the body and helps with movement. Bones also store some of the body's nutrients and produce specific types of cells. Humans are born with 237 bones. However, many of these bones fuse during childhood, and adults have only 206 bones. Bones can have a rough or smooth texture and come in four basic shapes: long, flat, short, and irregular.

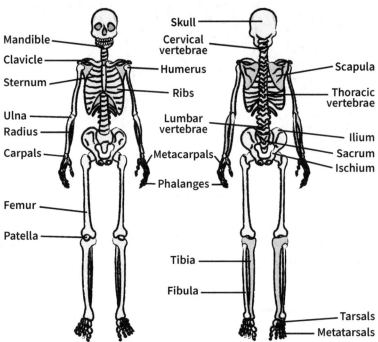

Figure 9.14. The Skeletal System

The **muscular system** allows the body to move and also moves blood and other substances through the body. The human body has three types of muscles. Skeletal muscles are voluntary muscles (meaning they can be controlled) that are attached to bones and move the body. Smooth muscles are involuntary muscles (meaning they cannot be controlled) that create movement in parts of the digestive tract, blood vessels, and the reproduction system. Finally, cardiac muscle is the involuntary muscle that contracts the heart, pumping blood throughout the body.

Some skeletal muscles, such as the diaphragm and those that control blinking, can be voluntarily controlled but usually operate involuntarily.

The **immune system** protects the body from infection by foreign particles and organisms. It includes the **skin** and mucous membranes, which act as physical barriers, and a number of specialized cells that destroy foreign substances in the body. The human body has an adaptive immune system, meaning it can recognize and respond to foreign substances once it has been exposed to them. This is the underlying mechanism behind vaccines.

The immune system is composed of **B CELLS**, or B lymphocytes, that produce special proteins called **ANTIBODIES** that bind to foreign substances, called **ANTIGENS**, and neutralize them. **T CELLS**, or T lymphocytes, remove body cells that have been infected by foreign invaders like bacteria or viruses. **HELPER T CELLS** coordinate production of antibodies by B cells and removal of infected cells by T cells. **KILLER T CELLS** destroy body cells that have been infected by invaders after they are identified and removed by T cells. Finally, **MEMORY CELLS** remember antigens that have been removed so the immune system can respond more quickly if they enter the body again.

Memory B cells are the underlying mechanisms behind vaccines, which introduce a harmless version of a pathogen into the body to activate the body's adaptive immune response.

The **NERVOUS SYSTEM** processes external stimuli and sends signals throughout the body. It is made up of two parts. The central nervous system (CNS) includes the brain and spinal cord and is where information is processed and stored. The brain has three parts: the cerebrum, cerebellum, and medulla. The **CEREBRUM** is the biggest part of the brain, the wrinkly gray part at the front and top, and controls different functions like thinking, vision, hearing, touch, and smell. The **CEREBELLUM** is located at the back and bottom of the brain and controls motor movements. The **MEDULLA**, or brain stem, is where the brain connects to the spinal cord and controls automatic body functions like breathing and heartbeat.

The peripheral nervous system (PNS) includes small cells called **NEURONS** that transmit information throughout the body using electrical signals. Neurons are made up of three basic parts: the cell body, dendrites, and axons. The cell body is the main part of the cell where the organelles are located. Dendrites are long arms that extend from the main cell body and communicate with other cells' dendrites through chemical messages passed across a space called a synapse. Axons are extensions from the cell body and transmit messages to the muscles.

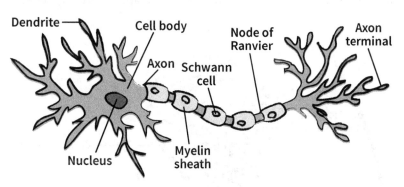

Figure 9.15. Neuron

The **ENDOCRINE SYSTEM** is a collection of organs that produce **HORMONES**, which are chemicals that regulate bodily processes. These organs include the pituitary gland, hypothalamus, pineal gland, thyroid gland, parathyroid glands, adrenal glands, testes (in males), ovaries (in females), and the placenta (in pregnant females). Together, the hormones these organs produce regulate a wide variety of bodily functions, including hunger, sleep, mood, reproduction, and temperature. Some organs that are part of other systems can also act as endocrine organs, including the pancreas and liver.

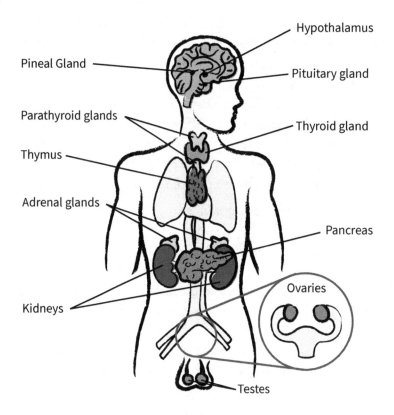

Figure 9.16. Endocrine System

The reproductive system includes the organs necessary for sexual reproduction. In males, sperm is produced in the TESTES (also known as TESTICLES) and carried through a thin tube called the VAS DEFERENS to the URETHRA, which carries sperm through the PENIS and out of the body. The PROSTATE is a muscular gland approximately the size of a walnut

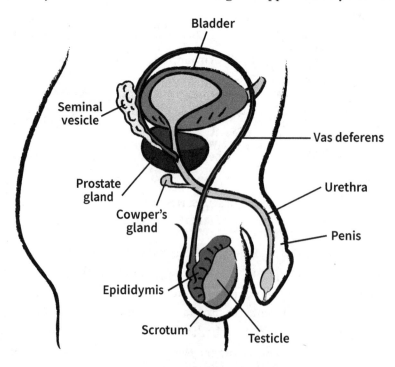

Figure 9.17. Male Reproductive System

that is located between the male bladder and penis and produces a fluid that nourishes and protects sperm.

In the female reproductive system, eggs are produced in the OVARIES and released roughly once a month to move through the FALLOPIAN TUBES to the UTERUS. If an egg is fertilized, the new embryo implants in the lining of the uterus and develops over the course of about nine months. At the end of GESTATION, the baby leaves the uterus through the cervix, and exits the body through the VAGINA. If the egg is not fertilized, the uterus will shed its lining.

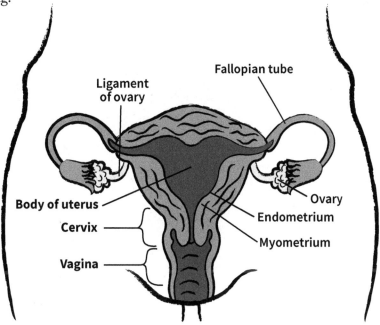

Figure 9.18. Female Reproductive System

EXAMPLES

1. Which of the following structures are small air sacs that function as the site of gas exchange in the lungs?

    A) capillaries

    B) bronchi

    C) alveoli

    D) cilia

    Answer:

    C) **is correct.** The alveoli are sacs found at the terminal end of each bronchiole in the lungs and are the site of gas exchange with the blood.

2. Where in the digestive tract are most of the nutrients absorbed?

    A) small intestine

    B) rectum

    C) stomach

    D) large intestine

Answer:

A) is correct. Most nutrients are absorbed by the small intestine.

Test Your Knowledge

Read the question, and then choose the most correct answer.

1. Which of the following is NOT a nucleobase of DNA?

   A) adenine

   B) guanine

   C) thymine

   D) uracil

2. Which of the following is a monomer used to build carbohydrates?

   A) glucose

   B) thymine

   C) aspartic acid

   D) histone

3. Which of the following processes uses the information stored in RNA to produce a protein?

   A) replication

   B) translation

   C) transcription

   D) mutation

4. The information stored in DNA is used to make which of the following molecules?

   A) amino acids

   B) proteins

   C) fatty acids

   D) monosaccharides

5. Which of the following is NOT present in an animal cell?

   A) nucleus

   B) mitochondria

   C) cytoplasm

   D) cell wall

6. Which of the following cell organelles are the site of lipid synthesis?

   A) smooth endoplasmic reticulum

   B) ribosome

   C) rough endoplasmic reticulum

   D) Golgi apparatus

7. Which of the following cellular processes does NOT use ATP?

   A) facilitated diffusion

   B) DNA replication

   C) active transport through the cell membrane

   D) movement of the mot complex in a flagellum

8. Which of the following molecules can be found in abundance in a fatigued muscle?

   A) glucose

   B) lactic acid

   C) ATP

   D) myoglobin

9. Why do some photosynthetic structures, like leaves, appear green?

   A) The epidermis of the leaf absorbs red and blue light.

   B) The epidermis of the leaf absorbs green light.

   C) The chlorophyll of the leaf absorbs red and blue light.

   D) The chlorophyll of the leaf absorbs green light.

10. The Calvin cycle produces one molecule of glucose from which of the following three molecules?

    A) ATP, NADPH, and O_2

    B) ATP, NADPH, and CO_2

    C) CO_2, H_2O, and ATP

    D) CO_2, H_2O, and O_2

11. The result of meiosis and cytokinesis is

    A) two haploid (1n) cells.

    B) four haploid (1n) cells.

    C) two diploid (2n) cells.

    D) four diploid (2n) cells.

12. Alleles for brown eyes (B)are dominant over alleles for blue eyes (b). If two parents are both heterozygous for this gene, what is the percent chance that their offspring will have brown eyes?

    A) 25

    B) 50

    C) 75

    D) 100

13. If a plant that is homozygous dominant (T) for a trait is crossed with a plant that is homozygous recessive (t) for the same trait, what will be the phenotype of the offspring if the trait follows Mendelian patterns of inheritance?

    A) All offspring will show the dominant phenotype.

    B) All offspring will show the recessive phenotype.

    C) Half the offspring will show the dominant trait, and the other half will show the recessive phenotype.

    D) All the offspring will show a mix of the dominant and recessive phenotypes.

14. A female who carries the recessive color blindness gene mates with a color-blind male, resulting in a male child. Which of the following numbers represents the likelihood the offspring will also be color blind?

    A) 25 percent

    B) 50 percent

    C) 100 percent

    D) 0 percent

15. Type AB blood—the expression of both A and B antigens on a red blood cell surface—occurs as the result of which of the following?

    A) incomplete dominance

    B) recombination

    C) codominance

    D) independent assortment

16. Which of the following is NOT a condition of natural selection?

    A) differential reproduction

    B) competition between species

    C) overproduction of offspring

    D) inheritance of traits

17. Which of the following is the type of nonrandom mating that leads to changes in allele frequency?

    A) sexual selection

    B) genetic drift

    C) migration

    D) gene flow

18. Which of the following aquatic biomes are located where freshwater streams empty into the ocean?

    A) wetlands

    B) coral reef

    C) estuaries

    D) littoral

19. Which of the following scenarios accurately describes primary succession?

   A) The ground is scorched by a lava flow; later the establishment of lichens begins on the volcanic rock, leading to the eventual formation of soils.

   B) A meadow is destroyed by a flood; eventually small grasses begin to grow again to begin establishing a healthy meadow ecosystem.

   C) A fire destroys a section of a forest; once the ashes clear, small animals begin making their homes within the area.

   D) A farmer overuses the land causing all the minerals and nutrients in the soil to be used up. Some leftover grass seeds in the soil begin to sprout, repopulating the land.

20. A barnacle is attached to the outside of the whale to collect and consume particulate matter as the whale moves through the ocean. The barnacle benefits, while the whale is unaffected.
   The phenomenon described is an example of

   A) predation

   B) commensalism

   C) mutualism

   D) parasitism

21. Which of the following organisms generate their own food through photosynthesis and make up the first level of the energy pyramid?

   A) heterotrophs

   B) autotrophs

   C) producers

   D) consumers

22. Which of the following is composed only of members of the same species?

   A) ecosystem

   B) community

   C) biome

   D) population

23. Which of the following type of muscle is responsible for voluntary movement in the body?

   A) cardiac

   B) visceral

   C) smooth

   D) skeletal

24. Which of the following organs is an accessory organ that food does NOT pass through as part of digestion?

   A) pharynx

   B) mouth

   C) small intestine

   D) liver

25. Which of the following is NOT a function of the respiratory system in humans?

   A) to exchange gas

   B) to produce sound and speech

   C) to distribute oxygen to the rest of the body

   D) to remove particles from the air

Answer Key

1. **D) is correct.**

   Uracil (U) is a pyrimidine found in RNA, replacing the thymine (T) pyrimidine found in DNA.

2. **A) is correct.**

   Glucose is a monosaccharide that can be used to build larger polysaccharides.

3. **B) is correct.**

   Translation is process of matching codons in RNA to the correct anti-codon to manufacture a protein.

4. **B) is correct.**

   Proteins are the expressed products of a gene.

5. **D) is correct.**

   The cell wall is the structure that gives plant cells their rigidity.

6. **A) is correct.**

   The smooth endoplasmic reticulum is a series of membranes attached to the cell nucleus and plays an important role in the production and storage of lipids. It is called smooth because it lacks ribosomes on the membrane surface.

7. **A) is correct.**

   Facilitated diffusion is a form of passive transport across the cell membrane and does not use energy.

8. **B) is correct.**

   Lactic acid, a byproduct of anaerobic respiration, builds up in muscles and causes fatigue. This occurs when the energy exerted by the muscle exceeds the amount of oxygen available for aerobic respiration.

9. **C) is correct.**

   Light passes through the epidermis and strikes the pigment chlorophyll, which absorbs the wavelengths of light that humans see as red and blue and reflects the wavelengths of light that the human eye perceives as green.

10. **B) is correct.**

    Glucose is produced from CO_2 by the energy stored in ATP and the hydrogen atoms associated with NADPH.

11. **B) is correct.**

    Four haploid (1n) cells are produced during meiosis.

12. **C) is correct.**

    The Punnett square shows that there is a 75 percent chance the child will have the dominant B gene, and thus have brown eyes.

	B	b
B	BB	Bb
b	Bb	bb

13. **A) is correct.**

    Because each offspring will inherit the dominant allele, all the offspring will show the dominant phenotype. The offspring would only show a mix of the two phenotypes if they did not follow Mendelian inheritance patterns.

14. **B) is correct.**

    The offspring has a 50 percent chance of inheriting the dominant allele and a 50 percent chance of inheriting the recessive allele from his mother.

things. Often this new land is the result of lava flows or glacial movement.

15. **C) is correct.**

Type AB blood occurs when two equally dominant alleles (A and B) are inherited. Since they are both dominant, one does not mask the other; instead, both are expressed.

16. **B) is correct.**

Competition between species is not necessary for natural selection to occur, although it can influence the traits that are selected for within a population.

17. **A) is correct.**

Sexual selection changes allele frequency because it leads to some members of the population reproducing more frequently than others.

18. **C) is correct.**

Estuaries are found at the boundary of ocean and stream biomes and are very ecologically productive areas.

19. **A) is correct.**

Primary succession can only occur on newly exposed earth that was not previously inhabited by living

20. **B) is correct.**

In a commensal relationship, one species benefits with no impact on the other.

21. **C) is correct.**

Producers are a kind of autotroph that are found on the energy pyramid and produce food via photosynthesis.

22. **D) is correct.**

A population is all the members of the same species in a given area.

23. **D) is correct.**

Skeletal muscles are attached to the skeletal system and are controlled voluntarily.

24. **D) is correct.**

The liver is an accessory organ that detoxifies ingested toxins and produces bile for fat digestion.

25. **C) is correct.**

The cardiovascular system distributes oxygen to the rest of the body.

ten

PHYSICAL SCIENCE

The Structure of the Atom

All matter is composed of very small particles called ATOMS. Atom can be further broken down into subatomic particles. PROTONS, which are positive, and NEUTRONS, which are neutral, form the nucleus of the atom. Negative particles called ELECTRONS orbit the nucleus.

While electrons are often depicted as orbiting the nucleus like a planet orbits the sun, they're actually arranged in cloud-like areas called SHELLS. The shells closest to the nucleus have the lowest energy and are filled first. The high-energy shells farther from the nucleus only fill with electrons once lower-energy shells are full.

The outermost electron shell of an atom is its VALENCE SHELL. The electrons in this shell are involved in chemical reactions. Atoms are most stable when their valence shell is full (usually with eight electrons), so the atom will lose, gain, or share electrons to fill its valence shell.

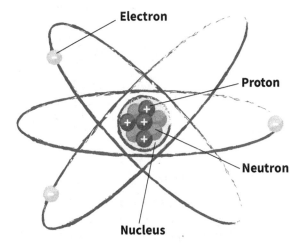

Figure 10.1. Structure of the Atom

A neutral atom will have an equal number of protons and electrons. When a neutral atom loses or gains electrons, it gains or loses charge accordingly, forming an ION. An ion with more protons than electrons has a positive charge and is called a CATION. An ion with more electrons than protons has a negative charge and is considered an ANION.

For example, the element oxygen (O) has eight protons and eight electrons. A neutral oxygen atom is represented simply as O. However, if it gains two electrons, it becomes an anion with a charge of –2 and is written as O^{2-}.

The attractive and repulsive forces in an atom follow the universal law that "like charges repel and opposite charges attract."

All atoms with the same number of protons are the same ELEMENT and cannot be further reduced to a simpler substance by chemical processes. Each element has a symbol, which is a one- or two-letter abbreviation for the element's name. The number of protons in an atom is that atom's ATOMIC NUMBER.

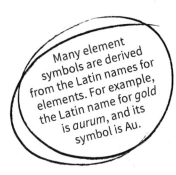

Many element symbols are derived from the Latin names for elements. For example, the Latin name for gold is *aurum*, and its symbol is Au.

Along with atomic charge, atoms have measurable mass. Protons and neutrons are significantly more massive than electrons (about 1,800 times), so the mass of electrons is not considered when calculating the mass of an atom. Thus, an element's MASS NUMBER is the number of protons and neutrons present in its atoms.

EXAMPLES

1. What is the charge of an atom with five protons and seven electrons?

    A) 12
    B) −12
    C) 2
    D) −2

    Answer:

    D) is correct. The total charge of an atom is the difference between the number of protons and electrons. Subtract the number of electrons from the number of protons: 5 − 7 = −2.

2. Which ion has the greatest number of electrons?

    A) K^+
    B) Cl^-
    C) Ca^+
    D) P^{3-}

    Answer:

    C) is correct. Calcium has an atomic number of 20 (found on the Periodic table), meaning it has 20 protons. For a Ca ion to have a charge of 1+, it must have nineteen electrons. All the other ions have eighteen electrons.

The Periodic Table of the Elements

Elements are arranged on the PERIODIC TABLE OF THE ELEMENTS by their atomic number, which increases from top to bottom and left to right on the table. Hydrogen, the first element on the periodic table, has one proton while helium, the second element, has two, and so on.

The rows of the periodic table are called PERIODS, and the vertical columns are called GROUPS. Each group contains elements with the same number of valence electrons, meaning the elements have similar chemical properties.

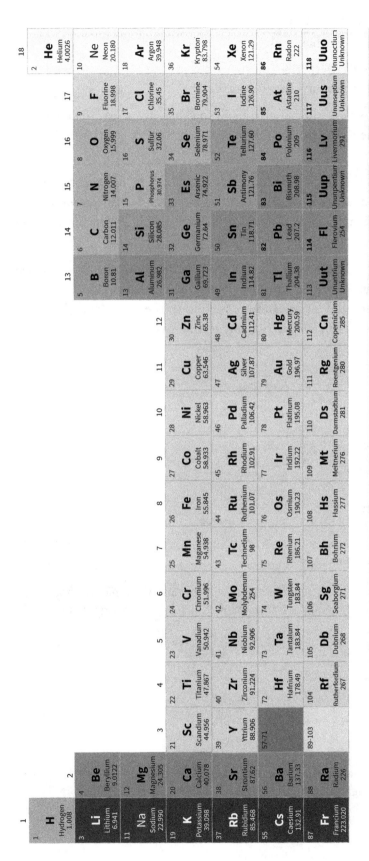

Figure 10.2. Periodic Table of the Elements

The majority of the elements in the periodic table are metals. Metals have the following properties:

- They are hard, opaque, and shiny.
- They are ductile and malleable.
- They conduct electricity and heat.
- With the exception of mercury, they are solids.

METALS begin on the left side of the periodic table and span across the middle of the table, almost all the way to the right side. Examples of metals include gold (Au), tin (Sn), and lead (Pb).

NONMETALS are elements that do not conduct electricity and tend to be more reactive than metals. They can be solids, liquids, or gases. The nonmetals are located on the right side of the periodic table. Examples of nonmetals include sulfur (S), hydrogen (H), and oxygen (O).

METALLOIDS, or semimetals, are elements that possess both metal and nonmetal characteristics. For example, some metalloids are shiny but do not conduct electricity well. Metalloids are located between the metals and nonmetals on the periodic table. Some examples of metalloids are boron (B), silicon (Si), and arsenic (As).

EXAMPLES

1. Bismuth is a
   A) metal.
   B) nonmetal.
   C) metalloid.
   D) transition element.

   Answer:

   A) is correct. Bismuth is a metal.

2. The lithium ion Li^+ combines with the fluorine ion F^- to form the ionic compound LiF. Which of the following elements is fluorine most likely to also form an ionic compound with?
   A) nickel (Ni)
   B) beryllium (Be)
   C) sodium (Na)
   D) argon (Ar)

   Answer:

   C) is correct. Lithium and sodium are both in Group 1 of the periodic table, so they have similar chemical properties. Sodium will form the ion Na^+ and join with F^- to form NaF.

Chemical Bonds

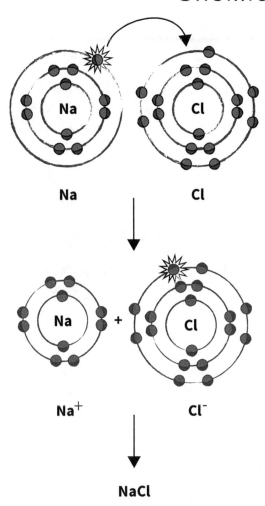

Na

Cl

Na⁺   +   **Cl⁻**

NaCl

Figure 10.3. The Ionic Bond in Table Salt

CHEMICAL BONDS are attractions between atoms that create molecules, which are substances consisting of more than one atom. There are three types of bonds: ionic, covalent, and metallic.

In an **IONIC BOND**, one atom "gives" its electrons to the other, resulting in one positively and one negatively charged atom. The bond is a result of the attraction between the two ions. Ionic bonds form between atoms on the left side of the periodic table (which will lose electrons) and those on the right side (which will gain electrons). Table salt (NaCl) is an example of a molecule held together by an ionic bond.

A **COVALENT BOND** is created by a pair of atoms sharing electrons to fill their valence shells. In a **NONPOLAR** covalent bond, the electrons are shared evenly. In a **POLAR** covalent bond, the electrons are shared unevenly. One atom will exert a stronger pull on the shared electrons, giving that atom a slight negative charge. The other atom in the bond will have a slight positive charge. Water (H_2O) is an example of a polar molecule.

The polar nature of water is responsible for many of its unique properties. The small charges within a water molecule cause attraction between the molecules. The molecules then "stick" to each other (cohesion) and to other surfaces (adhesion).

Metals can form tightly packed arrays in which each atom is in close contact with many neighbors. The valence electrons are free to move between atoms and create a "sea" of delocalized charge. Any excitation, such as an electrical current, can cause the electrons to move throughout the array. The high electrical and thermal conductivity of metals is due to this ability of

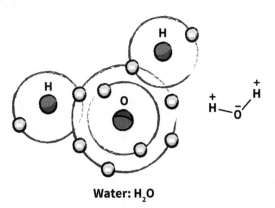

Water: H₂O

Figure 10.4. Polar Covalent Bond

electrons to move throughout the lattice. This type of delocalized bonding is called
METALLIC BONDING.

EXAMPLE

Which of the following compounds is held together by a polar covalent bond?

A) LiF

B) CO_2

C) H_2

D) NaOH

Answer:

B) is correct. Carbon and oxygen are both nonmetals that combine through a covalent bond. Oxygen has a strong pull on their shared electrons, so CO_2 is polar. In hydrogen gas (H_2), the identical hydrogen atoms share electrons equally, so the compound is nonpolar. Choices A) and D) are ionic compounds.

Properties of Matter

MATTER is any substance that takes up space. The amount of matter in an object is that object's **MASS**, which is measured in grams or kilograms. Mass is different from **WEIGHT**, which is a measure of the gravitational force exerted on an object. An object's mass never changes, but its weight will change if the gravitational force changes. The **DENSITY** of an object is the ratio of an object's mass to its volume.

Objects weigh less on the moon than on the earth because the pull of gravity on the moon is lower than that on earth. However, the mass of the object is the same no matter where in the universe it goes.

Properties of substances are divided into two categories: physical and chemical. **PHYSICAL PROPERTIES** are those that are measurable and can be seen without changing the chemical makeup of a substance. In contrast, **CHEMICAL PROPERTIES** are those that determine how a substance will behave in a chemical reaction. Chemical properties cannot be identified simply by observing a material. Instead, the material must be engaged in a chemical reaction in order to identify its chemical properties. A **PHYSICAL CHANGE** is a change in a substance's physical properties, and a **CHEMICAL CHANGE** is a change in its chemical properties.

Table 10.1. Properties of Matter

PHYSICAL PROPERTIES	CHEMICAL PROPERTIES
mass	heat of combustion
temperature	flammability
density	toxicity
color	chemical stability
viscosity	enthalpy of formation

TEMPERATURE is the name given to the kinetic energy of all the atoms or molecules in a substance. While it might look like matter is not in motion, in fact, its atoms have kinetic energy and are constantly spinning and vibrating. The more energy the atoms have (meaning the more they spin and vibrate) the higher the substance's temperature.

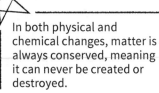

In both physical and chemical changes, matter is always conserved, meaning it can never be created or destroyed.

HEAT is the movement of energy from one substance to another. Energy will spontaneously move from high-energy (high-temperature) substances to low-energy (low-temperature) substances.

EXAMPLE

Which of the following describes a physical change?

A) Water becomes ice.

B) Batter is baked into a cake.

C) A firecracker explodes.

D) An acid is neutralized with a base.

Answer:

A) is correct. When water changes form, it does not change the chemical composition of the substance. Once water becomes ice, the ice can easily turn back into water by increasing its temperature.

States of Matter

All matter exists in different STATES (or phases) that depend on the energy of the molecules in the matter. SOLID matter has densely packed molecules and does not change volume or shape. LIQUIDS have more loosely packed molecules and can change shape but not volume. GAS molecules are widely dispersed, and gases can change both shape and volume.

Changes in temperature and pressure can cause matter to change states. Generally, adding energy (in the form of heat) changes a substance to a higher energy state (e.g., solid to liquid). Transitions from a high to lower energy state (e.g., liquid to solid) release energy. Each of these changes has a specific name, summarized in the table below.

Table 10.2. Changes in State of Matter

NAME	FROM	TO	OCCURS AT	ENERY CHANGE
evaporation	liquid	gas	boiling point	uses energy
condensation	gas	liquid	boiling point	releases energy
melting	solid	liquid	freezing point	uses energy
freezing	liquid	solid	freezing point	releases energy
sublimation	solid	gas	---	uses energy
deposition	gas	solid	---	releases energy

EXAMPLE

The process that takes place when water reaches its boiling point is called

A) condensation.

B) evaporation.

C) melting.

D) sublimation.

Answer:

B) is correct. Evaporation is the process of conversion from liquid to gas that occurs at the boiling point.

Chemical Reactions

A **CHEMICAL REACTION** occurs when one or more substances react to form new substances. **REACTANTS** are the substances that are consumed or altered in the chemical reaction, and the new substances are **PRODUCTS**. Equations are written with the reactants on the left, the products on the right, and an arrow between them. The state of the chemical compounds are sometimes noted using the labels *s* (solid), *l* (liquid), *g* (gas), or *aq* (aqueous, meaning a solution).

The equation below shows the reaction of hydrogen gas (H_2) and chlorine gas (Cl_2) to form hydrogen chloride (HCl), an acid.

$$H_2 \ (g) + Cl_2 \ (g) \rightarrow 2HCl \ (aq)$$

Chemical reactions follow the **LAW OF CONSERVATION OF MATTER**, which states that matter cannot be created or destroyed. In a reaction, the same types and numbers of atoms that appear on the left side must also appear on the right. To **BALANCE** a chemical equation, coefficients (the numbers before the reactant or product) are added. In the equation above, a coefficient of two is needed on HCl so that two hydrogen and two chlorine atoms appear on each side of the arrow.

There are five main types of chemical reactions; these are summarized in the table below.

Table 10.3. Types of Reactions

TYPE OF REACTION	GENERAL FORMULA	EXAMPLE REACTION
Synthesis	$A + B \rightarrow C$	$2H_2 + O_2 \rightarrow 2H_2O$
Decomposition	$A \rightarrow B + C$	$2H_2O_2 \rightarrow 2H_2O + O_2$
Single displacement	$AB + C \rightarrow A + BC$	$CH_4 + Cl_2 \rightarrow CH_3Cl + HCl$
Double displacement	$AB + CD \rightarrow AC + BD$	$CuCl_2 + 2AgNo_3 \rightarrow Cu(NO_3)_2 + 2AgCl$
Combustion	$C_xH_yO_z + O_2 \rightarrow CO_2 + H_2O$	$2C_8H_{18} + 25O_2 \rightarrow 10CO_2 + 18H_2O$

Energy is required to break chemical bonds, and it is released when bonds form. The total energy absorbed or released during a chemical reaction will depend on the individual bonds being broken and formed. A reaction that releases energy is EXOTHERMIC, and a reaction that absorbs energy is ENDOTHERMIC.

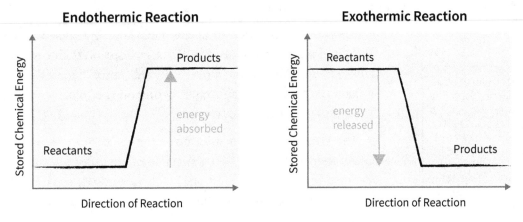

Figure 10.5. Stored Energy in Endothermic and Exothermic Reactions

EXAMPLES

1. Which of the following types of reactions is shown below?

   $Pb(NO_3)_2 + K_2CrO_4 \rightarrow PbCrO_4 + 2KNO_3$

   A) combustion

   B) decomposition

   C) double displacement

   D) single replacement

   Answer:

   C) is correct. In the reaction, the Pb and K exchange their anions in a double-displacement reaction.

2. Which of the following equations is a balanced equation?

   A) $2KClO_3 \rightarrow KCl + 3O_2$

   B) $KClO_3 \rightarrow KCl + 3O_2$

   C) $2KClO_3 \rightarrow 2KCl + 3O_2$

   D) $6KClO_3 \rightarrow 6KCl + 3O_2$

   Answer:

   C) is correct. In this equation, there are equal numbers of each type of atom on both sides (2 K atoms, 2 Cl atoms, and 6 O atoms).

Mixtures

When substances are combined without a chemical reaction to bond them, the resulting substance is called a MIXTURE. Physical changes can be used to separate mixtures. For example, heating salt water until the water evaporates, leaving the salt behind, will separate a salt water solution.

In a mixture, the components can be unevenly distributed, such as in trail mix or soil. These mixtures are described at HETEROGENEOUS. Alternatively, the components can be HOMOGENEOUSLY, or uniformly, distributed, as in salt water.

A SOLUTION is a special type of stable homogeneous mixture. The components of a solution will not separate on their own and cannot be separated using a filter. The substance being dissolved is the SOLUTE, and the substance acting on the solute, or doing the dissolving, is the SOLVENT.

Solutions can exist as solids, liquids, or gases. For example, carbonated water has a gaseous solute (CO_2) and a liquid solvent (water). A solution formed by combining two solid metals, such as stainless steel, is an **alloy**.

The SOLUBILITY of a solution is the maximum amount of solute that will dissolve in a specific quantity of solvent at a specified temperature. Solutions can be saturated, unsaturated, or supersaturated based on the amount of solute dissolved in the solution.

- A SATURATED solution has the maximum amount of solute that can be dissolved in the solvent.

- An UNSATURATED solution contains less solute than a saturated solution would hold.

- A SUPERSATURATED SOLUTION contains more solvent than a saturated solution. A supersaturated solution can be made by heating the solution to dissolve additional solute and then slowly cooling it down to a specified temperature.

EXAMPLES

1. Which of the following is a heterogeneous mixture?

    A) a mixture in which the atoms or molecules are distributed unevenly

    B) a mixture in which two substances are in different states

    C) a mixture of covalent and ionic compounds

    D) a mixture of polar and nonpolar molecules

    Answer:

    A) is correct. A heterogeneous mixture is any non-uniform mixture, which means that the atoms or molecules are unevenly distributed.

2. Which of the following terms describes a solution in which more solvent can be dissolved?

    A) unsaturated

    B) saturated

    C) supersaturated

    D) homogeneous

    Answer:

    A) is correct. An unsaturated solution has less solute than can be dissolved in the given amount of solvent.

Acids and Bases

Acids and bases are substances that share a distinct set of physical properties. ACIDS are corrosive, sour, and change the color of vegetable dyes like litmus from blue to red. BASES, or alkaline solutions, are slippery, bitter, and change the color of litmus from red to blue.

There are a number of different ways to define acids and bases, but generally acids release hydrogen ions (H^+) in solution, while bases release hydroxide (OH^-) ions. For example, hydrochloric acid (HCl) ionizes, or breaks apart, in solution to release H^+ ions:

$$HCl \rightarrow H^+ + Cl$$

The base sodium hydroxide (NaOH) ionizes to release OH^- ions:

$$NaOH \rightarrow Na^+ + OH^-$$

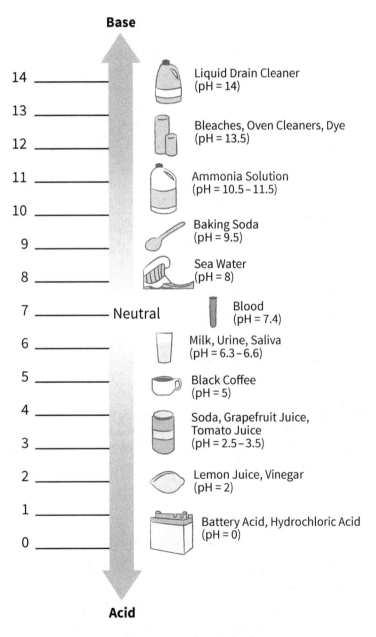

Base

14 — Liquid Drain Cleaner (pH = 14)

13 —
12 — Bleaches, Oven Cleaners, Dye (pH = 13.5)

11 — Ammonia Solution (pH = 10.5 – 11.5)

10 —
9 — Baking Soda (pH = 9.5)

8 — Sea Water (pH = 8)

7 — Neutral — Blood (pH = 7.4)

6 — Milk, Urine, Saliva (pH = 6.3 – 6.6)

5 — Black Coffee (pH = 5)

4 — Soda, Grapefruit Juice, Tomato Juice (pH = 2.5 – 3.5)

3 —
2 — Lemon Juice, Vinegar (pH = 2)

1 — Battery Acid, Hydrochloric Acid (pH = 0)

0 —

Acid

Figure 10.6. The pH Scale

Acids and bases combine in a NEUTRALIZATION REACTION. During the reaction, the H^+ and OH^- ions join to form water, and the remaining ions combine to form a salt:

$$HCl + NaOH \rightarrow H_2O + NaCl$$

A **buffer**, or buffer solution, is a solution that resists changes in pH when small quantities of acids or bases are added. A buffer can do this because it contains a weak acid to react with any added base and a weak base to react with any added acid.

The strength of an acid or base is measured on the **pH SCALE**, which ranges from 1 to 14, with 1 being the strongest acid, 14 being the strongest base, and 7 being neutral. A substance's pH value is a measure of how many hydrogen ions are in the solution. The scale is logarithmic, meaning an acid with a pH of 3 has ten times as many hydrogen ions as an acid with a pH of 4. Water, which separates into equal numbers of H^+ and OH^- ions, has a neutral pH of 7.

EXAMPLES

1. Which of the following is the product of a neutralization reaction?

    A) a base

    B) a buffer

    C) hydrogen ions

    D) a salt

    Answer:

    D) is correct. A neutralization reaction occurs when an acid and a base combine to form a salt and water.

2. What will happen to the pH of a nitric acid solution that is diluted by a factor of ten?

    A) The pH will go up ten units.

    B) The pH will go down ten units.

    C) The pH will go up one unit.

    D) The pH will go down one unit.

    Answer:

    C) is correct. The pH will go up: diluting an acid will decrease the concentration of H^+ ions, and higher pH values represent lower concentrations of H^+ ions. Diluting the acid by a factor of ten will change the pH one unit because the pH scale is logarithmic.

Motion

To study motion, it is necessary to understand the concept of scalars and vectors. **SCALARS** are measurements that have a quantity but no direction. **VECTORS**, in contrast, have both a quantity and a direction. **DISTANCE** is a scalar: it describes how far an object has traveled along a path. Distance can have values such as 54 m or 16 miles. **DISPLACEMENT** is a vector: it describes how far an object has traveled from its starting position. A displacement value will indicate direction, such as 54 m east or –16 miles.

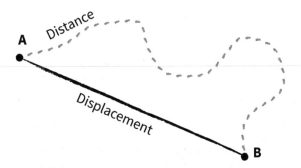

Figure 10.7. Distance versus Displacement

SPEED describes how quickly something is moving. It is found by dividing distance by time, and so is a scalar value. **VELOCITY** is the rate at which an object changes position. Velocity is found by dividing displacement by time, meaning it is a vector value. An object that travels a certain distance and then returns to its starting point has a velocity of zero because its final position did not change. Its speed, however, can be found by dividing the total distance it traveled by the time it took to make the trip.

ACCELERATION describes how quickly an object changes velocity. It is also a vector: when acceleration is in the same direction as velocity, the object will move faster. When the acceleration is in the opposite direction of velocity, the object will slow down.

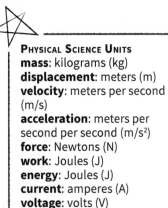

PHYSICAL SCIENCE UNITS
mass: kilograms (kg)
displacement: meters (m)
velocity: meters per second (m/s)
acceleration: meters per second per second (m/s²)
force: Newtons (N)
work: Joules (J)
energy: Joules (J)
current: amperes (A)
voltage: volts (V)

EXAMPLE

A person starts from rest and increases his velocity to 5 m/s over a time period of 1 second. What is his acceleration?

A) −5 m/s²

B) 0 m/s²

C) 5 m/s²

D) 10 m/s²

Answer:

C) is correct. Acceleration is the change in velocity over the change in time:

$$a = \frac{v}{t} = \frac{(5 \text{ m/s} - 0 \text{ m/s})}{1 \text{ s}} = \textbf{5 m/s}^2$$

Forces

A push or pull that causes an object to move or change direction is called a **FORCE**. Forces can arise from a number of different sources.

- **GRAVITY** is the attraction of one mass to another mass. For example, the earth's gravitational field pulls objects toward it, and the sun's gravitational field keeps planets in motion around it.

- **ELECTRICAL FORCE** is the creation of a field by charged particles that will cause other charged objects in that field to move.
- **TENSION** is found in ropes pulling or holding up an object.
- **FRICTION** is created by two objects moving against each other.
- **NORMAL FORCE** occurs when an object is resting on another object.
- **BUOYANT FORCE** is the upward force experienced by floating objects.

In 1687, Isaac Newton published **THREE LAWS OF MOTION** that describe the behavior of force and mass. Newton's first law is also called the **LAW OF INERTIA**. It states that an object will maintain its current state of motion unless acted on by an outside force.

Newton's **SECOND LAW** is an equation, $F = ma$. The equation states that increasing the force on an object will increase its acceleration. In addition, the mass of the object will determine its acceleration: under the same force, a small object will accelerate more quickly than a larger object.

An object in equilibrium is either at rest or is moving at constant velocity; in other words, the object has no acceleration, or $a = 0$. Using Newton's second law, an object is in equilibrium if the net force on the object is 0, or $F = 0$ (this is called the equilibrium condition).

Newton's **THIRD LAW** states that for every action (force), there will be an equal and opposite reaction (force). For instance, if a person is standing on the floor, there is a force of gravity pulling him toward the earth. However, he is not accelerating toward the earth; he is simply standing at rest on the floor (in equilibrium). So, the floor must provide a force that is equal in magnitude and in the opposite direction to the force of gravity.

EXAMPLES

1. When a car moving forward stops abruptly, which of the following describes what happens to the driver if she is wearing a seat belt?

    A) The driver's body will continue to move forward due to inertia, and the seat belt will apply the required force to keep her in her seat.

    B) The driver is inside the car, so she will stop with the car whether or not she is wearing a seat belt.

    C) Due to inertia, the driver's body wants to be at rest, so she will stop automatically once the car stops moving.

    D) The driver's body will slow down because inertia is passed from the seat belt in the car to the driver.

    Answer:

    A) is correct. The driver's body will continue moving forward due to inertia. A force is required to slow the driver down (Newton's first law).

2. Which example describes an object in equilibrium?

    A) a parachutist after he jumps from an airplane

    B) an airplane taking off

    C) a person sitting still in a chair

    D) a soccer ball when it is kicked

Answer:

C) is correct. A person sitting in a chair is not accelerating. All the other choices describe objects that are accelerating, or changing velocity.

Work

WORK is a scalar value that is defined as the application of a force over a distance. It is measured in Joules (J).

A person lifting a book off the ground is an example of someone doing work. The book has a weight because it is being pulled toward the earth. As the person lifts the book, her hand and arm are producing a force that is larger than that weight, causing the book to rise. The higher the person lifts the book, the more work is done.

The sign of the work done is important. In the example of lifting a book, the person's hand is doing positive (+) work on the book. However, gravity is always pulling the book down, which means that during a lift, gravity is doing negative (−) work on the book. If the force and the displacement are in the same direction, then the work is positive (+). If the force and the displacement are in opposite directions, then the work is negative (−). In the case of lifting a book, the net work done on the book is positive.

EXAMPLE

Which situation requires the most work done on a car?

A) pushing on the car, but it does not move

B) towing the car up a steep hill for 100 meters

C) pushing the car 5 meters across a parking lot

D) painting the car

Answer:

B) is correct. A steep hill requires a large force to counter the gravitational force. The large distance will also lead to a large amount of work done. Less work is done in choice C), and no work is done in choice A). Choice D) is incorrect because painting the car is "work," but not the technical definition of work. The car is not moving while being painted, so no work is done on the car.

Energy

ENERGY is an abstract concept, but everything in nature has an energy associated with it. Energy is measured in Joules (J). There are many types of energy:

◆ mechanical: the energy of motion

◆ chemical: the energy in chemical bonds

◆ thermal: the energy of an object due to its temperature

◆ nuclear: the energy in the nucleus of an atom

◆ electric: the energy arising from charged particles

- magnetic: the energy arising from a magnetic field

There is an energy related to movement called the KINETIC ENERGY (KE). Any object that has mass and is moving will have a kinetic energy.

POTENTIAL ENERGY (PE) is the energy stored in a system; it can be understood as the potential for an object to gain kinetic energy. There are several types of potential energy.

- ELECTRIC POTENTIAL ENERGY is derived from the interaction between positive and negative charges.
- Compressing a spring stores ELASTIC POTENTIAL ENERGY.
- Energy is also stored in chemical bonds as CHEMICAL POTENTIAL ENERGY.
- The energy stored by objects due to their height is GRAVITATIONAL POTENTIAL ENERGY.

Energy can be converted into other forms of energy, but it cannot be created or destroyed. This principle is called the CONSERVATION OF ENERGY. A swing provides a simple example of this principle. Throughout the swing's path, the total energy of the system remains the same. At the highest point of a swing's path, it has potential energy but no kinetic energy (because it has stopped moving momentarily as it changes direction). As the swing drops, that potential energy is converted to kinetic energy, and the swing's velocity increases. At the bottom of its path, all its potential energy has been converted into kinetic energy (meaning its potential energy is zero). This process repeats as the swing moves up and down. At any point in the swing's path, the kinetic and potential energies will sum to the same value.

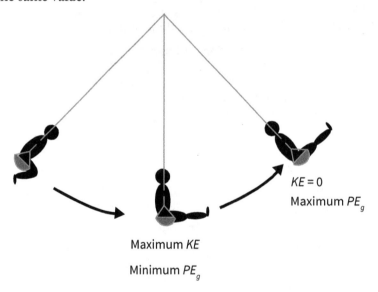

$KE = 0$
Maximum PE_g

Maximum KE

Minimum PE_g

Figure 10.8. Conservation of Energy in a Swing

EXAMPLES

1. Imagine a roller coaster that does not have its own power and starts on a hill at a height of 100 meters. There is no air resistance or friction. It falls down to a height of 50 meters in the first dip and begins to move up the next hill, which is 200 meters high. What will happen to the coaster on this hill?

A) It will slow down but will make it over the 200 meter hill.

B) It will make it 150 meters up the hill and move back down to the first dip.

C) It will make it 100 meters up the hill and move back down to the first dip.

D) It will make it 75 meters up the hill and move back down to the first dip.

Answer:

C) is correct. Its maximum energy is from its starting point, the potential energy at 100 meters, so it can never move higher than 100 meters.

2. A pendulum with mass *m* is swinging back and forth. Which of the following statements about the pendulum's speed is true?

    A) The maximum speed of the mass will occur when it's closest to the ground.

    B) The maximum speed of the mass will occur when it's farthest from the ground.

    C) The mass will always travel at the same speed.

    D) The maximum speed of the mass will occur when it is halfway between its lowest and highest point.

Answer:

A) is correct. The mass always has the same total energy. When the height is the lowest, the potential energy is at its minimum, and so the kinetic energy is at its maximum. When kinetic energy is high, the mass's velocity will be at its height.

Waves

Energy can also be transferred through **WAVES**, which are repeating pulses of energy. Waves that travel through a medium, like ripples on a pond or compressions in a Slinky, are called **MECHANICAL WAVES**. Waves that vibrate up and down (like the ripples on a pond) are **TRANSVERSE WAVES**, and those that travel through compression (like the Slinky) are **LONGITUDINAL WAVES**. Mechanical waves will travel faster through denser mediums; for example, sound waves will move faster through water than through air.

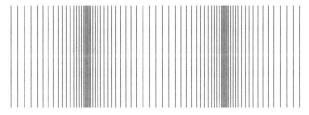

Longitudinal Wave

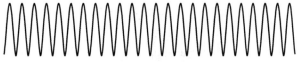

Transverse Wave

Figure 10.9. Types of Waves

Waves can be described using a number of different properties. A wave's highest point is called its **CREST**, and its lowest point is the **TROUGH**. A wave's **MIDLINE** is halfway between the crest and trough; the **AMPLITUDE** describes the distance between the midline and the crest (or trough). The distance between crests (or troughs) is the **WAVELENGTH**. A wave's **PERIOD** is the time it takes for a wave to go through one complete cycle, and the number of cycles a wave goes through in a specific period of time is its **FREQUENCY**.

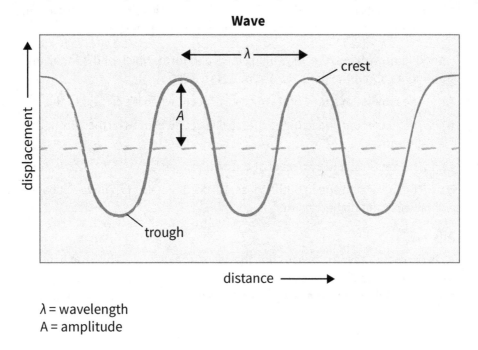

λ = wavelength
A = amplitude

Figure 10.10. Parts of a Wave

SOUND is a special type of longitudinal wave created by vibrations. Our ears are able to interpret these waves as particular sounds. The frequency, or rate, of the vibration determines the sound's **PITCH**. **LOUDNESS** depends on the amplitude, or height, of a sound wave.

The **DOPPLER EFFECT** is the difference in perceived pitch caused by the motion of the object creating the wave. For example, as an ambulance approaches an observer, the siren's pitch will appear to increase, and then as the ambulance moves away, the siren's pitch will appear to decrease. This occurs because sound waves are compressed as the ambulance approaches the observer and are spread out as the ambulance moves away from the observer.

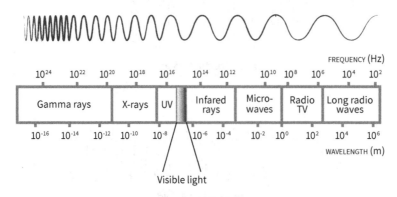

Figure 10.11. The Electromagnetic Spectrum

ELECTROMAGNETIC WAVES are composed of oscillating electric and magnetic fields and thus do not require a medium through which to travel. The electromagnetic spectrum classifies the types of electromagnetic waves based on their frequency. These include radio waves, microwaves, X-rays, and visible light.

The study of light is called OPTICS. Because visible light is a wave, it will display properties that are similar to other waves. It will REFLECT, or bounce off, surfaces, which can be observed by shining a flashlight on a mirror. Light will also REFRACT, or bend, when it travels between substances. This effect can be seen by placing a pencil in water and observing the apparent bend in the pencil.

Curved pieces of glass called LENSES can be used to bend light in a way that affects how an image is perceived. Some microscopes, for example, make objects appear larger through the use of specific types of lenses. Eyeglasses also use lenses to correct poor vision.

The frequency of a light wave is responsible for its color, with red/orange colors having a lower frequency than blue/violet colors. White light is a blend of all the frequencies of visible light. Passing white light through a prism will bend each frequency at a slightly different angle, separating the colors and creating a rainbow. Sunlight passing through raindrops can undergo this effect, creating large rainbows in the sky.

EXAMPLES

1. Which type of wave is a longitudinal wave?

   A) ocean wave

   B) light wave

   C) sound wave

   D) X-ray wave

   Answer:

   C) is correct. Sound waves are longitudinal waves because the vibrations travel in the same direction as the energy.

2. Which of the following events is caused by refraction?

   A) a rainbow during a rainstorm

   B) an echo in a cave

   C) a candle appearing in a mirror

   D) the Doppler effect

   Answer:

   A) is correct. The light of the sun hits rain droplets and bends into a band of colors. The bending of waves is refraction.

Electricity and Magnetism

ELECTRIC CHARGE is created by a difference in the balance of protons and electrons, which creates a positively or negatively charged object. Charged objects create an ELECTRIC FIELD that spreads outward from the object. Other charged objects in that field will experience a force: objects that have opposite charges will be attracted to each other, and objects with the same charge will be repelled, or pushed away, from each other.

Because protons cannot leave the nucleus, charge is created by the movement of electrons. STATIC ELECTRICITY, or electrostatic charge, occurs when a surface has a buildup of charges. For example, if a student rubs a balloon on her head, the friction will cause electrons to move from her hair to the balloon. This creates a negative charge on the balloon and a positive charge on her hair; the resulting attraction will cause her hair to move toward the balloon.

ELECTRICITY is the movement of electrons through a conductor, and an electric circuit is a closed loop through which electricity moves. Circuits include a VOLTAGE source, which powers the movement of electrons known as CURRENT. Sources of voltage include batteries, generators, and wall outlets (which are in turn powered by electric power stations). Other elements, such as lights, computers, and microwaves, can then be connected to the circuit and then powered by its electricity.

MAGNETS are created by the alignment of spinning electrons within a substance. This alignment will occur naturally in some substances, including iron, nickel, and cobalt, all of which can be used to produce permanent magnets. The alignment of electrons creates a magnetic field, which, like an electric or gravitational field, can act on other objects. Magnetic fields have a north and a south pole that act similarly to electric charges: opposite poles will attract, and same poles will repel each other. However, unlike electric charge, which can be either positive or negative, a magnetic field ALWAYS has two poles. If a magnet is cut in half, the result is two magnets, each with a north and a south pole.

Electricity and magnetism are closely related. A moving magnet creates an electric field, and a moving charged particle creates a magnetic field. A specific kind of temporary magnet known as an ELECTROMAGNET can be made by coiling a wire around a metal object and running electricity through it. A magnetic field will be created when the wire contains a current but will disappear when the flow of electricity is stopped.

EXAMPLES

1. What part of the atom flows through a circuit to power a light bulb?

   A) protons

   B) neutrons

   C) electrons

   D) nucleus

   Answer:

   C) is correct. Electrons are negatively charged subatomic particles that exist outside the nucleus of an atom. A power source forces moving electrons through a circuit.

2. Which metal attracts magnets?

A) iron

B) copper

C) silver

D) gold

Answer:

A) is correct. Magnets readily attract iron. The other metals are not attracted to magnets.

GO ON

Test Your Knowledge

Read the question, and then choose the most correct answer.

1. Which of the following determines the atomic number of an atom?

   A) the number of electrons orbiting the nucleus

   B) the number of protons in the nucleus

   C) the number of protons and neutrons in the nucleus

   D) the number of protons and electrons in the atom

2. How many neutrons are in an atom of the element $^{88}_{38}Sr$?

   A) 38

   B) 88

   C) 50

   D) 126

3. Refer to the periodic table on page 39. Which element is a metalloid?

   A) rubidium

   B) vanadium

   C) antimony

   D) iodine

4. Which of the following is NOT a typical property of metals?

   A) Metals have low densities.

   B) Metals are malleable.

   C) Metals are good conductors of electricity and heat.

   D) Metals in solid state consist of ordered structures with tightly packed atoms.

5. Which element has chemical properties most similar to sulfur?

   A) fluorine

   B) argon

   C) phosphorus

   D) oxygen

6. Which of the following groups on the periodic table will typically adopt a charge of +1 when forming ionic compounds?

   A) alkaline earth metals

   B) lanthanides

   C) actinides

   D) alkali metals

7. Match the elements with the type of bond that would occur between them.

Elements	Bond
magnesium and bromine	
carbon and oxygen	
solid copper	

   A) ionic

   B) metallic

   C) covalent

8. Label each compound as polar or nonpolar.

Compound	Polar	Nonpolar
H_2O		
F_2		
HF		

9. How many electrons are included in the double bond between the two oxygen atoms in O_2?

A) 2

B) 4

C) 6

D) 8

10. Which of the following describes a physical change?

A) Water becomes ice.

B) Batter is baked into a cake.

C) An iron fence rusts.

D) A firecracker explodes.

11. Which of the following processes produces a gas from a solid?

A) melting

B) evaporation

C) condensation

D) sublimation

12. Which of the following is a double replacement reaction?

A) HNO_3 (aq) + NaOH (aq) → $NaNO_3$ (aq) + H_2O (l)

B) CS_2 (g) + CO_2 (g) → 2COS (g)

C) $2N_2O$ (g) → $2N_2$ (g) + O_2 (g)

D) $BaCl_2$ (aq) + H_2SO_4 (aq) → 2HCl (aq) + $BaSO_4$ (s)

13. Balance the following chemical equation:
$P_4 + O_2 + H_2O → H_3PO_4$

A) 1:8:6:4

B) 1:2:2:4

C) 1:2:6:4

D) 1:5:6:4

14. Which of the following is NOT a homogeneous mixture?

A) air

B) sandy water

C) brass

D) salt dissolved in water

15. Which trait defines a saturated solution?

A) Both the solute and solvent are liquid.

B) The solute is distributed evenly throughout the solution.

C) The solute is unevenly distributed throughout the solution.

D) No more solute can be dissolved in the solution.

16. Which of the following is NOT a definition of an acid?

A) A substance that contains hydrogen and produces H^+ in water.

B) A substance that donates protons to a base.

C) A substance that reacts with a base to form a salt and water.

D) A substance that accepts protons.

17. A ball is tossed straight into the air with a velocity of 3 m/s. What will its velocity be at its maximum height?

A) −3 m/s

B) 0 m/s

C) 1.5 m/s

D) 3 m/s

18. How far will a car moving at 40 m/s travel in 2 seconds?

    A) 10 m

    B) 20 m

    C) 40 m

    D) 80 m

19. If a baseball thrown straight up in the air takes 5 seconds to reach its peak, how long will it need to fall back to the player's hand?

    A) 2.5 seconds

    B) 9.8 seconds

    C) 5.0 seconds

    D) 10.0 seconds

20. Which of the following is a measure of the inertia of an object?

    A) mass

    B) speed

    C) acceleration

    D) force

21. A box sliding down a ramp experiences all of the following forces EXCEPT

    A) tension.

    B) friction.

    C) gravitational.

    D) normal.

22. A person with a mass of 80 kg travels to the moon, where the acceleration due to gravity is 1.62 m/s². What will her mass be on the moon?

    A) greater than 80 kg

    B) 80 kg

    C) less than 80 kg

    D) The answer cannot be determined without more information.

23. If a force of 300 N is pushing on a block to the right and a force of 400 N is pushing on a block to the left, what is the net force on the block?

    A) 0 N

    B) 100 N to the left

    C) 300 N to the right

    D) 400 N to the left

24. A man is pushing against a heavy rock sitting on a flat plane, and the rock is not moving. The force that holds the rock in place is

    A) friction.

    B) gravity.

    C) normal force.

    D) buoyant force.

25. Which of the following describes what will happen when positive work is done on an object?

    A) The object will gain energy.

    B) The object will lose energy.

    C) The object will increase its temperature.

    D) The object will decrease its temperature.

26. What type of energy is stored in the bond between hydrogen and oxygen in water (H_2O)?

    A) mechanical

    B) chemical

    C) nuclear

    D) electric

27. A microscope makes use of which property of waves to make objects appear larger?

    A) diffraction

    B) amplitude

    C) reflection

    D) refraction

28. Which measurement describes the distance between crests in a wave?

   A) amplitude

   B) wavelength

   C) frequency

   D) period

29. Two negative charges are being held 1 meter apart. What will the charges do when they are released?

   A) They will move closer together.

   B) They will move farther apart.

   C) They will stay 1 meter apart and move in the same direction.

   D) They will stay 1 meter apart and not move.

30. The north poles of two magnets are held near each other. At which distance will the magnets experience the most force?

   A) 0.1 meters

   B) 1 meters

   C) 10 meters

   D) 100 meters

GO ON

Answer Key

1. **B) is correct.**

   Atomic number is defined as the total number of protons in the nucleus of an atom.

2. **C) is correct.**

   Subtracting the atomic number from the mass number gives the number of protons:
   $A - Z =$
   $88 - 38 = 50$.

3. **C) is correct.**

   Antimony is a metalloid. Rubidium is a metal, vanadium is a transition metal, and iodine is a halogen.

4. **A) is correct.**

   Because metals tend to consist of ordered, tightly packed atoms, their densities are typically high (not low).

5. **D) is correct.**

   Oxygen is in the same group as sulfur and is also a nonmetal.

6. **D) is correct.**

   By losing one electron and thereby adopting a +1 charge, alkali metals achieve a noble gas electron configuration, making them more stable.

7.

Elements	Bond
magnesium and bromine	**A) is correct.** Ionic bonds form between elements on the left side of the periodic table and the right side.
carbon and oxygen	**C) is correct.** Nonmetals tend to form covalent bonds.
solid copper	**B) is correct.** Solid metals are held together by metallic bonding.

8.

Compound	Polar	Nonpolar
H_2O	O attracts electrons more strongly than H, and H_2O is bent such that the charges on each O do not balance.	
F_2		Because the two atoms are the same, they share electrons equally.
HF	F attracts electrons more strongly than H, creating a polar molecule.	

9. **B) is correct.**

The two oxygen atoms in a covalent double bond share two pairs of electrons, or four total.

10. **A) is correct.**

When water changes form, it does not change the chemical composition of the substance. Once water becomes ice, the ice can easily turn back into water.

11. **D) is correct.**

Sublimation is the phase change in which a material moves directly from the solid phase to the gas phase, bypassing the liquid phase.

12. **D) is correct.**

This reaction is a double replacement reaction in which the two reactants change partners. Ba^{+2} combines with SO_4^{-2} and H^{+1} combines with Cl^{-1}.

13. **D) is correct.**

$$\_P_4 + \_O_2 + \_H_2O \rightarrow \_H_3PO_4$$

Add a 4 on the right side to balance the four P atoms on the left.

$$\_P_4 + \_O_2 + \_H_2O \rightarrow 4H_3PO_4$$

There are now twelve H atoms on the right, so add a 6 to H_2O on the left.

$$\_P_4 + \_O_2 + 6H_2O \rightarrow 4H_3PO_4$$

There are sixteen O on the right, so add a 5 to O_2 on the left.

$$P_4 + 5O_2 + 6H_2O \rightarrow 4H_3PO_4$$

14. **B) is correct.**

Sandy water is not a homogeneous mixture. Sand and water can be easily separated, making it a heterogeneous mixture.

15. **D) is correct.**

No more solute can be dissolved into a saturated solution.

16. **D) is correct.**

Acids increase the concentration of hydrogen ions in solution and do not accept protons.

17. **B) is correct.**

The velocity of a projectile is zero at its maximum height.

18. **D) is correct.**

Displacement is equal to velocity multiplied by time:

$d = vt = (40 \text{ m/s})(2 \text{ s}) = 80 \text{ m}$

19. **C) is correct.**

The time to the peak and the time to fall back to the original height are equal.

20. **A) is correct.**

Mass is a measure of an object's inertia.

21. **A) is correct.**

Tension is the force that results from objects being pulled or hung.

22. **B) is correct.**

The mass of an object is constant, so the mass would still be 80 kg. (However, the person's weight would be lower on the moon than on the earth.)

23. **B) is correct.**

The total force on an object is found by adding all the individual forces: 300 N + (−400 N) = −100 N (where negative is to the left).

24. **A) is correct.**

When the man pushes on the rock, static friction points opposite the direction of the applied force with the same magnitude. The forces add to zero, so the rock's acceleration is also zero.

25. **A) is correct.**

The object will gain energy.

26. **B) is correct.**

Chemical energy is stored in the bonds between atoms.

27. **D) is correct.**

Lenses refract, or bend, light waves to make objects appear larger.

28. **B) is correct.**

Wavelength is the length of each cycle of the wave, which can be found by measuring between crests.

29. **B) is correct.**

Like charges repel each other, so the two charges will move apart from each other.

30. **A) is correct.**

Magnetic force is inversely proportional to the distance between two objects, so the smallest distance will create the largest force.

eleven

EARTH AND SPACE SCIENCE

Astronomy

ASTRONOMY is the study of space. Our planet, **EARTH**, is just one out of a group of planets that orbit the sun, which is the star at the center of our solar system. Other planets in our solar system include Mercury, Venus, Mars, Jupiter, Saturn, Uranus, and Neptune. Every planet, except Mercury and Venus, has **MOONS**, or naturally occurring satellites that orbit a

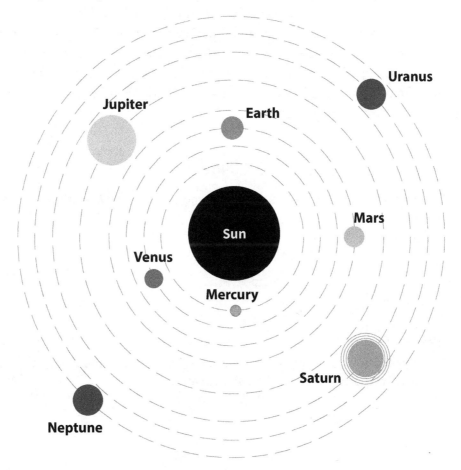

Figure 11.1. Solar System

planet. Our solar system also includes ASTEROIDS and COMETS, small rocky or icy objects that orbit the Sun. Many of these are clustered in the ASTEROID BELT, which is located between the orbits of Mars and Jupiter.

Our solar system is a small part of a bigger star system called a GALAXY. (Our galaxy is called the Milky Way.) Galaxies consist of stars, gas, and dust held together by gravity and contain millions of STARS, which are hot balls of plasma and gases. The universe includes many types of stars, including supergiant stars, white dwarfs, giant stars, and neutron stars. Stars form in NEBULAS, which are large clouds of dust and gas. When very large stars collapse, they create BLACK HOLES, which have a gravitational force so strong that light cannot escape.

Earth, the moon, and the sun interact in a number of ways that impact life on our planet. When the positions of the three align, eclipses occur. A LUNAR ECLIPSE occurs when Earth lines up between the moon and the sun; the moon moves into the shadow of Earth and appears dark in color. A SOLAR ECLIPSE occurs when the moon lines up between Earth and the sun; the moon covers the sun, blocking sunlight.

The cycle of day and night and the seasonal cycle are determined by the earth's motion. It takes approximately 365 days, or one YEAR, for Earth to revolve around the sun. While Earth is revolving around the sun, it is also rotating on its axis, which takes approximately twenty-four hours, or one DAY. As the planet rotates, different areas alternately face toward the sun and away from the sun, creating night and day.

The earth's axis is not directly perpendicular to its orbit, meaning the planet tilts on its axis. The SEASONS are caused by this tilt. When the Northern Hemisphere is tilted toward the sun, it receives more sunlight and experiences summer. At the same time that the Northern Hemisphere experiences summer, the Southern Hemisphere, which receives less direct sunlight, experiences winter. As the earth revolves, the Northern Hemisphere will tilt away from the sun and move into winter, while the Southern Hemisphere tilts toward the sun and moves into summer.

EXAMPLE

What term describes what occurs when the moon moves between the earth and the sun?

A) aurora

B) lunar eclipse

C) black hole

D) solar eclipse

Answer:

D) is correct. When the moon moves between the earth and the sun, a solar eclipse occurs, blocking sunlight from the planet.

Geology

GEOLOGY is the study of the minerals and rocks that make up the earth. A MINERAL is a naturally occurring, solid, inorganic substance with a crystalline structure. There are several properties that help identify a mineral, including color, luster, hardness, and density. Examples of minerals include talc, diamonds, and topaz.

Although a ROCK is also a naturally occurring solid, it can be either organic or inorganic and is composed of one or more minerals. Rocks are classified based on their method of formation. The three types of rocks are igneous, sedimentary, and metamorphic. IGNEOUS ROCKS are the result of tectonic processes that bring magma, or melted rock, to the earth's surface; they can form either above or below the surface. SEDIMENTARY ROCKS are formed from the compaction of rock fragments that results from weathering and erosion. Lastly, METAMORPHIC ROCKS form when extreme temperature and pressure cause the structure of pre-existing rocks to change.

Luster describes how light reflects off the surface of a mineral. Terms to describe luster include dull, metallic, pearly, and waxy.

The ROCK CYCLE describes how rocks form and break down. Typically, the cooling and solidification of magma as it rises to the surface creates igneous rocks. These rocks are then subject to WEATHERING, the mechanical and/or chemical processes by which rocks break down. During EROSION the resulting sediment is deposited in a new location. As sediment is deposited, the resulting compaction creates new sedimentary rocks. As new layers are added, rocks and minerals are forced closer to the earth's core where they are subjected to heat and pressure, resulting in metamorphic rock. Eventually, they will reach their melting

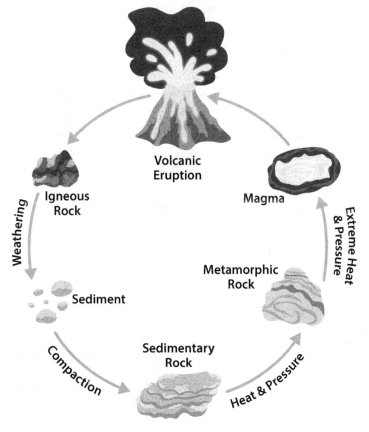

Figure 11.2. The Rock Cycle

point and return to magma, starting the cycle over again. This process takes place over hundreds of thousands or even millions of years.

PALEONTOLOGY, the study of the history of life on Earth, is sometimes also considered part of geology. Paleontologists study the rock record, which retains biological history through FOSSILS, the preserved remains and traces of ancient life. Fossils can be used to learn about the evolution of life on the planet, particularly bacteria, plants, and animals that have gone extinct. Throughout Earth's history, there have been five documented catastrophic events that caused major extinctions. For each mass extinction, there are several theories about the cause but no definitive answers. Theories about what triggered mass extinctions include climate change, ice ages, asteroid and comet impacts, and volcanic activity.

The surface of the earth is made of large plates that float on the less dense layer beneath them. These TECTONIC PLATES make up the lithosphere, the planet's surface layer. Over 200 million years ago, the continents were joined together in one giant landmass called PANGEA. Due to CONTINENTAL DRIFT, or the slow movement of tectonic plates, the continents gradually shifted to their current positions.

The magnitude of an earthquake refers to the amount of energy it releases, measured as the maximum motion during the earthquake. This can indirectly describe how destructive the earthquake was.

The boundaries where plates meet are the locations for many geologic features and events. MOUNTAINS are formed when plates collide and push land upward, and TRENCHES form when one plate is pushed beneath another. In addition, the friction created by plates sliding past each other is responsible for most EARTHQUAKES.

VOLCANOES, which are vents in the earth's crust that allow molten rock to reach the surface, frequently occur along the edges of tectonic plates. However, they can also occur at hotspots located far from plate boundaries.

The outermost layer of the earth, which includes tectonic plates, is called the LITHOSPHERE. Beneath the lithosphere are, in order, the ASTHENOSPHERE, MESOSPHERE, and CORE. The core includes two parts: the OUTER CORE is a liquid layer, and the INNER CORE is composed of solid iron. It is believed the inner core spins at a rate slightly different from the rest of the planet, which creates the earth's magnetic field.

EXAMPLE

Which type of rock forms when lava cools and solidifies?

A) igneous

B) sedimentary

C) metamorphic

D) sandstone

Answer:

A) is correct. Igneous rocks form when liquid rock cools and solidifies.

Hydrology

The earth's surface includes many bodies of water that together form the HYDROSPHERE. The largest of these are the bodies of salt water called OCEANS. There are five oceans: the Arctic, Atlantic, Indian, Pacific, and Southern. Together, the oceans account for 71 percent of the earth's surface and 97 percent of the earth's water.

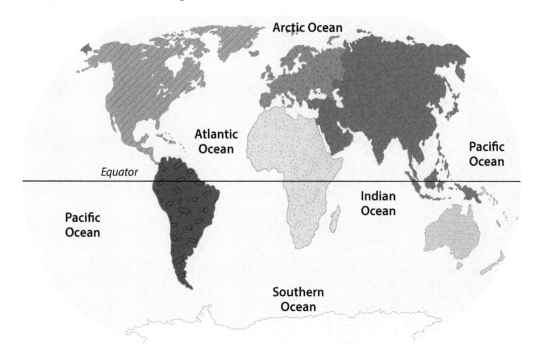

Figure 11.3. The Earth's Oceans

Oceans are subject to cyclic rising and falling water levels at shorelines called TIDES, which are the result of the gravitational pull of the moon and sun. The oceans also experience WAVES, which are caused by the movement of energy through the water.

Other bodies of water include LAKES, which are usually freshwater, and SEAS, which are usually saltwater. **RIVERS** and streams are moving bodies of water that flow into lakes, seas, and oceans. The earth also contains groundwater, or water that is stored underground in rock formations called AQUIFERS.

Much of the earth's water is stored as ICE. The North and South Poles are usually covered in large sheets of ice called polar ice. **GLACIERS** are large masses of ice and snow that move. Over long periods of time, they scour Earth's surface, creating features such as lakes and valleys. Large chunks of ice that break off from glaciers are called ICEBERGS.

The WATER CYCLE is the circulation of water throughout the earth's surface, atmosphere, and hydrosphere. Water on the earth's surface evaporates, or changes from a liquid to a gas, and becomes water vapor. Plants also release water vapor through transpiration. Water vapor in the air then comes together to form clouds. When it cools, this water vapor condenses into a liquid and falls from the sky as precipitation, which includes rain, sleet,

97 percent of the water on earth is saltwater. 68 percent of the remaining freshwater is locked up in ice caps and glaciers.

snow, and hail. Precipitation replenishes groundwater and the water found in features such as lakes and rivers, thus starting the cycle over again.

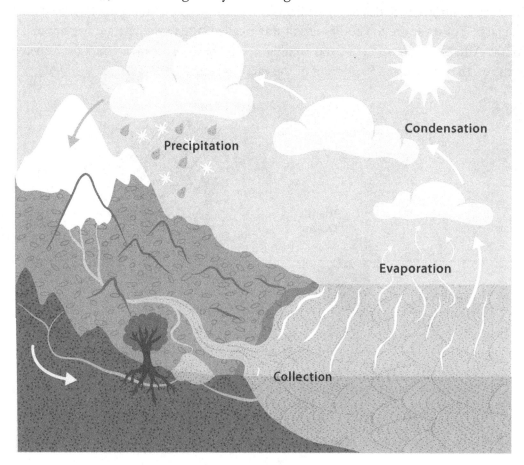

Figure 11.4. The Water Cycle

EXAMPLE

During the water cycle, groundwater is replenished by

A) transpiration.

B) glaciers.

C) lakes.

D) precipitation.

Answer:

D) is correct. Precipitation such as rain and snow seep into the ground to add to the groundwater supply.

Meteorology

Above the surface of Earth is the mass of gases called the **ATMOSPHERE**. The atmosphere includes the **TROPOSPHERE**, which is closest to the earth, followed by the **STRATOSPHERE**, **MESOSPHERE**, and **THERMOSPHERE**. The outermost layer of the atmosphere is the **EXOSPHERE**, which is located 6,200 miles above the surface. Generally, temperature in the atmosphere decreases with altitude. The OZONE LAYER, which captures harmful radiation from the sun, is located in the stratosphere.

The HUMIDITY, or amount of water vapor in the air, and the TEMPERATURE are two major atmospheric conditions that determine weather, the day-to-day changes in atmospheric conditions. A WARM FRONT occurs when warm air moves over a cold air mass, causing the air to feel warmer and more humid. A COLD FRONT occurs when cold air moves under a warm air mass, causing a drop in temperature.

Between each layer, a boundary exists where conditions change. This boundary takes the first part of the name of the previous layer followed by "pause." For example, the boundary between the troposphere and stratosphere is called the tropopause.

Sometimes, weather turns violent. Tropical cyclones, or hurricanes, originate over warm ocean water. Hurricanes have destructive winds of more than 74 miles per hour and create large storm surges that can cause extensive damage along coastlines. Hurricanes, typhoons, and cyclones are all the same type of storm; they just have different names based on where the storm is located. HURRICANES originate in the Atlantic or Eastern Pacific Ocean, TYPHOONS in the Western Pacific Ocean, and CYCLONES in the Indian Ocean. TORNADOES occur when unstable warm and cold air masses collide and a rotation is created by fast-moving winds.

The long-term weather conditions in a geographic location are called CLIMATE. A climate zone is a large area that experiences similar average temperature and precipitation. The three major climate zones, based on temperature, are the polar, temperate, and tropical zones. Each climate zone is subdivided into subclimates that have unique characteristics. The TROPICAL CLIMATE ZONE (warm temperatures) can be subdivided into tropical wet, tropical wet and dry, semiarid, and arid. The TEMPERATE CLIMATE ZONES (moderate temperatures) include Mediterranean, humid subtropical, marine West Coast, humid continental, and subarctic. The POLAR CLIMATE ZONES (cold temperatures) include tundra, highlands, nonpermanent ice, and ice cap. Polar climates are cold and experience prolonged, dark winters due to the tilt of the earth's axis.

EXAMPLE

Which layer of the atmosphere absorbs harmful ultraviolet radiation from the sun?

A) mesosphere

B) stratosphere

C) troposphere

D) thermosphere

Answer:

B) is correct. The stratosphere contains a sublayer called the ozone layer, which absorbs harmful ultraviolet radiation from the sun.

GO ON

Test Your Knowledge

Read the question, and then choose the most correct answer.

1. Which planet orbits closest to Earth?
   - **A)** Mercury
   - **B)** Venus
   - **C)** Jupiter
   - **D)** Saturn

2. What is the name of the phenomenon when a star suddenly increases in brightness and then disappears from view?
   - **A)** aurora
   - **B)** black hole
   - **C)** eclipse
   - **D)** supernova

3. How long does it take the earth to rotate on its axis?
   - **A)** one hour
   - **B)** one day
   - **C)** one month
   - **D)** one year

4. Which statement about the solar system is true?
   - **A)** Earth is much closer to the sun than it is to other stars.
   - **B)** The moon is closer to Venus than it is to Earth.
   - **C)** At certain times of the year, Jupiter is closer to the sun than Earth is.
   - **D)** Mercury is the closest planet to Earth.

5. When Earth moves between the moon and the sun, it is called a
   - **A)** solar eclipse.
   - **B)** lunar eclipse.
   - **C)** black hole.
   - **D)** supernova.

6. Which planet does not have a moon?
   - **A)** Mercury
   - **B)** Earth
   - **C)** Jupiter
   - **D)** Saturn

7. What is the term for the top layer of the earth's surface?
   - **A)** lithosphere
   - **B)** atmosphere
   - **C)** biosphere
   - **D)** asthenosphere

8. Which action is an example of mechanical weathering?
   - **A)** Calcium carbonate reacts with water to form a cave.
   - **B)** An iron gate rusts.
   - **C)** Tree roots grow under the foundation of a house and cause cracks.
   - **D)** Feldspar turns to clay when exposed to water.

9. Which of the following is caused by geothermal heat?
   - **A)** geysers
   - **B)** tsunamis
   - **C)** tornadoes
   - **D)** hurricanes

10. Which of the following holds the largest percentage of earth's freshwater?

    A) glaciers and ice caps

    B) groundwater

    C) lakes

    D) oceans

11. Which of the following best describes how igneous rocks are formed?

    A) Sediment is compacted by pressure in the earth to form rock.

    B) Magma comes to the earth's surface and cools to form rock.

    C) Chemical weathering changes the composition of a rock to form new rock.

    D) Ancient plant and animal life is calcified to create rock.

12. Which of the following is true as altitude increases in the troposphere?

    A) Temperature and pressure increase.

    B) Temperature increases and pressure decreases.

    C) Temperature and pressure decrease.

    D) Temperature decreases and pressure increases.

13. Which statement about hurricanes and tornadoes is true?

    A) Hurricanes and tornadoes spin in opposite directions.

    B) Tornadoes do not occur in warm climates.

    C) Tornadoes have a low wind velocity.

    D) Hurricanes are formed over warm ocean water.

14. Which two properties are used to classify climate zones?

    A) latitude and temperature

    B) temperature and precipitation

    C) elevation and latitude

    D) precipitation and tilt of Earth's axis

15. Which of the following best describes continental drift?

    A) The mass extinction of the earth's species that occurred when a meteor struck the earth.

    B) The spinning of the earth's inner core that creates the earth's magnetic field.

    C) The formation of land masses from cooled magma.

    D) The movement of tectonic plates in the lithosphere.

Answer Key

1. **B) is correct.**

   Venus's orbit is closest to Earth and is the second planet from the sun.

2. **D) is correct.**

   Before a star collapses, the star burns brighter for a period of time and then fades from view. This is a supernova.

3. **B) is correct.**

   Earth takes approximately twenty-four hours to rotate on its axis.

4. **A) is correct.**

   The sun is about ninety-three million miles from Earth; the next closest star is about twenty-five trillion miles away.

5. **B) is correct.**

   A lunar eclipse is when Earth moves between the moon and the sun.

6. **A) is correct.**

   Only the first two planets, Mercury and Venus, lack moons.

7. **A) is correct.**

   The lithosphere is the top layer of the earth's surface.

8. **C) is correct.**

   Mechanical weathering involves breaking a substance down without changing the composition of the substance.

9. **A) is correct.**

   Geysers are caused by geothermal heating of water underground.

10. **A) is correct.**

    Glaciers and ice caps contain approximately 68.7% of all of Earth's freshwater supply, which is the largest percentage of the resources listed.

11. **B) is correct.**

    Igneous rock is formed when magma (melted rock) is brought to the earth's surface and cools.

12. **C) is correct.**

    Temperature and pressure both decrease with altitude in the troposphere.

13. **D) is correct.**

    Hurricanes require warm ocean water to form.

14. **B) is correct.**

    Climate zones are classified by temperature and precipitation.

15. **D) is correct.**

    Continental drift is the movement of tectonic plates that lead to the current position of the continents.

Follow the link below for your second Science GED practice test:
www.acceptedinc.com/ged-2018-online-resources

PART IV:
SOCIAL STUDIES

twelve

UNITED STATES HISTORY

North America Before European Contact

Prior to European colonization, diverse Native American societies controlled the continent; they would later come into economic and diplomatic contact, and military conflict, with European colonizers and United States forces and settlers.

Major civilizations that would play an important and ongoing role in North American history included the **Iroquois** and **Algonquin** in the Northeast. Both of those tribes would also be important allies of the English and French, respectively, in future conflicts, in that part of the continent.

Later, the young United States would come into conflict with the **Shawnee**, **Lenape**, **Kickapoo**, **Miami**, and other tribes in the Midwest during early western expansion. These tribes formed the Northwest Confederacy to fight the United States.

In the South, major tribes included the **Chickasaw**, **Choctaw**, and **Creek** (Muscogee), who were the descendants of the **Mississippi Mound Builders** or Mississippian cultures, societies that built mounds from around 2,100 to 1,800 years ago as burial tombs or the bases for temples. It is thought that the **Cherokee** migrated south to present-day Georgia sometime long before European contact, where they remained until they were forcibly removed in 1832.

Farther west, tribes of the Great Plains like the **Sioux**, **Cheyenne**, **Apache**, **Comanche**, and **Arapaho** would later come into conflict with American settlers as westward expansion continued. Traditionally nomadic or semi-nomadic, these tribes depended on the **buffalo** for survival.

The **Navajo** controlled territory in the Southwest. The Navajo were descendants of the **Ancestral Pueblo** or **Anasazi**, who had settled in the Four Corners area.

In the Pacific Northwest, fishing was a major source of sustenance, and Native American peoples like the **Coast Salish** and **Chinook** created and used canoes to engage in the practice.

Ultimately, through both violent conflict and political means, Native American civilizations lost control of most of their territories and were forced onto reservations by the United States. Negotiations continue today over rights to land and opportunities and reparations for past injustices.

Colonial North America

The Americas were quickly colonized by Europeans after Christopher Columbus first laid claim to them for the Spanish, and the British, French, and Spanish all held territories in North America throughout the sixteenth, seventeenth, eighteenth, and nineteenth centuries.

Spanish *CONQUISTADORS* explored what is today the Southwestern United States, claiming land inhabited by local tribes for Spain. Spanish colonization not only included the control and settlement of land but also the mission to spread Christianity. The Spanish Crown granted *ENCOMIENDAS*, land grants to individuals to establish settlements, allowing the holder to ranch or mine the land and demand tribute and forced labor from local Native peoples.

Forced labor and diseases like SMALLPOX had decimated Native American populations in Mexico and the Southwest. Consequently, to exploit these resource-rich lands, Spanish colonizers took part in the European-driven TRANS-ATLANTIC SLAVE TRADE, kidnapping African people or purchasing them on the West African coast, bringing them to the Americas, and forcing them into slavery in mines and plantations in the Western Hemisphere.

Eventually France would control much of the Great Lakes and the Mississippi region through Louisiana and New Orleans, valuable trade routes. French explorers included **Jacques Cartier** and **Samuel de Champlain**, who founded New France.

Unlike Spain, which sought not only profit but also to settle the land and convert Native Americans to Christianity, France was mainly focused on trade. French explorers reached the Northeast and the eastern Great Lakes region as early as the seventeenth century in search of fur and beaver pelts.

While the Spanish and French arrived generally as single men for trade, who would intermarry with local inhabitants, the English brought their families and settled in North America, with the goal of establishing agricultural settlements. In the sixteenth century, Sir Walter Raleigh established the Roanoke colony in present-day Virginia; while this settlement disappeared by 1590, interest in colonization reemerged as JOINT-STOCK COMPANIES sought royal charters to privately develop colonies on the North American Atlantic coast.

The first established colony, JAMESTOWN, was also located in Virginia, which became so profitable that the English Crown took it over as a colony in 1624. Tobacco and rice grew in Virginia, the Carolinas, and Georgia. Appropriate for plantation farming, these crops required unskilled labor, and the southern colonies became socially stratified, with a society composed mainly of large numbers of enslaved Africans, indentured servants, and landowners.

In New England, **SEPARATISTS**, members of the Church of England who believed it had strayed too far from its theological roots, had come to North America seeking more religious freedom. The first group of Separatists, the Pilgrims, arrived on the *Mayflower* in 1620 and had drawn up the **MAYFLOWER COMPACT**, guaranteeing government by the consent of the governed. They were later joined by the **PURITANS**, who had been persecuted in England. These philosophies would later inform the American Revolution.

Despite differences from the South, social stratification existed in New England as well: according to Puritan belief, wealth and success showed that one was a member of the **ELECT**, or privileged by God. Poorer farmers were generally tenant farmers; they did not own land and rarely made a profit.

The North American colonial economy was part of the **ATLANTIC WORLD**, taking part in the **TRIANGULAR TRADE** between the Americas, Africa and Europe, where people from Africa who were enslaved were exchanged in the Americas for raw materials shipped to Europe to be processed into goods for the benefit of the colonial powers. Sometimes those goods were also exchanged for slaves in Africa. In this way, North America was part of the **COLUMBIAN EXCHANGE**, the intersection of goods and people throughout the Atlantic World.

The mid-Atlantic colonies were also founded on the basis of religious tolerance in the Quaker spirit inspired by the Quaker William Penn.

British policy toward the Colonies had been one of **SALUTARY NEGLECT**, allowing them great autonomy. However, an emerging culture of independence in the Thirteen Colonies caught the attention of the British Crown; it passed the **NAVIGATION ACTS** in 1651 to prevent colonial trade with any other countries. An early sign of colonial discontent, **BACON'S REBELLION** in 1676 against Governor Berkeley of Virginia embodied the growing resentment of landowners, who wanted to increase their own profit rather than redirect revenue to Britain.

American colonists were also increasingly influenced by Enlightenment thought. John Locke's *SECOND TREATISE* was published in 1689; critical of absolute monarchy, it became popular in the Colonies. Locke argued for **REPUBLICANISM**: that the people must come together to create a government for the protection of themselves and their property, thereby giving up some of their natural rights. However, should the government overstep its bounds, the people have the right to overthrow it and replace it.

In the mid-eighteenth century, a sense of religious fervor called the **GREAT AWAKENING** spread throughout the Colonies; people became devoted to God beyond the confines of traditional Christianity. The Great Awakening helped develop a more singularly North American religious culture. It also created a divide between traditional European Christianity and emerging North American faiths.

Meanwhile, North America served also as a battleground for France and England, already in conflict in Europe and elsewhere. In the mid-seventeenth century, the two colonial powers fought the proxy Beaver and Chickasaw wars in alliances with Native American tribes in the Northeast and Southeast.

The Seven Years' War broke out in Europe in 1756; this conflict between the British and French in North America was known as the **FRENCH AND INDIAN WAR**. Following defeats by strong colonial military leaders like **GEORGE WASHINGTON** and despite its strong alliances and long-term presence on the continent, France eventually surrendered. Britain gained control of French territories in North America—as well as Spanish Florida—in the 1763 TREATY OF PARIS which ended the Seven Years' War. In the Proclamation of 1763, Britain also promised Native American tribes that it would not expand its colonies farther west.

Revolution and the Early United States

As a result of the French and Indian War and subsequent unrest, Britain once again discarded its colonial policy of salutary neglect. Furthermore, Britain was in desperate need of cash, as the war had nearly bankrupted the country. The Crown sought ways to increase its revenue from the Colonies.

King George III enforced heavy taxes and restrictive acts in the colonies to generate income for the Crown and punish disobedience. These included the SUGAR ACT in 1764 and the QUARTERING ACT, requiring colonists to provide shelter to British troops stationed in the region.

The 1765 STAMP ACT, the first direct tax on the colonists, triggered more tensions. Any document required a costly stamp, the revenue reverting to the British government.

As a result, colonists began boycotting British goods and engaging in violent protest. In response, officials enforced the punitive TOWNSHEND ACTS which imposed more taxes and restrictions on the colonies. Samuel Adams continued to stir up rebellion with his COMMITTEES OF CORRESPONDENCE, which distributed anti-British propaganda.

Protests against the Quartering Act in Boston led to the BOSTON MASSACRE in 1770, when British troops fired on a crowd of protesters. By 1773, colonists protested the latest taxes on tea levied by the TEA ACT in the famous BOSTON TEA PARTY by dressing as Native Americans and tossing tea off a ship in Boston Harbor. In response, the government passed the INTOLERABLE ACTS, closing Boston Harbor and bringing Massachusetts back under direct royal control.

In response to the Intolerable Acts, colonial leaders met in Philadelphia at the FIRST CONTINENTAL CONGRESS in 1774 and issued the *DECLARATION OF RIGHTS AND GRIEVANCES*, presenting colonial concerns to the King, who ignored it. However, violent conflict began in 1775 at LEXINGTON AND CONCORD, when American militiamen (MINUTEMEN) had gathered to resist British efforts to seize weapons and arrest rebels in Concord. On June 17, 1775, the Americans fought the British at the BATTLE OF BUNKER HILL; despite American losses, the number of casualties the rebels inflicted caused the king to declare that the colonies were in rebellion. Troops were deployed to the colonies; the Siege of Boston began.

In May 1775, the SECOND CONTINENTAL CONGRESS met at Philadelphia to debate the way forward. Debate between the wisdom of continued efforts at compromise and negotiations and declaring independence continued. THOMAS PAINE published his pamphlet *COMMON SENSE*; taking Locke's concepts of natural rights and the obligation of a people to rebel against an oppressive government, it popularized the notion of rebellion against Britain.

By summer of 1776, the Continental Congress agreed on the need to break from Britain; on July 4, 1776, it declared the independence of the United States of America and issued the DECLARATION OF INDEPENDENCE, drafted mainly by THOMAS JEFFERSON and heavily influenced by Locke. Pro-revolution Americans were known as PATRIOTS; those against were TORIES. The American Revolution had begun.

GEORGE WASHINGTON was appointed head of the Continental Army and led a largely unpaid and unprofessional army; despite early losses and the military and financial superiority of the British, Washington and the colonists gained ground due to strong leadership, superior knowledge of the land, and international support. In the 1783 TREATY OF PARIS, the United States was recognized as a country. The American Revolution would go on to inspire revolution around the world.

Joy in the victory over Great Britain was short-lived. Fearful of tyranny, the Second Continental Congress had provided for only a weak central government, adopting the ARTICLES OF CONFEDERATION to organize the Thirteen Colonies—now states—as a loosely united country. However, it soon became clear that the Articles of Confederation were not strong enough to keep the nation united.

ALEXANDER HAMILTON and JAMES MADISON called for a CONSTITUTIONAL CONVENTION to write a Constitution as the foundation of a stronger federal government. Madison and other FEDERALISTS like JOHN ADAMS believed in SEPARATION OF POWERS, republicanism, and a strong federal government.

> The new country was heavily in debt. Currency was weak, and high taxes led to instability in the form of minor rebellions like **Shays' Rebellion**, a revolt of indebted farmers, and the **Whiskey Rebellion**. Furthermore, debt and disorganization made the country appear weak and vulnerable to Great Britain and Spain. If the United States was to remain one country, it needed a stronger federal government.

Despite the separation of powers provided for in the Constitution, ANTI-FEDERALISTS like THOMAS JEFFERSON called for even more limitations on the power of the federal government. The first ten amendments to the Constitution, or the BILL OF RIGHTS, a list of guarantees of American freedoms, was a concession to the anti-Federalists, who would later become the DEMOCRATIC-REPUBLICAN PARTY (eventually, the Democratic Party).

In order to convince the states to ratify the Constitution, Hamilton, Madison, and John Jay wrote the *FEDERALIST PAPERS*, articulating the benefits of federalism. Likewise, the Bill of Rights helped convince the hesitant. In 1791, the Constitution was ratified. GEORGE WASHINGTON was elected president, with John Adams serving as vice president; Washington appointed Hamilton as Secretary of the Treasury and Jefferson as Secretary of State.

Federalists favored taxation and centralized financial management, which Anti-Federalists—who became known as DEMOCRATIC-REPUBLICANS—vehemently opposed. The US tried to remain neutral in international affairs but was accosted by Britain and France at sea and in conflict in the Northwest Indian Wars.

In President Washington's FAREWELL ADDRESS, he recommended the United States follow a policy of neutrality in international affairs, setting a precedent for early American history. Vice President John Adams, a Federalist, became the second president.

During the Adams administration, the Federalists passed the harsh ALIEN AND SEDITION ACTS that increased executive power. Divisions between the Federalists and the Democratic-Republicans were deeper than ever and the presidential elections of 1800 were tense and controversial; nevertheless, Thomas Jefferson was elected to the presidency in 1801 in a historical non-violent transfer of power.

Jefferson shrank the federal government. The Alien and Sedition Acts were repealed. Economic policies favored small farmers and landowners, in contrast to Federalist policies, which supported big business and cities. However, Jefferson also oversaw the **LOUISIANA PURCHASE**, which nearly doubled the size of the United States. This troubled some Democratic-Republicans, who saw this as federal overreach, but the Louisiana Purchase would be a major step forward in westward expansion.

Figure 12.1. Louisiana Purchase

Continuing British provocation at sea and in the northwest led to the **WAR OF 1812**. Growing nationalism in the United States pressured Madison into pushing for war after the **BATTLE OF TIPPECANOE** in Indiana, when **GENERAL WILLIAM HENRY HARRISON** fought the **NORTHWEST CONFEDERACY**, a group of tribes led by the Shawnee leader **TECUMSEH**. Despite the Confederacy's alliance with Britain, the United States prevailed. Congress declared war under Madison with the intent to defend the United States, end chaotic trade practices and treatment of Americans on the high seas, and penetrate British Canada.

The war resulted in no real gains or losses for either the Americans or the British. Yet at the war's end, the United States had successfully defended itself as a country and reaffirmed its independence. Patriotism ran high.

With the Louisiana Purchase, the country had almost doubled in size. In the nineteenth century, the idea of **MANIFEST DESTINY**, or the sense that it was the fate of the United States to expand westward and settle the continent, prevailed. The **MONROE DOCTRINE**, James Monroe's policy that the Western Hemisphere was "closed" to any further European colonization or exploration, asserted US hegemony in the region.

Westward expansion triggered questions about the expansion of slavery, a divisive issue. Slavery was profitable for the southern states which depended on the plantation economy, but increasingly condemned in the North with the growing ABOLITIONIST movement. The MISSOURI COMPROMISE, also known as the COMPROMISE OF 1820, allowed Missouri to join the union as a slave state, but provided that any other states north of the THIRTY-SIXTH PARALLEL (36°30') would be free. However, more tension and compromises over the nature of slavery in the West were to come.

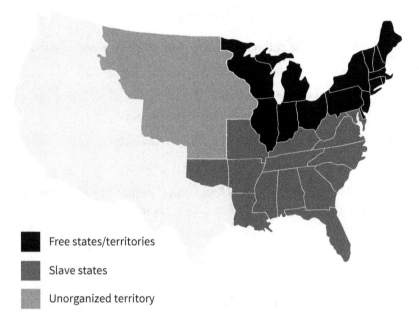

Figure 12.2. Missouri Compromise

Demographics were changing throughout the early nineteenth century. Technological advances such as the COTTON GIN had allowed exponential increases in cotton; therefore, more persons were enslaved than ever before, bringing more urgency to the issue of slavery. In addition, IMMIGRATION from Europe to the United States was increasing—mainly Irish Catholics and Germans. Reactionary NATIVIST movements like the KNOW-NOTHING PARTY feared the influx of non-Anglo Europeans, particularly Catholics, and discrimination was widespread, especially against the Irish. Other technological advances like the RAILROADS and STEAMSHIPS were speeding up westward expansion and improving trade throughout the continent; a large-scale MARKET ECONOMY was emerging. With early industrialization and changing concepts following the Second Great Awakening, women were playing a larger role in society, even though they could not vote.

Most states had extended voting rights to white men who did not own land or substantial property: UNIVERSAL MANHOOD SUFFRAGE. Elected officials would increasingly come to better reflect the electorate, and the brash war hero Andrew Jackson was popular among the "common man." During this period, the TWO-PARTY SYSTEM also emerged.

Jackson's popularity with the "common man," white, male farmers and workers who felt he identified with them, and the fact that owning property was no longer a requirement to vote, gave him the advantage and a two-term presidency. Jackson rewarded his supporters, appointing them to important positions as part of the SPOILS SYSTEM.

Jackson's administration faced economic crises that exacerbated divisions between northern, industrial interests that supported tariffs, and southern, agrarian interests that opposed them. Jackson also supported further continental expansion, which brought conflict with Native Americans. The 1830 **INDIAN REMOVAL ACT** forced thousands of people to travel mainly on foot, with all of their belongings, to Indian Territory (today, Oklahoma) on the infamous **TRAIL OF TEARS**, to make way for white settlers.

EXAMPLE

What advantage did the colonists have in the American Revolution?

A) vast financial wealth and resources

B) superior weaponry and equipment

C) strong leadership and knowledge of the terrain

D) a professional military and access to mercenaries

Answer:

C) is correct. The colonial military had strong leaders and an intimate knowledge of the terrain; many of its military leaders were born and raised in North America.

Civil War and Westward Expansion

In 1845, Texas, which had declared independence from Mexico in 1836, joined the Union; this event, in the context of US westward expansion, triggered the **MEXICAN-AMERICAN WAR**. As a result, the United States obtained territory in the Southwest, including gold-rich California. The population of California would grow rapidly with the **GOLD RUSH** as prospectors in search of gold headed west to try their fortunes. However, Californians of Hispanic descent who had lived in the region under Mexico lost their land and also suffered from racial and ethnic discrimination.

Meanwhile, social change in the Northeast and growing Midwest continued. As the market economy and early industry developed, so did an early **MIDDLE CLASS**. Activists like **SUSAN B. ANTHONY** and **ELIZABETH CADY STANTON** worked for women's rights. Women were also active in the temperance movement.

Reform movements continued to include abolitionism, which ranged from moderate to radical. An activist leader and writer, slave **FREDERICK DOUGLASS** publicized the movement along with the American Anti-Slavery Society and publications like Harriet Beecher Stowe's *Uncle Tom's Cabin*. The radical abolitionist **JOHN BROWN** led violent protests against slavery.

Competing factions in Congress had continued to battle over the expansion of slavery, resulting in the unsuccessful 1846 **WILMOT PROVISO**; the **COMPROMISE OF 1850**, which admitted the populous California as a free state; and the **FUGITIVE SLAVE ACT**, which allowed slave owners to pursue escaped slaves to free states and recapture them. Congress passed the **KANSAS-NEBRASKA ACT OF 1854** effectively repealing the Missouri Compromise. Violence broke out in Kansas between pro- and anti-slavery factions in what became known as **BLEEDING KANSAS**.

In 1856, an escaped slave, **DRED SCOTT**, took his case to the Supreme Court to sue for freedom. The Court upheld the Fugitive Slave Act, nullified the Missouri Compromise, and essentially decreed that African Americans were not entitled to rights under US citizenship.

In 1858, a series of debates between Illinois senate candidates, Republican **ABRAHAM LINCOLN** and Democrat **STEPHEN DOUGLAS**, showed the deep divides in the nation over slavery and states' rights. During the **LINCOLN-DOUGLAS DEBATES**, Lincoln spoke out against slavery, while Douglas supported the right of states to decide its legality on their own. In 1860, Lincoln was elected to the presidency. Given Lincoln's outspoken stance against slavery, South Carolina seceded immediately thereafter, followed by Mississippi, Alabama, Florida, Louisiana, Georgia, and Texas. They formed the Confederate States of America, or the **CONFEDERACY**, on February 1, 1861.

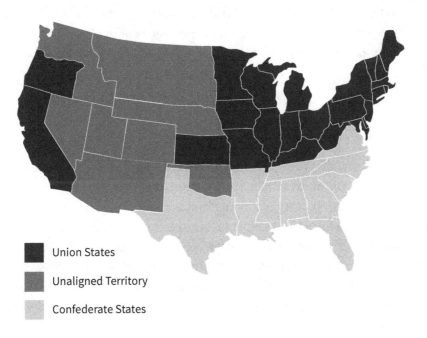

Union States

Unaligned Territory

Confederate States

Figure 12.3. Union and Confederacy

Shortly after secession, Confederate forces attacked Union troops in Charleston Harbor, South Carolina; the **BATTLE OF FORT SUMTER** sparked the Civil War. As a result, Virginia, Tennessee, North Carolina, and Arkansas seceded and joined the Confederacy.

The Confederacy had experienced military leadership and vast territory. The Union had a larger population (strengthened by immigration) and stronger industrial capacity (including weapons-making capacity). Both sides believed the conflict would be short-lived; however it became clear that the war would not end quickly.

The Union developed a blockade to prevent the Confederacy from trading internationally, since the South depended on international cotton trade for much of its income. Several years of bloody battles and economic stagnation resulted in Confederate surrender at Appomattox, Virginia, on April 9, 1865, where

Gettysburg, Pennsylvania, was the site of the bloodiest battle in US history up to that point. President Lincoln later delivered the Gettysburg Address there, in which he framed the Civil War as a battle for human rights and equality.

General Lee surrendered to General Grant. The war ended shortly after and **RECON-STRUCTION** began.

On January 1, 1863, President Lincoln had already decreed the end of slavery in the rebel states with the **EMANCIPATION PROCLAMATION**. Before his assassination just a few days after Confederate surrender, Lincoln had crafted the **TEN PERCENT PLAN** permitting a Southern state's readmission to the Union if ten percent of the population swore allegiance to the Union. However Lincoln's vice president, Andrew Johnson, enforced Reconstruction weakly and the white supremacist **KU KLUX KLAN** emerged; likewise, states developed the oppressive **BLACK CODES** to limit the rights of African Americans.

Congress passed the **CIVIL RIGHTS ACT** in 1866, granting citizenship to African Americans and guaranteeing African American men the same rights as white men (later reaffirmed by the **FOURTEENTH AMENDMENT**). Eventually former Confederate states also had to ratify the 1865 **THIRTEENTH AMENDMENT**, which abolished slavery; the **FOURTEENTH AMENDMENT**, which upheld the provisions of the Civil Rights Act; and the **FIFTEENTH AMENDMENT**, which in 1870 granted African American men the right to vote.

In 1867, a Republican-led Congress passed the **RECONSTRUCTION ACTS**, placing former Confederate states under the control of the US Army, effectively declaring martial law, but modernizing Southern education systems, tax collection, and infrastructure. The **FREEDMEN'S BUREAU** was tasked with assisting freed slaves in the South.

While enslaved African Americans had been freed, many were not aware of this; others still remained voluntarily or involuntarily on plantations. All slaves were eventually freed; however, few had education or skills. Furthermore, oppressive social structures remained: the **JIM CROW LAWS** enforced **SEGREGATION** in the South. In 1896, the Supreme Court upheld segregation in *PLESSY V. FERGUSON* when a mixed-race man, Homer Plessy, was forced off a whites-only train car. When Plessy challenged the law, the Court held that segregation was, indeed, constitutional; according to the Court, *separate but equal* did still ensure equality under the law. This would remain the law until *BROWN V. BOARD OF EDUCATION* in 1954.

Resentment over the Reconstruction Acts never truly subsided, and military control of the South finally ended with the **COMPROMISE OF 1877**, which resolved the disputed presidential election of 1876, granting Rutherford B. Hayes the presidency and removing Union troops from the South.

While the Civil War raged, and during the chaotic post-war Reconstruction period, settlement of the West continued. California had already grown in population due to the gold rush. In the mid-nineteenth century, **CHINESE IMMIGRANTS** came in large numbers to California. While Chinese Americans faced racism, Americans of European descent were encouraged to settle the Frontier by the **HOMESTEAD ACT OF 1862**. Meanwhile, ranching and herding cattle became popular and profitable. White settlers also hunted the buffalo; mass buffalo killings threatened Native American survival.

Americans of Asian descent moved beyond California and settled in western cities like Denver. They were an important part of the labor force that built the transcontinental railroads.

Meanwhile, the Great Plains and Rockies were already populated with the Sioux, Cheyenne, Apache, Comanche, Arapaho, Pawnee, and others. Conflict between Native American tribes and white settlers was ongoing. The **GHOST**

DANCE MOVEMENT united Plains tribes in a spiritual movement and in the belief that whites would eventually be driven from the land. In 1890, the military forced the Sioux to cease this ritual; the outcome was a massacre at WOUNDED KNEE and the death of the Sioux chief, SITTING BULL.

In 1887, the DAWES ACT ended federal recognition of tribes, withdrew tribal land rights, and forced the sale of reservations—tribal land. It also dissolved Native American families: children were sent to boarding schools, where they were forced to assimilate to the dominant American culture.

Back in the Northeast, the market economy and industry were flourishing. The GILDED AGE saw an era of rapidly growing income inequality, justified by theories like SOCIAL DARWINISM and the GOSPEL OF WEALTH, which argued that the wealthy had been made rich by God and were socially more deserving of it.

EXAMPLE

Following the Civil War, the United States ratified the Thirteenth, Fourteenth and Fifteenth Amendments to the Constitution. What did these amendments guarantee?

A) an end to slavery, equal rights for all Americans, and voting rights for all Americans, respectively

B) an end to slavery, equal rights for all Americans, and voting rights for all African Americans, respectively

C) an end to slavery, equal rights for all American men, and voting rights for all African American men, respectively

D) an end to slavery, equal rights for Americans, and voting rights for African American men, respectively

Answer:

D) is correct. The Thirteenth Amendment abolished slavery; the Fourteenth Amendment promised equal protection under the law to all U.S. citizens; the Fifteenth Amendment ensured that (male) African Americans and former slaves could vote.

Industrialization and the Progressive Era

Following the war, the INDUSTRIAL REVOLUTION accelerated in the United States. The Industrial Revolution had begun on the global level with textile production in Great Britain, had been fueled in great part by supplies of Southern cotton, and was evolving in the United States with the development of heavy industry—what would come to be called the SECOND INDUSTRIAL REVOLUTION. Westward expansion required railroads; railroads required steel, and industrial production required oil: all these commodities spurred the rise of powerful companies like John D. Rockefeller's Standard Oil and Andrew Carnegie's US Steel.

The creation of MONOPOLIES and TRUSTS helped industrial leaders consolidate their control over the entire economy. MONOPOLIES let the same business leaders control the market for their own products. Business leaders in varying industries (monopolies) organized into TRUSTS, ensuring their control over each other's industries.

With limited governmental controls or interference in the economy, American CAPITALISM—the free market system—was dominated by the elite. Government corruption led only to weak restrictive legislation like the INTERSTATE COMMERCE ACT of 1887, which was to regulate the railroad industry, and the SHERMAN ANTITRUST ACT (1890), which was intended to break up monopolies and trusts, in order to allow for a fairer marketplace. However, these measures would remain largely toothless until President Theodore Roosevelt's "trust-busting" administration in 1901.

To continue fueling economic growth, the United States needed more markets abroad. *NEW IMPERIALISM* described the US approach to nineteenth and early twentieth century imperialism as practiced by the European powers. Rather than controlling territory as the European powers did, the US sought economic connections with countries around the world.

While the free markets and trade of the CAPITALIST economy spurred national economic and industrial growth, the WORKING CLASS, many of whom were immigrants, suffered from dangerous working conditions and other abuses. As the railroads expanded westward, white farmers, Native Americans, and Mexican Americans suffered: they lost their land to corporate interests. African Americans in the South, though freed from slavery, were also struggling under SHARECROPPING, in which many worked the same land owned by former slaveholders, leasing land and equipment at unreasonable rates and unable to profit.

The PEOPLE'S (POPULIST) PARTY formed in response to corruption and industrialization injurious to farmers (later, it would also support reform in favor of the working class and women and children). Farmers were also concerned about fiscal policy and debt.

Jacob Riis' groundbreaking book and photo essay *How the Other Half Lives* revealed the squalor and poverty the poor urban classes endured, leading to more public calls for reform. Check it out to get a better understanding of life in the early twentieth century and prepare for images you might see on GED questions. It's available online for free!

At the same time, the LABOR MOVEMENT emerged to support mistreated industrial workers in urban areas using STRIKES and COLLECTIVE BARGAINING to gain protections and fair pay for the unskilled workers who had come to cities seeking industrial jobs. With the continual rise of the MIDDLE CLASS, women took a more active role in advocating for the poor and for themselves. Women activists also aligned with labor and the emerging PROGRESSIVE MOVEMENT to ensure better treatment for workers and immigrants.

With the Progressive THEODORE ROOSEVELT'S ascension to the presidency in 1901, the Progressive Era reached its apex. The *TRUST-BUSTER* Roosevelt broke up monopolies and obtained fairer treatment for workers. The Progressive Era also saw a series of acts to protect workers, health, farmers, and children.

Roosevelt also continued overseas expansion following McKinley's SPANISH-AMERICAN WAR (1898 – 1901), in which the US gained control over Spanish territory in the Caribbean, Asia, and the South Pacific. The ROOSEVELT COROLLARY to the Monroe Doctrine promised US intervention in Latin America in case of European aggression, asserting US dominance in the region.

The United States Becomes a Global Power

Debate had arisen within the US between **INTERVENTIONISM** and **ISOLATIONISM**—whether the US should intervene in international matters or not. Interventionists believed in spreading US-style democracy, while isolationists believed in focusing on development at home. This debate became more pronounced with the outbreak of World War I in Europe.

Several inflammatory events triggered US intervention in WWI. With victory in 1918, the US had proven itself a superior global military and industrial power. Interventionist **PRESIDENT WOODROW WILSON** played an important role in negotiating the peace. However, divisions between interventionists and isolationists continued.

On the home front, fear of homegrown radicals—particularly of communists and anarchists—and xenophobia against immigrants led to the **RED SCARE** in 1919 and a series of anti-immigration laws. In response to widespread xenophobia and a sentiment of isolationism following the First World War, Congress limited immigration specifically from Asia, Africa, Eastern Europe, and Southern Europe with the racist **EMERGENCY QUOTA ACT** of 1921 and **NATIONAL ORIGINS ACT** of 1924.

The **GREAT MIGRATION** of African Americans to the North that had begun after the Civil War continued, but tensions increased with urban race riots in 1919. In the South, the Ku Klux Klan was growing in power, and blacks faced intimidation, violence, and death. **LYNCHINGS**, in which African Americans were kidnapped and murdered, sometimes publicly, occurred frequently. At the same time, African American culture flourished with the **HARLEM RENAISSANCE** and become an integral part of a growing American popular culture.

Following WWI, the United States had experienced an era of consumerism and corruption. The government sponsored **LAISSEZ-FAIRE** policies and supported **MANUFACTURING**, flooding markets with cheap consumer goods. Union membership suffered; so did farmers, due to falling crop prices. While mass-production helped the emerging middle class afford more consumer goods and improve their living standards, many families resorted to **CREDIT** to fuel consumer spending. These risky consumer loans, **OVERSPECULATION** on crops and the value of farmland, and weak banking protections helped bring about the **GREAT DEPRESSION**. On October 29, 1929, or *BLACK TUESDAY*, the stock market collapsed. During the same time period, a major drought occurred in the Great Plains, affecting farmers throughout the region. Millions of Americans faced unemployment and poverty.

Figure 12.4. Soup Kitchen During the Great Depression

Following weak responses by the Hoover administration, **FRANKLIN DELANO ROOSEVELT** was elected to the presidency in 1932. FDR offered Americans a *NEW DEAL*: a plan to bring the country out of the Depression. During the *FIRST HUNDRED DAYS* of FDR's administration, a series of emergency acts (known as an *ALPHABET SOUP* of acts due to their many acronyms) was passed for the immediate repair of the banking system. A number of acts also provided relief to the poor and unemployed.

Japanese-Americans faced oppression and discrimination at home simply due to their race. Forced into internment camps, Japanese Americans challenged this violation of their rights in *Korematsu v. US*; however, the Supreme Court ruled that this forced displacement was constitutional. In 1988, the US government apologized for its actions.

The entire world suffered from the Great Depression, and Europe became increasingly unstable. With the rise of the radical Nazi Party in Germany, the Nazi leader Adolf Hitler led German takeovers of several European countries and became a threat to US allies, bombing Britain. However, the United States, weakened by the Great Depression and reluctant to engage in international affairs due to continuing public and political support for isolationism, remained militarily uncommitted in the war.

After the Japanese attack on **PEARL HARBOR** on December 7, 1941, the US entered World War II on the side of the Allies in Europe and the Pacific. The war ended with Japanese surrender in 1945 after the US bombed the Japanese cities **HIROSHIMA** and **NAGASAKI**, the only times that **ATOMIC WEAPONS** have been used in conflict. With most of Europe destroyed, the victorious United States and the Soviet Union emerged as the two global **SUPERPOWERS**.

The US-led **MARSHALL PLAN** was a program to rebuild Europe, but the USSR consolidated its presence and power in eastern European countries, forcing them to reject aid from the Marshall Plan. This division would destroy the alliance between the Soviets and the West, leading to the **COLD WAR** between the two superpowers and the emergence of a **BIPOLAR WORLD**.

With the collapse of the relationship between the USSR and the US, distrust and fear of **COMMUNISM** grew. Accusations of communist sympathies against public figures ran rampant during the **MCCARTHY ERA** in the 1950s, reflecting domestic anxieties.

President Harry S. Truman's **TRUMAN DOCTRINE** stated that the US would support any country threatened by authoritarianism (communism), leading to the **KOREAN WAR** (1950 – 1953), a conflict between the US and Soviet-backed North Korean forces, which ended in a stalemate. The policy of **CONTAINMENT**, to contain Soviet (communist) expansion, defined US foreign policy. According to **DOMINO THEORY**, once one country fell to communism, others would quickly follow.

Meanwhile, in Southeast Asia, communist forces in North Vietnam were gaining power. Congress never formally declared war in Vietnam but gave the president authority to intervene militarily there through the **GULF OF TONKIN RESOLUTION** (1964). However, the resulting protracted conflict—the **VIETNAM WAR**—also led to widespread domestic social unrest.

EXAMPLE

How did the United States change in the 1920s?

A) The Great Migration ceased.

B) African American culture became increasingly influential.

C) The Great Depression caused high unemployment.

D) Thanks to the New Deal, millions of Americans found jobs.

Answer:

B) is correct. The Harlem Renaissance is one example of the emergence of African American culture in the public imagination; as US popular culture developed, African American contributions had a strong influence.

Postwar and Contemporary United States

During the 1960s, the US experienced social and political change, starting with the election of the young and charismatic **JOHN F. KENNEDY** in 1960. Kennedy and his successor after his assassination, **LYNDON B. JOHNSON**, embraced **LIBERALISM**, believing that government should fight poverty at home, and play an interventionist role abroad (in this era, by fighting communism). **JOHNSON**'s administration envisioned a **GREAT SOCIETY**, passing legislation in support of the poor and of civil rights in the tradition of the Progressives. Johnson launched a **WAR ON POVERTY**, passing reform legislation to support the poor, providing housing, health care, and education.

The **CIVIL RIGHTS MOVEMENT**, led by activists like the **REV. DR. MARTIN LUTHER KING, JR.** and **MALCOLM X**, fought for African American rights in the South, including the abolition of segregation, and also for better living standards for blacks in northern cities. Civil rights came to the forefront with the 1954 Supreme Court case *BROWN V. BOARD OF EDUCATION*, when the Court found segregation unconstitutional.

Civil rights became a major domestic political issue with widespread public support. Civil rights workers organized the **MARCH ON WASHINGTON** in 1963, when Dr. King delivered his famous *I HAVE A DREAM* speech. In 1964, Congress passed the **CIVIL RIGHTS ACT**, which outlawed segregation. However, African Americans' voting rights were still not sufficiently protected. In 1965, led by President Lyndon B. Johnson, Congress passed the **VOTING RIGHTS ACT**, which forbade restrictions impeding the ability of African Americans to vote.

Figure 12.5. March on Washington

The Civil Rights Movement extended beyond the Deep South. **Cesar Chavez** founded the **United Farm Workers (UFW)**, which organized Hispanic and migrant farm workers in California and the Southwest to advocate for unionizing and collective bargaining. The Civil Rights Movement also included **feminist** activists who fought for fairer treatment of women in the workplace and for women's reproductive rights. The **American Indian Movement (AIM)** addressed injustices and discrimination suffered by Native Americans, achieving more tribal autonomy. The 1969 **Stonewall riots** occurred in New York City in response to police repression of the gay community. These riots and subsequent organized activism are seen as the beginning of the LGBT rights movement.

Conservatism strengthened in response to the heavy role of government in public life throughout the 1960s, high rates of government spending, and social challenges to traditional values. During the administration of the conservative President **Richard Nixon**, the conflict in Vietnam ended and a diplomatic relationship with China began. Nixon also oversaw economic reforms. However, the **Watergate scandal**, when the president was involved in a break-in at the headquarters of the **Democratic National Committee**, forced Nixon to resign. Nixon's resignation further destroyed many Americans' faith in their government.

At the same time, LBJ's overseas agenda in Vietnam was increasingly unpopular due to high casualties, the draft (which forced young American males to fight overseas) and what seemed to many to be the purposelessness of the war. Protests swept the nation against the war, and popular counterculture usurped government authority and challenged traditional values.

After political and economic instability in the 1970s, the conservative president **Ronald Reagan** championed domestic tax cuts and an aggressive foreign policy against the Soviet Union. However, tax cuts forced Congress to cut or eliminate social programs that benefitted millions. Enormous military investment—the **arms race** with the Soviet Union—helped bring about the end of the Cold War with the 1991 fall of the USSR and later, a new era of globalization. It also increased government debt. Finally, the Reagan Revolution ushered in an era of conservative values in the public sphere.

With the collapse of the Soviet Union, the balance of international power changed. The bipolar world became a unipolar world, and the United States was the sole superpower. US intervention in the Middle East during the **Gulf War**, or **Operation Desert Storm** (1991)—cemented its status as the world's sole superpower.

With the election of President **Bill Clinton** in 1992, the US took an active role in international diplomacy. Society became increasingly liberal. Technology like the **internet** facilitated national and global communication, media, and business; minority groups like the LGBT community engaged in more advocacy; and environmental issues became more visible.

As part of **globalization**, the facilitation of global commerce and communication, the Clinton administration prioritized free trade. The United States signed the **North American Free Trade Agreement (NAFTA)** with Mexico and Canada, removing trade restrictions throughout North America. Many American jobs went overseas, especially manufacturing jobs, where labor was cheaper, benefitting companies but causing unemployment. Furthermore, globalization began facilitating the movement of people as methods of communication and transportation transformed. **Immigration reform** would be a major issue into the twenty-first century.

By the end of the twentieth century, the United States had established itself as the dominant global economic, military, and political power. Due to its role in global conflict from the Spanish-American War onward, the US had established a military presence worldwide. The US dominated global trade. American popular culture was widely popular.

However, globalization also facilitated global conflict. On **SEPTEMBER 11, 2001 (9/11)**, the terrorist group AL **QAEDA** attacked the US, triggering an aggressive military and foreign policy under the administration of President **GEORGE W. BUSH**, who declared a *WAR ON TERROR*, an open-ended global conflict against terrorist organizations and their supporters. The US attacked al Qaeda bases in Afghanistan. President Bush believed in the doctrine of **PREEMPTION**, that if the US was aware of a threat, it should preemptively attack the source of that threat. Preemption would drive the invasion of Iraq in 2003.

At home, Congress passed the **USA PATRIOT ACT** to respond to fears of more terrorist attacks on US soil. This legislation gave the federal government unprecedented—and, some argued, unconstitutional—powers of surveillance over the American public.

Despite the tense climate, social liberalization continued in the US. Following the Bush administration, during which tax cuts and heavy reliance on credit helped push the country into the **GREAT RECESSION**, the first African American president, **BARACK OBAMA**, was elected in 2008. Under his presidency, the US emerged from the recession, ended its occupations of Iraq and Afghanistan, passed the Affordable Care Act, which reformed the healthcare system, and legalized same-sex marriage. The Obama administration also oversaw the passage of consumer protection acts, increased support for students, and safety nets for homeowners.

Yet change persists in the United States. In 2016, the country was deeply divided as the television personality and real estate developer **DONALD TRUMP** was elected president on a platform of conservatism and isolationism. However his opponent, former senator and Secretary of State **HILLARY RODHAM CLINTON**, won the popular vote. Many Americans viewed Trump as racist and sexist, and grassroots opposition movements developed. Still, his supporters remained committed. Some argued he understood the harms of rising income inequality better than Clinton, despite her work to support the poor and working class. Some researchers believe the election showed deeper divisions among Americans than had previously been understood.

EXAMPLE

Which of the following BEST describes the approach taken by the Reagan administration to counter the Soviet Union?

A) bilateral diplomacy

B) direct military confrontation

C) engagement in multilateral pact such as the United Nations

D) escalation of arms production and proxy warfare

Answer:

D) is correct. The Reagan administration focused on arms buildup, weapons spending, and supporting anti-Soviet movements around the world.

Test Your Knowledge

Read the question, and then choose the most correct answer.

1. Which of the following was a major difference between British and French colonization of the Americas?

    A) French colonists tended to be single men who intermarried with local residents, while British colonists brought their entire families to settle permanently, forming insular communities.

    B) British colonists tended to be single men who intermarried with local residents, while French colonists brought their entire families to settle permanently, forming insular communities.

    C) French colonists were more likely to form alliances with Native American tribes, while the British shunned them.

    D) British colonists had more economic interests in the Americas than the French did.

2. Why was the Mayflower Compact an important contribution to the foundation of American government?

    A) It provided for equal treatment of all Christians under the law.

    B) It was the first treaty between European settlers (the Pilgrims) and Native Americans.

    C) It laid out terms for government with the consent of the governed.

    D) It allowed people of all faiths to practice their religions freely under the law.

3. What advantage did the colonists have in the American Revolution?

    A) vast financial wealth

    B) superior weaponry

    C) strong leadership and knowledge of the terrain

    D) a professional military and access to mercenaries

4. How did the views of the Federalists and the Anti-Federalists differ during the Constitutional Convention?

    A) The views of the Federalists and Anti-Federalists did not significantly differ at the Constitutional Convention.

    B) The Anti-Federalists did not believe in a Constitution at all, while the Federalists insisted on including the Bill of Rights.

    C) The Anti-Federalists favored a stronger Constitution and federal government, while Federalists were concerned that states would risk losing their autonomy.

    D) The Federalists favored a stronger Constitution and federal government, while Anti-Federalists were concerned that states would risk losing their autonomy.

5. Why was the Louisiana Purchase controversial?

   A) Observers feared it would destabilize the relationship between the United States and France.

   B) Many people were concerned about federal overreach, given the scope of the purchase.

   C) Americans worried about maintaining stable relationships with the Native Americans living west of the Mississippi River.

   D) Citizens thought the United States could not control the enormous amount of land it had gained.

6. What was an important consequence of the War of 1812?

   A) The United States gained territory from Britain in the Northeast, including the state of Maine.

   B) The United States captured military technology from British troops fleeing the unsuccessful siege of Washington, DC.

   C) The United States purchased the Port of New Orleans from the French.

   D) The United States developed a sense of a strong national identity following its successful expulsion of the British and defense of its borders.

7. What was one reason for the election of Andrew Jackson to the presidency?

   A) Jackson was able to find a solution to the first Nullification Crisis.

   B) Allowing white men who did not own property to vote was a boon to Jackson, who was popular with the "common man."

   C) Jackson's popularity with landowners in Northern states guaranteed him the funds he needed to win the presidency.

   D) Jackson and his vice president, John C. Calhoun, were a strong and popular team when running for election.

8. The Mexican-American War resulted in which of the following gains for the United States?

   A) territory south of the Rio Grande

   B) the Southwest and California

   C) Oregon and Washington State

   D) western land including Idaho

9. Immigration to the United States, particularly from famine-hit Ireland, increased in the nineteenth century. What was one widespread response?

   A) the nativist movement, which promoted the rights of Native Americans

   B) the "Know-Nothing" movement, a nativist, anti-immigrant, anti-Catholic society

   C) the "Know-Nothing" movement, a nativist, anti-immigrant, anti-Protestant society

   D) the privileging of Chinese immigrants over white Irish immigrants

10. Although women did not gain the right to vote until the ratification of the Nineteenth Amendment in 1920, activists like Elizabeth Cady Stanton and Susan B. Anthony began advocating for women's rights as early as the Seneca Falls Convention of 1848. Why did the women's movement gain traction in the mid-nineteenth century?

    A) European literary thought supporting women's rights became popular in the northern states.

    B) As the abolitionist movement grew, abolitionists also came to oppose the oppression of women, recognizing their limited rights under the law and in society.

    C) The development of a middle class gave some women the time and the means to engage in progressive activism.

    D) Women settling the Frontier became increasingly vocal about equality at a national level, since men and women were nominally equal in many remote, isolated western settlements.

11. What did the Missouri Compromise accomplish?

    A) It admitted Missouri as a free state.

    B) It admitted California as a free state.

    C) It allowed slavery in New Mexico and Utah to be decided by popular sovereignty.

    D) It banned slavery north of the thirty-sixth parallel, so that new states formed in northern territories would be free.

12. How did the Lincoln-Douglas Debates impact the nation before the 1860 presidential election?

    A) They reflected the national mood: that the country was deeply divided over the question of slavery and whether states had the right to determine its legality.

    B) They reflected the national mood: that the country was deeply divided over the question of slavery—Lincoln called for abolition, while Douglas favored the practice.

    C) They reinvigorated the debate over slavery, which had been overshadowed by debate over states' rights.

    D) They reinvigorated the debate over states' rights, which had been overshadowed by debate over slavery.

13. What assets did the Confederacy have during the Civil War?

    A) The Confederacy had superior weaponry and production resources.

    B) The Confederacy maintained brisk trade with Europe, enabling it to fund the war.

    C) The Confederacy benefitted from strong military leadership and high morale among the population.

    D) The Confederacy's strong infrastructure allowed it to transport supplies and people efficiently throughout the South.

14. In the Emancipation Proclamation, President Lincoln declared an end to slavery

A) in Kentucky and Missouri.

B) in the Union only.

C) in slave states that had not seceded from the Union.

D) in the rebel states.

Read the following excerpt from Jefferson Davis' speech explaining his retirement from the US Senate to join Mississippi as it seceded from the United States. He would go on to become the president of the Confederacy. Answer the questions that follow.

It has been a conviction of pressing necessity, it has been a belief that we are to be deprived in the Union of the rights which our fathers bequeathed to us, which has brought Mississippi into her present decision.

She has heard proclaimed the theory that all men are created free and equal, and this made the basis of an attack upon her social institutions; and the sacred Declaration of Independence has been invoked to maintain the position of the equality of the races. That Declaration of Independence is to be construed by the circumstances and purposes for which it was made. The communities were declaring their independence…that there was no divine right to rule; that no man inherited the right to govern; that there were no classes by which power and place descended to families, but that all stations were equally within the grasp of the body-politic.

These were the great principles they announced; these were the purposes for which they made their declaration… They have no reference to the slave; else, how happened it that among the items of arraignment made against George III was that he endeavored to do just what the North has been endeavoring of late to do—to stir up insurrection among our slaves? Had the Declaration announced that negroes were free and equal, how was the prince to be arraigned for stirring up insurrection among them?

…When our Constitution was formed, the same idea was rendered more palpable, for there we find provision made for that very class of persons as property; they were not put upon the footing of equality with white men…but, so far as representation was concerned, were discriminated against as a lower caste, only to be represented in the numerical proportion of three-fifths.

– Jefferson Davis, *On Retiring from the Senate*, US Congress, Senate, Congressional Globe, 36th Congress, 2nd Session, p. 487.

15. How does Jefferson Davis use American history to justify slavery?

A) He argues that the Declaration of Independence asserted *political* equality rather than *racial* equality. He believed that no men (presumably no white men) had the right to rule over others (presumably other white men).

B) He reminds the Senate of the Three-Fifths Compromise, in which the states agreed that to count a state's population, slaves would count as three-fifths of a person (although they could not vote).

C) He reminds the Senate that King George III was accused of inciting rebellion among slaves to weaken the Revolution.

D) all of the above

16. How does Jefferson Davis describe the society of Mississippi?
    A) Mississippi believed that all men were free and equal.
    B) Mississippi's social institutions were based on the premise that all men were NOT free and equal.
    C) Mississippi's social institutions were based on freedom and equality for all people, women and men.
    D) Mississippi did not support the Declaration of Independence.

Read the following sentence from the speech and answer the question that follows.

It has been a conviction of pressing necessity, it has been a belief that we are to be deprived in the Union of the rights which our fathers bequeathed to us, which has brought Mississippi into her present decision.

17. Given how Jefferson Davis develops the text that follows this sentence, which of the following BEST explains the specific rights that Mississippi fears it will lose under the Union?
    A) the right to secede from the Union
    B) the right to make its own laws
    C) the right to legally enslave black people
    D) the right to trade internationally

18. What did the Reconstruction Acts do?
    A) They immediately improved conditions for African Americans in the South.
    B) They rapidly benefitted the Southern economy.
    C) They were widely considered fair in Congress and by Southerners.
    D) They imposed Northern military control over the South.

19. How did the US government break down tribal bonds and weaken Native American societies?
    A) through policies of assimilation
    B) by forcing Native American children to go to white schools and reject their cultures
    C) by forcing Native Americans to move onto reservations
    D) all of the above

20. The Interstate Commerce Act and the Sherman Anti-Trust Act
    A) immediately went into effect to regulate the railroad industry and break up monopolies.
    B) remained largely toothless until the First World War.
    C) remained largely toothless until the administration of Theodore Roosevelt.
    D) immediately went into effect to promote congressional efforts to regulate interstate commerce.

21. The United States remained relatively neutral in international conflicts for much of its early history. Which of the following conflicts is considered to be its first major assertion of international power overseas?

   A)   the Spanish-American War

   B)   the First World War

   C)   the Texan Revolution

   D)   the War of 1812

22. The United States entered WWI largely because of which of the following?

   A)   the Zimmerman Telegram

   B)   the rise of Nazi Germany

   C)   the assassination of Franz Ferdinand

   D)   the attack on the *Lusitania*

23. Segregation was found unconstitutional by which of the following Supreme Court decisions?

   A)   *Brown v. Board of Education*

   B)   *Plessy v. Ferguson*

   C)   *Scott v. Sanford*

   D)   *Korematsu v. US*

24. What was the relevance of the Gulf of Tonkin Resolution?

   A)   It gave Congress the power to declare war against the North Vietnamese forces.

   B)   It authorized the president to take military action against North Vietnamese forces.

   C)   It authorized the military to take action against North Vietnamese forces.

   D)   It authorized the president to take military action against South Vietnamese forces.

25. What was the significance of the Voting Rights Act of 1965?

   A)   It gave African Americans the right to vote in the segregated states.

   B)   It gave Americans under the age of twenty-one the right to vote.

   C)   It ended segregation in voting.

   D)   It ended restrictions that prevented African Americans from voting in many states with histories of institutionalized racism.

26. How did Cesar Chavez and the United Farm Workers impact Hispanic Americans?

   A) They supported Mexicans who wanted to join the Bracero program and become guest workers in the United States.

   B) They supported Mexican American agricultural workers in California and the Southwest and provided a foundation for later advocacy groups working for Hispanic Americans.

   C) They worked on behalf of Texas farmers to coordinate agreements with agricultural workers from Mexico.

   D) They worked on behalf of the California state government to negotiate temporary worker agreements with Mexico.

27. Which of the following events is generally considered to mark the beginning of the movement for LGBT civil rights in the United States?

   A) the first Gay Pride marches in New York, Chicago, and San Francisco

   B) the election of Harvey Milk to the San Francisco Board of Supervisors

   C) activism and dialogue surrounding the AIDS crisis

   D) the Stonewall Riots in New York City

28. Which of the following best explains the impact of the Watergate scandal on the United States?

   A) President Nixon was impeached.

   B) President Nixon declined to seek a second term of office.

   C) Americans lost faith in the federal government.

   D) Americans began supporting third party candidates more.

29. NAFTA accomplished which of the following?

   A) opened borders between the U.S., Canada, and Mexico, allowing for free movement of goods and people between these three countries

   B) initiated free trade between the US, Mexico, and Canada, facilitating and strengthening trade between these three countries

   C) created a union similar to the European Union in North America, in which Canada, Mexico, and the U.S. shared similar policy goals and consulted each other on matters of shared concern

   D) established common immigration procedures between Mexico, the US, and Canada

30. What was a consequence of Operation Desert Storm, the 1991 Gulf War?

   A) The United States occupied Iraq.

   B) Iraq occupied Kuwait under an international agreement.

   C) The United States became the world's sole superpower.

   D) The United States and the former Soviet Union, now represented by the Russian Federation, improved their cooperation at the United Nations.

Answer Key

1.

A) **Correct.** French colonists were generally single men seeking profit; if they stayed, they were more likely than the British to intermarry.

B) Incorrect. The British were more likely to establish settler colonies; entire families settled and formed communities in the colonies.

C) Incorrect. Both the British and the French formed strategic alliances with tribes as was expedient.

D) Incorrect. Both the British and the French had major economic interests in the Americas.

2.

A) Incorrect. The Mayflower Compact was written by one Christian group—Separatists.

B) Incorrect. The Mayflower Compact articulated terms of governance among European settlers; it was not a treaty with other parties.

C) **Correct.** As a governing document, the Mayflower Compact was notable in that it provided for governance with the consent of the governed, a departure from British rule.

D) Incorrect. The Mayflower Compact was written by Separatists.

3.

A) Incorrect. While some colonists were quite wealthy, colonial wealth paled in the face of British wealth.

B) Incorrect. The colonists did not have superior weaponry.

C) **Correct.** The colonial military did have strong leaders, and an intimate knowledge of the terrain, many having been born there.

D) Incorrect. Britain had an experienced military with substantial experience fighting in Europe and elsewhere. In addition, King George III hired Hessian mercenaries from Germany to supplement British troops.

4.

A) Incorrect. The views of the Federalists and Anti-Federalists differed a great deal.

B) Incorrect. The Bill of Rights was a compromise measure; it was not originally a Federalist contribution.

C) Incorrect. The reverse was true.

D) **Correct.** The Federalists were the driving force behind a stronger Constitution that would empower the United States federal government. The Anti-Federalists favored state sovereignty and ensured the passage of the Bill of Rights to protect certain rights not explicitly guaranteed in the Constitution itself.

5.

A) Incorrect. France and the early United States had a complex relationship, but this was not the central reason for US anxiety over the Louisiana Purchase.

B) **Correct.** Despite Jefferson's position as an Anti-Federalist Democrat, he had used executive powers as president to negotiate the purchase without congressional consultation, considered by many to be federal overreach.

C) Incorrect. The needs of Native Americans were not a pressing issue for most Americans; many considered strategic control of land and, eventually, westward expansion, to be necessary.

D) Incorrect. This was not the most pressing concern for most Americans, who were still preoccupied with preventing a dictatorship.

6.

A) Incorrect. The United States did not win any territory in the War of 1812.

B) Incorrect. The United States made no major gains in military technology.

C) Incorrect. The United States already controlled New Orleans.

D) Correct. A spirit of patriotism pervaded among many Americans, given that the country had successfully held off the British.

7.

A) Incorrect. This did not occur until after Jackson had been elected president.

B) Correct. Jackson was extremely popular among the lower classes and rural farmers of the South; universal manhood suffrage expanded the electorate, giving him a huge advantage.

C) Incorrect. Jackson was unpopular with the elite landowners of the North.

D) Incorrect. Jackson and Calhoun were fierce rivals with a poor personal and professional relationship.

8.

A) Incorrect. The United States never controlled the land south of the Rio Grande, which remains part of Mexico to this day.

B) Correct. Following the war, the United States took control of the Southwest (today, Arizona, New Mexico, and adjacent areas), as well as California.

C) Incorrect. These areas came under US control in the 1846 Oregon Treaty with the British.

D) Incorrect. Idaho emerged from portions of the Washington and Dakota Territories.

9.

A) Incorrect. Nativists promoted the rights of white Americans who had been born in North America and whose families had been born there for generations, not Native Americans.

B) Correct. The Know-Nothings were an underground nativist and anti-immigrant group.

C) Incorrect. The Know-Nothings were particularly anti-Catholic, not anti-Protestant; immigrants from Ireland and Southern Europe were mainly Catholic, while white Americans were mainly Protestant.

D) Incorrect. Chinese and other Asian immigrants were rarely, if ever, privileged over white immigrants.

10.

A) Incorrect. There was no major literary movement explicitly supporting women's rights (although significant women writers like Jane Austen and the Bronte sisters wrote novels with strong female characters).

B) Incorrect. While some abolitionists also believed in improving women's rights, women's suffrage was not part of the abolitionist platform.

C) Correct. Middle and upper-middle class women had more time for activism and charity, as they did not have to work.

D) Incorrect. Women's status on the Frontier may have varied, but Frontier women did not play a major political role in the nineteenth century women's rights movement.

11.

A) Incorrect. The Missouri Compromise allowed slavery in Missouri.

B) Incorrect. California was not admitted as a state until 1850.

C) Incorrect. This was a feature of the Compromise of 1850.

D) **Correct.** The Missouri Compromise prohibited slavery north of the thirty-sixth parallel in new US territories, permitting slavery in Missouri.

12.

A) **Correct.** The Lincoln-Douglas Debates showed how divided the country was over slavery.

B) Incorrect. Douglas was not so much in favor of slavery as he was a proponent of states' rights.

C) Incorrect. Slavery and states' rights were intertwined.

D) Incorrect. The question of slavery was at the root of the debate over states' rights.

13.

A) Incorrect. The South's technological resources were inferior to those of the North.

B) Incorrect. European countries ceased trade with the South, finding alternative sources of cotton in protest of slavery.

C) **Correct.** The Confederacy had excellent military leaders; many Confederate leaders and much of the population strongly believed in the right of states to make decisions without federal interference, not only about slavery but also about trade and other issues.

D) Incorrect. The Confederacy had limited infrastructure.

14.

A) Incorrect. The Emancipation Proclamation applied to rebel states; Missouri and Kentucky did not secede.

B) Incorrect. Lincoln freed the slaves in the Confederacy with the Emancipation Proclamation, not in the Union.

C) Incorrect. The Emancipation Proclamation applied to the rebel states.

D) **Correct.** The Emancipation Proclamation freed the slaves in the Confederacy.

15.

A) Incorrect. Davis does argue that the Declaration of Independence asserted political equality, rather than racial equality, but this is not the only correct answer.

B) Incorrect. Davis does invoke the Three-Fifths Compromise, in which the states agreed that to count a state's population, slaves would count as three-fifths of a person (although they could not vote).

C) Incorrect. Davis does recall the accusations against King George III, but there is a better answer here.

D) **Correct.** Davis referred to all these points in his speech.

16.

A) Incorrect. Davis claims the opposite.

B) **Correct.** Davis justifies his departure based upon the right of Mississippi as a state to maintain a society based on the premise that all men were *not* free and equal.

C) Incorrect. Davis claims the opposite, and he does not even mention women.

D) Incorrect. Davis invokes the Declaration of Independence to support his argument.

17.

A) Incorrect. Davis invokes Mississippi's right to a society based on inequality; he does not express fears of being unable to secede.

B) Incorrect. Davis is worried about more than just Mississippi's right to make its own laws; he sees new interpretations of the law as a threat to Mississippi's social fabric.

C) **Correct.** Davis asserts that Mississippi has the right to maintain slavery, since "the theory that all men are created free and equal, and this made the basis of an attack upon her social institutions."

D) Incorrect. Davis is concerned about the interpretation of the Declaration of Independence to mean that all people, regardless of race, enjoy equality. He is not fearful of Mississippi's right to trade internationally.

18.

A) Incorrect. Conditions for most freed slaves did not immediately improve; they continued to face widespread violence and discrimination.

B) Incorrect. With damage to agricultural land and existing infrastructure, the Southern economy and many Southerners suffered; Reconstruction programs did not immediately take effect.

C) Incorrect. Radical Republicans felt that the Reconstruction Acts did not go far enough in punishing the South; others in Congress felt they were too harsh. Likewise, many in the South felt they were unfair.

D) **Correct.** The Reconstruction Acts effectively placed the South under martial law.

19.

A) Incorrect. Assimilation destroyed many people's connection with their cultures and traditions, but this answer choice is incomplete in the context of the other options.

B) Incorrect. Again, forcing children to leave their families for white schools destroyed their connection with their languages, cultures, and traditions. Moreover, these actions injured their personal bonds with their families and communities—further weakening tribal societies. However, this answer choice is insufficient, given the other answer choices available.

C) Incorrect. Forcing people to leave their homelands for assigned living spaces on reservations fostered social breakdown by interrupting traditional connections with land and dispossessing people of their homes. Again, however, this answer choice is incomplete

D) **Correct.** All of the above are true.

20.

A) Incorrect. The Interstate Commerce Act and the Sherman Anti-Trust Act were ineffective until the Roosevelt administration; they were even used to break up labor unions and farmer's organizations rather than for their intended purpose.

B) Incorrect. During Theodore Roosevelt's presidency, the Interstate Commerce Act and the Sherman Anti-Trust Act were finally used to break up monopolies and to ensure a fairer marketplace.

C) **Correct.** It was not until Theodore Roosevelt came into office that these acts were effectively used for their intended purpose: to create a fair market in the United States by eliminating trusts and monopolies.

D) Incorrect. They were not immediately implemented.

21.

A) **Correct.** The United States was the aggressor in the Spanish-American War—it was never definitively proven that the *Maine* was actually attacked by Spain. Furthermore, the war was fought in several different theaters worldwide.

B) Incorrect. The First World War took place after all these conflicts.

C) Incorrect. The Texan Revolution occurred before Texas joined the United States.

D) Incorrect. The War of 1812 was partially due to British provocations and took place entirely on US and British Canadian soil.

22.

A) **Correct.** The Zimmerman Telegram, a German offer to assist Mexico in attacking the U.S., forced the United States to enter WWI, following a series of other German provocations.

B) Incorrect. Nazi Germany did not exist until the 1930s.

C) Incorrect. While the assassination of Franz Ferdinand triggered the First World War in Europe, the United States did not enter the conflict until later.

D) Incorrect. The attack on the *Lusitania* angered many Americans but did not alone trigger U.S. entry into the conflict.

23.

A) **Correct.** *Brown v. Board of Education* found that keeping races separate (in this case, in segregated schools) could not ensure that all people would receive equal treatment, and that segregation was therefore unconstitutional.

B) Incorrect. *Plessy v. Ferguson* upheld segregation.

C) Incorrect. *Scott v. Sandford* upheld and strengthened the Fugitive Slave Act, thereby upholding the Kansas-Nebraska Act and effectively abolishing the Missouri Compromise.

D) Incorrect. *Korematsu v. US* ruled the constitutionality of the Japanese internment camps during WWII.

24.

A) Incorrect. The Gulf of Tonkin Resolution allowed the president flexibility in committing forces. According to the Constitution, Congress has the power to declare war.

B) **Correct.** The Gulf of Tonkin Resolution gave the president power to commit military troops in Vietnam without Congressional authorization.

C) Incorrect. The president is the Commander in Chief, and Congress empowers the president to take lengthy military action.

D) Incorrect. The United States was allied with South Vietnamese forces.

25.

A) Incorrect. Black men gained the right to vote with the Fifteenth Amendment; black women could vote after the ratification of the Nineteenth Amendment (although in practice, African American men and women were often denied this right).

B) Incorrect. Americans eighteen years of age and older were able to vote after the ratification of the Twenty-Sixth Amendment.

C) Incorrect. Segregation in public places ended with the Civil Rights Act.

D) **Correct.** The Voting Rights Act abolished discriminatory restrictions that prevented African

Americans from exercising their right to vote.

26.

A) Incorrect. Cesar Chavez and the UFW organized Mexican and Mexican American workers already present in the United States. They focused on the rights of workers in the United States.

B) Correct. Cesar Chavez and the UFW advocated for the rights of Mexican and Mexican American farmworkers in the United States, who were often disadvantaged. The activism of the UFW set a precedent for later advocacy in support of Hispanic Americans.

C) Incorrect. Cesar Chavez and the UFW were mainly active in California and the Southwest, not Texas. Furthermore, they advocated for workers, not farmers.

D) Incorrect. Cesar Chavez and the UFW did not work for any government; they organized and supported farm workers in the United States.

27.

A) Incorrect. Gay Pride rallies and marches were not major features of the public landscape until after the Stonewall Riots.

B) Incorrect. Milk's election was an important development in LGBT rights as openly gay public figures were rare, but his election occurred after the Stonewall Riots.

C) Incorrect. Again, the public discourse and activism that resulted from the AIDS crisis helped bring LGBT issues into the mainstream public sphere, but these events happened in the 1980s and 1990s.

D) Correct. Generally viewed as the beginning of the LGBT rights movement, the Stonewall Riots occurred in response to ongoing police harassment of the gay community in New York City and resulted in a more organized push for civil rights.

28.

A) Incorrect. President Nixon resigned.

B) Incorrect. Watergate unfolded during Nixon's second term.

C) Correct. Watergate destroyed many Americans' trust in the government, which had already been weakened after the turbulent 1960s and the Vietnam War.

D) Incorrect. Watergate did not change the two-party system.

29.

A) Incorrect. NAFTA permitted free trade among the three countries, but national borders remain, and movement of people is restricted.

B) Correct. NAFTA is a free trade agreement among the three countries.

C) Incorrect. NAFTA is not a political agreement; it is an economic one.

D) Incorrect. NAFTA is not an immigration agreement; it addresses international trade.

30.

A) Incorrect. The United States did not occupy Iraq until the 2003 Iraq War.

B) Incorrect. Iraq was driven from Kuwait in 1991 by US-led forces.

C) Correct. Having led the coalition that defeated Iraq in the 1991 Gulf War, the United States proved its position as the sole superpower after the collapse of the Soviet Union.

D) Incorrect. The relationship between the United States and the Russian Federation, while not destabilized by the Gulf War, did not necessarily improve because of it.

thirteen

CIVICS AND GOVERNMENT

The Constitution

Any study of the United States government must begin with its founding document: the **CONSTITUTION**. It was written as both an expression of ideals and as a practical framework for the functioning of the country. Designed to be a "living document," the Constitution and how it is interpreted has changed in the almost 230 years since it was written. However, its core principles have not. They continue to serve as the foundation and guiding light of American government and politics. In order to understand the government that emerged from the US Constitution, it is necessary to understand its historical context.

Historical Background

In 1781 the Second Continental Congress had convened to organize a government for the emerging nation. The colonies had broken away from Britain because of what they viewed as the oppressive rule of an overbearing central government. As a result, the first government they created, whose framework was called the **ARTICLES OF CONFEDERATION**, was intentionally weak. Called a "firm league of friendship," it was designed to create a loose confederation between the colonies (now states) while allowing them to retain much of their individual sovereignty.

As a result, the Articles established a political system which consisted of a **UNICAMERAL LEGISLATURE** (only one house) with extremely limited authority. The Congress of the Confederation, as it was called, did not have the power to levy taxes or raise an army. Any laws had to be passed by a two-thirds vote, and any changes to the Articles had to be passed unanimously—essentially an impossible feat. The legislature was intentionally subordinate to the states. Representatives were selected and paid by state legislatures.

It quickly became clear that this government was too weak to be effective, and by 1787 the new government of the United

While influenced by philosophy, the Constitution is actually a very practical document. It lays out the overarching structure of the government. However, each decision made about the structure of the government was an attempt to either prevent the re-emergence of tyranny or fix the mistakes of the first, failed government.

States was already in crisis. Without the power to levy taxes, the federal government had no way to alleviate its debt burden from the war. In addition, without an organizing authority, states began issuing their own currencies and crafting individual trade agreements with foreign nations, halting trade and sending inflation through the roof. Without a national judicial system, there was no mechanism to solve the inevitable economic disputes.

Discontent was particularly strong among farmers, who were losing their property at devastating rates. Violence exploded in 1786 when Daniel Shays led a rebellion against Massachusetts tax collectors and banks. Unable to raise an army, the Congress of the Confederation was powerless to intervene. The rebellion was finally suppressed when citizens of Boston contributed funds to raise a state militia. **SHAYS' REBELLION** made it clear that the new government was unable to maintain order.

A convention of the states was called to address problems in the young United States. At the **CONSTITUTIONAL CONVENTION** in 1787, a decision was made to completely throw out the old Articles and write a new governing document from scratch. There were five main goals for the new Constitution:

1. the protection of property
2. granting increased, but limited, power to the federal government
3. the protection of and limitations on majority rule
4. the protection of individual rights
5. the creation of a flexible framework for government

It was clear that a stronger central government was needed. However, the states did not want a central government that was so strong that it would oppress the states or the people. The solution? Increase the power of the government, but prevent the concentration of power by *dividing* it.

Each of these reflects the desire to balance authority and liberty, the core of the framework of the American government.

The federal government was reorganized under the Constitution, shifting from a one-body political system to a three-branch system as conceived by the Enlightenment philosopher **MONTESQUIEU**. In addition to a now bicameral (two house) legislature, a legitimate executive branch was added as well as a judicial. Following Montesquieu's model of **SEPARATION OF POWERS**, the now-increased powers of the federal government were divided among these branches. In addition, each branch was given powers that would limit the power of the other branches in a system called **CHECKS AND BALANCES**. For example:

♦ The executive branch—via the role of president—has the power to veto (reject) laws passed by the legislature.

♦ The legislative branch can override the president's veto (with a two-thirds vote) and pass the law anyway.

♦ The judicial branch can determine the constitutionality of laws (the principle of **JUDICIAL REVIEW**).

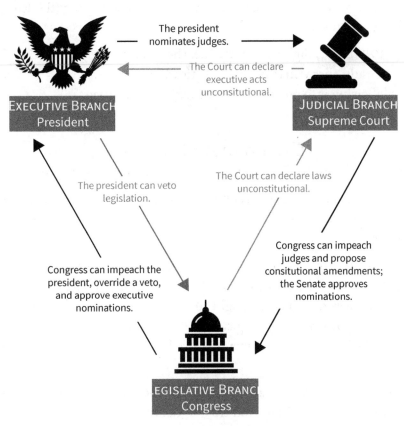

The president
nominates judges.

The Court can declare
executive acts
unconsitutional.

EXECUTIVE BRANCH
President

JUDICIAL BRANCH
Supreme Court

The president can veto
legislation.

The Court can declare laws
unconstitutional.

Congress can impeach the
president, override a veto,
and approve executive
nominations.

Congress can impeach
judges and propose
consitutional amendments;
the Senate approves
nominations.

LEGISLATIVE BRANCH
Congress

Figure 13.1. Checks and Balances

Enlightenment Philosophy

The founders of the United States were all educated in the philosophy of the ENLIGHTEN-MENT. Several key elements of this philosophy are reflected in the Constitution.

RULE OF LAW: The very desire for a written constitution—a law above all others—reflected Enlightenment thinking, as it ensures a rule of law, rather than a rule of man. In a nation ruled by man, governance is at the whim of an individual or small group of individuals. Decisions are arbitrary based on the interests and needs of those in authority. In a nation ruled by law, governance is based on a body of written, or otherwise codified, law (such as the Constitution). No individual can make a governing decision in conflict with those laws.

REASON: The Constitution is a document based on reason, and is therefore relatively simple and straightforward. It lays out the structure of government without detailing every single function of that government. Rather than simply empowering authority, the Constitution aims to limit government while still allowing it to fulfill its function. It also insists that governing decisions are made outside the scope of religion, by actively separating the two.

SOCIAL CONTRACT: The document begins "We the People…" because the founders believed that government was a social contract, legitimized only by the consent of the people. This is also known as POPULAR SOVEREIGNTY. The Constitution protects individual liberty, life, and property, the fundamental natural laws laid out by the Enlightenment philosopher JOHN LOCKE.

SOCIAL PROGRESS: Enlightenment thinkers believed strongly that social progress was possible. As a result, the writers of the Constitution built in a means for *amending* the Constitution, allowing it to progress with the nation it governed.

Governmental Powers

Governmental powers in the Constitution can be divided into six types:

EXPRESSED POWERS or ENUMERATED POWERS are powers that are specifically granted to the federal government only. An example of an expressed power is the power to make treaties with foreign nations.

IMPLIED POWERS are powers the federal government has that are not in the Constitution. They derive from the elastic clause of the Constitution, Article I, Section 8. The ELASTIC CLAUSE gives Congress the right to "make all laws necessary and proper" for carrying out other powers. For example, over time as new technologies have emerged, such as radio and television, the commerce clause has been expanded to allow the federal government to regulate them.

The idea of implied powers was supported by the Supreme Court in *McCulloch v. Maryland* (1819). The state of Maryland tried to tax the Maryland branch of the Bank of the United States. When the bank refused to pay the tax, the case landed in the Maryland Court of Appeals; the court ruled that the Bank of the United States was unconstitutional, as the Constitution did not expressly give the federal government the power to operate a bank. Later, the Supreme Court overturned the ruling, citing the elastic clause.

RESERVED POWERS are powers that are held by the states through the Tenth Amendment, which states that all powers not expressly given to the federal government belong to the states. For example, the management of public education is a reserved power.

INHERENT POWERS are powers that derive specifically from US sovereignty and are inherent to its existence as a nation. For example, the powers to make treaties and to wage war are both inherent powers.

CONCURRENT POWERS are powers that are shared equally by both the national and state government. The power to tax and the power to establish courts are both concurrent powers.

PROHIBITED POWERS are powers that are denied to both the national government and the state governments. Passing bills of attainder (laws that declare someone guilty without a trial) is a prohibited power.

The separation of powers limited the powers within the federal government, but did not address the power relationship between the federal government and the states. Under the Articles, the federal government was completely beholden to the states for its very existence. However, it was clear that complete state sovereignty did not work. Instead, the Constitution created a FEDERAL relationship between the two levels of government. FEDERALISM is a system in which both the state government and federal government retain sovereignty by dividing up the areas for which they are responsible.

Under the Constitution, the federal government is charged with matters that concern the population at large: for example, handling federal lands, coining money, and maintaining an army and navy. It also handles conflicts between the states via the federal judiciary and by regulating interstate trade. Matters of regional or local concern are handled by state or local governments. This relationship is best codified in the Tenth Amendment, which states that any powers not explicitly given to the federal government are reserved for the states. However, according to the SUPREMACY CLAUSE (Article VI, Clause 2) the Constitution is the "supreme law of the land." Therefore, in cases of conflict between the states and the federal government, the federal government's authority generally supersedes that of the states.

The division of power has shifted over time with more power going to the federal government as its scope has expanded. The federal government also can exert influence over state governments through GRANT-IN-AID, money that is provided for a particular purpose. The federal government can attach stipulations to this funding. For example, grant-in-aid was given to the states in the late 1970s for highway improvement. However, states who accepted the money were required to set the drinking age at twenty-one years old in their state. This was a way for the government to influence law that was technically beyond their purview.

EXAMPLE

In the American federal system of government, the power of state governments derives from

A) the Constitution

B) the people of the nation

C) the state legislatures

D) the people of that state

Answer:

D) is correct. Each state government is a democratic republic in which authority is derived from the consent of the governed.

Organization of the Federal Government

The Legislative Branch

At the writing of the Constitution, the branch of the federal government endowed with the most power was the legislative branch. Called CONGRESS, this branch is composed of a bicameral legislature (two houses). Based on the British model, most colonies—and then states—had bicameral legislatures with an upper and lower house. While this structure was not originally adopted under the Articles of Confederation, the framers chose it when reorganizing the government. This was in large part due to a dispute at the convention over the structure of the legislative body—specifically the voting power of each state.

Small states advocated equal representation, with each state having the same number of representatives, each with one vote. Called the NEW JERSEY PLAN, this plan distributed decision-making power equally among the states, regardless of land mass or population. The more populous states found this system to be unfair. Instead, they argued for a plan called the VIRGINIA PLAN, based on PROPORTIONAL REPRESENTATION. Each state would be assigned a number of representatives based on its population (enslaved people deprived of their rights would even be counted among the population, benefiting those states with large slave populations). In the end, the GREAT COMPROMISE was reached. There would be two houses: the HOUSE OF REPRESENTATIVES (the lower house) would have proportional representation, and the SENATE (the upper house) would have equal representation.

The bicameral system had other advantages. The House of Representatives would be directly elected by the people, and the Senate by the state legislatures. This supported the federal structure of the government: one house would serve the needs of the people directly, and the other would serve the needs of the states. Also, it curbed federal power by fragmenting it and slowing down the legislative process.

The structure and powers of Congress are outlined in Article I of the Constitution. As the most representative branch of government, the legislative branch was also designed to be the most powerful. Hence, it has the most expressed powers in the Constitution. Section Eight contains eighteen clauses listing specific powers which can be divided into peacetime powers and war powers:

Table 13.1. Powers of Congress

CLAUSE	PEACETIME POWERS	CLAUSE	WAR POWERS
1	to establish and collect taxes, duties, and excises	11	to declare war; to make laws regarding people captured on land and water
2	to borrow money	12	to raise and support armies
3	to regulate foreign and interstate commerce	13	to provide and maintain a navy
4	to create naturalization laws; to create bankruptcy laws	14	to make laws governing land and naval forces
5	to coin money and regulate its value; regulate weights and measures	15	to provide for summoning the militia to execute federal laws, suppress uprisings, and repel invasions
6	to punish counterfeiters of federal money	16	to provide for organizing, arming, and disciplining the militia and governing it when in the service of the Union
7	to establish post offices and roads		
8	to grant patents and copyrights		
9	to create federal courts below the Supreme Court		
10	to define and punish crimes at sea; define violations of international law		
17	to exercise exclusive jurisdiction over Washington, D.C. and other federal properties		
18	to make all laws necessary and proper to the execution of the other expressed powers (elastic clause)		

The **HOUSE OF REPRESENTATIVES** is the house which was designed to directly represent the people, and it was originally the only part of the federal government that was directly elected by the citizens. It is the larger of the houses with the number of representatives from each state based on the states' population (**PROPORTIONAL REPRESENTATION**). Every state is guaranteed at least one representative. Apportionment of representatives is based on the census, so seats are reapportioned every ten years with the new census.

At the convention, Southern states argued that their (non-voting) slave population should count towards their overall population, therefore entitling them to more representatives. Northern states with few slaves disagreed. This issue was settled with the **THREE-FIFTHS COMPROMISE** which declared that each slave would be counted as three-fifths of a person for the purpose of the census. (Women, who could not vote until the ratification of the Nineteenth Amendment, were also counted in the census.)

The size of the House grew every ten years along with the population of the United States until 1929, when Congress set the number at 435 voting representatives where it has remained since. Today, each member of Congress represents approximately 700,000 people. Residents of Washington D.C. and territories held by the United States (Guam, American Samoa, and the US Virgin Islands) are represented by non-voting observers; Puerto Rico is represented by a resident commissioner.

Each state legislature divides its state into essentially equally populated congressional districts. This process can become political, with political parties attempting to draw the lines to ensure the maximum number of seats for their party. This is called **GERRYMANDERING**. The Supreme Court has made several rulings to limit gerrymandering, including requiring each district to have equal population and contiguous or connected lines. It is also unconstitutional to draw lines based solely on race.

Members of the House of Representatives are elected for two-year terms in an effort to keep them beholden to the people. The Constitution lays out basic requirements for membership in the House. In order to qualify, candidates must be at least twenty-five years old, have been a US citizen for at least seven years, and live in the state they are representing at the time of the election. The leader of the House is called the **SPEAKER OF THE HOUSE**. He or she is the leader of the majority party in the House.

Although it is technically considered the lower house, there are still powers that belong only to the House of Representatives:

- All revenue bills must start in the house. While the Senate may amend the bills, the framers wanted to keep fiscal power in the hands of the house most beholden to the people.
- The House may bring charges of **IMPEACHMENT** against the president or a Supreme Court justice. Impeachment is the process by which a federal official can be officially charged with a crime. If found guilty, he or she is removed from office. In order to impeach a president or justice, a simple majority is required. Only two presidents have ever been tried for impeachment: Andrew Johnson and Bill Clinton.
- The House must choose the president if there is no majority in the Electoral College. The House has only selected the president once: in 1824, Andrew Jackson, John Quincy Adams, and Henry Clay split the electoral vote. Jackson

had the plurality (the greatest percentage), but did not win a majority. The vote went to the House, and, after some backroom politics, they voted for John Quincy Adams.

The SENATE was designed to be the house of the states. To signify that no one state is more important than any other, representation in the Senate is apportioned equally, with two senators per state, making a total of 100 senators. The framers designed the Senate so that representatives were chosen by the state legislatures; there was no direct connection between the Senate and the people. However, as the power of the federal government grew, the people increasingly came to think of it as representing themselves rather than their states. Corrupt state legislatures sold Senate seats to the highest bidder rather than electing the most qualified individual. As a result, the Senate seemed disconnected from the democratic process, a corrupt millionaire's club.

The tension between the people's perception of their relationship to the federal government and the mechanism of Senate elections came to a head during the Progressive Era. Political machinations led to deadlocks in state legislatures over appointments, leaving Senate seats vacant for months at time. In 1913, the SEVENTEENTH AMENDMENT to the Constitution was ratified; it required the direct election of senators by the people of a state.

As the upper house, the Senate was designed to have greater autonomy with stricter qualifications. Senators are elected for six year terms to allow them time to make decisions that might not be popular but that are best for the nation. They are staggered in three groups; one group is up for election every two years. This ensures that all senators do not face re-election at the same time, allowing for more consistent governance.

To be a senator, candidates must be at least thirty years old, have been a citizen of the United States for nine years, and—at the time of the election—live in the state they will represent. The president of the Senate is the US vice president. However, he or she only has the power to vote in case of a tie. The vice president is often absent from the Senate, in which case the PRESIDENT PRO TEMPORE presides. He or she is generally the longest-serving member of the Senate.

Much like the House, the Senate has certain unique powers:

- Whereas the House has the power to impeach, the Senate acts as the jury in the impeachment of a president and determines his or her guilt. In order to remove, or oust, a president from office, the Senate must vote two-thirds in favor. Removal has never happened in American history.

- The Senate approves executive appointments and appointments to federal positions in the judicial system. These include, among others, members of the Supreme Court and other federal courts, the attorney general, cabinet members, and ambassadors.

- The Senate ratifies (approves) all treaties signed by the president. The president is in charge of foreign relations and is responsible for negotiating all treaties; however, as part of the system of checks and balances, the president requires the Senate's approval before any treaty becomes a permanent agreement.

The primary function of the legislature is to write and pass laws. Approximately 5,000 bills are introduced in Congress each year, only 2.5 percent of which become laws. There are no restrictions on who can write a bill. In fact, most are not written by Congress, but begin either in the executive branch or are written by special interest groups. A member of Congress is required, however, to introduce the bill. With the exception of revenue bills, bills can start in either house. Since the two houses have parallel processes, the same bill often starts in both houses at the same time.

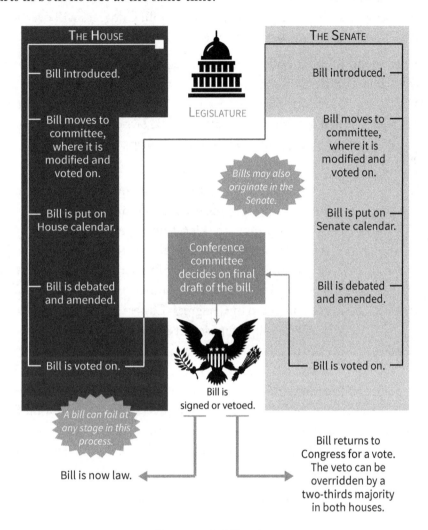

Figure 13.2. Bill to Law

Once it is placed in the "hopper," the bill is assigned a number and sent to the appropriate committee. Committees and their subcommittees are where most of the hard work of lawmaking is actually done. Here bills are read, debated, and revised. It is also where most bills die, by either being TABLED (put aside) in subcommittee or committee, or by being voted down. If a bill does get voted out of committee, it goes to the floor for debate. In the House of Representatives, the powerful RULES COMMITTEE not only determines which bills make it to the floor for debate, but also sets time limits for debate on each bill.

In the Senate, debate is unlimited. This allows for a unique tactic called the FILIBUSTER, in which a senator or group of senators continues debate indefinitely to delay the passage of a bill. Sixty votes are needed to end a filibuster, so senators often attempt to gather sixty or more votes for a bill before it comes to the floor to ensure it is not filibustered.

After debate has ended, the members of each house vote on the bill. If it passes out of both houses, it moves to the CONFERENCE COMMITTEE which must transform the two very different draft bills (as different revisions and amendments were made as the bill made its way through each house) into one. Once that is done, the unified bill returns to both houses for a final vote. If it passes, it then proceeds to the president for signature or veto. If the president does veto the bill, it returns to Congress where both houses can vote again. If two-thirds of each house vote in favor of the bill, Congress will override the veto and the bill will become law anyway. However, this rarely happens.

Congress is responsible for another significant legislative process: amending the Constitution. The framers understood that they could not possibly foresee every threat to state sovereignty and personal liberty nor every need that would require government management. So they added Article V to the Constitution, which lays out a procedure for amending it. This is one of the most significant aspects of the Constitution as it makes it a "living document."

The process by which laws are written and passed is intentionally cumbersome and complicated. The framers of the Constitution believed that the longer the process took, the more deliberation there would be, decreasing the risk of abuse of power.

Amendments to the Constitution can either come from Congress or from the state legislatures. For Congress to propose an amendment to the Constitution, two-thirds of each house must vote in favor of the amendment. Alternatively, an amendment can be proposed if two-thirds of the states call for a national constitutional convention. All amendments to date, however, have been proposed by Congress. Either way, once the amendment has been officially proposed, it is not ratified until three-quarters of state legislatures (or special conventions convened by each state) approve it. There are twenty-seven amendments to the Constitution, the first ten of which were passed immediately in 1791.

These first ten amendments, called THE BILL OF RIGHTS, were a condition for ratification imposed by those who thought the new government wielded too much power. These ANTI-FEDERALISTS argued that individual liberty had to be explicitly protected from federal intervention. According to the amendments, the government may not:

Amendment I: prohibit freedom of religion, speech, press, petition and assembly

Amendment II: prohibit the right to bear arms

Amendment III: quarter troops in citizens' homes

Amendment IV: conduct unlawful search and seizures

Amendment V: force anyone to testify against themselves or be tried for the same crime twice

Amendment VI: prohibit the right to a fair and speedy trial

Amendment VII: prohibit the right to a jury trial in civil cases (remember the original Constitution only guaranteed a jury in criminal cases)

Amendment VIII: force citizens to undergo cruel and unusual punishment

Amendment IX: violate rights that exist but are not explicitly mentioned in the Constitution

Amendment X: usurp any powers from the states not given to them in the Constitution (so all other powers not listed in the Constitution belong to the states)

While the only official way to change the Constitution is through the amendment process, other loopholes for change exist within its framework. These include:

- **CLARIFYING LEGISLATION:** Using the ELASTIC CLAUSE, much legislation has been passed whose purpose is to clarify or expand the powers of the federal government. For example, the Constitution only provides directly for the Supreme Court, but empowers Congress to create other courts. The Judiciary Act of 1789 created the federal judiciary.

- **EXECUTIVE ACTIONS:** Although Congress holds most lawmaking power, the president is able to issue executive actions which have the force of law without having to involve Congress. The most famous of these is Abraham Lincoln's Emancipation Proclamation.

- **JUDICIAL DECISIONS:** In *Marbury v. Madison* (1803) the Supreme Court established the precedent of JUDICIAL REVIEW, the power of the Supreme Court to determine the constitutionality of laws. *Marbury v. Madison* not only illustrated how judicial decisions can expand federal power in general, but it also broadened the power of the Supreme Court in particular, laying the groundwork for future decisions that would have a similar impact.

- **POLITICAL PARTIES:** The rise of political parties changed the political landscape as well. Some aspects of American politics—like how the Speaker of the House is chosen and nomination conventions for presidential candidates—have come from political parties rather than through a formal legislative process.

Although Congress was made much more powerful by the Constitution, a real fear of tyranny existed among the framers. While Section VIII of the Constitution lists the powers of Congress, Section IX lists what Congress cannot do. Most notable are:

1. **NO SUSPENSION OF HABEAS CORPUS:** A writ of habeas corpus is a legal demand a prisoner can make to appear in court in order to profess their innocence. Essentially a means of preventing unreasonable imprisonment, habeas corpus was viewed as an essential element of a just government. The Constitution forbids its suspension except in cases of rebellion or invasion. (Abraham Lincoln, during the Civil War, was the first president to suspend habeas corpus.)

2. **NO BILLS OF ATTAINDER:** A bill of attainder is a law that declares an individual or a group guilty of a crime without holding a trial. Much like with the writ of habeas corpus, this was seen as an essential protection in a fair society.

3. **NO EX POST FACTO LAWS:** An ex post facto law is a law which punishes an individual or group for breaking a law that was not a law when the act was committed. For example, slavery was abolished in 1865. If an ex post facto law was passed at that time, it would have punished anyone who had owned slaves before 1865.

4. **No titles of nobility:** It was important to the framers to provide safe-guards against a return to monarchy. Therefore, they prohibited an American nobility of any kind.

EXAMPLE

Why did the framers give the House of Representatives the power to start revenue bills?

A) Based on their qualifications, members of the House would have more economic knowledge.

B) Members of the House would be less influenced by outside forces and political parties than members of the Senate.

C) The House was more truly a national legislature; therefore, it should be in charge of the national budget.

D) The frequency of elections for House of Representatives would make them more responsive to the will of the people in terms of spending.

Answer:

D) is correct. The framers thought it was important that those who spent the money be held most accountable to the people to avoid corruption and misuse.

The Executive Branch

Defined by Article II of the Constitution, the executive branch enforces all federal law. Article II only provides for a president, vice president, and an unspecified number of executive departments. However, the federal government has expanded considerably over the past 225 years, in large part due to the expansion of the executive branch. Today, the executive branch is also responsible for administering a federal bureaucracy that spends $3 trillion a year and employs 2.7 million people.

Of the three mentioned, the president is the only executive role that is specifically defined in the Constitution. The president serves a term of four years and may be re-elected up to two times. While the term length was set in the original Constitution, the term limit was added in the Twenty-Second Amendment in 1951, in response to Franklin Delano Roosevelt's four elections to the presidency. Many felt that allowing unlimited terms opened the door for a de facto dictator and threatened liberty.

In order to qualify for the presidency, candidates must be natural-born American citizens, at least thirty-five years old, and have resided in the United States for at least fourteen years. While the Constitution does not specifically list requirements for the vice presidency, it does state that the vice president becomes the president in case of death, resignation, or impeachment. As a result, the vice president must meet the same qualifications as the president.

The CABINET consists of the heads of the executive departments and may advise the president on a variety of matters. It is not directly referred to at all in the Constitution. Instead, it was derived from one line in Section 2: "[the president] may require the opinion, in writing, of the principal officer in each of the executive departments, upon any subject relating to the duties of their respective offices." However, the cabinet as we know it today was established immediately under George Washington. He established four executive departments, so the first cabinet consisted of four positions: the Secretary of State, the Secretary of the Treasury, the Secretary of War (now, the Secretary of Defense) and the Attorney General, or head of the Justice Department. Over time, eleven new executive departments were added, for a total of fifteen cabinet positions.

1. Department of State
2. Department of the Treasury
3. Department of Defense
4. Department of Justice
5. Department of Interior
6. Department of Agriculture
7. Department of Commerce
8. Department of Labor
9. Department of Energy
10. Department of Education
11. Department of Housing and Urban Development
12. Department of Transportation
13. Department of Veterans Affairs
14. Department of Health and Human Services
15. Department of Homeland Security

These fifteen departments employ more than two-thirds of all federal employees.

In addition to managing their departments, the members of the cabinet are also all in the line of presidential succession as established by the Presidential Succession Act (first passed in 1792 but most recently amended in 1947). The line of succession is as follows: following the vice president is the Speaker of the House, then the president pro tempore of the Senate, followed by each cabinet member in the order of the department's creation, beginning with the Secretary of State and ending with the Secretary of Homeland Security.

Article II is considerably shorter than Article I because the framers intended the role and powers of the president to be more limited than those of Congress. However, the president does have a number of expressed powers.

One of the most significant presidential powers is the power to appoint federal officials. The president's APPOINTMENT POWER is far-ranging and includes cabinet members, heads of independent agencies, ambassadors, and federal judges. Through this power, the president not only controls the entirety of the executive branch as well as foreign policy, but also wields significant and long-term influence over the judicial branch. This power, however, is not unlimited. Based on the advise and consent clause of the Constitution, the Senate must approve all presidential appointments. The president does have the power

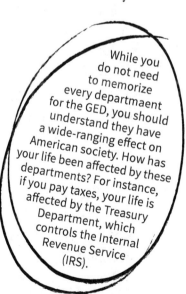

While you do not need to memorize every departmaent for the GED, you should understand they have a wide-ranging effect on American society. How has your life been affected by these departments? For instance, if you pay taxes, your life is affected by the Treasury Department, which controls the Internal Revenue Service (IRS).

to remove any of his or her appointees from office—with the exception of judges—without Senate approval.

The first line of section 2 of Article II declares the president COMMANDER-IN-CHIEF of the army and navy. In this role, the president is the supreme leader of US military forces. He or she can deploy troops and dictate military policy. However, this power is checked as well. While the president controls the military, Congress retains the power to declare war. Presidents have circumvented this check in the past, however, by deploying troops without requesting a formal declaration of war. In the twentieth century, this happened most notably in the Vietnam War, which was never officially declared. In 1964, Congress passed the Gulf of Tonkin Resolution in response to the perceived attack on an American ship in the Gulf of Tonkin. The resolution essentially gave the president a blank check for military action in Vietnam, which led to a rapid and massive escalation of US military spending and troops. Because of this, in 1974 Congress passed the WAR POWERS RESO-LUTION; this resolution requires the president to inform Congress within forty-eight hours of a troop deployment and restricts deployment unsupported by congressional authorization to sixty days.

The president is also considered the CHIEF DIPLOMAT of the United States. In this capacity, the president has the power to recognize other nations, receive ambassadors, and negotiate treaties. However, any treaties negotiated by the president must be approved by the Senate before taking effect.

Many of the president's diplomatic powers are informal. In the twentieth century, the US became a superpower, transforming the role of the president into that of a world leader as well as the leader of the nation. As a result, the president is now expected to manage international crises, negotiate executive agreements with other countries, and monitor and maintain confidential information related to the security of the nation and to the rest of the world.

While the executive and judicial branches are quite separate, the president has powers intended to check the power of the judicial branch. Primarily, this is the power to appoint federal judges. The president may also grant pardons and reprieves for individuals convicted of federal crimes. The purpose of this is to provide a final option for those who have been unfairly convicted. This is one of the president's more controversial powers, as pardons are often seen to be politically motivated or a tool for those with political or personal connections.

Like the judicial branch, the president is constitutionally accorded some LEGISLATIVE POWERS in order to limit the powers of the legislative branch. All laws that are passed end up on the president's desk. He or she has the choice to either sign the bill—in which case it becomes a law—or to VETO the bill. The president's veto prevents the bill from becoming law (unless Congress overrides the veto). The president is required to either fully accept or fully reject a bill; he or she may not veto only sections of it. This is called a LINE-ITEM VETO, and the Supreme Court declared it unconstitutional in 1996. If the president does not wish to take such a clear stand on a bill, he or she can also simply ignore it. If the president does nothing for ten days, the bill automatically becomes law, even without a signature. If, however, there are less than ten days left in Congress's session, and the president does not sign the bill, it automatically dies. This is called a POCKET VETO.

The president also has the power to convene both houses of Congress to force them to consider matters requiring urgent attention.

While this is technically the extent of the president's legislative powers, in reality the position has a much greater legislative impact. The president sets the policy agenda both as the leader of his or her party and through the STATE OF THE UNION address. Section 3 of Article II states, "He [or she] shall from time to time give to the Congress information of the state of the union, and recommend to their consideration such measures as he [or she] shall judge necessary and expedient." This has evolved into an annual formalized address to Congress in which the president lays out executive legislative priorities.

Many bills originate in the executive branch, either from the president's office or from one of the executive departments. The president also often uses the power of the veto to influence legislation. By threatening to veto, the president can force changes to bills that align more with her or his political agenda.

Almost half of Article II is dedicated to describing the process of electing the president. The framers wanted to ensure the president represented all of the states and was immune from the mob rule of democracy. As a result, they created the ELECTORAL COLLEGE. Over the years, the political parties have expanded the process into a nine-month series of elections by various groups of people.

The first step in choosing a president is selecting the candidates. Originally, this was done in smoke-filled back rooms; it then became the provenance of party caucuses and then conventions, eventually evolving into the current system of primaries and caucuses. In a PRIMARY election, members of a political party in a state vote at a polling place for whom they believe is the best candidate for their party. In ten states, a CAUCUS system is used, in which members of a party in a state gather together at party meetings and vote for the candidate using raised hands or by gathering in groups.

Then, in July of the election year, the party holds a NATIONAL NOMINATING CONVENTION. Historically, this is where the candidate was chosen after days of heated debate and dealings. However, because of the primary and caucus systems, delegates at the convention arrive already knowing whom their state supports. The delegates vote for the candidate who won their primary or caucus. The candidate with the most votes becomes the party's nominee.

Presidential elections are held nationwide every four years on the Tuesday following the first Monday in November. Today, all American citizens over the age of eighteen are allowed to vote, but this was not always the case. The framers viewed the electorate as a small, select segment of the population. However, no voter qualifications are written into the Constitution; those were left to the states. In 1789, in every state, only propertied white men—one in fifteen white men—were allowed to vote. Starting with the removal of property qualifications during the Jacksonian era (1830s), views of democracy began to change, and the electorate expanded. Aside from property requirements, each expansion resulted from a new amendment to the Constitution.

GO ON

Table 13.2. Constitutional Amendments Expanding Voting Rights

AMENDMENT	YEAR	PROVISION
Fifteenth	1870	All male citizens, regardless of race, are allowed to vote.
Nineteenth	1920	Women are allowed to vote.
Twenty-Third	1961	Residents of the District of Columbia are allowed to vote in presidential elections.
Twenty-Fourth	1964	Poll taxes, an indirect restriction of black voting rights, are prohibited.
Twenty-Sixth	1971	All citizens over the age of eighteen are allowed to vote (in most states the voting age had previously been twenty-one years).

While the popular vote is tallied on Election Day, it does not determine the outcome of the presidential election. That is the job of the Electoral College. The **ELECTORAL COLLEGE** is composed of electors from each state who vote for the president. Electors are apportioned based on population; the number of a state's electors is the same as its number of representatives plus its number of senators (so each state has at least three electors).

In the January following the election, electors gather in their states to cast their votes for president. Technically, electors are not bound to vote in line with their state's popular vote. However, rarely has an elector taken advantage of this, and it has never affected the outcome of an election. Today, most states are winner-take-all, meaning the electors are expected to all vote in line with the outcome of the state's popular vote. The president must win a majority—not a plurality—of the Electoral College in order to win. This is 270 votes.

A state's number of electors is equal to its number of representatives plus its number of senators (which is two for every state). So, every state (and Washington, DC) has at least three electoral votes. There are a total of 538 votes available.

The Electoral College was designed to elect a president for a nation that was scattered and had greater regional than national loyalty. It favors small states and minority groups, giving them greater influence on the election than they would have in a direct election system. Today many people feel that the Electoral College is outdated and ill-fitting. They argue it is undemocratic, and that it gives undue importance to certain states based on their number of electoral votes. Instead, they support a direct election system.

EXAMPLE

The Electoral College represents which of the beliefs of the framers of the Constitution?

A) Government derives its authority from the consent of the people.

B) Concentration of power can lead to tyranny.

C) The federal government derives its authority from the states.

D) The federal government needs greater power to provide stability to the nation.

The Judicial Branch

The Constitution's framework for the judicial branch is the least detailed of the three branches. It is also a passive branch. Where the legislative branch creates laws, and the executive branch takes actions to enforce those laws, the judicial branch can only weigh in when an actual case is presented to it. It may not rule or make decisions based on hypotheticals. Yet this branch has grown to be at least as influential as the other two branches both in setting policy and molding the size and shape of the federal government.

The United States has a complex DUAL COURT SYSTEM; each state has its own multi-part judicial system in addition to the federal one. Even though federal district courts handle over 300,000 cases a year, ninety-seven percent of criminal cases are heard in state and local courts. While the federal courts hear more civil cases than criminal, the majority of these are still handled within the states. Because of the federal system, state courts have JURISDICTION—or the authority to hear a case—over most cases. Only cases that meet certain criteria (e.g. a dispute between two states, a case involving federal employees or agencies, or a violation of federal law) are heard in federal courts. Most cases also can only be APPEALED—or reviewed by a higher court—up to the state supreme court. For the federal Supreme Court to review a state supreme court's decision, there must be an issue involving the interpretation of the federal Constitution.

The federal court system is composed of three levels of courts. First are the district courts. There are ninety-four district courts in the country, served by 700 judges. They handle 80 percent of all federal cases. The next level of courts are the twelve circuit courts of appeal. These courts review district court decisions and the decisions of federal regulatory agencies.

Article III, the article of the Constitution which discusses the judicial branch, only details the Supreme Court. It then empowers Congress to create the rest of the judiciary, which it did beginning with the Judiciary Act of 1789.

At the top is the SUPREME COURT. Sometimes called the "court of last resort," the Supreme Court reviews cases from the circuit court and from state supreme courts, and is the final arbiter of constitutionality. Decisions made by the Supreme Court establish PRECEDENTS, rulings that guide future court decisions at all levels of the judicial system.

While the Constitution delineates which kinds of cases the Supreme Court may hear, its real power was established by the precedent of an early case, *Marbury v. Madison* (1803). In this case, William Marbury—citing the Judiciary Act of 1789—sought relief from the court when James Madison, Secretary of State to the newly inaugurated Thomas Jefferson, did not deliver the federal appointment Marbury was given under the previous president, John Adams. The court, under Chief Justice John Marshall, ruled that while Madison was in the wrong, the section of the Judiciary Act allowing Marbury to petition the Supreme Court was unconstitutional because it extended the jurisdiction of the court beyond the scope established in Article III. This established JUDICIAL REVIEW, the Supreme Court's power to determine the constitutionality of laws. This has become the most significant function of the court, and has allowed it to shape public policy.

You do not need to memorize all the important Supreme Court cases to do well on the GED. Instead, focus on understanding why they were important and how they affected US government and society.

There are nine justices who serve on the Supreme Court. Appointed by the president and approved by the Senate, Supreme Court justices serve for life. The Constitution does not provide any criteria for serving on the court. However, unofficial requirements do exist: justices must demonstrate competence through high level credentials or through prior experience. Today, all of the justices on the Supreme Court hold law degrees from major universities and first served in federal district or appellate courts. They also generally share policy preferences with the president who appointed them, although judicial inclinations do not always neatly align with political ones.

There are several significant Supreme Court cases to know, some of which are listed in Table 2.3.

Table 13.3. Supreme Court Cases

CASE NAME	RULING
Marbury v. Madison (1803)	This case established judicial review.
McCulloch v. Maryland (1819)	The court ruled that states could not tax the Bank of the United States; this ruling supported the implied powers of Congress.
Dred Scott v. Sandford (1857)	The Supreme Court ruled that enslaved persons were not citizens; it also found the Missouri Compromise unconstitutional, meaning Congress could not forbid expanding slavery to US territories.
Plessy v. Ferguson (1896)	This case established the precedent of separate but equal (segregation).
Korematsu v. US (1945)	This case determined that the internment of Japanese Americans during WWII was lawful.
Brown v. Board of Education (1954)	The Supreme Court overturned Plessy v. Ferguson; it ruled that separate but equal, or segregation, was unconstitutional.
Gideon v. Wainwright (1963)	The Supreme Court ruled that the court must provide legal counsel to poor defendants in felony cases.
Miranda v. Arizona (1966)	This ruling established that defendants must be read their due process rights before questioning.
Tinker v. Des Moines (1969)	This case established "symbolic speech" as a form of speech protected by the First Amendment.
Roe v. Wade (1973)	This case legalized abortion in the first trimester throughout the United States.
Bakke v. Regents of University of California (1978)	This case ruled that while affirmative action was constitutional, the university's quota system was not.

CASE NAME	RULING
Citizens United v. Federal Elections Commission (2010)	The court ruled that restricting corporate donations to political campaigns was tantamount to restricting free speech; this ruling allowed the formation of influential super PACs, which can provide unlimited funding to candidates running for office.
Obergefell v. Hodges (2015)	The court ruled that same-sex marriage was legal throughout the United States.

Civil Liberties and Rights

Influenced by the ideas of the Enlightenment and fresh from revolution, the framers of the Constitution valued CIVIL LIBERTIES. Civil liberties are rights—provided for either directly by the Constitution or through its historical interpretations—which protect individuals from arbitrary acts of the government. The framers protected some liberties explicitly in the Constitution via the prohibited powers, and expanded on them in the BILL OF RIGHTS. Each of these amendments restricts the actions of the federal government rather than actually granting a freedom to the people.

The liberties most central to the American identity are articulated in the FIRST AMENDMENT: speech, press, petition, assembly, and religion. The first four are all closely related. No liberty is truly unlimited, however, and the court has imposed restrictions on FREEDOM OF SPEECH over time. It has upheld laws banning libel, slander, obscenity, and symbolic speech that intends to incite illegal actions.

The FREEDOM OF RELIGION comes from two clauses in the First Amendment: the ESTABLISHMENT CLAUSE and the FREE EXERCISE CLAUSE. The first prohibits the government from establishing a state religion or favoring one religion over another. The second prohibits the government from restricting religious belief or practice. Again, this is not unlimited. The court has found that religious practice can be banned if it requires engagement in otherwise illegal activity. There are also continuing debates on allowing prayer in schools and granting vouchers to students to attend parochial schools.

Most of the civil liberties written into the body of the Constitution addressed the rights of the accused, including prohibitions on bills of attainder, ex post facto laws, and denials of writs of habeas corpus. Three of the amendments in the Bill of Rights address this as well.

The FOURTH AMENDMENT restricts unlawful searches and seizures. In *Mapp v. Ohio* (1961), the Supreme Court ruled that evidence obtained illegally—so in violation of the Fourth Amendment—could not be used in court. This EXCLUSIONARY RULE is very controversial, and the courts have struggled since to determine when and how to apply it.

The FIFTH AMENDMENT protects the accused from self-incrimination. Drawing on this amendment, the Supreme Court ruled in *Miranda v. Arizona* (1966) that arrestees must be informed of their due process rights before interrogation in order to protect them from self-incrimination. These rights, along with those in the Sixth Amendment, are now colloquially known as MIRANDA RIGHTS.

The **SIXTH AMENDMENT** guarantees the accused the right to a fair, speedy, and public trial, as well as the right to counsel in criminal cases. While originally this only applied at the federal level, in *Gideon v. Wainwright* (1963) the Supreme Court ruled that states must provide counsel to those who cannot afford it.

What rights do Americans enjoy under these constitutional amendments and court rulings? To do well on the exam, it is more important to have an understanding of citizens' rights than to memorize each court case and amendment.

The Court's ruling in *Gideon v. Wainwright* was based on the Fourteenth Amendment's **EQUAL PROTECTION CLAUSE**. Ratified in 1868, the amendment's original purpose was to ensure the equal treatment of African Americans under the law after the abolition of slavery. However, its use has been expanded far beyond that original purpose. The equal protection clause has been used to protect the **CIVIL RIGHTS**—protections against discriminatory treatment by the government—of individuals of a variety of groups.

The courts have regularly protected political and legal equality, as well as equality of opportunity (like the *Brown v. Board of Education* decision in 1954). However, the courts do not recognize a right to economic equality. The Supreme Court also recognizes the need for reasonable classifications of people, and allows discrimination along those lines. For example, age restrictions on alcohol consumption, driving, and voting are all considered constitutional.

The Supreme Court has also used the **FOURTEENTH AMENDMENT** over time to extend federal civil liberties to the state level. Today, all states are held to the same standard as the federal government in terms of civil liberties.

The second part of the Fourteenth Amendment extends the Fifth Amendment's **DUE PROCESS** guarantees to the state level. "No person shall be deprived of life, liberty or property without the due process of law…" While this typically refers to the processes of the accused, as discussed above, it has also come to represent certain unnamed, or implied, rights. At the heart of most of these **IMPLIED RIGHTS** is the right to privacy, which is not specifically protected in the Constitution. However, the court has ruled that it is implied by the Fourth, Fifth, and Fourteenth Amendments. This was the basis for its decision to legalize abortion in *Roe v. Wade* (1973).

EXAMPLE

Which of the following is NOT considered protected speech?

A) burning the American flag

B) writing an article criticizing the government

C) publishing a false list of supposed KKK members

D) protesting outside of an abortion clinic

Answer:

C) is correct. Incorrectly alleging that someone is a member of a white supremacist group is considered libel (if written) or slander (if spoken). This is not protected by the Constitution.

Political Parties

Although the framers envisioned a political system without political parties, by the election of 1800, two official parties existed. A **POLITICAL PARTY** is a group of citizens who work together in order to win elections, hold public office, operate the government, and determine public policy. Some countries have one-party systems; others have multiple parties.

Although party names and platforms have shifted over the years, the United States has maintained a two-party system. Since 1854, our two major parties have been the **DEMOCRATIC PARTY** and the **REPUBLICAN PARTY**. Democrats generally follow a liberal political ideology, while Republicans have a conservative ideology. The parties operate at every level of government in every state. Although many members of a party serve in elected office, political parties have their own internal organization. Parties are hierarchical: they are comprised of national leaders, followed by state chairpersons, county chairpersons, and local activists.

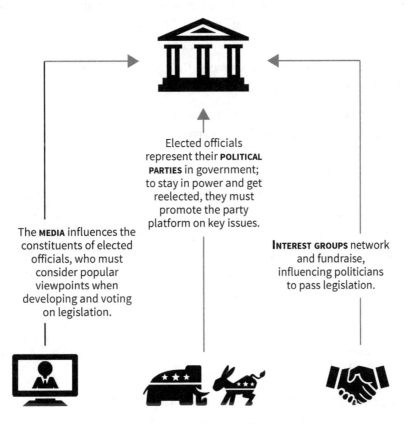

The **MEDIA** influences the constituents of elected officials, who must consider popular viewpoints when developing and voting on legislation.

Elected officials represent their **POLITICAL PARTIES** in government; to stay in power and get reelected, they must promote the party platform on key issues.

INTEREST GROUPS network and fundraise, influencing politicians to pass legislation.

Figure 13.3. Political Influence

The parties serve an important role in the American political system, fulfilling functions that aid government operations. These include:

- recruiting and nominating candidates for office
- running political campaigns
- articulating positions on various issues
- connecting individuals and the government

In Congress, parties have become integral to the organization of both houses. The leadership of each house is based on the leadership of whichever party has the majority.

The majority party also holds all of the committee chairs, assigns bills to committees, holds a majority in each committee, controls the important Rules Committee, and sets the legislative agenda.

While still very important, the power of political parties has declined dramatically since the beginning of the twentieth century. In response to the dominance and corruption of political machines, many states implemented **DIRECT PRIMARIES** to circumvent the parties. Individual politicians can now build power without the party machinery.

Although the United States has a two-party system, third parties still emerge from time to time. These parties are always relatively small and come in three types:

1. **CHARISMATIC LEADERSHIP PARTIES** are dominated by an engaging and forceful leader. Examples include the Bull Moose Party (Teddy Roosevelt, 1912), the American Independent Party (George Wallace, 1972), and the Reform Party (Ross Perot, 1992 and 1996).

2. **SINGLE-ISSUE PARTIES** are organized around one defining issue. Examples include the Free Soil Party and the Know Nothing Party in the 1840s, and the Right to Life Party in the 1970s and 1980s.

3. **IDEOLOGICAL PARTIES** are organized around a particular non-mainstream ideology. Examples include the Green Party and the Libertarian Party.

Although they rarely succeed in gaining major political office, these third parties play an important role in American politics. The two main parties tend toward the middle in an attempt to garner the majority of votes. Third parties, on the other hand, target select populations and are thus able to express strong views on controversial issues. Because their views are usually shared by the most extreme elements of one of the major parties, their stances often push the major parties into more radical positions. They also can affect the outcome of an election, even without winning it. By siphoning off a segment of the vote from one of the dominant parties, they can "spoil" the election for that party. For example, in the 2000 presidential election, Ralph Nader, the Green Party candidate, did not win any electoral votes. However, he drew away votes that most likely otherwise would have gone to Al Gore, contributing to George W. Bush's election.

EXAMPLE

Third parties primarily impact presidential elections by

A) increasing voter turnout.

B) preventing either party from winning a majority in the Electoral College.

C) encouraging more voters to officially join a political party.

D) bringing forward issues to be adopted by the major parties later.

Answer:

D) is correct. This is by far the most significant role third parties play. They are able to discuss more controversial issues and espouse more radical positions. This often pushes the major parties to discuss the issues as well and take a stand.

Other Groups

Organizations and individuals who are not politicians or employed by the government still have a role to play in politics. Washington, DC and state capitals are home to many interest groups, and the media is key in governance.

Interest Groups

An **INTEREST GROUP** is a private organization made up of individuals who share policy views on one or more issues. Organized together, the group then tries to influence public opinion to its own benefit. Interest groups play an important role in American politics. Much like political parties (and often even more directly than political parties), they connect citizens to the government. They act as a two-way street, both bringing their members' concerns and perspective to government officials and sharing information with their members about government policy. They wield more influence than the average citizen: they speak for many, and they raise money to influence policymakers, thereby influencing policy.

Most interest groups focus on one core issue or on a set of issues and draw their membership from people interested in those issues. For example, the National Rifle Association (NRA) focuses on protecting the right to gun ownership. Other organizations focus on a specific group of people, and then determine their interests based on the interests of that group. The AARP (American Association of Retired Persons) is an example of this type of interest group. It determines which issues are most relevant to senior citizens (who make up their membership), and pursues those issues. In addition, large corporations, industry organizations, agricultural groups, professional associations, and unions act as interest groups.

> Interest groups play an increasingly dominant role in American political life. The number of groups increased from 6,000 in 1959 to 22,000 in 2010.

Interest groups **LOBBY** lawmakers to try to effect the change they wish to see. To lobby means to attempt to persuade policymakers to make a certain decision. There are about 30,000 lobbyists in Washington D.C., making $2 billion a year. It is their full-time job to advance the agenda of their interest groups. They do this by testifying before congressional committees, meeting with aides, connecting influential constituents to lawmakers, drafting legislation, and providing relevant technical information to members of Congress.

When all else fails, interest groups will turn to the courts to help them achieve their goals. They write amicus briefs (supporting documents arguing for a side) in Supreme Court cases or initiate court cases to challenge existing laws. They also can play a significant role in determining who is nominated to the federal courts, including the Supreme Court.

Another tool interest groups use to influence policymakers is the **POLITICAL ACTION COMMITTEE**, also known as a PAC. These are committees that interest groups form with the purpose of raising money to support the campaigns of specific candidates who can further their interests. PACs are limited to contributions of $5000 per candidate per election. In 2010, however, the Supreme Court ruled in *Citizens United v. Federal Elections Commission* that limiting corporate donations to candidates was tantamount to limiting free speech. This controversial decision resulted in the creation of super PACs which have no limits on spending.

The role of lobbying, and most specifically PACs and super PACs, in American politics is a hotly debated one. Some political analysts are concerned that politics and money have become too closely tied together. Others argue that the sheer number of special interest groups is a benefit because they each balance each other out. In order to accomplish anything, politicians must bargain and compromise, creating solutions that are ultimately better for more people. Others still argue that rather than creating solutions, the number of competing interests leaves politicians scared to take any action for fear that they will anger one interest group or another.

Mass Media

Any means of communication—newspapers, magazines, radio, television, or blogs—that reaches a broad and far-reaching audience is considered part of the MASS MEDIA. Although certainly not a formal part of the political process, the mass media has a significant impact on American politics. It connects people to the government by providing them with inside information on its people and processes, through reports, interviews, and exposés. The media also can help set the political agenda by drawing attention to issues through its coverage. For example, the medical treatment of veterans became a significant political issue after two lengthy exposés in the *Washington Post* on the conditions at Walter Reed Medical Center in 2007.

Mass media has also reshaped American campaigns. Campaigns have become more candidate-centered rather than issue-centered, as candidates now must consider their image on television and other video sources. They also have to be media savvy, making appearances on popular nightly shows and radio programs. The need for a strong media presence is largely responsible for the increase in campaign spending, as candidates work to maintain an up-to-date web presence and spend millions of dollars on television advertising space. Candidates' lives and pasts are also more visible to the public as journalists research their backgrounds to a further extent than ever before. In the 1960 presidential campaign, John F. Kennedy and Richard Nixon engaged in the first televised presidential debate in American history. Those who listened to it on the radio declared Nixon—who was confident in speech, but sweaty and uncomfortable on camera—the winner, while those who watched it on television saw the suave and image-savvy Kennedy as the victor. Many credit this debate for Kennedy's eventual win, demonstrating the new importance of crafting a public image for politicians.

EXAMPLE

Throughout the twentieth and twenty-first centuries, changes in politics have coincided with the emergence of new media or a change in the organization of media. This shows that:

A) Politics is responsive to changes in how people communicate.

B) Media has a greater impact on the functioning of government than other political systems.

C) There is no connection between the functioning of media and politics.

D) New media develops in response to political changes.

Answer:

A) is correct. Politicians are always trying to find the best way to connect to their constituencies; therefore they must be adaptable to new media as it emerges. Also, new media changes the way in which politics is reported, which then changes the way it functions.

Test Your Knowledge

Read the question, and then choose the most correct answer.

1. Which of the following illustrated the problems with the Articles of Confederation?

    A) conflict between Federalists and Anti-Federalists

    B) Shays' Rebellion

    C) the Revolutionary War

    D) conflict between slave and free states

2. Which of the following is a safeguard against federal overreach built into the U.S. Constitution?

    A) a system of checks and balances, in which a president can only be elected to two consecutive terms

    B) a system of checks and balances, in which the House, Senate, and president are able to limit each other

    C) a system of checks and balances, in which the president—a civilian leader—controls the military

    D) a system of checks and balances, in which the three branches of government—executive, legislative, and judicial—are able to limit each other

3. Which group insisted on including the Bill of Rights in the Constitution in order to ratify it?

    A) Constitutionalists

    B) Revolutionaries

    C) Federalists

    D) Anti-Federalists

4. Which of the following best explains the Three-Fifths Compromise?

    A) Three-fifths of the states would be permitted to own slaves.

    B) Three-fifths of the states needed to ratify amendments before they could go into effect.

    C) To account for a state's population size, a slave would count for three-fifths of a person.

    D) Three-fifths of the states had to ratify the Constitution before it could go into effect.

5. John Locke's theory of a social contract is best reflected in which section of the Constitution?

    A) the Bill of Rights

    B) Article V, which refers to amending the Constitution

    C) the Preamble

    D) Article VII, which refers to ratification

6. Which of the following is an accurate example of checks and balances?

   A) The president signs treaties, and the Senate ratifies them.

   B) A bill becomes a law when Congress votes on it and the Supreme Court declares it constitutional.

   C) The Senate appoints justices to the Supreme Court, and the House of Representatives approves them.

   D) Congress has the power to remove the president, and the Supreme Court has the power to remove members of Congress.

7. Which clause of the Constitution best supports the idea of the rule of law?

   A) the Supremacy Clause

   B) the Elastic Clause

   C) the Advise and Consent Clause

   D) the Due Process Clause

8. The Bill of Rights was added to the Constitution

   A) in response to the Supreme Court's ruling in *Marbury v. Madison*.

   B) by the first Congress immediately after ratification.

   C) by Congress slowly over the first twenty years of the nation's existence.

   D) through George Washington's signature before he left office.

9. When the president vetoes a bill, he or she is effectively

   A) sending it back to conference committee.

   B) rejecting one part of the bill.

   C) rejecting the whole bill.

   D) declaring the bill unconstitutional.

10. Constitutional amendments have been proposed to make abortion illegal, to ban same-sex marriage, and to prohibit flag burning. What can be deduced from these movements?

    A) It is easy to amend the Constitution.

    B) People sometimes disagree with Supreme Court decisions.

    C) Some people believe that the Constitution is outdated.

    D) Americans tend to avoid complicated social issues.

11. The executive can check the legislative branch by doing which of the following?

    A) The president can remove members of Congress.

    B) The president selects the Speaker of the House.

    C) The president can pocket veto laws passed by Congress.

    D) The president can line-item veto laws passed by Congress.

12. At the Constitutional Convention, what did small states and large states disagree about?

   A) the creation of an executive branch

   B) the federal power to tax

   C) the method of electing Senators

   D) representation in the legislature

13. Which of the following is the most common critique of the Electoral College system?

   A) A president can be elected without winning the majority of the popular vote.

   B) It threatens the two-party system.

   C) It gives too much power to small states.

   D) Electors have too often voted for candidates not listed on the ballot.

14. Which of the following concepts most directly pertains to the relationship between national and state governments?

   A) federalism

   B) separation of powers

   C) checks and balances

   D) proportional representation

15. What lasting impact did *Marbury v. Madison* and *McCulloch v. Maryland* have?

   A) They ensured the Bill of Rights applied to enslaved persons as well as free.

   B) They restricted congressional power.

   C) They expanded the powers of the federal government.

   D) They drew a clear line between the executive and judicial branches.

16. To which of the following does the Supreme Court's power of judicial review NOT apply?

   A) laws passed by Congress

   B) laws passed by state legislatures

   C) executive orders

   D) lower-court decisions

17. The Bill of Rights expressly prohibits all of the following EXCEPT
    A) unlawful searches.
    B) double jeopardy.
    C) poll taxes.
    D) cruel and unusual punishment.

18. Which of the following constitutional rights is fully unrestricted?
    A) the freedom to say anything
    B) the freedom to go anywhere
    C) the freedom to believe anything
    D) the freedom to keep anything private

19. What contributed to the declining power of political parties in the twentieth century?
    A) the rise of third parties
    B) the influence of mass media
    C) increasing alignment of party platforms
    D) more direct primaries

20. What purpose do political parties serve in American politics?
    A) They ensure fair and democratic elections.
    B) They guard against tyranny.
    C) They nominate candidates and run campaigns.
    D) They provide structure for the organization of both houses of Congress.

Answer Key

1.

A) Incorrect. Federalists and Anti-Federalists disagreed on many points, but their disagreements were political, not military.

B) **Correct.** Daniel Shays led a rebellion against tax collectors in 1786. Congress could not raise an army and was powerless to intervene. It became clear that the Articles of Confederation needed to be strengthened.

C) Incorrect. The Revolutionary War, or the American Revolution, was fought before the Articles of Confederation were written.

D) Incorrect. Conflict between slave states and free states led to the Civil War later on in American history.

2.

A) Incorrect. An individual president was not limited to two terms of service until the twentieth century.

B) Incorrect. The system of checks and balances, as built into the Constitution, includes the judicial branch.

C) Incorrect. While civilian oversight of the military is an important part of the American government, this answer choice does not properly describe the system of checks and balances reinforced by the three branches of government.

D) **Correct.** The Constitutional system of checks and balances is comprised of the three branches of government, which limit each other, thereby limiting federal power.

3.

A) Incorrect. Today, *Constitutionalists* refers to politicians and members of the judiciary who believe in following the Constitution today exactly as it was written; it was not a term used in the late eighteenth century.

B) Incorrect. The Revolution was over by the time of the Constitutional Convention.

C) Incorrect. Federalists were content with the Constitution as it was written.

D) **Correct.** Anti-Federalists would not accept the Constitution without the Bill of Rights, believing it did not go far enough to protect individual and states' rights.

4.

A) Incorrect. At the time, slavery was legal throughout the United States.

B) Incorrect. Three-quarters of the states must ratify amendments in order for them to take effect.

C) **Correct.** The Three-Fifths Compromise accounted for slaves as part of a state's population (although they could not vote or enjoy the same rights as white citizens).

D) Incorrect. Nine states needed to ratify the Constitution for it to go into effect.

5.

A) Incorrect. The Bill of Rights is an example of Locke's theory of natural rights: it lists rights protected from government interference.

B) Incorrect. Article V is an example of the rule of law: it states that the only way to override the provisions of the Constitution is to legally change it.

C) **Correct.** The Preamble states, "We the People," supporting the idea that the government exists with the consent of the governed.

D) Incorrect. Article VII is an example of federalism: the federal government could not exist without the approval of the states.

6.

A) **Correct.** The Constitution empowers the president to make treaties with the advice and consent of the Senate.

B) Incorrect. For a bill to become a law, Congress votes on it, and the president must sign it. The Supreme Court rules on it only if a relevant case comes before the court.

C) Incorrect. The president appoints justices to the Supreme Court and the Senate approves them.

D) Incorrect. Congress does have the power to impeach and remove the president, but members of Congress can only be removed by the House or the voters.

7.

A) **Correct.** The Supremacy Clause declares the Constitution the highest law in the land. The only way to change the Constitution is through the amendment process; no individual has authority higher than the Constitution.

B) Incorrect. The Elastic Clause, also known as "necessary and proper," provides room for Congress to utilize powers not specifically listed in the Constitution. It does not assert the law's authority over individuals.

C) Incorrect. The Advise and Consent Clause gives the Senate the power to approve presidential appointees. This is a prime example of a check on executive authority.

D) Incorrect. The Due Process clause is one of the clauses of the Fourteenth Amendment. It guarantees all citizens fair treatment under the law. While it does deal with the relationship between individuals and the law, it does not explicitly restrict any individual's authority from superseding the law.

8.

A) Incorrect. *Marbury v. Madison* did not address individual liberties.

B) **Correct.** Including the Bill of Rights in the Constitution was a condition of ratification for several states.

C) Incorrect. The first ten amendments were added to the Constitution collectively and immediately.

D) Incorrect. The president does not have the authority to add amendments to the Constitution.

9.

A) Incorrect. A bill is only in conference committee in order to unify versions of the bill before it goes to the president.

B) Incorrect. This would be a line-item veto, which the Supreme Court has declared unconstitutional.

C) **Correct.** A veto is a formal rejection of a bill by the president. The only way for a vetoed bill to become a law is through a two-thirds vote in both houses of Congress.

D) Incorrect. The president does not determine the constitutionality of laws; that is the job of the Supreme Court.

10.

A) Incorrect. While all of these amendments have been proposed, none of them have ever been ratified. This shows it is actually quite difficult to amend the Constitution.

B) **Correct.** Each of these amendments was proposed either after a Supreme Court decision or in anticipation of one. For example, in 1973 the Supreme Court determined in *Roe v. Wade* that abortions are legal. Now, the only way to change that would be through a new decision or constitutional amendment.

C) Incorrect. None of the issues listed above are addressed in the Constitution. The desire to add these amendments is not a sign of dissatisfaction with the Constitution itself; instead, support for these amendments is an attempt to override the Supreme Court.

D) Incorrect. These attempts at constitutional amendments demonstrate the ways in which Americans grapple with difficult issues.

11.

A) Incorrect. Each house has the authority to remove members for inappropriate or illegal activity. In most cases however, members of Congress lose their seats when their constituencies vote them out.

B) Incorrect. The Speaker of the House is selected by the majority party and is typically the congressional leader of that party.

C) **Correct.** If a bill arrives at the president's desk within ten days of the end of the term, he or she can cause the bill to fail simply by doing nothing. This is called a pocket veto.

D) Incorrect. The president must either wholly accept or reject a bill. He or she may not reject only certain parts of it.

12.

A) Incorrect. Disagreement over the executive was between those who supported a strong central government and those who wanted to safeguard state sovereignty.

B) Incorrect. The inability of the national government to tax was one of the key issues that led to the Convention. All delegates agreed on its importance.

C) Incorrect. The size of a state has no bearing on the method of electing Senators.

D) **Correct.** Small states wanted equal apportionment of representation in the legislature, while large states wanted proportional representation.

13.

A) **Correct.** As the American political system has moved closer to a direct democracy, many people feel that the Electoral College is anachronistic. They believe the president should be the candidate who wins the majority vote of the people.

B) Incorrect. The two-party system is unaffected by the Electoral College. In fact, because it is a winner-takes-all system in most states, it is nearly impossible for a third party to win any electoral votes.

C) Incorrect. States will small populations do have increased representation in the Electoral College. However, large states still have a much greater impact on the outcomes of elections.

D) Incorrect. While electors have occasionally voted differently than the popular vote in their state, this has been very rare and has never impacted the outcome of an election. Today, most electors are bound by law to follow the state's popular vote.

14.

A) **Correct.** Federalism is a political system in which power is shared between the national and state governments.

B) Incorrect. The separation of powers describes how power is distributed throughout the federal government. It does not address the states.

C) Incorrect. Checks and balances refers to the ways branches of government limit each other's power. This term does not address the states.

D) Incorrect. Proportional representation is how representation is determined in the House of Representatives: it is based on the population of each state. However, this term does not address the relationship between the states and the national government.

15.

A) Incorrect. Neither *Marbury v. Madison* nor *McCulloch v. Maryland* addressed the status of enslaved persons.

B) Incorrect. While *Marbury v. Madison* did address an act of Congress, it did not restrict congressional power. *McCulloch v. Maryland* interpreted the elastic clause as an expansion of Congress's powers.

C) **Correct.** *Marbury v. Madison* expanded the power of the judiciary by establishing judicial review (the power to determine the constitutionality of laws). *McCulloch v. Maryland* expanded congressional power by establishing its right to create a national bank.

D) Incorrect. Neither case addressed the relationship between the executive and judicial branches.

16.

A) Incorrect. The Supreme Court may determine the constitutionality of laws passed by Congress. In fact, the case that created the power of judicial review, *Marbury v. Madison*, dealt with a law passed by Congress (the Judiciary Act of 1789).

B) **Correct.** The Supreme Court's power—as well as the rights and powers listed in the Constitution—only apply to the federal government. The states are beholden to their own constitutions, which are interpreted by their own supreme courts.

C) Incorrect. As acts of the federal government, executive orders are subject to judicial review.

D) Incorrect. Using a writ of certiorari, the Supreme Court has the power to demand any case within its jurisdiction be sent up for review.

17.

A) Incorrect. The Fourth Amendment prohibits unlawful searches and seizures.

B) Incorrect. The Fifth Amendment prohibits trying someone twice for the same crime.

C) **Correct.** The Twenty-Fourth Amendment prohibits poll taxes; however, this amendment is not part of the Bill of Rights.

D) Incorrect. The Eighth Amendment prohibits cruel and unusual punishment.

18.

A) Incorrect. Freedom of speech can be restricted if it is obscene, defamatory, or intentionally incites others to violence.

B) Incorrect. The right to travel is an implied right and can be limited if a more important government interest is involved. For example, individuals may not enter a prison whenever they want. The more important government interest is society's safety.

C) **Correct.** While religious practice can be restricted if it violates pre-existing, neutral laws, religious (or nonreligious) belief can never be.

D) Incorrect. The right to privacy is also an implied right and may be restricted when a more important government interest is involved.

19.

A) Incorrect. Third parties have never had a serious impact on American political structure.

B) Incorrect. While mass media has come to play a more significant role in politics, both parties have used that to their advantage.

C) Incorrect. While both parties tend toward the middle, they have maintained opposing viewpoints on many issues throughout the twentieth century and continue to do so today.

D) **Correct.** The increase in direct primaries allowed candidates to bypass political machines, decreasing their importance in the overall system.

20.

A) Incorrect. While each party does monitor the other to an extent during elections, it is simply to increase its own chances of winning.

B) Incorrect. Political parties do act as watchdogs of each other, so they often help to identify abuses of power. However, this is a byproduct of their behavior, not their primary function.

C) **Correct.** Political parties developed and persist as a means of organizing people with similar political views in order to ensure that public officials who support those views are in office.

D) Incorrect. The parties do play a role in structuring the Senate and House of Representatives, but this is not their primary purpose.

fourteen

ECONOMICS

Economists study how goods and services are produced and distributed. Economic activity is generally assumed to occur on the market (although there are different economic systems).

The **MARKET** refers to how goods and services are bought and sold. Historically, a market was an actual location where merchants would buy and sell goods; this remains true today. However, the term *market* also refers more abstractly to commercial networks of buying, selling, and production on the local, regional, national, and international scale. There are different types of markets: investors buy and sell stocks and bonds in the financial markets, individuals can find food and clothing in the retail market, and the housing market varies from city to city and region to region as home prices rise and fall.

PRODUCTION is the creation of goods and services that are sold on the market for profit. Producers, or **FIRMS**, **PROFIT** when they sell a product for a higher price than it cost to create the product. Goods and services are **DISTRIBUTED** through the market: that is, they are made available for **CONSUMPTION**, or purchase.

LABOR refers to the work done by humans in an economy to produce goods and services. **CAPITAL** is something that produces income. Capital might be a farmer's tractors, a restaurant's kitchen equipment, or a contractor's tools. Labor turns capital into goods and services that are then sold on the market. The people that do the labor are compensated for it with **WAGES**.

Types of Economic Systems

There are four kinds of economic systems.

A **TRADITIONAL ECONOMY** is a pre-industrialized economy, guided by tradition, and often using **BARTERING** rather than currency. For instance, farmers in medieval societies might have traded crops for handmade goods like tools.

A PURE COMMAND ECONOMY is usually found in COMMUNIST societies. In a pure command economy, the government—rather than the market—determines all aspects of production. Today, they are very rare; North Korea is an example.

A PURE MARKET ECONOMY, also known as CAPITALISM, is governed by the laws of supply and demand with no outside interference. The economist ADAM SMITH theorized that the "INVISIBLE HAND" of the market would direct activity to maximize economic efficiency. Government should let the economy behave freely—a concept called LAISSEZ-FAIRE, or "let do" in French. Pure market economies are usually found where there is weak or no government, for instance in parts of Somalia.

A MIXED ECONOMY is governed by both the market and the government. The people may decide what is produced by what they are willing to buy, but the government regulates different aspects of the economy with regards to the safety of the population. Most modern economies are mixed economies. The United States economy is based on capitalism, but it is a mixed economy because the government intervenes in some aspects.

EXAMPLE

In the 1870s in the United States, Americans favored laissez-faire economics, minimizing government regulations and controls on business. This most closely resembles which type of economy?

A) traditional

B) market

C) command

D) mixed

Answer:

B) is correct. Laissez-faire economics essentially means to leave the market alone to function. The United States came close to having a pure market economy in the 1870s.

Functions of the Market

There are several defining principles of a market economy.

PRIVATE PROPERTY: The market favors private ownership of most economic resources. Private ownership leads to innovation and investment, which in turn lead to growth. It also allows for trade (of services and goods). Economists often point to the inefficiency of the United States Postal Service (USPS) as compared to private carriers like FedEx or UPS to illustrate this point. FedEx and UPS have an incentive to provide better service, in order to stay in business and grow. The better their services, the more likely consumers are to choose them, keeping their businesses alive and thriving. USPS, as a publicly owned entity, is guaranteed survival by the government. So even if the USPS provides bad service, it will not lose government support (though customers may choose to send packages by FedEx or UPS instead).

FREEDOM OF CHOICE: In a market economy, all individuals are free to acquire, use, and sell resources without restriction or regulation. This allows market forces to function properly. Two important elements in the market are supply and demand. If there was a restriction on buying large cars, for example, this would artificially alter demand, and throw off the functioning of the automobile market.

Private property and freedom of choice create the two primary driving forces of the market: self-interest and competition.

Economists assume that people are motivated by SELF-INTEREST as they use their own resources. The seller in the market wants to maximize resources (or profit). The buyer wants to maximize utility (or happiness). As a result, the seller offers goods that will maximize the happiness of buyers in order to attract sales. Self-interest, then, leads to innovation and quality, as it creates a market where the best products are available to buyers. For example, Apple has noted that technological integration brings buyers a great deal of happiness, so the company works to continually innovate new ways of integrating technology (like the Apple watch) in its quest for profit.

Because all individuals are motivated by self-interest, new sellers will enter the market when they determine that there is a possibility for profit. And, because all individuals have freedom of choice, buyers will buy from the sellers whose products maximize their happiness (either through prices or quality). Therefore, sellers compete with each other to attract buyers by appealing to their maximum happiness. COMPETITION leads to lower prices and higher quality.

Consequently, the primary communication tool of the market is PRICE. Because of competition, prices are set by the market rather than by individuals. As a result, price signals buyers and sellers who, in turn, use it to make decisions about how to use their resources. Prices communicate the relative value of products in the market and deliver to both sellers and buyers what they seek through their own self-interest: profit and happiness, respectively.

Economic Behavior

Economists assume that all people have unlimited wants; however, there are limited resources to satisfy those wants. This concept is called SCARCITY. Scarcity forces individuals to make a CHOICE, to select one want over another. In making choices, people seek to maximize their UTILITY, the point of greatest happiness.

For example, a student wants to go to the movies with her friends, but also wants to do well on her exams the next day. Her resource—in this case, time—is limited, so she must choose between the options. She will weigh the cost, or value lost, of not studying for her exam, against the benefit, or value attained, of seeing the movie, and vice versa. The value of the option *not* selected is called the OPPORTUNITY COST. So, the opportunity cost of staying home to study is the lost fun of seeing the movie and strengthening the bonds with friends.

Resources, also called FACTORS OF PRODUCTION, fall into four basic categories:

1. labor
2. land/natural resources
3. physical capacity
4. entrepreneurial ability, or know-how

Each of the four factors of production is necessary for producing anything in the marketplace. They are considered some of the most basic parts of the business equation.

EXAMPLE

Which of the following is NOT an example of the principle of scarcity?

A) a pharmaceutical company lowers the price of a commonly used drug

B) overfishing in key coastal waters

C) drought reduces the amount of pumpkins sold in fall farmer's markets

D) flu season ramps up and flu vaccines are hard to find

Answer:

A) is correct. The lowered price by itself does not create scarcity, as the supply of the drug is not impacted.

Demand and Supply

The LAW OF DEMAND is simple. As the price for a good or service increases, the demand for it will decrease. In other words, if the price goes up, purchases usually go down. For example, a coffee shop sells coffee for $1 a cup and sales skyrocket. The coffee shop then quadruples the price to $4 a cup, and sales plummet.

Whereas demand addresses the behavior of buyers, supply deals with the behavior of sellers. The LAW OF SUPPLY states that as the price of a good increases, suppliers will increase the quantity of the good they supply. This is because of INCREASING MARGINAL COSTS: as suppliers increase the amount they are supplying, the marginal costs of production (the costs of capital, labor, etc.) increase as well. Therefore, they will only increase supply if price is high enough to offset that cost.

For example, at the holidays, a toy company decides to double its supply of its most popular toy. In order to do this, the company must hire more workers, keep the factory open longer, run the machines longer, pay more in electricity, and pay more in packing materials and shipping costs to get the toys to the stores. If they decided to triple the supply, these costs would only increase. So, the price of the toy would need to be high enough to generate enough revenue to offset these additional costs.

The interplay of supply, demand, and price is used to describe the state of the market. When the quantity demanded equals the quantity supplied at a given price, the market is in a state of EQUILIBRIUM. Essentially, this means that both suppliers and buyers are satisfied with the price.

When the quantity demanded exceeds the quantity supplied, a SHORTAGE, or EXCESS DEMAND, exists. Shortages occur when prices are low because low prices lead to high demand but low supply. For example, if the market price of a television is $20, demand for these inexpensive TVs will be high, but increasing supply would be too expensive for producers because they are not making enough money to offset production costs. Therefore, producers would not make more TVs to meet demand, keeping the supply low.

When the quantity supplied exceeds the quantity demanded, a **SURPLUS**, or **EXCESS SUPPLY**, exists. Again, this is caused by the supply and demand's opposing relationships to price. If the TVs are now $2,000 each, fewer buyers will be willing to purchase one. However, the high price allows the supplier to clearly outstrip the costs of production.

When have you been affected by price changes due to demand and supply? For instance, stores heavily discount leftover Valentine's Day candy on February 15 because demand for it drops after the holiday.

The market always tends toward equilibrium. So, in the case of a shortage, buyers will offer to pay more for the television, and suppliers will begin to increase supply. This trend will continue until they reach equilibrium. On the flip side, when a surplus exists, suppliers will lower prices in order to attract buyers, thereby increasing demand until equilibrium is reached.

The Basic Categories of Financial Assets

STOCKS AND BONDS are securities, monetary units that can be exchanged. Public and private interests and individuals may invest in stocks as stockholders, or in bonds as lenders. Stocks and bonds are traded on the **STOCK MARKET**, a venue where private individuals, businesses, government agencies, and even foreign investors and foreign countries can invest.

Stocks are essentially shares of any given company or corporation that has "gone public" or offered its stock for sale to the highest bidder, whomever that may be. In the last century, the value of the stock market has come to reflect the state of the American economy as never before.

In 1929, the stock market was the precursor to an economic downturn that history has called the **GREAT DEPRESSION**. It was not just an American economic downturn. Most of the world was affected by the stock market crash in 1929 and the decade of depression that followed. The graph below shows the pitfalls of more than a decade of questionable buying practices by investors of all economic demographics.

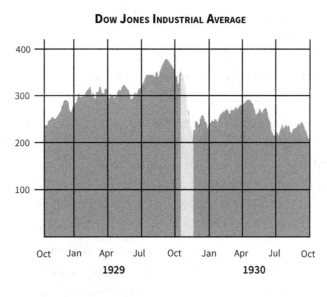

Stock Market Crash

Figure 14.1. Stock Market Crash and Consequences

The American economy is still more or less a mirror reflection of the American stock market. Its movement, both up and down, is the fodder of presidential campaigns and Congressional debate. For smaller investors, the risks and rewards can be high. There are fortunes to be made and lost for anyone who wants to take the risk. This graph explores the three different stock measures over a period of several years.

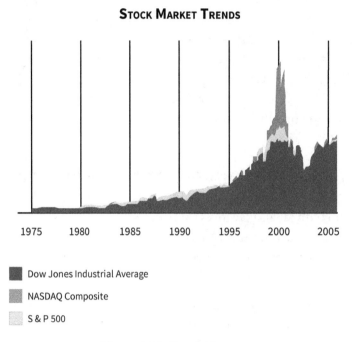

STOCK MARKET TRENDS

Dow Jones Industrial Average

NASDAQ Composite

S & P 500

Figure 14.2. Stock Measures

MONEY MARKET FUNDS invest in short-term investments like treasury bonds. These are considered safe and solid investments much like bank deposits, but encompass a broader scope for large scale investors.

The Allocation of Resources

ALLOCATION OF RESOURCES, or how resources are distributed across an economy, can fall to either the government or the market, depending on the type of economy. Within a specific firm, the allocation of resources is determined by profit maximization: how can the resources be used most efficiently?

One of the best ways to explain government control of the allocation of resources is to look at rationing during the Second World War in the United States. Rather than allow the public to hoard goods and create shortages, the federal government decided to control the flow of goods to civilians by allocating only a small amount of goods to the public on a weekly and monthly basis. Most resources are limited. In this case, economists determine the best way to allocate resources that does the least harm to all parties.

PUBLIC GOODS are products that an individual can consume without reducing their availability to other individuals. Public goods are also equally available to all. Basic television, plumbing infrastructure, and sewage systems are all examples of public goods. Some people now argue that internet access should be a public good. In a pure market economy, the market would provide for all public goods. However, in reality, often private markets fail to provide the allocatively efficient level of public goods, and providing them falls to the government.

EXAMPLE

Which of the following is NOT an example of a public good?

A) public parks

B) streetlights

C) air travel

D) radio broadcasts

Answer:

C) is correct. Air travel is not available to everyone; it is restricted by price. Also, once one person "consumes" air travel by taking up a seat on a plane, the passenger prevents someone else from "consuming" that good.

Government Intervention

In the United States, one of the government's most important roles in the economy is to foster **COMPETITION** to guarantee a fair market and help ensure that consumers have choices. **ANTITRUST LAWS** promote a competitive market environment. Antitrust laws exist to protect consumers from illegal mergers and other unfair business practices. Antitrust laws emerged out of the Progressive movement of the nineteenth century in response to the monopolies and trusts dominated by banking and heavy industry in the Second Industrial Revolution.

The richest businessmen of the nineteenth century were called **ROBBER BARONS** because they controlled vast amounts of money and property. For the robber barons, controlling all aspects of one given industry was simply good business practice. For example, a steel magnate might control the steel industry of a given region of the United States. That means he or she controls the mines where raw ingredients are mined from the earth as well as the

Understanding the US government's basic role in the economy will be an asset on the GED.

miners, even providing company houses and a company store. Furthermore, the magnate controls the railroad that hauls raw ingredients to the steel foundries and the railroads that carry the finished product to its destination.

Competition is key to a market economy and a capitalist system. Establishing a **TRUST**—control over the entire industrial process—defeats that purpose. It was for that reason that the US government set out to break the trusts of the late nineteenth and early twentieth centuries.

THE GOVERNMENT ALSO INTERVENES IN THE FORM OF TAXATION. IN THEORY, PRO-GRESSIVE TAXES tax the income of the wealthy more than other groups in society. These taxes increase gradually as income rises for an individual, but in a free market economy, taxes are adjusted to account for income losses in business, charitable contributions, and other circumstances. Therefore, in reality, tax rates may vary considerably across income levels.

Other forms of taxation include PROPORTIONAL and REGRESSIVE TAXES. PROPORTIONAL TAXES are similar to flat rate taxes in that all taxpayers are taxed at the same rate or at the same proportion of their incomes. REGRESSIVE TAXES affect everyone at the same rate without a sliding proportional scale, making life more expensive for the lower classes.

EXAMPLE

Which of the following statements is true of antitrust laws?

A) They are designed to modify perfect competition markets.

B) They are designed to protect controlling firms in trusts.

C) They are designed to shift markets towards monopolies.

D) They are designed to decrease the power of monopolists.

Answer:

D) is correct. With the rise of the robber barons and the consolidation of market power in several industries (including steel, railroads, and oil), the government took action to reduce that power and restore balance in the market.

The Federal Reserve

THE FEDERAL RESERVE behaves as a central bank of the United States and ensures the safety of the American monetary system. In the century since its inception, the role of the Fed has expanded tremendously, but the Fed's primary role at the end of the day is to maximize employment and stabilize prices in the United States.

The Federal Reserve was created in 1913 to help thwart the rising numbers of financial panics that seized the nation every few years. The Fed was created to stabilize the US money supply and to moderate interest rates. As mentioned earlier, the Fed's duties have also expanded to include monitoring and maintaining reserves for US banks. With its own seal and flag, the Federal Reserve is among the most important components of the US federal government.

The Federal Reserve is the arbiter of interest rates for mortgages, the stock market, and any other monetary policy involving interest (such as money markets). EQUILIBRIUM INTEREST RATES, regulated by the Fed, occur only when interest rates and the money supply are roughly equivalent.

The interest rate set by the Federal Reserve is established by a number of factors, including the federal funds rate, the interest that the Federal Reserve charges banks. Figure 3.4 shows the fluctuating interest rates that banks have paid in recent decades and how they ultimately trickled down to consumers.

Figure 14.3. The Federal Reserve

The Federal Reserve also monitors MONETARY STABILIZATION: efforts to keep prices, unemployment, and the money supply, among other fiscal indicators, relatively stable. Monetary stabilization helps to prevent the economy from oscillating between inflation and recession.

You do not need to memorize every responsibility of the Fed for the GED, but you should know its purpose.

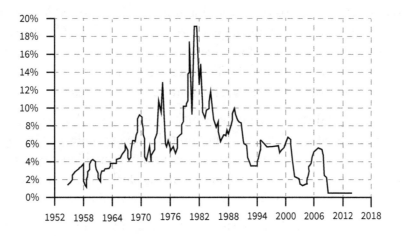

Figure 14.4. Federal Funds Rate

EXAMPLE

Which of the following is NOT a responsibility of the Federal Reserve?

A) to set interest rates

B) to determine government spending

C) to maximize employment

D) to stabilize prices

Answer:

B) is correct. Although the Federal Reserve plays an important role in fiscal policy, it has no control over government spending.

Fiscal Policy

FISCAL POLICY is an approach to economic management in which the government is deeply involved in managing the economy. When an individual or firm spends or saves money, those choices impact that individual's or firm's own finances. When the government makes similar choices, the government's decisions impact the economy as a whole. These economic decisions are called MULTIPLIERS.

Countries experience business cycles. In a BUSINESS CYCLE, businesses tend to expand and grow. Consumer spending and employment increase. Then, the economy experiences a period of contraction and slowdown. The contraction period is known as RECESSION and is marked by unemployment, low wages, and low consumer spending. A particularly harsh recession is a DEPRESSION. After a period of time, recession is followed by RECOVERY, which may be stimulated by government intervention, and growth begins anew.

In INFLATION, the price of goods and services in an economy outpaces the ability of the local currency to purchase them. Inflation is not necessarily related to the business cycle.

In EXPANSIONARY FISCAL POLICY, the government either increases spending or decreases taxes to counteract a recession. When the economy experiences inflation, government uses CONTRACTIONARY FISCAL POLICY: reducing government spending or increasing taxes.

A TARIFF is a tax or duty paid on anything imported or exported into or from a given country. Low tariffs encourage foreign goods to enter the market. Countries may do this to stimulate trade or in exchange for other trade agreements. For example, the North American Free Trade Agreement (NAFTA) essentially eliminated tariffs among Canada, the United States, and Mexico. This is also known as FREE TRADE.

High tariffs protect domestic industry by making foreign goods more expensive. This is known as PROTECTIONISM. However, they also risk slowing trade. For example, between World War I and World War II, the United States passed a very high protectionist tariff. In response, other countries instituted retaliatory tariffs to block American trade as Americans had blocked foreign trade. Consequently, world trade ground to a halt.

When governments make changes to spending and taxes, it affects the government's budget. When revenue (primarily money from taxes) exceeds spending, the government has a SURPLUS. When spending exceeds revenues, the government has a DEFICIT. A deficit is not the same thing as a debt. A deficit is simply the gap between what the government has spent and what it has earned. In order to cover that deficit, it must borrow money, generating government debt. National debt develops over years of deficits.

Changes in CURRENCY are caused by and impact the strength of a nation's economy. CURRENCY APPRECIATION occurs when a country's money gains value in national and international markets. This increases foreign investment, as other countries are able to gain more value for their money. However, a strong currency makes that nation's exports more expensive, which can affect trade.

CURRENCY DEPRECIATION occurs when a country's money loses value in national and international markets. Currency depreciation may point to instabilities in the nation's economy (such as high rates of inflation). However, when carried out in an intentional and orderly manner, it can increase a nation's global competiveness by lowering the cost of its exports. For example, China has used intentional currency depreciation to build a strong export-based economy and foster economic growth.

EXAMPLE

Which of the following would NOT be an example of contradictory fiscal policy?

A) freezing annual increases on government employees' salaries

B) reducing the operating hours of national parks

C) increasing property taxes

D) financing a new dam

Answer:

D) is correct. If the government builds a new dam, it injects new spending into the economy, thereby expanding the economy.

Test Your Knowledge

Read the question, and then choose the most correct answer.

1. Which of the following is NOT a basic factor of production?

   A) labor

   B) land

   C) consumers

   D) capital

2. In the production possibility curve below, economic growth would be indicated if the curve moved

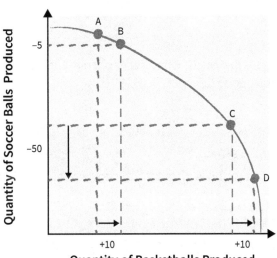

   Quantity of Basketballs Produced

   A) from point C to point A.

   B) from point A to point B.

   C) from point A to point D.

   D) from point D to point C.

3. According to the law of demand, when the price of cucumbers increases, which of the following should happen?

   A) The quantity of cucumbers demanded increases.

   B) The quantity of cucumbers demanded falls.

   C) The demand for cucumbers falls.

   D) The demand for cucumbers increases.

4. Which of the following is the best example of a public good?

   A) tickets to a popular concert

   B) electricity

   C) an energy bar

   D) a newspaper subscription

5. The price of the type of tomatoes used in ketchup drops dramatically. At the same time, the price of mustard, a substitute for ketchup, increases. What impact will these two events have on the supply and price of ketchup?

    A) Price falls, but quantity is hard to determine.

    B) Price rises, but quantity is hard to determine.

    C) Price is hard to determine, but quantity rises.

    D) Price is hard to determine, but quantity falls.

6. What is the role of the Federal Reserve?

    A) to coin money

    B) to control government spending

    C) to determine tax policy

    D) to stabilize prices

7. If the price of razor blades increases, what will happen to the demand for shaving cream, a complementary good?

    A) Demand will increase.

    B) Demand will decrease.

    C) Demand will stay the same.

    D) Demand for shaving cream is unrelated to demand for razor blades.

8. What is the purpose of antitrust laws?

    A) to transition monopolies into oligopolies

    B) to transition monopolies and oligopolies into perfectly competitive markets

    C) to maintain a perfectly competitive market

    D) to transition a perfectly competitive market into an oligopoly

9. Which of the following statements is true about a mixed economy?

    A) The "invisible hand" of the market alone determines allocation.

    B) Government departments determine decisions related to production.

    C) The private sector and the free market work together to determine economic decisions.

    D) Government and the market both solve economic problems.

10. Which of the following is NOT a principle of the pure market?

    A) freedom of choice

    B) self-interest

    C) competition

    D) government safety net

Answer Key

1.

A) Incorrect. Labor is an essential factor of production, involved in all economic activity.

B) Incorrect. While some industries may no longer require physical land, most do. Land is still considered a basic factor of production.

C) Correct. Consumers provide the demand for products. They do not play a role in production.

D) Incorrect. All businesses require capital to start and to maintain production. This is an essential factor of production.

2.

A) Incorrect. Point C represents under-utilization of resources. Movement from C to A simply demonstrates that resources are now being used at their full potential.

B) Incorrect. Movement along the production possibility frontier indicates a shift in the ratio of output for the two products. This is not economic growth but simply a reallocation of resources.

C) Correct. Economic growth is shown by an overall outward shift in the production possibility curve, as would happen if A moved to D.

D) Incorrect. Movement from D to C would indicate an inefficient use of resources, not a shift in overall economic growth.

3.

A) Incorrect. Price and quantity demanded have an inverse relationship. When prices rise, consumers are less willing to buy the product.

B) Correct. The law of demand states that, holding all else constant, an increase in price causes a fall in demand.

C) Incorrect. Demand—rather than quantity demanded—is affected by changes in determinants of demand, including consumer income and prices of substitute or complimentary goods.

D) Incorrect. Demand only increases when consumer income increases or there is a change to another determinant of demand. Changes in price impact quantity demanded.

4.

A) Incorrect. Use of the tickets prevents others from seeing the concert; therefore, the tickets cannot be a public good.

B) Correct. When one person turns on the lights in their house, it does not prevent anyone else from turning on their own lights.

C) Incorrect. Once eaten, an energy bar cannot be eaten by anyone else, making it a private good.

D) Incorrect. Although a newspaper can be read by many people, once that newspaper is delivered it cannot be delivered to anyone else. Sharing something is not the same as it being available to all regardless of consumption.

5.

A) Incorrect. With two opposing forces on the ketchup market, it is impossible to tell the impact on price without knowing which force is stronger. The hypothetical does not give us that information.

B) Incorrect. There are too many factors in this situation to determine the impact on price without more specific information.

C) **Correct.** Price cannot be determined from the information given; however, the lowered tomato price will increase the supply of ketchup, and the higher mustard price will increase the demand for ketchup. Together, these will increase the overall supply of ketchup.

D) Incorrect. If tomatoes became more expensive or mustard less expensive, the supply of ketchup would fall because both would act as deterrents to ketchup production. However, that is not the case in this situation.

6.

A) Incorrect. The U.S. Mint coins money; the Federal Reserve controls the flow of money in the economy.

B) Incorrect. The Federal Reserve has no power over government spending. That is within the purview of Congress.

C) Incorrect. Like government spending, tax policy is controlled by Congress. The Internal Revenue Service is responsible for the collection of taxes.

D) **Correct.** The Federal Reserve's job is to stabilize prices in order to prevent inflation and keep the economy strong.

7.

A) Incorrect. The price of razor blades has an inverse relationship to the demand for both razor blades and the complementary good of shaving cream.

B) **Correct.** If the price of razor blades increases, the demand for razor blades will decrease. Because shaving cream is a complementary good, the demand for each product is linked. As a result, the demand for shaving cream will decrease as well.

C) Incorrect. Demand for shaving cream and demand for razor blades are linked together. Therefore, changes in the price of one affects the demand of the other.

D) Incorrect. Because shaving cream is required for the use of razor blades, the two are complementary goods and are linked in terms of demand.

8.

A) Incorrect. Anti-trust laws target both monopolies and oligopolies equally, and striving to prevent a concentration of market power.

B) **Correct.** Anti-trust laws break up single firms or several large firms that control an industry in order to return that industry to a perfectly competitive market.

C) Incorrect. Anti-trust laws were created in response to the increasing concentration of power in the hands of a few across industries. When they were written, few perfectly competitive markets existed in the United States.

D) Incorrect. This is the opposite of the goal of anti-trust laws, which break up groups that hold a disproportionate share of market power.

9.

A) Incorrect. Only in a pure market does the market operate entirely independently of government.

B) Incorrect. The government makes decisions about production in a command economy.

C) Incorrect. The private sector is a player in the free market and cannot collude with it to guide the economy.

D) **Correct.** A mixed economy utilizes both market forces and government intervention to ensure the economy benefits the greatest number of people.

10.

A) Incorrect. The freedom to choose which products to buy and sell is essential to the functioning of the economy.

B) Incorrect. Self-interest drives the market as buyers seek to maximize utility and sellers seek to maximize profit. The result is the best quality products at the best price.

C) Incorrect. Like self-interest, competition is an important force in the market. Competition leads to innovation and higher quality products.

D) **Correct.** Market theory states that the market self-corrects, tending towards equilibrium. In this case any government interaction acts only to impede the functioning of the market.

fifteen

GEOGRAPHY AND THE WORLD

Geography

Human-Environment Interaction

Humans have always modified the environment to suit their needs. For example, with the advent of agriculture, humans began loosening the topsoil to make planting easier. A looser topsoil is more susceptible to erosion from wind and rain, allowing greater changes to the physical landscape. Cities are also a prime example. Cities significantly reduce the amount of exposed ground in an area and lead to a concentration of fuel and resource consumption.

The environment has also shaped human activity. For example, the main economic activities of a place—farming, fishing, trade—have historically been determined, in large part, by the physical characteristics of the place. People living in deserts have traditionally been nomadic because restricted access to food and water requires them to continually move around in search of it. Climate impacts clothing, housing, and work and leisure patterns. For example, a period of rest in the middle of the day is common in cultures in hot climates.

One of the most significant ways humans have impacted their environment is through the use of natural resources. Some resources are **RENEWABLE RESOURCES**, meaning they are virtually unlimited or can be grown and regrown. Wind, sun, and plants are all examples of renewable resources. Other resources are **NONRENEWABLE RESOURCES** because they cannot be replaced once they are consumed. Iron ore, coal, and petroleum are three of the most important nonrenewable resources.

Consuming nonrenewable resources—and consuming renewable resources too quickly—is a growing concern as industrialization has greatly increased overall consumption. Many countries are searching for ways to promote **SUSTAINABLE DEVELOPMENT**, the use of natural resources and the growth of new ones at a rate that can be maintained from one generation to

Trees can be considered both renewable and nonrenewable. If managed properly, they can be replanted and grown again. However, the rapid consumption of old growth forests uses up a resource that essentially cannot be replaced. Also, the land trees are on is often repurposed for farm land, urbanization, or mining, resulting in a permanent loss of the resource.

the next. The UNITED NATIONS COMMISSION ON SUSTAINABLE DEVELOPMENT defines several criteria for global sustainable development: caring for the soil, avoiding overfishing, preserving the forest, protecting species from extinction, and reducing air pollution.

Other sustainability efforts focus on indirect factors impacting the earth's natural resources. For example, efforts to reduce fuel consumption are motivated by both the finite quantity of oil and also by the GREENHOUSE EFFECT caused by industrialization. Industrial production unleashes carbon dioxide, methane, and other gases. These create a vapor that transforms radiation into heat, which leads to GLOBAL WARMING, an overall rise in the earth's temperature. As a result, the ice caps are melting prematurely, leading to rising sea levels and changes in oceanic patterns.

EXAMPLE

Which of the following statements is true about sustainable development?

A) Sustainable development requires a prohibition on the use of nonrenewable resources.

B) Sustainable development only applies to energy resources like wind, sun, oil, and coal.

C) Sustainable development requires the proper management of renewable resources like trees and fish.

D) Sustainable development contributes to the greenhouse effect and increases global warming.

Answer:

C) is correct. The goal of sustainable development is to ensure resources are available to the next generation. Therefore, renewable resources must be managed to make sure consumption does not outpace the rate of replacement.

Human Characteristics of Place

The human characteristics of a place make up its CULTURE. These characteristics include the shared values, language, and religion of the people living in a location or region. Culture also includes the ways people feed, clothe, and shelter themselves. Cultures can be very specific or regional, like FOLK CULTURES, or they can be diffuse and widespread, like POPULAR CULTURE.

There are eight locations where formal culture—meaning the development of agriculture, government, and urbanization—began. These locations are known as CULTURE HEARTHS.

In the Americas, culture began in Andean America and Mesoamerica. In Africa, the culture hearths were in West Africa and the Nile River Valley. In the Middle East, culture began in Mesopotamia, and in Asia, hearths existed in the Indus River Valley, the Ganges River delta, and along the Wei and Huang Rivers in China. In each of these hearths, similar innovations—the seeds of culture—developed completely independently of one another.

SETTLEMENTS are the cradles of culture. They allow for the development of political structures, the management of resources, and the transfer of information to future generations. While settlements differed greatly, they did all share some commonalities. Settlements all began near natural resources that can support life, namely water and a reliable food source. The success and growth of a settlement was based on its proximity to these natural resources and its ability to collect and move raw materials. As each of these characteristics reached a new level of sophistication, population in that area began to concentrate near the point of resource allocation and production.

The spatial layout of these settlements, then, was determined by the environment and the primary function of the settlement. For example, European villages were clustered on hillsides to more easily protect against invaders and to leave the flat areas for farming. Settlements that rose up around trade, like those on the outskirts of the Saharan desert, concentrated around access to the trade routes and were generally more dispersed.

Later in history, successful settlements also needed an ample work force, and the ability to produce and deliver finished products elsewhere. Once transportation methods were developed, the populations of these settlements became mobile, allowing for a faster diffusion of culture, and—eventually—the development of industrial centers. These industrial centers became cities. A CITY is a major hub of human settlement with a high population density and a concentration of resource creation or allocation. Today, more than half of the world's population lives in cities. In more developed regions the percentages are even higher. With the development of cities, three types of areas emerged: URBAN (in the city itself), SUBURBAN (near the city), and RURAL (AWAY FROM THE CITY). In some cases, urban and suburban areas or multiple urban areas merge into a MEGALOPOLIS, or super-city. The Northeast Corridor from Washington, DC, to Boston is one such example.

EXAMPLE

The majority of people in the world today live in

A) urban areas.

B) suburban areas.

C) rural areas.

D) megalopolises.

Answer:

A) is correct. More than half of the world's population lives in cities.

Development and Globalization

As areas develop and economies grow, manufacturing becomes increasingly important to the functioning of the economy. This phenomenon is called INDUSTRIALIZATION. Because industrialization requires a shift in the labor force, it pairs with a decline in subsistence farming: the rural labor force moves to cities.

Industrialization is a relatively recent phenomenon. The INDUSTRIAL REVOLUTION began in Great Britain in the 1760s, then diffused to Western Europe and North America by 1825. The discovery of new energy sources like coal (which was later replaced by oil) and technological advancements that allowed machines to replace human labor led to the emergence of manufacturing centers and a shift in the functioning of the economy. As people left rural areas in search of manufacturing jobs, urban areas grew: this phenomenon is called URBANIZATION.

Economic growth is strongly connected to DEVELOPMENT, the use of technology and knowledge to improve the living conditions of people in a country. While economic in its foundation, development focuses on a range of quality of life issues like access to basic goods and services, education, and healthcare. Countries on the wealthier side of the spectrum are called MORE DEVELOPED COUNTRIES (MDCs), while those on the poorer side are called LESS DEVELOPED COUNTRIES (LDCs). MDCs are concentrated primarily in the Northern Hemisphere. Their primary economic concern is maintaining growth. LDCs, found mostly in the Southern Hemisphere, face the challenge of improving their economic conditions by stimulating significant and sustainable economic growth.

GLOBALIZATION is the trend of increasing interdependence and spatial interaction between disparate areas of the world economically, politically, and culturally. At its core, globalization is an economic trend; however it has significant cultural and political impacts as well. For example, the exportation of American fast food restaurants, like McDonald's, to other parts of the world reflects the capitalist drive to find new markets. Furthermore, the introduction of this type of food has a significant impact on one of the major distinguishing cultural traits of other countries—their cuisine.

The primary driving force of globalization is MULTINATIONAL CORPORATIONS (MNCs) or TRANSNATIONAL CORPORATIONS (TNCs). These are companies whose headquarters are located in one country and whose production is located in one or more different countries. The process of moving production to a different country is called OUTSOURCING. Outsourcing benefits the MNC because of reduced labor costs, lower tax rates, cheaper land prices, and usually fewer regulations on safety and environmental standards.

DEMOGRAPHY is the study of human population. More than half of the world's population today lives in cities. While this is a relatively recent change, the population has always been unevenly distributed based on resources. So, as cities have become better at obtaining and allocating resources, they have attracted more people. Seventy-five percent of all people live on only 5 percent of the earth's land.

While much of the world's wealth is concentrated in North America and Western Europe, 80 percent of people live in poor, developing countries in South America, Asia, and Africa. The most populated area in the world is East Asia, which is home to 25 percent of the world's population. In terms of population, East Asia is followed by Southeast Asia, and then Europe, from the Atlantic Ocean to the Ural Mountains.

Over the last 300 years, the population of Earth has exploded; population has been growing at an exponential rate, meaning the more people are added to the population, the faster it grows. In 1765, the global population was 300 million people. Today it is six billion. This increase has raised concerns for many demographers, particularly in the areas with a higher population concentration. To determine if an area is at risk, demographers determine its CARRYING CAPACITY, the number of people the area can support.

The carrying capacity of various areas can differ greatly depending on technology, wealth, climate, available habitable space, access, and INFRASTRUCTURE, or institutions that support the needs of the people. When a country exceeds its carrying capacity, it suffers from OVERPOPULATION. Countries in danger of overpopulation may attempt to restrict their growth, like China did through its one-child policy.

In spite of the population boom, some countries actually suffer from UNDERPOPULATION. They have a much greater carrying capacity—due to their high levels of production, amount of land, or abundance of natural resources—than their population uses.

MIGRATION is the permanent relocation of an individual or group from one home region to another region. As globalization has increased, so has global mobility, both in frequency and length of migrations. Some migration is internal—people moving from one place to another within the same region, like urbanization. Other migration involves people moving from one region of the world to another. Many immigrants have migrated to the United States from other countries around the world.

PUSH FACTORS are the negative aspects of the home region that make someone want to leave it; PULL FACTORS are the positive aspects of the new region that make someone want to move there. Push factors include high taxes, high crime rates, resource depletion, and corrupt governments. Migrants who cross international borders fleeing persecution, governmental abuse, war, or natural disaster are called REFUGEES. People who migrate intra-nationally by moving from one part of a country to another are called INTERNALLY DISPLACED PERSONS.

Not all migration is voluntary. History has many examples of FORCED MIGRATION, when a group of people is forcibly removed from their home and brought to a new region. The African slave trade and the removal of Native American tribes from the Southeastern United States are both examples of forced migration.

According to the UN, at least 40 percent of Syria's population was internally displaced in 2014, fleeing violence in that country's civil war. In 2015, millions of refugees from Syria and elsewhere in the Middle East, Asia, and North Africa began migrating to Europe, seeking safety from violent conflict.

EXAMPLE

Canada produces more resources than its population can consume. This is an example of

A)   overpopulation.

B)   carrying capacity.

C)   underpopulation.

D)   graying population.

Answer:

C) is correct. When a country does not have enough people to utilize its resources, it is underpopulated.

GO ON

World History

Early Civilizations and the Great Empires

Around 2500 BCE (or possibly earlier) the SUMERIANS emerged in the Near East (eventually expanding into parts of Mesopotamia). Developing irrigation and advanced agriculture, they were able to support settled areas that developed into cities. They also developed CUNEIFORM, the earliest known example of writing to use characters to form words.

Around the eighteenth century BCE, BABYLONIA dominated Southern Mesopotamia and ASSYRIA to the north. King Hammurabi in Babylonia had developed courts and an early codified rule of law—THE CODE OF HAMMURABI—which meted out justice on an equal basis: "an eye for an eye, a tooth for a tooth."

To do well on the GED, focus on understanding historical trends and why they occurred. Don't worry about memorizing dates.

Meanwhile, development had been under way in the NILE VALLEY in ancient EGYPT. Despite the surrounding Sahara Desert, the fertile land on the banks of the Nile River lent itself to agriculture, and the early Egyptians were able to develop settled communities thanks to agriculture and irrigation. Known for their pyramids, art, and pictorial writing (HIEROGLYPHS), the ancient Egyptians emerged as early as 5000 BCE; evidence of Egyptian unity under one monarch, or PHARAOH, dates to around 3000 BCE.

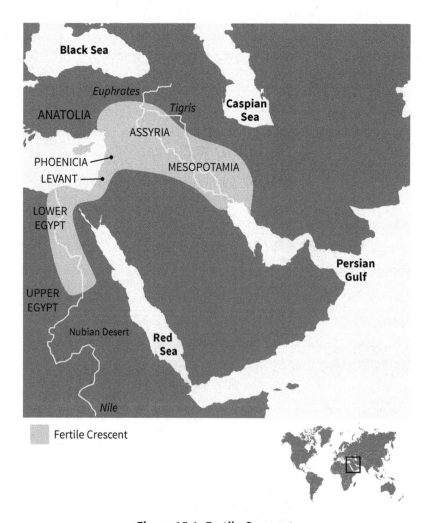

Fertile Crescent

Figure 15.1. Fertile Crescent

Early civilizations also developed farther east. The **INDUS VALLEY CIVILIZATIONS** flourished in the Indian Subcontinent and the Indus and Ganges river basins. The **HARAPPAN** civilization was based in Punjab from around 3000 BCE. Concurrent with the Roman Empire, the **GUPTA EMPIRE** emerged in India. During this period, known as the Golden Age of India, the region was economically strong; there was active trade by sea with China, East Africa, and the Middle East in spices, ivory, silk, cotton, and iron, which was highly profitable as an export.

In China, the **SHANG DYNASTY**, the first known dynasty, ruled the **HUANG HE** or **YELLOW RIVER** area around the second millennium BCE and developed the earliest known Chinese writing, which helped unite Chinese-speaking people throughout the region. The concept of the **MANDATE OF HEAVEN**, in which the emperor had a divine mandate to rule, emerged from the understanding that land was divinely inherited. **CONFUCIUS** taught harmony and respect for hierarchy.

Under the Qin and Han Dynasties, China developed centralized administration, expanded infrastructure, standardization in weights and measures, standardized writing, a standardized currency, and strict imperial control. The administrative **BUREAUCRACY** established by the emperor was the foundation of Chinese administration until the twentieth century. In addition, the Emperor constructed the **GREAT WALL OF CHINA**.

Throughout Mesoamerica, civilizations like the **OLMEC** had developed irrigation as early as 1200 BCE to expand and enrich agriculture, similar to developments in the Fertile Crescent. In South America, artistic evidence remains of the **CHAVIN**, **MOCHE**, and **NAZCA** peoples, who preceded the later Inca civilization and empire.

The **MAYA** came to dominate the Yucatan peninsula around 300. They developed a complex spiritual belief system accompanied by relief art, and built pyramidal temples that still stand today. In addition, they developed a detailed calendar and a written language using pictographs similar to Egyptian hieroglyphs; they studied astronomy and mathematics. Maya political administration was organized under monarchical city-states until around 900, when the civilization began to decline.

PERSIA conquered the Babylonians in the sixth century BCE. Persian rule extended from the Indus Valley to Egypt, and north to **ANATOLIA** by about 400 BCE, where the Persians encountered the ancient **GREEKS**.

Greece was comprised of **CITY-STATES** like **ATHENS**, the first known **DEMOCRACY**, and the military state **SPARTA**. Historically these city-states had been rivals; however, they temporarily united to defeat Persia. Much of Greece became unified under Athens following the war. During this **GOLDEN AGE** of Greek, or Hellenic Age, civilization, art, architecture, and philosophy emerged that would influence European civilization. **SOCRATES** began teaching, influencing later philosophers like **PLATO** and **ARISTOTLE**, who established the basis for modern western philosophical and political thought.

The term *democracy* comes from the Greek word **demokratia**—"people power." It was participatory rather than representative; officials were chosen by groups rather than elected. Athens was the strongest of the many small political bodies.

In Italy, the city of **ROME** was founded as early as the eighth century BCE; it became strong thanks to its importance as a trade route for the Greeks and other Mediterranean peoples.

Originally a kingdom, Rome became a **REPUBLIC** and elected lawmakers (senators) to the **SENATE**. The Romans developed highly advanced infrastructure, including aqueducts and roads, some still in use today. Economically powerful Rome began conquering areas around the Mediterranean with its increasingly powerful military, holding territory thanks to its infrastructure.

However, the Senate became corrupt, and divisions grew throughout the Republic between the wealthy ruling class and the working, poor, and military. The popular military leader **JULIUS CAESAR** forced the corrupt Senate to give him control and began to transition Rome from a republic to an empire. His nephew **OCTAVIAN** became the first emperor.

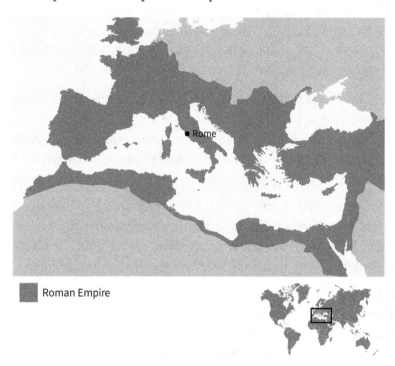

Figure 15.2. Pax Romana

At this time, Rome reached the height of its power, and the Mediterranean region enjoyed a period of stability known as the *PAX ROMANA*. Rome controlled the entire Mediterranean region and lands stretching as far north as Germany and Britain, territory into the Balkans, far into the Middle East, Egypt, North Africa, and Iberia. In this time of relative peace and prosperity, Latin literature flourished, as did art, architecture, philosophy, mathematics, science, and international trade throughout Rome and beyond into Asia and Africa. A series of emperors would follow and Rome remained a major world power, but it would never again reach the height of prosperity and stability that it did under Augustus.

EXAMPLE

Rome was able to maintain imperial control over a vast amount of territory thanks in part to

A) the idea that the Roman emperor had a divine mandate to rule: the Mandate of Heaven.

B) a powerful military and strong infrastructure (like roads) throughout the empire.

C) the concept of one god, and shared religion throughout the empire.

D) how easy it was to obtain Roman citizenship and all the benefits that came with it.

Answer:

B) is correct. Strong infrastructure facilitated trade, communication, and military movement throughout the empire, ensuring unity and security.

Feudalism through the Era of Expansion

After the fall of Rome, the Byzantine Empire—formerly the eastern part of the Roman Empire, based in Constantinople—remained a strong civilization and a place of learning. Constantinople was a strategically located commercial center that connected Asian trade routes with Europe. Later, missionaries traveled north to Slav-controlled Russia, spreading Christianity and literacy. Russian Christianity was influenced by the Byzantine doctrine, what would become Greek Orthodox Christianity.

Despite the chaos in Western Europe, the Christian Church in Rome remained strong, becoming a stabilizing influence. However, differences in doctrine between Rome and Constantinople became too wide to overcome. Beginning in 1054, a series of SCHISMS developed in the now-widespread Christian religion between the ROMAN CATHOLIC CHURCH and the GREEK ORTHODOX CHURCH over matters of doctrine and some theological concepts. Eventually the two would become entirely separate churches.

In Europe, the early Middle Ages (or *DARK AGES*) from the fall of Rome to about the tenth century, were a chaotic, unstable, and unsafe time. What protection and stability existed were represented and maintained by the Catholic Church and the feudal system.

Society and economics were characterized by decentralized, local governance, or FEUDALISM, a hierarchy where land and protection were offered in exchange for loyalty. Feudalism was the dominant social, economic, and political hierarchy of the European Middle Ages.

In exchange for protection, VASSALS would pledge FEALTY, or PAY HOMAGE TO LORDS, landowners who would reward their vassals' loyalty with land, or FIEFS. Economic and social organization consisted of MANORS, self-sustaining areas possessed by lords but worked by peasants. The peasants were SERFS, not slaves but not entirely free. Tied to the land, they worked for the lord in exchange for protection; however they were not obligated to fight. Usually they were also granted some land for their own use, but they could not leave the manor. While not true slaves, their lives were effectively controlled by the lord.

Warriors who fought for lords, called KNIGHTS, were rewarded with land and could become minor lords in their own right. Lords themselves could be vassals of other lords; that hierarchy extended upward to kings or the Catholic Church. The Catholic Church itself was a major landowner and political power. In a Europe not yet dominated by sovereign states, the POPE was not only a religious leader, but also a military and political one.

In what is considered the reemergence of centralized power in Europe, parts of Western and Central Europe were organized under Charlemagne, who was crowned emperor of the Roman Empire by Pope Leo III in **800 CE**. While in retrospect this seems long after the end of Rome, at the time many Europeans still perceived themselves as somehow still part of a Roman Empire.

Charlemagne brought stability to Western and Central Europe during a period when two powerful, organized, non-Christian civilizations—the Vikings in the north and the Islamic powers in the south—threatened what was left of western Christendom, and when insecurity was growing to the east with the decline of the Byzantines.

It was also under Charlemagne that the feudal system became truly organized, bringing more stability to Western Europe. The Catholic Church would dominate Europe from Ireland towards Eastern Europe—an area of locally controlled duchies, kingdoms, and alliances. In **962**, the pope crowned the first emperor of the Holy Roman Empire in Central Europe, a confederation of small states which remained an important European power until its dissolution in **1806**.

Meanwhile, in the wake of the decline of the Byzantine Empire, Arab-Islamic empires characterized by brisk commerce, advancements in technology and learning, and urban development arose in the Middle East.

In Arabia itself, Judaism, Christianity, and animist religions were practiced by the Arab majority. The Prophet Muhammad was born in Mecca around 570; he began preaching Islam around 613. Muhammad and his followers established Islam and Arab rule in the region, and the Arabs went on to conquer the Byzantine Empire and Persia in a series of *caliphates*, or empires: first the Umayyad caliphate based in Damascus, and then the Abbasid Caliphate based in Baghdad. By 750, they would control territory from Iberia (Spain) to parts of Central Asia and what is today Pakistan.

Stability permitted open trade routes, economic development, and cultural interaction throughout Asia, the Middle East, North Africa, and parts of Europe. Thanks to the universality of the Arabic language, scientific and medical texts from varying civiliza-

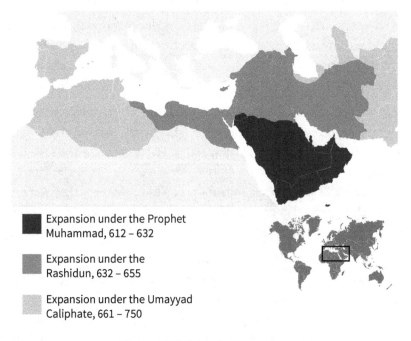

Expansion under the Prophet Muhammad, 612 – 632

Expansion under the Rashidun, 632 – 655

Expansion under the Umayyad Caliphate, 661 – 750

Figure 15.3. Islamic Expansion

tions—Greek, Persian, Indian—could be translated into Arabic and shared throughout the Islamic world. Arab thinkers studied Greek and Persian astronomy and engaged in further research. The Arabs studied mathematics and developed algebra, and fostered literary culture.

Around this time, the **SONG DYNASTY (960 – 1276)** controlled most of China. Under the Song, China experienced tremendous development and economic growth. Characterized by increasing urbanization, the Song featured complex administrative rule, including the difficult competitive written examinations required to obtain prestigious bureaucratic positions in government.

Most traditions recognized as Chinese emerged under the Song, including the consumption of tea and rice and common Chinese architecture. The Song engaged not only in overland trade along the Silk Road, exporting silk, tea, ceramics, jade, and other goods, but also sea trade with Korea, Japan, Southeast Asia, India, Arabia, and even East Africa.

International commerce was vigorous along the **SILK ROAD,** trading routes which stretched from the Arab-controlled Eastern Mediterranean to Song Dynasty China. The Silk Road reflected the transnational nature of Central Asia: the nomadic culture of Central Asia lent itself to trade between the major civilizations of China, Persia, the Near East, and Europe. Buddhism and Islam spread into China. Chinese, Islamic, and European art, pottery, and goods were interchanged between the three civilizations—early globalization. The Islamic tradition of the HAJJ, or the pilgrimage to Mecca, also spurred cultural interaction. Islam had spread from Spain throughout North Africa, the Sahel, the Middle East, Persia, Central Asia, India, and China; peoples from all these regions traveled and met in Arabia as part of their religious pilgrimage.

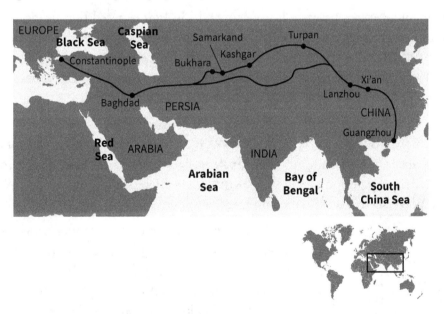

Figure 15.4. The Silk Road

Islam also spread along trans-Saharan trade routes into West Africa and the Sahel. Brisk trade between the gold-rich **KINGDOM OF GHANA** and Muslim traders based in Morocco brought Islam to the region around the eleventh century. The Islamic **MALI EMPIRE (1235 – 1500),** based farther south in **TIMBUKTU,** eventually extended beyond the original Ghanaian boundaries all the way to the West African coast, and controlled the valuable gold and salt trades. It became a center of learning and commerce. At the empire's peak, the ruler MANSA MUSA made a pilgrimage to Mecca in 1324. However, by 1500, the SONGHAI EMPIRE had overcome Mali and eventually dominated the Niger River area.

Loss of Byzantine territory to the Islamic empires meant loss of Christian lands in the Levant—including Jerusalem and Bethlehem—to Muslims. In **1095 CE**, the Byzantine emperor asked THE POPE for help to defend Jerusalem and protect Christians. With a history of Muslim incursions into Spain and France, anti-Muslim sentiment was strong in Europe and Christians there were easily inspired to fight them in the Levant, or HOLY LAND; the Pope offered lords and knights the chance to keep lands and bounty they won from conquered Muslims (and Jews) in this *crusade*. He also offered Crusaders INDULGENCES—forgiveness for sins committed in war and guarantees they would enter heaven. The CRUSADES continued over several centuries.

Meanwhile, the Abbasid Caliphate went into decline in the tenth century and control in the region splintered. The collapse of the Abbasid Caliphate led to instability and decentralization of power, and production and economic development declined. China closed its borders and trade on the Silk Road declined.

Despite conflict in Europe, Christians found they had more in common with each other than with Muslims, and united to fight in the Middle East. While the ongoing Crusades never resulted in permanent European control over the Holy Land, they did open up trade routes and information exchange between Europe and the Middle East, stretching all the way along the Silk Road to China. This increasing interdependence led to the European Renaissance.

Ongoing interactions between Europeans and Muslims exposed Europeans, who could now afford them thanks to international trade, to improved education and goods. However, the **BUBONIC (BLACK) PLAGUE** also spread to Europe as a result of global exchange, killing off a third of its population from 1347–1351. The plague had a worldwide impact: empires fell in its wake.

Back in Europe, instability reached its height throughout the thirteenth and fourteenth centuries known as the **HUNDRED YEARS' WAR** (1337 – 1453), a chaotic time of conflict between France and England. In Islamic Spain, Christian raids and conflict were ongoing during the lengthy period of the **RECONQUISTA**, which did not end until 1492 when Christian powers led by Ferdinand and Isabella united Spain as one Christian kingdom.

The GED will not test you on dates or names directly. Instead, you will be asked to analyze reading passages and images. However, you will need to be familiar with historical events and major figures to do well on the test.

In Southwest Asia, the **MONGOL INVASIONS** destroyed agriculture, city life and planning, economic patterns and trade routes, and social stability for some time. The **MONGOL EMPIRE** was based in Central Asia; led by **GENGHIS KHAN**, the Mongols expanded thanks to their abilities in horsemanship and archery. The continent was vulnerable: Central Asia lacked one dominant culture or imperial power; Southwest Asia was fragmented following the decline of the Abbasids. These weaknesses allowed the Mongols to take over most of Eurasia. In China, they did maintain infrastructure, but they established their own dynasty, the Yuan Dynasty, in 1271, with Mongols at the top of the social and political hierarchy.

Eventually in China, the Ming Dynasty reasserted Chinese control and continued traditional methods of administration; the construction of the FORBIDDEN CITY, the home of the Emperor in Beijing, helped consolidate imperial rule. The Ming also emphasized international trade; demand for ceramics in particular, in addition to silk and tea, was high abroad, and contact with seafaring traders like the Portuguese and Dutch in the sixteenth century was strong. The Ming also encouraged trade and exploration by sea.

In Russia, IVAN THE GREAT brought Moscow from Mongol to Slavic Russian control. In the late fifteenth century, Ivan had consolidated Russian power over neighboring Slavic regions. Through both military force and diplomacy, Ivan achieved Moscow's independence in 1480. Turning Russian attention toward Europe, he set out to bring other neighboring lands under Russian rule. Ivan achieved a centralized, consolidated Russia that was the foundation for an empire and a sovereign nation that sought diplomatic status with Europe.

A century later, IVAN THE TERRIBLE set out to expand Russia further, to integrate it into Europe, and to strengthen Russian Orthodox Christianity. Named the first TSAR, or emperor, Ivan reformed government, strengthening centralization and administrative bureaucracy and disempowering the nobility. He led the affirmation of orthodox Christianity and reorganized the military. However, overextension of resources and oppression depopulated the state and gave him the reputation as a despotic ruler.

Despite the instability inland, Indian Ocean trade routes had continued to function since at least the seventh century. These oceanic routes connected the Horn of Africa, the East African Coast, the Arabian Peninsula, Southern Persia, India, Southeast Asia, and China. The ocean acted as a unifying force throughout the region, and the MONSOON WINDS permitted Arab, Persian, Indian, and Chinese merchants to travel to East Africa in search of goods such as ivory and gold—and slaves.

Many civilizational advances were achieved on the backs of enslaved persons. The EAST AFRICAN SLAVE TRADE remained vigorous until the nineteenth century. Arabs, Asians, and other Africans kidnapped African people and sent them to lives of slavery throughout the Arab world and South Asia. Later, Europeans would take part in the trade, forcing Africans into slavery in colonies throughout South and Southeast Asia, and on plantations in Indian Ocean islands such as Madagascar.

The major East African port was ZANZIBAR, from which gold, coconut oil, ivory, other African exports, and enslaved people made their way to Asia and the Middle East. However, enslaved persons from Sub-Saharan Africa were also forced north overland to markets in CAIRO, where they were sold and dispersed throughout the Arab-Islamic empires and later, the Ottoman Empire.

Islam also spread throughout the African coast and inland; given the cosmopolitan nature of the coastline, the SWAHILI language adopted aspects of Arabic and other Asian languages.

Further north, the Ottoman Turks represented a threat to Central Europe. Controlling most of Anatolia from the late thirteenth century, the Ottomans spread west into the Balkans. In 1453 they captured Istanbul, from which the OTTOMAN EMPIRE would come to rule much of the Mediterranean world and eventually the Middle East and North Africa until the nineteenth century. Christians left Constantinople and Greece for

Italy, bringing Greek, Middle Eastern, and Asian learning with them and enriching the emerging European Renaissance.

Renaissance and Exploration

The **European Renaissance**, or *rebirth*, included the revival of ancient Greek and Roman learning, art, and architecture. However, the roots of the Renaissance stretched farther back to earlier interactions between Christendom, the Islamic World, and China during the Crusades and through Silk Road trade. Not only did the Renaissance inspire new learning and prosperity in Europe, enabling exploration, colonization, profit, and later imperialism, but it also led to scientific and religious questioning and rebellion against the Catholic Church and, later, monarchical governments.

The fall of Constantinople precipitated the development of **HUMANISM** in Europe, a mode of thought emphasizing human nature, creativity, and an overarching concept of truth in philosophy. Humanism represented a threat to religious, especially Catholic, orthodoxy, as it allowed for the questioning of religious teaching. Ultimately humanism would be at the root of the **REFORMATION** of the sixteenth century.

Art, considered not just a form of expression but also a science in itself, flourished in fifteenth century Italy, particularly in **FLORENCE**. Major figures who explored anatomy in sculpture, design and perspective, and innovation in architecture included Leonardo da Vinci, Bramante, Michelangelo, Rafael, and Donatello. Leonardo is particularly known for his scientific pursuits in addition to his artistic achievement. Interest in classical (ancient Greek and Roman) artistic work enjoyed a resurgence.

Meanwhile, scholars like Galileo, Isaac Newton, and Copernicus made discoveries in what became known as the **SCIENTIFIC REVOLUTION**, rooted in the scientific knowledge of the Islamic empires, which had been imported through economic and social contact initiated centuries prior in the Crusades. Scientific study and discovery threatened the power of the Church.

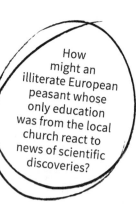

How might an illiterate European peasant whose only education was from the local church react to news of scientific discoveries?

Also in the mid-fifteenth century, **JOHANN GUTENBERG** invented the **PRINTING PRESS**; the first book to be published would be the Bible. With the advent of printing, texts could be more widely and rapidly distributed, and people had more access to information. Here lay the roots of the **ENLIGHTENMENT**, the basis for reinvigorated European culture and political thought that would drive its development for the next several centuries—and inspire revolution.

Transnational cultural exchange had also resulted in the transmission of technology to Europe. During the sixteenth century, European seafaring knowledge, navigation, and technology benefitted from Islamic and Asian expertise; European explorers and traders could now venture beyond the Mediterranean. Portuguese and Dutch sailors eventually reached India and China, where they established ties with the Ming Dynasty. Trade was no longer dependent on the Silk Road. Improved technology also empowered Europeans to explore overseas, eventually landing in the Western Hemisphere.

Interest in exploration grew in Europe during the Renaissance period. Technological advancements made complex navigation and long-term sea voyages possible, and economic growth resulting from international trade drove interest in market expansion. Global interdependence got a big push from Spain when King Ferdinand and Queen Isabella agreed to sponsor CHRISTOPHER COLUMBUS' exploratory voyage in 1492 to find a sea route to Asia, in order to speed up commercial trade there. Instead, he stumbled upon the Western Hemisphere, which was unknown to Europeans, Asians, and Africans to this point.

Columbus landed in the Caribbean; he and later explorers would claim the Caribbean islands and eventually Central and South America for Spain and Portugal. However, those areas were already populated by the major American civilizations.

By around 1400, two major empires dominated Central and South America: the Incas and the Aztecs. These two empires would be the last indigenous civilizations to dominate the Americas before European colonization of the Western Hemisphere.

Their military power and militaristic culture allowed the AZTECS to dominate Mexico and Mesoamerica and regional trade in precious objects. The main city of the Aztec empire, TENOCHTITLAN, was founded in 1325 and, at its height, home to several million people. Aztec civilization was militaristic in nature and divided on a class basis: it included slaves, indentured servants, serfs, an independent priestly class, military, and ruling classes. The Aztecs shared many beliefs with the preceding Mayan civilization.

Meanwhile, in the Andes, the INCAS had emerged. Based in CUZCO, the Incas had consolidated their power around 1300. Domesticated llamas and alpacas allowed the military to transport supplies through the mountains. Inca engineers built the citadel of MACHU PICCHU and imperial infrastructure, including roads throughout the Andes. They grew crops at high altitudes. To subdue local peoples, they moved conquered groups elsewhere in the empire and repopulated conquered areas with Incas.

With its weapons and technological superiority, Spain took over the silver- and gold-rich Mesoamerican and Andean territories. The Spanish *conquistador* Hernán Cortés conquered the Aztecs, and Francisco Pizarro the Incas. In the Caribbean islands, sugar became an important cash crop.

The economic system of MERCANTILISM developed, in which the colonizing or *MOTHER COUNTRY* took raw materials from the territories they controlled for the colonizers' own benefit. Governments amassed wealth through protectionism and increasing exports at the expense of other rising colonial powers. This eventually involved developing goods and then selling them back to those colonized lands at an inflated price. The *ENCOMIENDA* system granted European landowners the "right" to hold lands in the Americas and demand labor from the local inhabitants. Spreading Christianity was another important reason for European expansion. Local civilizations and resources were exploited and destroyed.

The COLUMBIAN EXCHANGE enabled mercantilism to flourish. Conflict and illness brought by the Europeans—especially SMALLPOX—decimated the Native Americans, and the Europeans were left without labor to mine the silver and gold or to work the land. AFRICAN SLAVERY was their solution.

Slavery was an ancient institution in many societies worldwide; however, with the Columbian Exchange slavery came to be practiced on a mass scale the likes of which the world had never seen. Throughout Africa and especially on the West African coast,

Europeans traded for slaves with some African kingdoms and also raided the land, kidnapping people. Europeans took captured Africans in horrific conditions to the Americas; those who survived were enslaved and forced to work in mining or agriculture for the benefit of expanding European imperial powers.

The Columbian Exchange described the **TRIANGULAR TRADE** across the Atlantic: Europeans took kidnapped African people from Africa to the Americas along the "Middle Passage," sold them at auction and exchanged them for sugar and raw materials; these materials were traded in Europe for consumer goods, which were then exchanged in Africa, and so on.

The Haitian Revolution nearly bankrupted France, and was one reason for the sale of its territory in Louisiana to the early United States. Haiti was the first independent state in Latin America.

Figure 15.5. Triangular Trade

Throughout this period, Africans did resist both on ships and later, in the Americas; **MAROON COMMUNITIES** of escaped slaves formed throughout the Western Hemisphere, the **UNDERGROUND RAILROAD** in the nineteenth-century United States helped enslaved persons escape the South, and **TOUSSAINT L'OUVERTURE** led a successful slave rebellion in Haiti, winning independence from the French for that country in 1803. However, the slave trade continued for centuries.

During the eighteenth century, Spain and Portugal were preeminent powers in global trade thanks to colonization and **IMPERIALISM**, the possession and exploitation of land overseas. However, Great Britain became an important presence on the seas; it would later dominate the oceans throughout the nineteenth century.

Reformation and Revolution

While Spain and Portugal consolidated their hold over territories in the Americas, conflict ensued in Europe. The power of the Catholic Church was threatened; new scientific discoveries and secular Renaissance thought were at odds with many teachings of the Church. The Catholic monk **MARTIN LUTHER** wrote a letter of protest to the Pope in 1517 known as the **NINETY-FIVE THESES**, outlining ways he believed the Church should reform. His ideas gained support, especially among rulers who wanted more power from the Church. Triggering the **REFORMATION**, or movement for reform of the Church, Luther's ideas led to offshoots of new versions of Christianity in Western Europe. Protestant thinkers like Luther and **JOHN CALVIN** addressed particular grievances, condemning the **INFALLIBILITY** of the Pope (its teaching that the Pope was without fault) and the selling of **INDULGENCES**, or guarantees of entry into heaven.

Conflict between Protestants and Catholics was fierce on the Continent as well. The **THIRTY YEARS' WAR** (1618 – 1648) began in Central Europe between Protestant nobles in the Holy Roman Empire who disagreed with the strict Catholic **FERDINAND II**, who ruled parts of Central Europe. Elected Holy Roman Emperor in 1619, Ferdinand II was a leader of the **COUNTER-REFORMATION**, attempts at reinforcing Catholic dominance throughout Europe during and after the Reformation in the wake of the Renaissance and related social change. Ferdinand was also closely allied with the Catholic **HABSBURG** Dynasty, which ruled Austria and Spain.

At the same time, France came into conflict with its Catholic neighbors—Habsburg-ruled Spain and Austria—despite their shared faith. Threatened by a strengthened Spain and Holy Roman Empire, France declared war. European politics began emphasizing state sovereignty over religious solidarity.

The tangled alliances between European powers resulted in widespread conflict. In the 1648 **TREATY OF WESTPHALIA**, European powers agreed to recognize **STATE SOVEREIGNTY** and practice **NON-INTERFERENCE** in each other's matters—at the expense of family and religious allegiance. 1648 marked a transition into modern international relations when politics and religion would no longer be inexorably intertwined.

The end of the Thirty Years' War represented the end of the notion of the domination of the Catholic Church over Europe and the concept of religious regional dominance, rather than ethnic state divisions. Over the next several centuries, the Church and religious empires would eventually lose control over ethnic groups and their lands, later giving way to smaller NATION-STATES.

International relations today are based on the principles of the Treaty of Westphalia.

Peace did not last, and in 1756, the SEVEN YEARS' WAR began between Prussia and Austria, drawing in other allied countries. In Europe, this war further cemented concepts of state sovereignty and delineated rivalries between European powers engaged in colonial adventure and overseas imperialism—especially Britain and France. It would kick-start British dominance in Asia. In North America, it was known as the French and Indian War; France lost its territory there to Britain.

This time of change in Europe would affect Asia. European concepts of social and political organization became constructed around national sovereignty and nation-states. European economies had become dependent upon colonies and were starting to industrialize, enriching Europe at the expense of the Americas, Africa, and increasingly Asia.

Industrialization and political organization allowed improved militaries, which put Asian governments at a disadvantage. The major Asian powers—India, China, the Ottoman Empire, and Persia—would eventually succumb to European influence or come under direct European control.

Monarchies in Europe had been weakened by the conflicts between Catholicism and Protestant faiths; despite European presence and increasing power overseas, as well as its dominance in the Americas, instability on the continent and in the British Isles made the old order vulnerable. Enlightenment ideals like democracy and republicanism, coupled with political instability, would trigger revolution against ABSOLUTE MONARCHY. Revolutionary actors drew on the philosophies of Enlightenment thinkers like JOHN LOCKE, JEAN-JACQUES ROUSSEAU, and MONTESQUIEU, whose beliefs, such as REPUBLICANISM, the SOCIAL CONTRACT, the SEPARATION OF POWERS, and the RIGHTS OF MAN would drive a series of revolutions.

In the seventeenth century, conflict following the ENGLISH CIVIL WAR between the ROYALISTS, who supported the monarchy, and the PARLIAMENTARIANS, who wanted a republic, eventually resulted in a constitutional monarchy.

The AMERICAN REVOLUTION, heavily influenced by Locke, broke out a century later. Chapter One, *US History*, contains details.

The FRENCH REVOLUTION was the precursor to the end of the feudal order in most of Europe. KING LOUIS XIV, the *Sun King* (1643 – 1715), had consolidated the monarchy in France, taking true political and military power from the nobility. Meanwhile, French Enlightenment thinkers like JEAN-JACQUES ROUSSEAU, MONTESQUIEU, and VOLTAIRE criticized absolute monarchy and the repression of freedom of speech and thought. In 1789, the French Revolution broke out.

The power of the Catholic Church had weakened and the Scientific Revolution and the Enlightenment had fostered social and intellectual change. Colonialism and mercantilism were fueling the growth of an early middle class: people who were not traditionally nobility or landowners under the feudal system were becoming wealthier and more powerful thanks to early capitalism. This class, the **BOURGEOISIE**, chafed under the rule of the nobility, which had generally inherited land and wealth (while the bourgeoisie earned their wealth in business).

In France, the problem was most acute as France had the largest population in Europe at the time. At the same time, France had one of the most centralized monarchies in Europe and entrenched nobilities. With a growing bourgeoisie and peasant class paying increasingly higher taxes to the nobility, resentment was brewing.

Louis XIV had strengthened the monarchy by weakening the nobility's control over the land and centralizing power under the king. However, his successors had failed to govern effectively or win the loyalty of the people; both the nobility and the monarch were widely resented. Furthermore, the bourgeoisie resented their lack of standing in government and society. Moreover, advances in medicine had permitted unprecedented population growth, further empowering the peasantry and bourgeoisie.

The French government was struggling financially, having supported the American Revolution, and needed to increase taxes. The burden of taxation traditionally fell on the Third Estate, the middle class and the poor peasants, not the wealthier nobility, who were unwilling to contribute. In fact, peasants had to **TITHE**, paying ten percent of their earnings to the nobles.

The Congress of Vienna was the first real international peace conference and set the precedent for European political organization.

After a poor harvest in 1788, unrest spread throughout the country. On July 14 the people stormed the **BASTILLE** prison. The peasantry then revolted in the countryside. The National Constituent Assembly was formed and took control. While unrest continued in France, the French Revolution is noteworthy for having inspired revolutionary movements throughout Europe and beyond.

In 1804 **NAPOLEON BONAPARTE** emerged as emperor of France and proceeded to conquer much of Europe. French occupation of Spain weakened that country enough that revolutionary movements in its colonies strengthened. Latin American countries led by **SIMÓN BOLIVAR** joined Haiti and the United States in revolution against colonial European powers. By 1815, other European powers had managed to halt France; at the **CONGRESS OF VIENNA** in 1815, European powers agreed on a **BALANCE OF POWER** in Europe.

EXAMPLE

Which of the following best describes the motivation for Protestant reformers?

A) Protestants, including Martin Luther, originally sought to develop a new form of Christianity separate from the Catholic Church.

B) Protestants like Martin Luther were unhappy with the teachings of the Church, including papal indulgences and corruption in the Church, and originally sought reform.

C) Protestants were initially influenced by European political leaders, who used them to limit the power of the Church.

D) Protestants such as Martin Luther wanted to topple the Catholic Church, believing it to have become too corrupt.

Nationalism, Industry, Imperialism

The nineteenth century was a period of change and conflict, and the roots of the major twentieth century conflicts—world war and decolonization—are found in it. Modern European social and political structures and norms, including NATIONALISM and the NATION-STATE, would begin to emerge. Economic theories based in the Industrial Revolution like SOCIALISM and eventually COMMUNISM gained traction with the stark class divisions brought on by URBANIZATION and industry.

Following the Napoleonic Wars, Prussia had come to dominate the German-speaking states that had composed the Holy Roman Empire. OTTO VON BISMARCK unified the linguistically and culturally German states of Central Europe. Prussian power had been growing, fueled by NATIONALISM and the NATION-STATE, or the idea that individuals with shared experience (including ethnicity, language, religion, and cultural practices) should be unified under one government. In 1871, the GERMAN EMPIRE became a unified state. Bismarck encouraged economic cooperation, instituted army reforms, and cultivated an image of Prussia as a defender of German culture and nationhood.

In the Balkans, Southwest Asia and North Africa, the Ottoman Empire was in decline. The Ottoman Empire had long been a major force in Europe, controlling the bulk of the Balkans. However, the empire had lost land in Europe to the Austrians and in Africa to British and French imperialists. In the Balkans, rebellion among small nations supported by larger European powers would put an end to Ottoman power in Europe for good.

Eventually tension between Russia and Austria-Hungary—which was supported by Germany—led to the breakdown of Russian relationships with those countries. At the same time, Russian relations with Great Britain and France improved. In 1894, Russia and France became allies. This alliance would culminate in the 1907 TRIPLE ENTENTE, setting the stage for the system of alliances at the heart of the First World War.

World War I was rooted in complex alliances among countries going back to the mid-nineteenth century.

Continued European involvement in the Balkans accelerated the ongoing loss of Ottoman influence there due to phenomena like nationalism, PAN-SLAVISM (by which Balkan nations like Serbia and Bulgaria were empowered to rebel against the Ottoman Empire by identifying with Russia), military and political power, and religious influence. The Balkan nations continued rebellion against Ottoman rule, and European powers proceeded into the area.

Eventually, instability in the region would lead to the First World War which was triggered by the assassination of the Austro-Hungarian ARCHDUKE FRANZ FERDINAND by the Serbian nationalist GAVRILO PRINCIP in Bosnia-Herzegovina in 1914.

Meanwhile, European powers were expanding their reach overseas. As colonialism in the fifteenth and sixteenth centuries had been driven by mercantilism, conquest, and Christian conversion, so was seventeenth, eighteenth and nineteenth century imperialism driven by capitalism, European competition, and conceptions of racial superiority.

In 1837, QUEEN VICTORIA ascended to the English throne. During her reign (1837 – 1901) the British Empire would expand enormously, controlling much of Sub-Saharan Africa, South Asia, and the Pacific. The concept of the *WHITE MAN'S BURDEN*, wherein white Europeans were "obligated" to bring their "superior" culture to other civilizations around the globe, also drove imperialism, popularizing it at home in Britain and elsewhere in Europe.

The European powers were immersed in what became known as the *SCRAMBLE FOR AFRICA*; the industrial economies of Europe would profit from the natural resources abundant in that continent, and the "white man's burden" continued to fuel colonization. At the **1884 BERLIN CONFERENCE**, control over Africa was divided among European powers without regard for or consultation with existing civilizations on the continent.

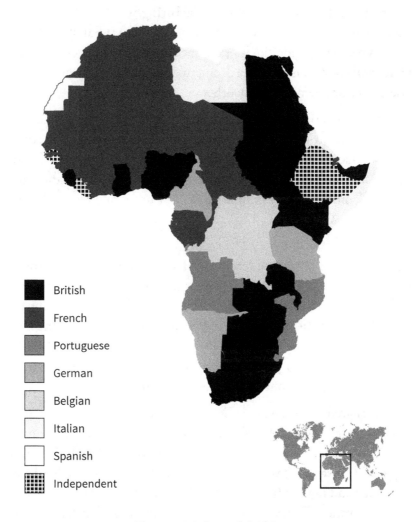

Figure 15.6. Imperial Africa

To gain access to closed **CHINESE** markets, Britain forced China to buy Indian opium; the **OPIUM WARS** ended with the **TREATY OF NANKING (1842)**. As a consequence, China lost great power to Britain and later, other European countries, which gained **SPHERES OF INFLUENCE**, or areas of China they effectively controlled, and **EXTRATERRITORIALITY**, or privileges in which their citizens were not subject to Chinese law.

However, not all non-European countries fell to European imperialism. ETHIOPIA was never colonized, having repelled Italian forces. In Asia, the Emperor Meiji promoted modernization of technology, especially the military, during the MEIJI RESTORATION of 1868. Japan proved itself a world power when it defeated Russia in the RUSSO-JAPANESE WAR in 1905, and would play a central role in twentieth century conflict.

Raw goods from colonies fueled European economic growth and development, leading to the INDUSTRIAL REVOLUTION in the nineteenth century. Industrialization began in Manchester, where factories produced textiles using cotton from the colonies. Poor people moved from rural areas to cities for higher-paying jobs in factories, beginning URBANIZATION.

Early industrial technology sped up the harvesting and transport of crops and their conversion to textiles. This accelerated manufacturing was based on CAPITALISM, the *LAISSEZ-FAIRE* (or FREE MARKET) theory developed by ADAM SMITH, who believed that an *INVISIBLE HAND* should guide the marketplace—that government should stay out of the economy regardless of abuses, as the economy would eventually automatically correct for inequalities, price problems, and any other problematic issues.

To access the raw materials needed to produce manufactured goods, Britain and other industrializing countries in Western Europe needed resources—hence the drive for imperialism. Cotton was harvested in India and Egypt for textile mills; minerals were mined in South Africa and the Congo for industry. Furthermore, as industrialization and urbanization led to the development of early middle classes in Europe and North America, imports of luxury goods from Asia increased to meet consumer demand. Colonial powers also profited by selling manufactured goods back to the colonies.

Largely unbridled capitalism had led to the dangerous conditions of the early Industrial Revolution; workers suffered from poor treatment and unsafe working environments. The German philosophers KARL MARX and FRIEDRICH ENGELS were appalled by these injustices. They developed SOCIALISM, the philosophy that workers, or the PROLETARIAT, should own the means of production and reap the benefits, rather than the BOURGEOISIE, who were only concerned with profit. Later, Marx and Engels wrote the *COMMUNIST MANIFESTO*, a pamphlet laying out their ideas and calling for revolution.

Communism inspired the Russian intellectuals VLADIMIR LENIN and LEON TROTSKY, paving the way for the political and economic organization of the Soviet Union. In Russia, Tsar Nicholas faced dissent at home due to a humiliating defeat by Japan in the 1905 Russo-Japanese War; discontent was fueled by longer-term economic hardship compared to industrial Europe and limited freedoms. Workers began striking, and peasants rebelled against oppressive taxation. Following a period of revolution and instability, Lenin's party, the BOLSHEVIKS, would gain power and eventually take over the country. Installing a communist government, they established the Soviet Union in 1921.

Twentieth Century

Global Conflicts

The assassination of the Austro-Hungarian Archduke **FRANZ FERDINAND** in Sarajevo on June 28, 1914, kicked off the **SYSTEM OF ALLIANCES** that had been in place among European powers, setting off the First World War.

Austria-Hungary declared war on Serbia, and Russia came to Serbia's aid. An ally of Austria-Hungary as part of the **TRIPLE ALLIANCE**, Germany declared war on Russia. Russia's ally France prepared for war; as Germany traversed Belgium to invade France, Belgium pleaded for aid from other European countries and so the United Kingdom declared war on Germany. After several provocations, in 1917 the United States would join

Figure 15.7. WWI Alliances

the war on the side of the TRIPLE ENTENTE (France, Russia, and the United Kingdom), helping defeat Germany.

Germany had been emphasizing military growth since the consolidation of the empire under Bismarck. Now, under KAISER WILHELM II, who sought expanded territories in Europe and overseas for Germany, it was a militarized state and an important European power.

According to the SCHLIEFFEN PLAN, Germany had planned to fight a war on two fronts against both Russia and France. However, Russia's unexpectedly rapid mobilization stretched the German army too thin on the Eastern Front, while it became bogged down in TRENCH WARFARE on the Western Front against the British, French, and later the Americans. Germany lost the war and was punished with the harsh TREATY OF VERSAILLES. The treaty brought economic hardship on the country by forcing it to pay REPARATIONS for the war. German military failure and consequent economic collapse set the stage for the rise of fascism and Adolf Hitler.

The treaty also created the **League of Nations**, an international organization designed to prevent conflict; however, it was largely powerless, especially because the United States did not join.

The end of WWI also marked the end of the Ottoman Empire, which was officially dissolved in 1923. From the end of the nineteenth century, the British had been increasing their influence throughout Ottoman territory in Egypt and the Persian Gulf, seeking control over the Suez Canal and petroleum resources in the Gulf. The Ottomans had already lost their North African provinces to France in the mid-nineteenth century.

In 1916, France and Britain concluded the SYKES-PICOT AGREEMENT, which secretly planned for the Middle East following the defeat of the Ottoman Empire. The agreement divided up the region into spheres of influence to be controlled by each power; Palestine would be governed internationally. In 1917, the secret BALFOUR DECLARATION promised the Jewish people an independent state in Palestine, but Western powers did not honor this agreement. The state of Israel was not established until 1948.

At the end of the war the area was indeed divided into MANDATES controlled by Britain and France. Most of those borders remain today dividing the modern Middle East. After the First World War, the nationalist Turkish leader MUSTAFA ATATURK kept European powers out of Anatolia and abolished the Caliphate in 1924, establishing modern Turkey.

The first international war to use industrialized weaponry, WWI was called "the Great War" because battle on such a scale had never before been seen.

After the dissolution of the Ottoman Empire, the future of the Middle East was uncertain. Despite its weaknesses, the Ottoman Empire had been the symbolic center of Islam, controlling Mecca and Medina. The Ottoman sultan held the title of Caliph, or the one entrusted with the leadership of those two cities holy in Islam. With the region broken up into European-controlled protectorates and an independent, nationalist, secular Turkey turned toward Europe, the social and political fabric of the region was becoming undone.

The roots of two competing ideologies, PAN-ARABISM and ISLAMISM, developed in this context. According to PAN-ARABISM, Arabs and Arabic speakers should be aligned regardless of international borders. Similar to Pan-Slavism, Pan-Arabism eventually became an international movement espousing Arab unity in response to European and US influence and presence later in the twentieth century. ISLAMISM or political Islam began as a social and political movement, where Islam, rather than Arabic and Arab culture, was a unifying factor. It influenced political thinkers and groups, including violent extremists, into the twenty-first century.

In the Soviet Union, following Lenin's death in 1924, the Secretary of the Communist Party, JOSEF STALIN, took power. The USSR became socially and politically repressive; the Communist Party and the military underwent PURGES where any persons who were a potential threat to Stalin's power were imprisoned or executed.

The general population suffered under the GREAT TERROR throughout the 1920s. Any hint of dissent was to be reported to the secret police and usually resulted in imprisonment in *GULAGS*, forced labor camps. Stalin also enforced RUSSIFICATION policies, persecuting ethnic and religious minorities.

In 1931, Stalin enforced the COLLECTIVIZATION of land and agriculture in an attempt to consolidate control over the countryside and improve food security. The government confiscated land and imprisoned landowners; by 1939, most farming and land was controlled by the government, and most peasants lived on collective land. Collectivizing the farms encouraged more peasants to become industrial workers. However, systemic disorganization in the 1920s and early 1930s resulted in famine and food shortages.

In the 1920s, around twenty million Russians were sent to the gulags, usually hundreds or thousands of miles from their homes. Millions died.

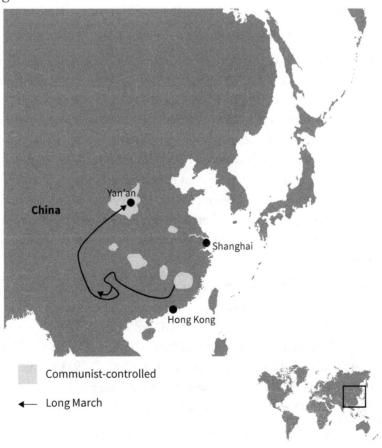

Figure 15.8. The Long March

As part of modernizing Russia, Stalin focused on accelerating industrial development. Targeting heavy industry, these **FIVE YEAR PLANS** increased production of industrial materials and developed major infrastructure. The USSR quickly became an industrial power, but at the expense of millions who lost their lives in purges, forced labor camps, and famine.

Similar rapid modernization occurred in East Asia. Japan had undergone rapid modernization as part of the Meiji Restoration in the nineteenth century. After the Russo-Japanese War, Japan turned towards imperialism throughout Asia, gaining control of parts of China, Korea, and the Pacific Islands in the early twentieth century, which Japan considered its *SPHERE OF INFLUENCE*.

While Japan was building its global reputation and military and economic strength in Asia, China was undergoing political change. Dynastic Chinese rule ended in 1911 with a revolution. After a short-lived republic, China came under the control of two rival factions: the **KUOMINTANG (KMT)**, or Nationalist Party led by **JIANG JIESHI (CHIANG KAI-SHEK)**, and the **CHINESE COMMUNIST PARTY (CCP)** led by **MAO ZEDONG**. In the 1920s and 1930s, parts of coastal and northern China were controlled by Japan; the KMT controlled much of the south, although peasants there supported the communists, and the CCP had been driven north by the KMT in the arduous **LONG MARCH**.

Meanwhile, Germany suffered under the provisions of the Treaty of Versailles. In 1919, a democratic government was established—the **WEIMAR REPUBLIC**. But debt from **REPARATIONS** owed for WWI set off **HYPERINFLATION**, impoverishing the country and its people. Economic crisis was amplified by the stock market crash in 1929 and the Great Depression. In this climate, the National Socialist Party, or **NAZI PARTY**, led by **ADOLF HITLER**, became powerful as an alternative to the ineffective Weimar government.

Hitler's charisma and popular platform—to cancel the Treaty of Versailles—allowed him to become chancellor and then *FÜHRER*, or *leader*, by 1934. Nazi ideals and effective propaganda appealed strongly to both industrial interests and workers in the face of global economic depression. Hitler and the Nazis consolidated total control by banning political parties and trade unions and establishing the violent **GESTAPO**, or secret police. They also set into motion their agenda of racism and genocide against Jewish people, Roma, Slavic people, homosexuals, disabled people, people of color, communists, and others. So-called "undesirables," particularly the Jews in Germany and eventually other European countries, were discriminated against, forced into ghettoes, and later imprisoned and murdered in **CONCENTRATION CAMPS**. At least six million European Jews were murdered by the Nazis in the **HOLOCAUST**.

Hitler sought to restore Germany's power and expand its reach by annexing **AUSTRIA** and part of what is today the Czech Republic. He invaded the rest of **CZECHOSLOVAKIA** and formed an alliance with **ITALY**. In 1939, Germany invaded **POLAND** in what is commonly considered the beginning of the **SECOND WORLD WAR (WWII)**. Europe descended into conflict again. Despite staying out of combat, in 1941 the **UNITED STATES** enforced the **LEND-LEASE ACT** which provided support and military aid to Britain. The two also released the **ATLANTIC CHARTER**, outlining common goals.

Japan joined the **AXIS** powers of Germany and Italy, bringing conflict in Asia into the Second World War. Japan had invaded and occupied parts of China and other parts of

East and Southeast Asia controlled by Europe, threatening European imperial and economic interests. In December of 1941, Japan attacked the United States at Pearl Harbor. Consequently, the US joined the war in Europe and in the Pacific, deploying thousands of troops in both theaters. In 1944, the Allies invaded France on **D-DAY**; as the US led forces from the west and the USSR pushed from the east, Germany surrendered in the spring of 1945.

The war in the Pacific would continue until the summer of 1945, when the US used atomic bombs against the Japanese cities of **HIROSHIMA** and **NAGASAKI**. The tremendous civilian casualties forced the Emperor to surrender; the Second World War came to an end.

> The Atlantic Charter described values shared by the US and Britain, including restoring self-governance in occupied Europe and liberalizing international trade.

The **CHINESE CIVIL WAR** between Mao Zedong's CCP and Jiang Jieshi's KMT had halted as Chinese forces united against Japanese invasion. By the end of the war, the CCP was stronger than ever, with widespread support from many sectors of Chinese society. By 1949 the communists had emerged victorious and China became a communist country.

Allied forces took the lead in rebuilding efforts: the US occupied areas in East Asia and Germany, while the Soviet Union remained in Eastern Europe. The Allies had planned to rebuild Europe according to the **MARSHALL PLAN**; however, Stalin broke his promise made at the 1945 **YALTA CONFERENCE** held by the Allies to allow Eastern European countries to hold free elections after the war. Instead, the USSR occupied these countries and they came under communist control. The **COLD WAR** had begun.

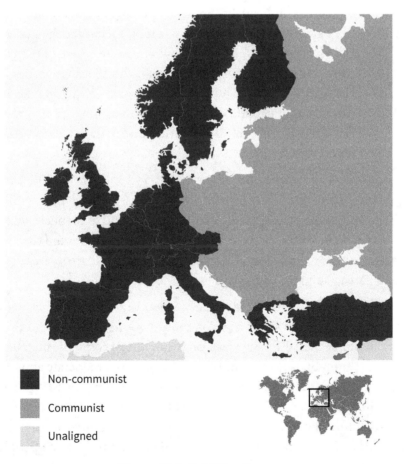

Non-communist

Communist

Unaligned

Figure 15.9. Cold War Europe

Stalin ensured that communists came to power in Eastern Europe, setting up satellite states at the Soviet perimeter. The Soviet rationale was to establish a buffer zone following its extraordinarily heavy casualties in WWII. Germany was divided into east and west, and eventually a wall built dividing the city of Berlin. An *IRON CURTAIN* had come down across Europe, dividing east from west.

Consequently, western states organized the North Atlantic Treaty Organization or **NATO**, a **COLLECTIVE SECURITY** agreement in the face of the Soviet expansionist threat. The United States adopted a policy of **CONTAINMENT**, the idea that communism should be *contained*, as part of the **TRUMAN DOCTRINE** of foreign policy.

In response, the Soviet Union created the **WARSAW PACT**, a similar organization consisting of Eastern European communist countries. **ATOMIC WEAPONS**, especially the development of the extremely powerful **HYDROGEN BOMB**, raised the stakes of the conflict. During the **CUBAN MISSILE CRISIS** in 1962, the world came closer than ever to nuclear war when the US found out the Soviet Union was building missile bases in communist Cuba. Diplomacy averted disaster.

According to the Truman Doctrine, communism needed to be contained. Furthermore, according to **DOMINO THEORY**, if one country became communist, then more would, too, like a row of dominoes falling. Therefore, the United States, by way of the United Nations, became involved in the **KOREAN WAR** (1950 – 1953) which divided the country into North and South Korea.

What factors caused the Cold War to erupt between the Allies and the Soviet Union?

United States pursued conflict in **VIETNAM** for almost a decade beginning in the early 1960s. Supporting anti-communist fighters, the US battled North Vietnamese forces, including the guerrilla fighters called **VIET CONG**, in a war for Vietnamese sovereignty throughout the 1960s. Despite being outnumbered, the Viet Cong's familiarity with the difficult terrain, support from Russia and China, and determination eventually resulted in victory. Extreme objection to the war within the United States, high casualties, and demoralization resulted in US withdrawal in 1973.

Toward the end of the 1960s and into the 1970s, the Cold War reached a period of **DÉTENTE**, or a warming of relations. The US and USSR signed the **NUCLEAR NON-PROLIFERATION TREATY**, in which they and other nuclear powers agreed not to further spread nuclear weapons technology. Later, the USSR and the US signed the **SALT I** (Strategic Arms Limitation Treaty), limiting strategic weaponry. Some cultural exchanges and partnerships in outer space took place also.

At the same time, the United States began making diplomatic overtures toward communist China. Despite its status as a communist country, China and the USSR had difficult relations due to their differing views on the nature of communism. Nikita Khrushchev, Soviet leader from Stalin's death until the 1970s, took a moderate approach to world communism, while Mao supported active revolution. Following the **SINO-SOVIET SPLIT** of the 1960s, China had lost much Soviet support for its modernization programs. Despite advances in agriculture and some industrialization, Mao's programs like the **GREAT LEAP FORWARD** and the **CULTURAL REVOLUTION** had taken a toll on the people. In 1972,

President Nixon visited China, establishing relations between the communist government and the United States.

The climate would change again, however, in the 1970s and 1980s. The US and USSR found themselves supporting opposing sides in regional conflicts throughout the world. PRESIDENT RONALD REAGAN pursued a militaristic policy, prioritizing weapons development with the goal of outspending the USSR on weapons technology. The ARMS RACE was underway.

Meanwhile, the former colonies of the fallen European colonial powers had won or were in the process of gaining their independence through DECOLONIZATION. These newly formed countries constituted the *THIRD WORLD*, an alternative to the countries directly dominated by the democratic-capitalist and communist spheres of the US and USSR. However, the global superpowers fought for dominance worldwide by arming different sides in smaller regional conflicts (fighting *proxy wars*) and influencing regional and global politics.

Already, the leader MOHANDAS GANDHI had led a peaceful independence movement in INDIA against the British, winning Indian independence in 1949. His assassination by Hindu radicals led to conflict between HINDUS and MUSLIMS in the SUBCONTINENT, resulting in PARTITION, the violent division of India into India, Pakistan and later, Bangladesh.

African countries became independent through both revolution and thanks to strong leadership by African nationalist leaders and thinkers. The APARTHEID regime in South Africa, where segregation between races was enforced and people of color lived in oppressive conditions, was not lifted until the 1990s; NELSON MANDELA led the country in a peaceful transition process.

In the Middle East, post-Ottoman *PROTECTORATES* became independent states with arbitrary borders drawn and rulers installed by the Europeans. The creation of the state of ISRAEL was especially contentious: in the 1917 BALFOUR DECLARATION, the British had promised the ZIONIST movement that the Jews would be given a homeland in the British-controlled protectorate of Palestine. However, the US assured the Arabs in 1945 that a Jewish state would not be founded there. Israel emerged from diplomatic confusion, chaos, and tragedy after the murder of millions of Jewish people in Europe, and violence on the ground in Palestine carried out by both Jews and Arabs. This legacy of conflict persists in the Middle East.

In Egypt, GAMAL ABDUL NASSER led the Pan-Arabist movement in the region, which included creating an Arab alliance against Israel. Arab allies fought Israel in the 1967 Six-Day War and again in the 1973 Yom Kippur War, but Israel held on to and even gained territory. In 1978, the US brokered a peace agreement between Egypt and Israel—the CAMP DAVID ACCORDS. By the 1970s, Pan-Arabism was no longer the popular, unifying movement it had once been.

PROXY WARS between the US and the USSR were fought around the world. In 1979, the USSR invaded AFGHANISTAN, an event which would contribute to the Soviet collapse; in response, the US began supporting anti-Soviet *MUJAHIDEEN* forces there. Other examples

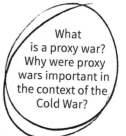

What is a proxy war? Why were proxy wars important in the context of the Cold War?

include the Nicaraguan Revolution, the **ANGOLAN CIVIL WAR**, the **MOZAMBICAN CIVIL WAR**, and conflict in the Horn of Africa.

While never officially colonized, **IRAN** had been under the oppressive regime of the western-supported **SHAH** for decades. By the 1970s, the Shah's corrupt, oppressive regime was extremely unpopular in Iran, but it was propped up by the West. Following the 1979 **IRANIAN REVOLUTION**, Islamist revolutionaries took over the country. The new theocracy was led by the **AYATOLLAH KHOMEINI**, who instituted political and social reforms, including stricter interpretations of Islamic laws and traditions. Later that year, radical students stormed the US embassy and held a number of staff hostage for over a year; the **IRAN HOSTAGE CRISIS** would humiliate the United States.

Following the Iranian Revolution, the Iraqi leader **SADDAM HUSSEIN** declared war against Iran. Saddam feared Iran would trigger a similar revolution there. Iraq also sought control over strategic territories. The Iran-Iraq war raged from 1980 – 1990.

EXAMPLE

The Warsaw Pact was a supranational organization created in response to

A) NATO.

B) the United Nations.

C) the European Union.

D) the League of Nations.

Answer:

A) is correct. Following the creation of NATO, a military alliance formed to counter the Soviet Union, the USSR and the countries of the Eastern Bloc came to an agreement on collective defense—the Warsaw Pact.

Post-Cold War World

In 1991, the Soviet Union fell when Soviet Premier **MIKHAIL GORBACHEV**, who had implemented reforms like *GLASNOST* and *PERESTROIKA* (or *openness* and *transparency*), was nearly overthrown in a coup. A movement led by **BORIS YELTSIN**, who had been elected president of Russia, stopped the coup. The USSR was dissolved later that year and Yeltsin became president of the Russian Federation. The war in Afghanistan and military over-spending in an effort to keep up with American military spending had weakened the USSR to the point of collapse, and the Cold War ended.

In 1990, Saddam Hussein, the leader of Iraq, invaded Kuwait and took over its oil reserves and production facilities. In response, an international coalition led by the United States expelled Iraq from Kuwait and protected Saudi Arabia, regaining control of the world's petroleum reserves in the **GULF WAR**. This event cemented the US status as the sole world superpower.

Despite stability throughout most of Europe, the changes following the fall of the Iron Curtain led to instability in the Balkans. The **BOSNIAN WAR** raged from 1992 to 1995, resulting in the deaths of thousands of civilians and another European genocide—this time, of Bosnian Muslims. Also following the Cold War, instability in the developing world continued as a result of colonialism and proxy wars. In 1994, conflict in Central Africa resulted in the RWANDAN GENOCIDE. In the 1980s, drought in the Horn of Africa led to widespread famine; humanitarian affairs and issues came into the public eye and the general public became more concerned about providing foreign aid.

The balance of economic and political power began to change. The **G-20**, the world's twenty most important economic and political powers, includes many former colonies and non-European countries. The **BRICS**—Brazil, Russia, India, China, and South Africa—are recognized as world economic and political leaders.

Steps toward European unification had begun as early as the 1950s; the EUROPEAN UNION, as it is known today, was formed after the MAASTRICHT TREATY was signed in 1992. As the former Soviet satellite states moved from communism to more democratic societies and capitalistic economies, more countries partnered with the EU and eventually joined it; as of 2015, twenty-eight countries are members, with more on the path to membership.

Continental integration exists beyond Europe. In Africa, the AFRICAN UNION, originally the Organization of African Unity, has become a stronger political force in its own right, organizing peacekeeping missions throughout the continent. An organization similar to the EU, the AU is a forum for African countries to organize and align political, military, economic, and other policies.

In this era of GLOBALIZATION, international markets became increasingly open through free-trade agreements like **NAFTA** (the North American Free Trade Agreement) and MERCOSUR (the South American free-trade zone). The WORLD TRADE ORGANIZATION oversees international trade. Technological advances like improvements in transportation infrastructure and the INTERNET made international communication faster, easier, and cheaper.

However, more reliable international transportation and faster, easier worldwide communication brought risks, too. In the early twenty-first century, the United States was attacked by terrorists on SEPTEMBER 11, 2001, resulting in thousands of civilian casualties. Consequently, the US launched a major land war in Afghanistan and another later in Iraq.

While benefits of international trade include lower prices and more consumer choice, unemployment often increases in more developed countries and labor and environmental violations are more likely in developing countries. How do you feel about international trade?

Following the attacks on 9/11, the United States attacked Afghanistan as part of the WAR ON TERROR. Afghanistan's radical Islamist TALIBAN government was providing shelter to the group that took responsibility for the attacks, AL QAEDA. Led by OSAMA BIN LADEN, al Qaeda was inspired by radical Islamism. Bin Laden had fought the Soviets with the US-supported Afghan *mujahideen* during the 1980s; despite that alliance, bin Laden and his followers were angered by US involvement in the Middle East throughout the 1990s and its support of Israel. While bin Laden was killed by the United States in 2011, and while control of Afghan security was turned over from the US to the US-backed government in 2014, the US still maintains a strong military presence in the country.

The IRAQ WAR began in 2003 when the US invaded that country under the faulty premises that Saddam Hussein's regime was involved with al Qaeda, supported international terrorism, and illegally possessed weapons of mass destruction. Iraq descended into chaos, with thousands of civilian and military casualties, Iraqi and American alike. While the country technically and legally remains intact under a US-supported government, the ethnically and religiously diverse country is de facto divided as a result of the disintegration of central power.

Elsewhere in the Middle East, reform movements began via the 2011 **ARAB SPRING** in Tunisia, Egypt, Bahrain, and Syria. Some dictatorial regimes have been replaced with democratic governments; other countries still enjoy limited freedoms or even civil unrest. In Syria, unrest erupted into civil war. One consequence has been enormous movements of **REFUGEES** into Europe. Uprisings in Israeli-occupied West Bank and Gaza have continued sporadically. Long-term peace efforts have failed and conflict continues.

EXAMPLE

In the twenty-first century, which phenomenon has so far characterized global governance?

A) international terrorism

B) globalized political and economic organization

C) worldwide war and conflict

D) the European Union and the African Union

Answer:

B) is correct. While the United States remains a leading world power, the emergence of international organizations like the BRICS, the EU, the G-20, and the AU has empowered other countries; furthermore, international trade agreements are helping mold the balance of power. However, the AU, EU, and other organizations do not dominate the world in their own right, so they do not characterize global governance. Nor has the world descended into total chaos, so conflict and terrorism do not characterize global governance, either.

Test Your Knowledge

Read the question, and then choose the most correct answer.

1. Boston, New York, Philadelphia, Baltimore, and Washington DC, as geographically close urban areas, form a(n)

    A) urban realm

    B) world city

    C) megalopolis

    D) transition zone

2. According to the map below, which city is located at approximately 39°N, 126°E?

    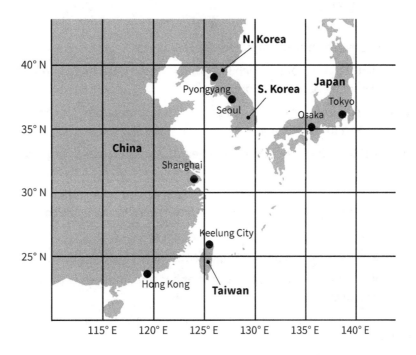

    A) Tokyo

    B) Keelung

    C) Pyongyang

    D) Pusan

3. Which of the following is a nonrenewable resource?

    A) coal

    B) wind

    C) plants

    D) fish

4. Which of the following would be considered a push factor for migration?

   A) a peace treaty being signed, ending civil war in a country

   B) a new law in the home country requiring a religious practice

   C) the discovery of oil in a certain region

   D) the relocation of a major company to its home region

5. Ancient Egypt was able to develop into a civilizational power due to which of the following?

   A) the Indus River valley

   B) the agricultural yield of Mesopotamia

   C) the Yellow River valley

   D) the Nile Valley

6. Why did Rome evolve into an empire from a republic?

   A) It was able to conquer so much land that it would have been impossible to maintain the Republic in its original form.

   B) The patricians of Rome amassed so much wealth that they were able to take over the Senate and establish an empire.

   C) Hannibal was able to overthrow the Senate and establish an empire in its place.

   D) The wealthy patricians of the Senate became corrupt, disregarding the interests of the plebeians who then supported Julius Caesar's coup.

7. How was the Mandate of Heaven an important concept in early Chinese history?

   A) It taught that the people in the area that became China were divinely fated to unite as one culture.

   B) It taught that the emperor had a divine mandate to rule the people in what would become China.

   C) It taught that China was a divinely important world power, meant to become a global leader.

   D) It taught that the emperor was a divine servant of the people of in the area that would become China.

8. Following the collapse of the Western Roman Empire, what was the status of serfs in Europe?

   A) Serfs, while bound to the land on the manors where they lived and forced to farm for the lords, were not enslaved, nor were they forced to fight for lords. Rather, they were to be protected.

   B) Serfs were agricultural slaves expected to farm the land on manors in order to support lords.

   C) Serfs were peasants on manors, expected to farm the land for lords but also able to farm their own land; they were free to leave manors if they wished but rarely did due to unsafe conditions.

   D) Serfs were agricultural slaves who were also expected to fight for lords when called upon for defense.

9. Despite never making significant land gains in the Levant, Europe benefitted from the Crusades through which of the following ways?

   A) Many knights returned from the Middle East with Middle Eastern, Muslim wives, bringing religious and ethnic diversity to Europe.

   B) Many knights returned to Europe with new language skills, helping reinvigorate trade on the Silk Road through Asia and Muslim-held lands into China.

   C) Crusaders returned to Europe with knowledge of Arab-Islamic technology, navigation, and science, eventually contributing to the Renaissance, the Scientific Revolution, and the colonial era.

   D) Crusaders returned to Europe with more knowledge of Eastern Orthodox Christianity, contributing to the rites and teachings of the Catholic Church after centuries of stagnation following the fall of the Roman Empire.

10. How did political stability or instability impact trade along the Silk Road?

    A) Stable imperial rule allowed for easier trade and travel, as roads were safe.

    B) Political instability made trading more profitable, since demand for scarce goods would rise.

    C) Political stability led traders to use sea routes, even when navigation technology was limited.

    D) Since trade was so profitable, political conditions did not impact the trade routes.

11. What was mercantilism?

    A) A political-economic system that enriched Spain by providing it with valuable raw materials, especially gold and silver.

    B) A financial system that placed particular value on merchants, allowing them to trade without taxes or duties.

    C) A colonial strategy established to counter the African slave trade by focusing on a marketplace of goods, not persons.

    D) A market strategy to enhance trade between indigenous populations in the Americas and Spain's European competitors like the Netherlands and Britain.

12. During the colonization of the Americas, the triangular trade across the Atlantic developed, and Africans suffered greatly; however, Africans still developed forms of resistance. Which of the following events or phenomena is an example of African resistance to slavery during this period?

    A) the Maroon communities

    B) the Seminole Wars

    C) the Underground Railroad

    D) the Ghost Dance movement

13. Which of the following best describes the motivation for Protestant reformers?

   A) Protestants, including Martin Luther, originally sought to develop a new form of Christianity separate from the Catholic Church.

   B) Protestants like Martin Luther were unhappy with the teachings of the Church, including papal indulgences and corruption in the Church, and originally sought reform.

   C) Protestants were initially influenced by European political leaders, who used them to limit the power of the Church.

   D) Protestants, including Martin Luther, originally sought to topple the Catholic Church, believing it to have become too corrupt.

14. Which of the following led to the French Revolution?

   A) food shortages, heavy taxation, and Enlightenment thought

   B) the rise of Napoleon and militarization of French culture

   C) the Congress of Vienna and shifting diplomatic alliances in Europe

   D) the reign of Louis XIV

15. How were European empires affected by nationalism in the eighteenth and nineteenth centuries?

   A) European empires like the Austro-Hungarian Empire benefitted from nationalism, as Austrians and Hungarians were more loyal to the imperial government.

   B) The Austro-Hungarian Empire lost its Balkan territories to the Ottoman Empire, which was perceived to be more tolerant of Muslim minorities.

   C) Given the nature of empire—consolidated rule over an extended region home to diverse peoples—nationalism threatened empire as ethnic groups began to advocate for representation in imperial government.

   D) Given the nature of empire—consolidated rule over an extended region home to diverse peoples—nationalism threatened empire as ethnic groups began to advocate for their own independent states.

16. Following the collapse of the Ottoman Empire after the First World War, European countries took control of the Middle East, establishing protectorates according to arbitrary boundaries and installing rulers in accordance with European strategic interests. What effect has this had on the Middle East in the twentieth and twenty-first centuries?

   A) The Middle East has not been greatly affected.

   B) Illegitimate national borders and rulers have led to instability in the region.

   C) Better governance, thanks to the protectorates, improved stability following the decline of the Ottoman Empire in the region.

   D) European investment in strategic resources supported long-term political stability in the Middle East.

17. Which of the following best explains the economic impact on Germany following the First World War?

   A) Overspeculation on German farmland caused the market to crash.

   B) The Great Depression and wartime reparations mandated by the Treaty of Versailles caused inflation to skyrocket, plunging the German economy into crisis.

   C) Germans were forced to pay extra taxes to cover reparations, and due to high prices, many could not afford to do so.

   D) The Reichsmark was removed from circulation and replaced with the dollar as a means of punishment, forcing many Germans into poverty.

18. What was one reason for the Sino-Soviet Split?

   A) the Chinese alliance with the United States

   B) the Soviet alliance with the United States

   C) the absence of the People's Republic of China from the United Nations

   D) the differences between the communist philosophies of China and the USSR

19. What was Apartheid?

   A) strict racial segregation associated with South Africa

   B) a type of slavery in South Africa

   C) a form of colonial government in South Africa

   D) rebellion against colonial South African government

20. After the Soviet invasion of Afghanistan and its subsequent withdrawal, what happened in Afghanistan?

   A) Afghanistan came under Indian influence, making it vulnerable to extremist movements like the Taliban.

   B) Afghanistan descended into a period of instability and civil war, making it vulnerable to extremist movements like the Taliban.

   C) Afghanistan temporarily united with Pakistan in an effort to regain stability.

   D) Afghanistan temporarily came under NATO administration in an effort to regain stability and prevent the development of extremist groups.

Answer Key

1.

A) Incorrect. An "urban realm" is not a geographic term. A realm is the largest unit the world can be divided into, and it includes multiple regions.

B) Incorrect. A world city is a locus of global economic, cultural, or political power. While New York City is a world city, these five cities do not make up one.

C) Correct. A megalopolis is a large urban area formed by the close proximity of multiple urban centers. These five cities are sometimes called the "BosWash megalopolis."

D) Incorrect. A transition zone is an area between culture regions where traits from both regions exist. It does not relate to urban zones.

2.

A) Incorrect. Tokyo is located at approximately 35°N, 140°E.

B) Incorrect. Keelung is located at approximately 25°N, 122°E.

C) Correct. Pyongyang is located at approximately 39°N, 126°E.

D) Incorrect. Pusan is located at approximately 35°N, 129°E.

3.

A) Correct. Coal is a finite resource. It is an organic rock formed over millions of years.

B) Incorrect. Wind is essentially infinite, as it is harnessed and not consumed.

C) Incorrect. While plants are consumed, they can be regrown relatively quickly.

D) Incorrect. Like plants, when properly managed, fish populations are self-sustaining.

4.

A) Incorrect. Ending conflict and bringing peace to an area would stabilize that area, making it more likely that the inhabitants would stay there. A peace treaty and resulting stability might even be a pull factor, attracting migrants from other places.

B) Correct. This new law would push out any individuals who did not wish to practice the religion.

C) Incorrect. The discovery of oil would lead to new job opportunities, acting as a pull factor in migration.

D) Incorrect. Relocating a company to its home region would likely provide new job opportunities in the home region, discouraging migration out.

5.

A) Incorrect. The Indus River is located in South Asia.

B) Incorrect. Mesopotamia is located in Southwest Asia.

C) Incorrect. The Yellow River is located in China.

D) Correct. The Nile River is located in North Africa.

6.

A) Incorrect. The Senate did not chose to dissolve itself and form an empire in order to better control land.

B) Incorrect. The patricians already controlled the Senate and most Roman wealth when the Republic fell.

C) Incorrect. Hannibal never overthrew the Senate.

D) Correct. Caesar, with the support of dissatisfied Romans, took over the weak and corrupt Senate.

7.

A) Incorrect. The Mandate of Heaven did not enforce cultural unity.

B) Correct. The Mandate of Heaven legitimized imperial governance.

C) Incorrect. The Mandate of Heaven did not dictate China's view of itself in the world.

D) Incorrect. According to the Mandate of Heaven, the emperor was a ruler, not a servant.

8.

A) Correct. Serfs were not slaves, but they were not entirely free as they were bound to the lord's land and had to farm it. However, the lord was obligated to protect them, and they were not expected to fight.

B) Incorrect. Serfs were not slaves and could not be individually bought or sold (although since they were tied to the land, they worked for whoever owned the land).

C) Incorrect. Serfs could not leave the manor.

D) Incorrect. Serfs were not slaves, nor were they expected to fight.

9.

A) Incorrect. Fighters did not return with Middle Eastern wives and diversity in Europe did not increase.

B) Incorrect. While some returning Europeans had learned a new language, this alone was not enough of a widespread phenomenon to impact international trade.

C) Correct. Crusaders had gained knowledge of navigation, technology, medicine, and science, helping spark the Scientific Revolution and the Renaissance. This knowledge transfer also helped bring about the colonial era.

D) Incorrect. In fact, at times the Orthodox Church and the Catholic Church worked together against Muslims.

10.

A) Correct. Stability allowed safer travel and a stronger international economy, with demand for international products.

B) Incorrect. Instability halted trade as it became unsafe to travel long distances in Asia.

C) Incorrect. Oceanic routes were not widely used until the fifteenth century because navigation improved during the European Renaissance and Scientific Revolution.

D) Incorrect. Despite the potential for profit, international commerce was impossible without security.

11.

A) Correct. Mercantilism enriched colonial powers at the expense of colonies, increasing their power relative to other European countries.

B) Incorrect. Mercantilism was advanced by the government; it was not market based.

C) Incorrect. The slave trade was an important element of mercantilism, enabling the cheap exploitation of labor and raw materials.

D) Incorrect. In a mercantilist economy, the government promoted protectionism and increasing exports.

12.

A) Correct. Maroon communities were communities of escaped slaves throughout the Americas.

B) Incorrect. The Seminole Wars were fought between the Seminole tribe and United States forces in Florida in the nineteenth century.

C) Incorrect. The Underground Railroad took place in the nineteenth century, after colonization of the Americas and the trans-Atlantic slave trade.

D) Incorrect. The Ghost Dance movement is an example of Native American resistance to westward expansion of the United States.

13.

A) Incorrect. Martin Luther was a Catholic monk; he originally sought reform within the Catholic Church.

B) **Correct.** Martin Luther and his followers opposed corruption in the Church and wanted changes.

C) Incorrect. The Reformation was not originally a political movement.

D) Incorrect. Again, Martin Luther originally wanted reform, not to overthrow the papacy or the Church.

14.

A) **Correct.** The peasants and bourgeoisie were dissatisfied with bearing the brunt of the heavy tax burden; meanwhile, poor harvests led to food shortages and panic in rural areas. These factors, along with Enlightenment thought and recent revolutions elsewhere, spurred the French Revolution.

B) Incorrect. Napoleon came to power after the French Revolution.

C) Incorrect. The Congress of Vienna occurred after the French Revolution.

D) Incorrect. The reign of Louis XIV weakened the nobility and centralized power under the king. In the long term, weakening the nobility and isolating them at Versailles contributed to the circumstances that enabled the French Revolution. However, his

reign alone did not cause it, and he was long dead by the time the Revolution began.

15.

A) Incorrect. Nationalism did not benefit the Austro-Hungarian Empire: smaller ethnic groups living in territory controlled by the empire wanted their independence due to nationalism.

B) Incorrect. The Austro-Hungarian Empire began losing control over its Balkan territories due to nationalism and interference from Russia, which supported Slavic minorities in the Balkans.

C) Incorrect. Nationalism drove ethnic groups to seek self-rule and independence, not representation in imperial government.

D) **Correct.** Nationalism triggered independence movements and advocacy.

16.

A) Incorrect. Many of the boundaries are the modern borders of Middle Eastern countries today, so the region has been greatly affected.

B) **Correct.** Borders did not take into account history or ethnic groups; installed rulers did not necessarily have legitimacy in the eyes of the people, leading to political instability and violence.

C) Incorrect. The protectorates did not improve governance or stabilize the region following the decline of the Ottoman Empire.

D) Incorrect. Outside investment in strategic resources (like oil) has contributed to instability in the region by providing support to illegitimate rulers and contributing to income inequality and conflict.

17.

A) Incorrect. This explanation is insufficient.

B) Correct. The main factors in post-WWI German economic collapse are all addressed here.

C) Incorrect. This explanation does not account for global economic depression.

D) Incorrect. This is untrue.

18.

A) Incorrect. China was not a US ally.

B) Incorrect. The Soviet Union was certainly not a US ally.

C) Incorrect. While the People's Republic of China was not represented at the UN, this was not the reason for the Sino-Soviet Split; the USSR recognized the PRC.

D) Correct. The Soviet establishment became increasingly alarmed at Maoist interpretations of communism, which differed from Marxism-Leninism.

19.

A) Correct. Apartheid was a policy of racial segregation and unequal treatment in South Africa.

B) Incorrect. While Apartheid was a system of oppression against blacks and other people of color, it was not legalized slavery.

C) Incorrect. Apartheid was a policy under independent South Africa.

D) Incorrect. Apartheid was a social policy, not a revolutionary philosophy.

20.

A) Incorrect. Afghanistan did not come under Indian influence, although it did become vulnerable to extremist influences.

B) Correct. Afghanistan became unstable and entered a period of civil war that ended only with the rise of the extremist Taliban. While the Taliban did stabilize much of the country, they also introduced an extremist, tribal ideology that oppressed women and minority groups and allowed terrorist groups to take hold.

C) Incorrect. While greatly influenced by Pakistan, Afghanistan did not unite with that country.

D) Incorrect. Technically, neither NATO nor any other international organization has governed Afghanistan, though a US-led international presence strongly influenced Afghan politics during the United States' war in Afghanistan in the early twenty-first century.

Click the link below for your second Social Studies GED practice test:
www.acceptedinc.com/ged-2018-online-resources

CPSIA information can be obtained
at www.ICGtesting.com
Printed in the USA
BVHW011644230221
600900BV00007B/448